"Favored Strangers"

"Favored Strangers"

Gertrude Stein and Her Family

Linda Wagner-Martin

Rutgers University Press
New Brunswick, New Jersey

Library of Congress Cataloging-in-Publication Data

Wagner-Martin, Linda.
   "Favored strangers" : Gertrude Stein and her family / Linda
Wagner-Martin.
     p.   cm.
   Includes bibliographical references (p.) and index.
   ISBN 0-8135-2169-6
     1. Stein, Gertrude, 1874–1946—Family. 2. Stein, Gertrude,
1874–1946—Friends and associates. 3. Women authors,
American—20th century—Family relationships. 4. Women
authors,   American—20th   century—Biography. 5. Paris
(France)—Intellectual life—20th century. 6. Americans—
France—Paris—History—20th Century. 7. Family—United
States—History—20th century. 8. Art—Collectors and col-
lecting—Biography. 9. Lesbians—France—Paris—Biogra-
phy. 10. Stein family. I. Title.
PS3537.T323Z87   1995
818'.5209—dc20
[B]   94-23700
                                           CIP

British Cataloging-in-Publication information available

Dedicated to the memory of my parents,
Sam and Esther Welshimer,
and to my children,
Doug, Tom, and Andrea

CONTENTS

At the Threshold

Dark eyes shining, she looked nervously about her. Gertrude Stein seemed suspended in the doorway, as if a frown or a terse word would send her immediately back out to Garden Street. No one frowned; one co-ed—dressed like her twin in a flat straw hat, pongee waist, and long skirt—actually smiled at her. In the vestibule of Fay House, its vermilion carpet more than a little worn, Gertrude steadied herself, took a deep breath, and began to walk toward the lovely open staircase. Her invitation to the first social event of the 1893 year—Mrs. Agassiz's Sunday tea—had read, "Second floor, Fay House, the Harvard Annex."

An aura of calm usually surrounded her, but today Gertrude was nervous. She was, in fact, almost in a panic, a familiar tightness in her chest making breathing difficult. Leo had taunted her that morning with the fact that she had never graduated from high school: what was she, a dropout, a Jew, a California rebel, doing in Cambridge, Massachusetts, enrolled as a special student in the Women's Annex at Harvard? Well, she knew older brothers could be difficult, and she knew she had read as much as most college freshmen. But Leo was right: she was frightened, not so much about the academics as about the rest of it—her clothes, her hats, her manners, her all-too-often dirty fingernails, and that raucous, uncontrollable laugh. It had gotten her into trouble her whole life.

She paused before starting up the stairs, and a soft voice beside her broke into her reverie: "Hello. My name is Adele, Adele Oppenheimer, and I'm from New York. Are you a freshman too?" Stein's hearty voice seemed too loud in her own ears: "You betcha," she said with her contagious smile, "and I'm Gertrude Stein, or Gertie, from lots of places—California for a long time, and now Baltimore."

Adele returned her smile, and the two women moved together toward the receiving line ahead. Already members of an intellectual elite, these soon-to-be bluestockings listened to the comments of the courtly Arthur Gilman, secretary of the Annex, and the dignified welcome of the famed Mrs. Agassiz, surrogate mother for all the college women. Then they set on the tea table in earnest, nearly eighty of them, finding their friends for the next four years among the dainty cucumber and watercress sandwiches and the ladyfingers. And by the end of the hour, more than a few people had heard the hearty laugh of the young woman from California. It was clear that Gertrude Stein—though she was far from the typical Annex student—was already making her mark on Cambridge.

One version of Gertrude Stein's life—the story of the idiosyncratic art collector and writer who ruled the expatriates in Paris with her immense personal power—has been told so often that it has become a piece of Americana, burnished to a high gloss through repetition. Unfortunately, that representation of Stein's life is so partial and so limiting that it tends to obscure her personal success story. Shadowed with tragedies, Stein's life shows her resilience, her imaginative courage, in its every aspect—not only in her collecting, her writing, and her encouragement of others' artistry.

In 1995, we understand that the experiences of childhood shape much of a person's adult character. It is one of the enigmas of current literary history that Gertrude Stein seems never to have been a child, an adolescent, a college woman, or a medical school student. Indeed, in most biographies, she makes her first appearance as a woman in her forties, part of the Paris salon at 27, rue de Fleurus, surrounded by Pablo Picasso, Ernest Hemingway, F. Scott Fitzgerald, and as many other men as the biographer can unearth. While Stein did spend many of her middle years in that environment, and while she did consider herself a teacher of younger writers and artists—women as well as men—her earlier years built the complex foundation for her productive, brilliant, but completely unorthodox adulthood. Her satisfied, happy life as the lesbian partner of Alice B. Toklas, another well-born and well-educated Jewish woman from California, is another untold part of Stein's biography, silenced by the attitudes of the polite society in which both Gertrude and Alice, and their families, lived their lives.

This book tells the stories of not only Gertrude Stein but her siblings—the first-born Michael, the handsome but uneducable Simon, the capable Bertha, and the bossily intellectual Leo. It makes the point that Gertrude was not just the youngest child—a daughter—in a patriarchal and in many ways traditional Jewish family; she was also the sister and, in some ways, the charge of the four older children. Their influence on her—their caring, support, and sometimes disdain—is a large part of her story. Without considering what it meant to be Gertrude Stein in the context of her family, one is left with little access into the intriguing personality of the woman who changed the way much of the world thinks about writing and painting today.

As the family's youngest child and second daughter, Gertrude—"Baby"—basked in the spotlight. She grew up thinking that whatever she did was charming, particularly when she turned to comedy. But beneath her winning manner ran a steely dogmatism: when Baby wanted to go outdoors (whether in Pittsburgh or Baltimore, Vienna or Paris), the family changed its plans to accommodate her. Milly Stein, her mother, was a classic enabler, juggling an irascible husband and five children as if getting along were easy. Years later, after her mother was dead, when Gertrude stayed out later than her father thought she should, even his physical punishments did not change her behavior. Years later still, when she and Alice Toklas set up housekeeping together under the clearly disapproving eyes of her older brothers and their families, Gertrude went her own way to find both personal happiness and artistic acclaim. And later still, when Ernest Hemingway appeared drunk in the Stein-Toklas Paris salon, calling her "Gertie" in a swaggering voice, she did not hesitate to throw him out—although she knew he was likely to become famous. Even during her last years, spent in Vichy France throughout World War II, she did not pretend to be anyone but herself—a Jewish-American woman of some prominence.

That Gertrude survived World War II is a miracle, but the story of her life is miraculous in other ways as well. The woman was indefatigable. She could be imperious and arrogant, but she was more often cordial and generous. What drove her through her seventy-four years was a will to accomplish, a drive to succeed at her art (whether that art was psychology, being a salon hostess, or writing). Luckily, much of her writing—whether published or not—has been preserved at Yale. There, I have read thousands of pages of her work, her handwriting staunchly flowing across the small pages of French school notebooks with hardly a correction. I have read and collected hundreds of her letters, scattered in libraries throughout the world. This biography also makes use of nearly two thousand published essays and books about both the Steins and the people connected with them. Most important, I have seriously studied the family papers, from letters from aunts helping to care for the Stein children after they had moved to Austria to letters from Michael shortly before his death, advising his baby sister (now in her sixties) about her income tax, thinking that the seventy years of correspondence that charts Gertrude Stein's life would provide essential insights.

Of those family papers, the most interesting source of information about early years is Milly Stein's diary, kept intermittently from the time Gertrude was three until she was eleven, when Milly's battle with cancer made scripting her family's lives impossible. Most biographers have discounted Milly's diary, because she was not given to retrospective monologues. Instead, her diary is a busy mother's journal, focused on what she considered matters of importance—the health of her children, their activities, and the whereabouts of her often-absent husband, whose business often took him continents away from his young family. Yet Milly's diary provides much of the story of the Stein children and their parents, successful first-generation Austrian Jewish emigrants to their promised land, America.

Chapel Hill, North Carolina
September 1994

ACKNOWLEDGMENTS

No book gets written without a great deal of help. I am grateful for the aid of other scholars in both Stein studies and American literature—Richard Bridgman, Leon Katz, Donald Gallup, Ulla Dydo, Joseph Barry, Wendy Steiner, Shari Benstock, Emily Toth, Cathy Davidson, Susan Koppelman, Townsend Ludington, Scott Donaldson, and E. M. Broner. The Beinecke Library, Yale University, deserves special thanks, as do the Harry Ransom Humanities Research Center, University of Texas; the Bancroft Library, University of California, Berkeley; and the Research Library, University of California, Los Angeles. The help of interlibrary loan and special collections librarians at both Michigan State University and University of North Carolina, Chapel Hill, was invaluable.

Stein and Toklas materials are used with the permission of appropriate libraries, Calman A. Levin, trustee for the Stein estate, and Edward Burns, trustee for the Toklas estate. Thanks also to Rose Raffel and Fabian Bachrach.

This biography has been completed with the assistance of research grants from the National Endowment for the Humanities and the American Council of Learned Societies. Time to write was provided by an NEH Senior Fellowship, the Rockefeller Research Center at Bellagio, and by the Institute of Arts and Humanities, University of North Carolina, Chapel Hill. For all kinds of practical help, I thank Elaine Markson, my agent, and research assistants Cathy Downs, Kelli Larson, Dianne Chambers, and Kelly Cannon.

Leslie Mitchner, my Rutgers editor, has been a true contributor to this book, especially at a very busy time, and I thank her for her many efforts. Without the assistance of my computer expert son, Tom, writing the biography would have taken even longer, and without the assistance of my spouse, Robert A. Martin, and my other children, Doug and Andrea Wagner, I would not even have begun.

For all the people with stories about Gertrude Stein, this book is for you.

"Favored Strangers"

"All happy families resemble one another,
but each unhappy family is unhappy in its own way."

Leo Tolstoy, *Anna Karenina*

"Happy or unhappy, families are all mysterious."

Gloria Steinem, "Ruth's Song"

PART 1

The Making of Americans
(1841–1903)

Three children of the Daniel and Amelia (Keyser) Stein family may have changed the direction of twentieth-century painting. One did change the direction of modern writing; another contributed to the development of American aesthetics. Gertrude, Leo, and Michael Stein give readers reason to be fascinated with the Austrian Jewish family whose history began with emigration to America during the 1800s. Simon and Bertha, the middle children, led less visible lives, but those too were typical for both Baltimore, where the Stein and Keyser families first settled, and San Francisco, where the children reached adulthood. In the interstices of the five children's development exists a complex story, one of ambition, fear, and ingenious survival.

The voices that tell the Steins' story themselves conflict—sometimes speaking in the German or French the children learned as preschoolers, more often in the vigorous American English they preferred. In the 1877 photograph, the dominance of the male tutor echoes the family orientation—the Stein family was a patriarchy, a mirror of Daniel Stein's ego, serving to image his material success. The boys dressed in expensive wool suits and the girls in velveteen dresses, the five children pose around a book as icon: good education was imperative. Ironically, the book is held by Simon, seriously learning disabled and therefore, eventually, an outcast. Michael, the oldest, was the dutiful son who did his father's bidding; the youngest boy, Leo, emanates worry even at age four. The girls—Gertrude at three and Bertha at six—seem more at ease, anchored by physical touch to their governess and therefore protected from some of the family pressure. As captured by the professional photographer, the children's expressions show that the occasion was solemn, as was much about life in the Stein household.

Coming to America

The story of Gertrude Stein and her siblings—Michael, Simon, Bertha, and Leo—is a second chapter in the familiar narrative of the immigrant family that arrives in America sure that it can conquer the continent. The American Dream bloomed particularly well in the imaginations of the German and Austrian Jews who flocked to the States in the mid-nineteenth century. Hard-working, firm in their commitment to succeed, the Steins and their friends also fled possible inscription in the national army.

The Michael Steins and Baltimore

The Stein family story begins in 1841 with the arrival of eighteen-year-old Meyer, who had sailed from Weigergruben, Bavaria, for Maryland. A few months later, he wrote to urge his parents, Michael and Hannah Seliger Stein, to come, even though they would have to leave behind four of their older children, three daughters and a son, who were already settled. On September 2, prompted by Hannah's enthusiasm for the plan, the family landed in Baltimore. With them on the *Pioneer* were four of their other sons—Samuel, ten; Daniel, not quite nine; Solomon, five; and Levi, two.

The Stein family emigration to America was not unusual. Although Jews in Germany were less persecuted than those in Russia under Alexander III, they faced legal and economic hardships as well as likely military service. Letters from German Jews already living in the United States spoke of an alternative: one could leave Europe and find work, freedom, and education elsewhere. By 1835 such letters, published in Jewish newspapers throughout Germany, stressed "the ease with which jobs were to be had and the large salaries that were paid." Opportunities for education were also good, and, most important, Jews were welcomed.

In the port and trade center of Baltimore, the Jewish population more than trebled during the decade, increasing from two hundred families in 1840 to seven hundred in 1850. The Steins were part of this migration. In southern cities like Baltimore, business opportunities for merchants, food providers, and second-hand store owners were good, and deeply ingrained prejudice against blacks reduced tendencies toward anti-Semitism. The city was attractive, too, because the state legislature had earlier amended the Maryland Constitution to permit those "professing the Jewish religion" both to practice law and to hold public office.

With his son Meyer's encouragement, Michael Stein, who had been a merchant in Austria, established a men's clothing store in Baltimore shortly before he died in 1846. Meyer then managed Stein Brothers Clothiers with the help of sixteen-year-old Samuel and Daniel, then fourteen—and with his mother's strong support. The store prospered through the 1850s, at least partly because Baltimore's Jewish population increased daily. In 1845 Lloyd Street Synagogue, the first temple in Maryland, was built; in 1854 the Young Men's Hebrew Association opened a Baltimore center. That same year Rabbi David Einhorn came from Austria to serve the Har Sinai Reform congregation, making it a national center of the Reform movement.

Most early German Jewish immigrants settled in East Baltimore (High, Lombard, Broadway, Exeter, and Aisquith streets), later moving southwest around Fayette, Hanover, Lexington, and Saratoga. During the 1870s, other Jewish families moved to beautiful central Baltimore—Madison and Linden avenues and Eutaw Place, the latter patterned after the Champs Elysées in Paris and Berlin's Ünter den Linden. There they were near museums, art galleries, Symphony Hall, Johns Hopkins University, and the Enoch Pratt Free Library. Wealthy Jewish immigrants entertained lavishly and gave debutante balls, but the Steins did not move in that company. Although they prided themselves on being intelligent, this first American generation of Steins had little formal education.

Baltimore barely survived the Civil War. While it was the only Southern city in which most Jews did not keep slaves, families in the non-Jewish German community lived "almost feudal lives, with ten or eleven servants [slaves]." Because of their shared nationality and language, most German Jews, too, adopted secessionist views. Rabbi Einhorn became so active an abolitionist, however, that in 1861 he was forced to flee Baltimore, abandoning a congregation now divided in its loyalties. At war's end, Jews were serving in both the Confederate and the Union armies, despite one of the most flagrant instances of anti-Semitism in America, in 1862, when U. S. Grant issued General Order No. 11, which barred Jews from the Tennessee Army. In 1863 President Lincoln revoked the order, and by 1865 Jews held important posts in the Union army: there were, in fact, nine generals, eighteen colonels, nine lieutenant colonels, and more than six hundred other Jewish officers.

None of the Steins fought in the Civil War. Like their parents, the boys valued both public success and private happiness. Although not Orthodox, each married within the Jewish community, prompted by both tradition and the belief that health and intelligence were genetically determined. The

Baltimore Steins grew to an impressive family: Meyer and his wife, Rose Rosenstock, had eight children, four of whom married and also had large families. Solomon, who married Pauline Bernard, fathered four children, as did Levi in his marriage to Betty Schiff. Samuel married twice, first to Julia Hamburger and later to Annie Heidelberger.

And on March 23, 1864, Daniel Stein—age thirty-two—married the twenty-two-year-old Amelia ("Milly") Keyser, one of eleven children. Moses and Bertha Keyser, early emigrants from Germany, occupied a higher place in Baltimore society than did the Steins, although Moses, a tanner turned merchant, was never wealthy. The forthright Amelia, whose quiet demeanor masked a hot temper, was happy to define herself as a helpmeet to Daniel and a loving daughter to her family; in Baltimore, she enjoyed music and the arts. With Daniel's financial help, her younger brother Ephraim later studied art abroad and became a significant sculptor. In 1877 Milly's younger sister Fanny married David Bachrach, a pioneer American photographer, and the Bachrach household became the center of the Keyser family. Nearly all the Keyser children remained in the Baltimore area: Milly's sisters were the "little aunts" of Gertrude's childhood memories.

Both the Stein and the Keyser families supported the South during the Civil War, but Daniel was an exception. His courtship of Milly might have recalled the Romeo and Juliet tragedy if in 1862 he and his brother Solomon had not opened a branch of Stein Brothers in Pittsburgh, perhaps as a way to escape political differences within the family. For Milly, however, marrying Daniel and moving to Pennsylvania meant the end of her comfortable extended family life: it would be a dozen years before the Steins returned to Baltimore.

The Daniel Steins and Allegheny

Daniel Stein's personal history is a fabric of stories about his unpredictable behavior; for example, his brother Solomon saw his role in the business as winning back the customers Daniel regularly drove away. After his children were born, Daniel threw his considerable energy into schemes for manipulating the five of them to succeed. The Stein household at 71 Beach Street in Allegheny (now northern Pittsburgh) included a nursemaid and, when Daniel's food fetishes allowed, a cook. In the five years between first-born Michael's birth on March 26, 1865, and Bertha's on October 10, 1870, Milly bore three other children, only one of whom—Simon—lived past infancy. For Milly, the children's deaths, coupled with her almost continuous pregnancies, exacerbated the tensions of life with Daniel. His rash enthusiasms, his quick anger, sometimes over trifles, and his unbending will meant that maintaining a peaceful household was difficult.

Often ignoring his other children, Daniel concentrated on Michael, who appeared to a be miniature of his father. Simon, a slow learner, was happiest eating, playing, and building things; Bertha found her pleasure in drawing; for both, studying was painful. Daniel, who defined *education* as mathematics, science, and classical languages, had no patience with children who were not quick in school. Rather than encourage Bertha in her drawing or Simon in his crafts, Daniel called them "dumb" and "stupid." The birth of Leo on May 11, 1872, added a gifted child to the family, as did Gertrude's arrival less than two years later.

Despite her growing family, Milly's existence in dirty, industrial Allegheny was lonely. Her sisters visited, but she missed Baltimore, its art and music, and her family and friends. In Pennsylvania, she and her children were thrown into an unconsciously competitive situation with Solomon's family. When the Daniel Steins lived on Beach Street, some distance from the store downtown on the corner of Wood and Fourth streets, competition between the young cousins was bearable. But after Daniel and Solomon built twin red brick homes side by side on elite Western Avenue, rivalry between Solomon's four children—Bird, Hattie, Amy, and Fred—and Daniel's five increased. Of the cousins, only Fred and Leo were friends throughout their lives.

Family lore attributes Daniel's final break with Solomon to Milly's enmity with her sister-in-law Pauline, but there was business-related stress as well. In 1872 the older brothers Meyer and Samuel had dissolved the parent clothing store in Baltimore and had gone into banking. In 1874 Daniel rationalized that a move to Austria would offer a chance to investigate banking abroad, as well as the means to give his children European educations. At this time, Daniel believed firmly that learning German and French in childhood was the only way to master these languages. Eager for change, he waited impatiently for Milly to give birth to the child who was planned to be their last. Gertrude was born shortly before 8 A.M. on February 3, 1874, and in the fall of that year, the Stein family sailed for Austria.

Life in Europe

Resembling her mother as much as Michael did his father, Gertrude was wide-eyed and smiling, "a perfect baby." Content to let the world move around her while she observed, she became the center of everyone's life, and in the strange Austrian surroundings, the family focused even harder on that center. When the Steins arrived in Europe, Michael was nine and a half; Simon, six; Bertha, four; Leo, two; and Gertrude an infant. To be abroad for the benefit of the children's educations sounded ideal, but living amid people speaking languages other than English was often traumatic for the youngsters. Even more traumatic was Daniel's absence: the family was hardly settled before business called him back to the States, leaving Milly in Austria with the children.

First in Gemünden and then in Vienna, the Stein household consisted of Milly, her unmarried sister Rachel, the children, and a staff of Herr Krajoletz, a Hungarian medical student who taught the boys (largely through collecting insects and leaves); a governess who was responsible for the girls; a cook; and a housemaid. Living in well-furnished rented houses, the children knew little change in their material circumstances. Milly, however, had many hours to reflect sadly on her last brief visit to the Linden Street house in Baltimore, with her children at the heart of the extended Keyser family. The relatives had been charmed by baby Gertrude's inquisitive eyes. But the question in her father's serious, shadowed face was, *To go to Austria to live— why?* And she had no good answer—except that her husband had convinced her that their children deserved European educations.

Milly disliked questioning Daniel's decisions. Comparatively uneducated herself, she admired his authority. But in fact, Daniel's education— "three winters of schooling in early boyhood"—gave him little understanding of the process of instruction. He was correct in arguing that Austrian music and art would be wonderful supplements to the children's lives, but they were only young children. Most of their days were spent in school or on outings to the Volksgarten, the Belvedere gardens, the Staatpark, and Schonbrunn or on hikes in the Tyrol on the River Traun, the home of Apollo butterflies. As the oldest child, Mike derived the greatest benefits. His German became fluent, and he studied hard for gymnasium classes, especially in classical languages. In 1875 he wrote his grandfather Keyser that his parents were visiting Switzerland and then "going on to the Rhine" so that Daniel— ever in search of improved health—could take "the grape cure." He also wrote in 1876 that his parents were traveling through Italy with Ephraim Keyser, leaving Aunt Rachel in charge of the children and the household staff.

Like most men of his class, Daniel saw children as necessary, but he left their care to his wife. It was not his role to try to understand their needs. One of the most telling memories of the Stein household was of tense mealtimes "where there was much fierce talking and much frowning, and then the father would end with pounding on the table and threatening and saying that he was the father they were the children, he was the master, they must obey." Leo, who later felt that he had grown up "rather Topsy-like," admitted to consistently "disagreeable" memories of his father, whom he described as "a stocky, positive, dominant, aggressive person . . . exceedingly disputatious." Yet, given accepted patterns for child rearing and family behavior, Daniel Stein looked at his handsome children and considered himself good husband and father—a fine provider, a properly stern disciplinarian, a man devoted to shaping his children's futures. He also saw himself as the quintessential American pioneer, taking his family on an international journey as he searched—sometimes desperately—for the American dream.

It was clear that the children spent a lot of time worrying about pleasing their father. Pleasing Daniel meant being obedient, and being obedient meant spending many hours daily in educational pastimes. The children who could learn easily—Michael, Leo, and Gertrude—studied hard, because being good at school was a proven way to please Daniel. Simon and Bertha, however, gradually stopped trying, and learned to live with their father's disapproval.

For Leo, hungry for Daniel's love, nothing he did was ever good enough. Self-critical and insecure, he remembered only his failures: it was he who got lost on family outings as well as on school trips; it was he who could not find the right leaf for his demanding tutor. (Just as he could never please his father, he could never satisfy his tutor.) Wanting desperately to be the smartest of the children, Leo worked hard to learn the German names for plants and insects, but his handwriting was unreadable, and memorization was difficult for him. The Stein home, often tense, was no place to relax, but neither was school. All Leo's memories of formal education are filled with unpleasantness and fear. A talkative child himself, he recalled a kindergarten teacher's pasting paper over a student's mouth because she would not stop whispering to her friend. Years later Leo still saw "the struggling, crying girl's face. It seemed to me like horrid brutality." Children are, of course, often scarred by such cruelty, no matter how innocent an adult's intentions; each of the five Stein children suffered long past childhood from the effects of their father's rigid and often unreasonable demands.

Being the youngest, and a winning charmer, Gertrude escaped most discipline. Aunt Rachel wrote that the baby "walks all alone . . . only fourteen months old . . . and imitates everything!" A few months later, Rachel continued, "Our little Gertie is a little Schnatterer. She talks all day long and so plainly. She outdoes them all. She's such a round little pudding, toddles around the whole day and repeats everything that is said or done." Gertrude amused herself no matter where the family lived: she collected pebbles and made designs of them; she carried her books through the house, fascinated by the color and shape of pictures even though she could not yet read. She loved her nurse, and she loved to "study" with her siblings, especially when their tutor Herr Krajoletz frightened her by growling like a tiger. With Leo, she learned to perform songs and poems. And as Rachel wrote in 1876, shortly before she returned to the States, Leo and Gertrude were well adjusted, as was Mike ("His whole time is occupied with his studies"). About Simon and Bertha, Rachel wrote with prescient accuracy: "Symey hasn't as much desire for learning, he likes comfort and ease too much: he likes to play all the time. . . . Bertha will be more like Symey as respects learning."

Living in Vienna, without Rachel and often without her husband, on January 1, 1878, Milly began to keep a diary. Her attempts to give expression to the nature of her life, to create some record of that surprising existence far removed from the easy pleasures of genteel Baltimore, are written in a tiny hand. Her short entries often refer to "dear Dan," who was frequently either traveling or ill with the indigestion that marked his life, and to the children, now ranging in age from four to twelve. Her diary records family visits to friends, museums, concerts—with the boys trying to escape the visits in order to skate. Bertha practiced piano. The boys had teeth pulled. Her entries often closed with a formulaic "Cloudy, cold, all well," a kind of mother's shorthand for the domestic matter most important to her—the children's health. As her January 26 entry noted, with Daniel an ocean away in Pittsburgh, Milly "called Dr. Steiner to see Gertrude. She having diarhea [sic]. He ordered powders." That entry closed with a benedictionlike phrase, "Thank God she is better." Two days later, Milly's single-line entry read, "Thank God the Baby is all right again."

According to the diary, when Gertrude celebrated her fourth birthday, her mother bought her a canary, for which Mike made a cage. Milly used the occasion to have "all the children's photos taken. Also Bertha and Baby." As a Jewish woman, Milly knew her daughters were in danger of being overlooked. Knowing well the comparative powerlessness of girls in the Jewish family, Milly balanced the traditional emphasis on male rites of passage and male education with attention to Bertha and Gertrude. Despite the Talmudic admonition that "Whoever teaches his daughter Torah, teaches her obscenity," she planned that her daughters, too, would be educated.

In Austria, Milly observed with curiosity the German "salon Jewesses," women who gained political and financial advantage through hostessing social and intellectual gatherings. Most of the time she happily accepted her modest role of wife, complete with the blood taboo. (Considered unclean for the seven days following the onset of her menstrual period, the Jewish wife could not so much as hand her husband a dish.) Milly did not want social prominence; what she wanted was a safe and happy family. Her chief talent as a mother was her ability to value each of her children as an individual. When Bertha passed a test "very well," Milly bought her a book as a reward. Whenever she could, she countered the adage "Woe to the father whose children are girls." Naturally, she loved her sons as well, often praising Mike for placing high in his class. Though her worries about the children's health continued (Bertha had a ringworm; Gertrude, a sore foot; Simon and Leo, coughs), she also described days of gentle pleasure: "I was out with the little ones Sunday." "May 19. All went to Parkersdorf—spent the day. It was lovely till about six o'clock. It commenced to rain. We got home all right at eight P.M.; [had] left at half past eight." Milly's energies as mother were dedicated to enjoying, and perhaps improving, her children's lives, even on twelve-hour trips on rainy Sundays.

During the fall of 1878, with Daniel back in the States on business, Milly decided that living in Paris would be more interesting than staying on in Austria. Dismissing her staff, on December 24 she moved to a flat at 32, rue Sheffer in Passy. Her husband arrived soon after the move, and during the winter they often took the children into Paris—to see exhibits at the Louvre; to visit the 1878 Exposition; to buy toys. The boys went to school, studied violin, and, with their mother, took riding lessons. After Daniel returned to the States in March, Bertha and Gertrude attended a school where breakfasts of soup and lunches of spinach were the high points. Gertrude also remembered an exciting afternoon at the school when the boys, on horseback, visited them.

Stein returned to France in the summer of 1878 to retrieve his family, booking passage to the States by way of London. He wanted the children to see another world capital. Of the weeks spent there, however, the younger children remembered only a huge, glittering theater where they saw *H.M.S. Pinafore*. Mike did recall a flamboyant shopping spree before they left France, however, when his usually prudent mother threw financial caution to the winds and bought caps, muffs, scarves, furs, extravagant hats, riding habits, a microscope, a full set of the French history of zoology, and gloves— dozens of pairs—to take back to the States. There, a new experience awaited them: their father had this time charted his course for the West.

The Steins in California

After the Steins' four years abroad, living with Milly's family in Baltimore during the 1879–80 winter was comforting. The Keysers doted hungrily on the children, particularly Gertrude and Bertha, and the young Steins also spent time with their parental cousins, aunts, and uncles. Uncle Meyer Stein, active at the Lloyd Street Synagogue after the death of his son in 1876, later became its president; like Grandfather Keyser, he was serious about his religion. In Baltimore, for the first time that the children remembered, they celebrated the Jewish high holy days and went to bar mitzvah ceremonies and parties. Both grandmothers were strongly religious and welcomed the five children as if they were prodigals. Gertrude's resemblance to her great-grandmother Keyser, rumored to have had Native American blood, made her a special family favorite.

Milly and the children explored the markets, the waterfront, and the art galleries. Gertrude practiced speaking English by counting "one little Indian two little Indians, three little Indian boys." Excited to be near so many relatives, especially cousins her own age, she later wrote, "One is always proud of the places your people come from." Meanwhile, Daniel traveled to California, visiting Los Angeles, San Jose, and Oakland before deciding that he would settle his family in the third city.

During the 1870s and 1880s, moving to California was fairly common for German Jewish families; many had known people who made fortunes during the 1849 Gold Rush. By 1880 San Francisco was called "the Paris of the West," and people moved there for many of the same reasons that had drawn them to Baltimore forty years earlier. There was already a substantial, prosperous Jewish community, and the best-educated congregations were Reform. California's great variety of racial and ethnic groups meant that—except for consistent discrimination against Asians—there was little visible prejudice. The area was also cosmopolitan, with cultural celebrations of many kinds. Public education was excellent, as were San Francisco's Jewish newspapers, published partly in German.

Diversity made imaginative business ventures possible as well. The successes of the merchant princes Levi Strauss, John Rosenfeld, and the Castle Brothers; the Alaska Fur Company; and countless bankers encouraged Daniel, who saw himself as comparably adventurous. Specifically, he had his eye on street railroad development, lured by tales of the fortunes made from the California Street Cable Railroad Company, an adjunct of the Central Pacific Railroad, owned by multimillionaires Collis Huntington, Leland Stanford, Charles F. Crocker, and Mark Hopkins.

But now far from wealthy, Stein chose to live in East Oakland, a bedroom community separated from the mainland by the bay. The children loved the ferry trips across, complete with Portuguese and Italian musicians who entertained passengers, especially when they got to help steer. As the terminus of the Central Pacific transcontinental rail route, Oakland was proud of its five banks, thirty-three churches, two daily papers, opera house, and the Oakland Free Library; it claimed to be "the most healthful city on the continent."

The excited family arrived after a long train trip, marked by Daniel's stopping the train when Bertha's hat blew out a window. The Steins took rooms in the new Tubbs' Hotel, built in 1870 on East Twelfth Street. The turreted five-story hotel, surrounded by gardens of geraniums, fuchsias, and roses, was both landmark and curiosity. Milly hired Anna Quarry as governess even though the children also started school. Daniel commuted by ferry and street railroad to his San Francisco office, where he brokered stock and invested in cable cars and street trolleys. Despite his somewhat erratic attendance at synagogue, he used his religious affiliation as an entry to the business community. Becoming friends with the popular Rabbi M. S. Levy, Daniel sporadically insisted that his children attend Sabbath School.

The next move for the Steins was to a furnished house at 461 East Twelfth Street, at the corner of Ninth Avenue. Besides the governess, Milly hired a cook for twenty dollars a month. From her monthly household allowance of three hundred dollars she paid all expenses, including the $55 house rental (in January 1881, she recorded in her diary expenses of $25.50 for coal, $18.30 for groceries, and $4.50 for milk). On April 28, 1881, according to Milly's diary, the Steins moved again, this time to the house the children would think of as home. For four years they would live in "the Old Stratton Place," which had been Joseph Stratton's house and was now owned by Mrs. M. F. Templeton. Renting for fifty dollars monthly, the frame house stood on a hilltop, surrounded by a ten-acre yard bordered with a rail fence. Shaggy eucalyptus trees lined the long drive. Milly and Daniel shopped for furniture in San Francisco, buying a high-backed sofa and walnut armchairs upholstered in rich brocade, an onyx table, a fashionable looking glass, and a bronze chandelier. They bought dogs and two birds, Bertha's "Billy" and "Dick," who belonged to Gertrude. Milly also bought chickens and a cow, planted a hedge of roses, and raised and preserved vegetables and fruits.

The children reveled in the space, the view, the apple and cherry orchards, and the pets. Nearby was Lake Merritt, a saltwater lake surrounded by a wildlife refuge, and at the hilly end of nearby Fruitvale Avenue was the wooded Dimond Canyon picnic area. Gertrude recalled "Saint Helena where we used to take the stage coach to go up into the mountains into the Etna Springs where we used to swim in mineral water and go down into the quick-silver mines . . . where the overseer could swear for fifteen minutes without repeating himself." To Gertrude, the yard of the Old Stratton Place was more important than the house. Until then, the Stein children had lived a hotel childhood, having to be well dressed for meals and outings. Just doing the girls' curls had taken much of each morning. Living on their California hilltop turned Gertrude into a thorough tomboy, as her exuberant description suggested: "The sun was always shining. . . . Sunday meant sunshine and pleasant lying on the grass with a gentle wind blowing . . . it meant the full satisfied sense of being stuffed up with eating, it meant sunshine and joking, it meant laughing and fooling, it meant warm evenings and running." Free from family oughts and shoulds, the Stein children equated California with freedom. Gertrude later recalled about those years "a great deal of fresh air as a necessity, and a great deal of eating as an excitement and as an orgy."

Guided by the middle-class ethic that daughters should be musical, Daniel purchased a four-hundred-dollar Sohmer piano, an extravagance that set the tone for the upwardly mobile household. Bertha and Gertrude took lessons and attempted duets. Prosperity continued: in July 1881 the Steins rented a horse and buggy, and Milly learned to drive Daniel to the ferry. In October Daniel bought two mares and a carriage with a single and double harness, so that the older boys could drive. The Steins were living out the materialist ethic that fellow Californian Harriet Levy described as a single "standard of excellence. . . . One standard of prestige existed as did one God: to have money was to be somebody."

Daniel Stein's pride in his prosperity was at odds with his address, however; the Old Stratton Place was in a lower-class neighborhood. The Steins' comparative wealth may have intensified what Leo remembered as the neighbors' anti-Semitism. Milly's diary shows that she tried to keep the elite friendships she had made at Tubbs' Hotel, but travel was difficult, and she was now in charge of a large house as well as the children. Years later, Gertrude recorded the family tensions: "More and more there was no visiting for them with the richer people who were the natural people for them to have as friends. . . . The father spent his days with rich men for he had his business with them, he was making his great fortune among them." When the children did go to "rich" households, "they would shrink behind their mother . . . as they grew older they almost hated the people who lived in that part of Gossols where people were richer." (Predictably, instead of building their confidence, Daniel treated his children's shyness as if it were a character flaw.) The Steins went into San Francisco for musical and dramatic performances, but being seen at the opulent Baldwin Theater or the Tivoli Opera House did not compensate for having the wrong address.

Gertrude also described the tension at home when the busy Daniel was there. Seldom calm, her father "walked up and down and his impatient feeling was irritable inside him and he would be muttering and talking to himself and jingling the money in his pockets then and more and more it came to be true of him that he walked up and down thinking, to himself inside him working, scheming." Gertrude's accounts bring Daniel's irascibility to vivid life. When his temper simmered near the boiling point, as it often did, his family tiptoed carefully around him.

The domestic atmosphere did not improve when Daniel insisted that everyone discuss schoolwork over meals. Mike was planning to go to the University of California in Berkeley. Simon, thirteen, had transferred to the Prescott School; he would soon drop out and try learning a trade at the Fulton Iron Works. Bertha at ten was torn between wanting to play with friends and shadowing her mother as she worked in the house. Leo, nine, and Gertrude, seven, busied themselves at Franklin School, where they and Bertha were placed in the fifth, sixth, and seventh levels. Just one level behind her older sister, Gertrude saw her relationship with Bertha as one of rivalry. Bertha liked to tease Leo and Gertrude that they would not have been born had the other two children not died (a situation that made the two youngest Steins uncomfortable). That the girls shared a bedroom also caused difficulty: Gertrude's messiness combined with her secure place in the family meant that Bertha had either to play maid for her little sister or to adjust to living in her clutter. For Gertrude, Bertha's teeth grinding as she slept was a constant annoyance.

Gertrude's young life seemed happy; she had immense strength of ego, fostered by her family's making her the center of their attention. Ordinarily, she liked school. She also liked being taken care of and said repeatedly that having a brother two years older "makes everything a pleasure to you, you go everywhere and do everything while he does it all for and with you." The inseparables, Leo and Gertrude, often read books and such children's magazines as *St. Nicholas* together. But even as a child, Gertrude was competitive. Not above asking her older brothers to draw pictures for her, she occasionally used their efforts to win contests. When one of her essays was chosen as the winner of another contest, she did not object to someone else's copying her effort over because her penmanship was bad; the important thing was having her work displayed.

Gertrude liked the variety of people in school: "California meant knowing lots of nationalities. And if you went to school with them and knew about their hair and their ways and all you were bound later not to be surprised." Her appreciation of difference started early. In contrast, Leo lost what confidence he had when he realized how different he was from other children: he had been educated abroad, and he was Jewish. He worried his way through elementary school, dreading every class: "I was never very good at recitation, since I was so frightfully self-conscious that to be called on in class always disconcerted me. The only time I shone was when the teacher would ask: does any one know anything about this or that, and then as I had far more general information than any of the others and since I had not been called on by name—how I detested my name—I could pour out my supplies." The sympathetic Gertrude remembered that Leo was very nervous whenever he had to recite: "You had to stand on the platform alone . . . it was no longer your brother but someone who certainly could not remember . . . he had not that kind of memory, I did not have that kind of memory either but I could hold it a little longer."

Because the Stein children's rank in class was important to Daniel, Milly sometimes badgered teachers for higher placements for them. Although she had confidence in her children, she also knew that if their academic progress did not satisfy their father, he was likely to start his own study program at home. She had weathered his shifting enthusiasms: his insistence that the family live abroad so the children could speak German and French had been countered with the present edict that they speak and read only English. In fact, by the time Daniel chose a second California governess, he had decided that homemaking skills were more important than language abilities.

Family Narratives

The Mother's Diaries

Recent literary theory suggests that women's writing often includes significant elements of disguise. Many women who write feel uneasy about presenting the truth; in some cases, they may also be shielding themselves from that truth, and their writing helps them construct lives they can accept. Milly Stein's writing exhibits both traits.

During fifteen years of marriage, Milly had become an all-sacrificing helpmeet. She had little to say about where her family lived, and now, in California, twenty-five hundred miles away from her family in Baltimore, she found herself doing a great deal of physical work in a house on a hilltop, isolated from the social life and friendships she enjoyed. She dealt regularly with a difficult spouse, and, although she referred to him consistently a "Dear," she knew that he caused more problems for her and the children than he solved. In her diary, however, a place for candor, Milly never said that her life was not what she had expected. She maintained her image of good wife almost to the end of her private script.

For the most part, her diaries continue to record a busy, stressful life. On December 23, 1881, the cook gave notice, so good-humored Milly prepared food for the holidays: "Dear Dan and the children helped me a good deal and we got along very nicely." Although she hired a new cook for $25 a month, as well as employing a governess for $50 and a yardman for $25, her diaries suggest that she was economizing: the monthly household allowance had shrunk from $300 to $250. Even the most necessary economies needed to be invisible, so as not to undercut Daniel's successful image. For the first time in her diaries, Milly itemized marketing expenses: "Fish, 60; Veg and fruits, 75; Knife for Simey, 65; School Books, 250." Soon after this entry, Daniel took her to visit Mr. Lauden to discuss "commencing a regular set of books. Dan bought a ledger and cash books for me." Later that week, Mr. Lauden came for dinner. No instruction in budgeting, however, could remedy the problem, which was a shortage of money. Milly tried to be inventive: part of her rationale for buying fresh cows was that she could churn butter; on January 14 she noted that although she sold one roll of butter for eighty cents, the dog ate the other. She was also proud of her success in hatching chicks ("13 out of the setting of 13 eggs . . . 20 out of the setting of 26"). In May she and the children picked peas, which they sold to friends by the sack; on Memorial Day everyone except Daniel worked on the lawn.

Gertrude remembered long days alone or playing with Leo, but Milly's diaries suggest continuous family activity. Friends and business associates visited, often for several days; children came home from school with the Steins; there were graduation, confirmation, and birthday parties and week-long stays by the dressmaker. In March the family visited McClure's Military Academy, thinking that Simon might benefit from going to school there. Milly and Daniel, often with the children, called on such friends as the Franks, Schlessingers, Roses, Lippmans, Greenbaums, Priesses, Levys, and Rosenbergs in Oakland and San Francisco. Only twice during 1882 did Milly mention going to synagogue to hear Mr. Levy preach, but the children went to Sabbath School. They also went to oculists, Chinese doctors, and Dr. Fine for "bilious attacks."

Milly's diary also became the repository of more private experiences. On September 10, 1882, Milly noted proudly, "Bertha took unwell for the first time. She will be twelve on the 11th of next month. She is feeling quite well considering." Menstruation, an essential bond between mother and daughter, was all the more powerful for its silent place in polite society. Along with health concerns, the children's schooling continued to dominate Milly's diary. There was an uproar when Bertha had to repeat a grade and pride when Mike entered the University of California—the first of his family to go to college. After he left home, Milly often spent time alone in his room, looking lovingly at the clothes he left behind. Later, her longest diary entries describe times when all the children were home together, as in December 1883: "They had a lively time throwing snowballs. They also made a sled and went out coasting, but it commenced to rain . . . so they came home dripping wett [sic]. . . . They say they had a fine time."

Milly's diary placidly charted the three years of life at the Old Stratton Place, until her tone changed in 1884. On January 1, Milly was too tired to take walks; on January 2, she had diarrhea. That spring, her entries were sporadic. She was lonesome for Mike, who had transferred to Johns Hopkins University in Baltimore after a year at Berkeley, and in June 1884, for the first time since the Steins had gone West in 1879, Milly visited both Baltimore and Allegheny. Her trip was ostensibly to discourage Mike from marrying, but by the time she arrived, he had already broken his engagement. It could be that Milly recognized that she was ill and went to doctors in Baltimore. At any rate, her plans changed from their original conception, which involved taking the other children along. Instead, during the several months of her absence, they lived with their governess's family in Marysville.

Once she returned from the East, Milly was more active, but that spring—evidently, as an economizing measure—the Steins dismissed their household help and moved into the Harrington house on Tenth Avenue. Milly's diary entry was terse: "Drove to the house for the last time in our carriage. Will give it up this evening. Will sleep in our new home tonight."

Somewhat out of character, in the midst of the move, Milly wrote a long entry about her forty-third birthday. After years of recording her family's life and her husband's travels, Milly stopped on April 16 to savor her day:

> At home my birthday. Sophie Miller gave me a pretty black crochet purse finished jet beads and steel bars and rings. Mrs. Miller sent me a pretty set of table mats. Bertha gave me a lovely dark garnet sideboard scarf of felt, finished on both sides with a strip of light blue satin. . . . Dan and the little ones gave me a large cake with the inscription of Happy Birthday to Dear Mama. . . . The children surprised me by inviting Mr. and Mrs. Rosenwald over to dinner. . . . The children played their duet. . . . Mrs. R. sang and we enjoyed ourselves.

Milly's portrait of the loving family was the last one she recorded in her diary; it was also the last year she was in good health and spirits.

The Children's Narratives

Many events in children's lives blur into a kaleidoscope of memory; when accounts are written decades later, events grow even less specific. It is not surprising, then, for two children from the same family to have different recollections. For Gertrude, who claimed that she benefited from being the youngest child and a daughter, childhood was at least bearable. For Leo— and, perhaps, the three more silent children—memories of early years were mixed.

At the center of the children's recollections, as in their mother's diaries, stands Daniel, the demanding father who insisted that his children succeed. His heroes were the Italian patriots Giuseppe Garibaldi and Camillo Cavour and the Hungarian revolutionary Louis Kossuth, Europeans who led armies during the 1848 revolutions. For his children, Daniel's encouragement was not always a blessing; if they failed, he felt shame—and saw that they felt it also. Despite his pose of rationality, he had an unpredictable temper, which his children had learned to avoid. Although Gertrude's memories of Daniel were never so negative as Leo's, she admitted that "all of them had it in them to be more or less afraid of their father when he was angry or even playing with them. They never knew then how the anger in him might drive him . . . when it might change in him to an outburst and then they never knew how far this burst would carry him."

When she went for walks with her father, and he casually took fruit from a stand, Gertrude was in torment. Would he pay for it? "The children would be most uncomfortable then and say something about not wanting it to him. 'What!' and he never listened to them . . . the father never really heard." Guilty of not hearing what his children wanted, perhaps more important, Daniel did not know what he wanted. Gertrude recalled times when he suggested a card game only to change his mind and give his hand to the governess; "the children would have then to play together a game none of them would have thought of beginning, and they had to keep on going for often he would stop in his walking to find which one was winning."

Happiest when making rules for his children, Daniel told them how and what they were to study, how they were to play and with whom, what health and fitness levels they were to attain, and what and when they were to eat. As Leo recalled, "My father was as insistent as he was positive, and at home he was often making rules which were never observed after the first few days. One of these rules . . . was that the children should eat everything that was put before them. It was an unfortunate fact that boiled turnips and carrots nauseated me, and generally I didn't eat them, but one Sunday we had visitors for dinner, and so my father was showing off his discipline and made me eat them anyway, and I was sick all the rest of the day."

One sure way of avoiding Daniel was to do things he did not do. Leo became bookish at least partly because his father was no reader. With the Steins' emphasis on getting good educations, reading and studying were legitimate pastimes; their parents would ask Simon to help with chores from which the studious Mike and Leo were exempt. In retaliation for this favoritism, Simon teased Leo by hiding his violin in the barn, where it absorbed smells the younger boy abhorred. Ensured both privilege and privacy through reading, Leo became Gertrude's mentor and encouraged her studious bent. The two went to libraries and art exhibits together and bought books from secondhand stores (their way of investing some of the family fortune during Daniel's recurring financial panics). Leo's interest in Gertrude was not unselfish: Simon and Bertha ridiculed his bookish life, whereas Gertrude liked to go places with him.

A tyrant within the household, Daniel confused his children by claiming that he had little power over them. Saying "You're the doctor," he pretended to let them make their own decisions. As they matured, however, and those decisions became crucial, he was less willing to stay out of their business. Being well disciplined was also a dilemma for the Steins. They knew that polite children deferred to authority, yet their authority figure was not only unpredictable; he was often simply mean. Leo remembered his disappointment when Daniel did not buy him a promised treat after he had had a tooth pulled. When he confronted Daniel about the broken promise, his father said he had been waiting for Leo to ask for the treat; by not asking, Leo had forfeited the reward.

Daniel also blustered his way through his role as sexual adviser. Conscious of what behavior would make his family look good, he told his sons only what they should *not* do. Leo was so frightened by what his father told him about sex that he could no more read bawdy stories—or even dime novels—than he could masturbate. His father's injunctions against unclean pastimes were strident, though unexplained, and he described as evil everything connected with any bodily process. One of Leo's earliest memories was of the (to him) shameful experience of wetting his pants after he had stayed out in the cold too long watching Mike skate, an event that most children would quickly forget. His paralyzing shyness with girls was further evidence of his sexual fear. When Anna, a smart classmate, sat nearby, which meant they would be exchanging papers for correction after spelling tests, he misspelled every word. With girls, as with his family, Leo's relationships were distant; until late in life, he signed his letters with only his name, forgoing any affectionate closing. He clearly felt uncertain about what kind of intimacy was appropriate, and his fear of the sexual stifled his natural impulses to be loving.

Understandably, the children spent as much time as they could away from their family. Parental unpredictability (Milly usually sided with her husband) and dissension among the children made daily life difficult. Leo and Gertrude enjoyed going off together, taking "all the dried bits of crust in the bread basket [and] tramping over the hills munching." Both remembered watching magnificent sunsets during the autumn of 1883 following the eruption of the Krakatoa volcano. With Simon, they collected insects and snakes and, with Mike and Bertha, played games outside on summer evenings. Gertrude loved everything about the outdoors; she later wrote about the pleasure of eating "radishes pulled with the black earth sticking to them . . . and to fill ones hat with fruit and sit on the dry ploughed ground and eat and think and sleep and read and dream and never hear them when they would all be calling." While their mother wrote about *the family* as if it were a single, cohesive unit, each of the children looked for ways of escape.

Milly's Death

Milly described her illness in her diary before it was diagnosed as cancer. The symptoms, tiredness and diarrhea, began in 1884; during 1885 her entries were terse: "At home—busy." Perhaps she thought her weariness stemmed from doing all the cooking and housework. In October 1885 the trusted Dr. Fine began applying the galvanic battery ("electric treatment"), a technique customary for abdominal pain. He prescribed salt baths and, as Milly's discomfort increased, an opium-based drug. Milly's entries became much more focused on herself: "am not well yet," "At home. Everything going on as usual," "Bertha . . . always goes with me to the Dr. I do not trust to walk alone." In December Fine started coming to the house to care for Milly. The children, after their initial annoyance at their mother's illness and her preoccupation with her health, grew afraid. With Mike in Baltimore and their mother in bed, there was no buffer between them and their father, nor was there anyone to give them the kind of care they expected.

In her diary for 1886, Milly focused entirely on her health. Family life appeared to have ended; except for noting that Bertha accompanied her to the doctor's, she mentioned few other people. Mike, the beloved oldest son, appears only once; Simon and Leo, not at all. There are only two entries about Gertrude, one describing her first menstrual period in language reminiscent of the entry about the onset of Bertha's menses ("Gertrude was unwell for the first time," Nov. 5, 1885). Not yet twelve, "Baby" experienced the abdominal pain that marked her mother's illness; to be told that her pain was normal whereas her mother's pain required treatment added confusion to her fear. She later wrote, "I wish I had died when I was a little baby. . . . I would not then have to think of being frightened by dying."

Milly's second mention of Gertrude was during the time Bertha had mumps and "Baby" was going to the doctor's with her mother. On one visit, Milly asked that they be weighed. Each five feet tall, the mother weighed 108 pounds; the daughter, 135. The stocky Gertrude loved potatoes roasted in meat juices, gravies, candy, pies, and cakes (one of the recipes in Milly's diary, "Mrs. Levy's Cake," called for an entire pound of butter). The hormonal changes in Gertrude's pubescent body, along with her steadily increasing weight, only intensified her anxiety.

Watching her mother go to the doctor's and continue to suffer even with medication and treatments, Gertrude didn't say much. No one noticed her silence; no one talked with her about her worries—not only about her mother's condition but about her own changing body. And without Milly the peacemaking mother, tempers erupted and doors slammed, closing people off from easy reconciliation. Instead of scolding and bustling from one to the other of her children, as she had done all their lives, she seemed not to notice them at all. When Milly spoke, it was to talk of *her* illness, *her* treatment, *her* pain—and she spoke less and less often.

She wrote less, too. Milly's diaries contain no information about her pain, loss of appetite, bowel dysfunction. Given Milly's sense of her role in life, there must have been guilt for abandoning the care of her family, and there was surely fear, but neither appears. The diary only reports her visits to the doctor's. From late 1885 to the March 12, 1886, entry that was almost the last, it becomes a list of relentless two-word phrases,

> To drs.
> To drs.
> To drs.
> To drs.
> To drs.

On March 12, she wrote "Did not go." The March 13 entry, her last, was "Dr. Fine."

The silences of Milly's diary are the silences of shock at the collapse of her world. These were modern times: science would cure her. She was only forty-three. Consistently healthy, she had never even been treated for "women's complaints," and her children were young—Gertrude was eleven; Mike, not yet twenty-one. Reared to defer to the authority of both men and professionals, she assumed Dr. Fine would find a solution. Milly had listened to her husband for more than twenty years, living her life as he wished; she would meet her illness as he, and his chosen physician, instructed. After six months of being the good patient, however, her modest diary shows that Milly no longer listened to Daniel's admonitions to stay confident and to ignore her pain. Finally, she did not even bother to record the process of her inevitable death.

During the several years of Milly's illness, Gertrude was shut off from both comfort and information. But because being angry with her sick mother was unforgivable, she hid her feelings of fear and abandonment, replacing them with angry depression. Just as Leo denied his anger toward his father, so Gertrude buried hers toward her mother, expressing it as indifference. When she later wrote about Milly's death, she called the cancer a "weakness": "She broke down a little, later, into weakness inside her. She more and more then had no strength in her, she more and more then was not important to her husband . . . she was lost then among her children who were then themselves inside in each one of them and fighting it out with all the world around them." Gertrude tried to diminish Milly's value: "She died away and left them and they all soon forgot that she had ever been important to them as a wife, a mother." Yet her denial of the centrality of her mother doesn't mask her real feelings.

Intent on rewriting the script of her desperate loss, Gertrude worked hard to justify her father's callous behavior toward both his wife and his children. She tried to establish rapport with him, but his customary hostility made that difficult. As Jessica Benjamin theorizes, when a daughter tries to find liberation in the father, she must also struggle against him—"his command of and contempt for her, her mother, and women in general." Gertrude's dilemma was complex: "How to be a subject in relation to her father (or any man like her father)? How to be like her father and still be female." The youngest Stein finally concluded, despite all her efforts to the contrary, that "fathers are depressing. Mothers may not be cheering but they are not as depressing as fathers."

Gertrude's identifying with her father and her fantasy about her mother's unimportance allowed her to "forget" the immense personal pain she felt both at Milly's death and, before that, at her mother's preferring Bertha for the first time in their lives. That people she loved could die meant that she also was mortal: "It was when I was between twelve and seventeen that I went through the dark and dreadful days of adolescence, in which predominated the fear of death." They were years of what she called "agony," years during which she had learned that "nothing is clear and nothing is sure, and nothing is safe."

Milly's death came, finally, with the family surrounding her, on July 29, 1888, more than two years after her last diary entry. Mike, graduated from Johns Hopkins, worked with Daniel at the Omnibus Cable Car company in San Francisco; Leo was preparing for college; Gertrude was starting high school; and Simon and Bertha worked—Simon for neighbors, and Bertha for her family. In some ways, Gertrude's sense that her mother had left the family much earlier was accurate, although each of the children felt her loss poignantly.

The Stein household, which had struggled to function during the three years of Milly's agonizing illness, disintegrated after the funeral. The children stayed up late and slept late. Clothes went unmended and unwashed. Holy days passed without notice. For people who enjoyed eating, the loss of regular mealtimes was unsettling: Bertha tried to cook, but Daniel's harsh criticism of her meals ended her efforts. To expect the teenage girl to run a household for six people, after two years of caring for her bedridden mother, was to demand the impossible. Bertha deserved better. On the brighter side, Gertrude and Leo—now fifteen and seventeen—got some meals by taking the ferry to San Francisco and arriving at Mike's office as he was finishing work; he would usually stake them to supper.

Daniel's Death

The children's memoirs include little about the years following their mother's death. Although household routine collapsed, the real cause of their silence was their ambivalence toward Daniel. Children who have lost one parent often become dependent on the other, even if they were previously distant from that person. As Gertrude wrote about these years, "we went on doing what we had done but naturally our father was more a bother than he had been." Milly had shielded Daniel from the children, but she had also protected them from him. After her death, new patterns evolved.

As the oldest son, Mike could bargain with his father: Daniel did not want to lose his affection. He saw Mike as the continuation of the family and valued his bond with him, as much as he could value any relationship. Properly deferential, Mike did what he thought best—for the family and for his father. Bertha, as the older daughter, had limited power. Being female decreased her value, and she diminished it further by accepting the comparatively powerless position that her mother had occupied.

Although he was older than Bertha and male to boot, Simon had no power at all, as his father's letter to him when he turned twenty-two made clear: "You may rest assured that unless you improve your mind by observation, reading, studying and learn to think for yourself, keep yourself tidy . . . be temperate in eating and drinking, in one word your mind must be educated and trained and strengthened to control the body, otherwise a man is very little higher than the lowest of animals." Upset at Simon's working as "a common farm hand," his father urged him to follow the American dream: "Your destiny is in your own hands, every person in this country has the same and equal chance . . . so if you fail, you have no one to blame but yourself." Daniel was less concerned that Bertha, too, had dropped out of school and was content to spend her time keeping house.

During Milly's illness, Gertrude began to behave more like Mike and Leo: she was outspoken and aggressive, and she became a serious reader. "Her bookish life commenced at this time. She read anything that was printed that came her way. . . . In the house were a few stray novels, a few travel books, her mother's well bound gift books. . . . She used to worry lest in a few years more she would have read everything and there would be nothing unread to read." She removed herself from the family, seeking intellectual refuge in reading and writing in her private journal (now lost), and she removed herself physically, leaving the house to read in libraries.

For Gertrude, the gender differences that Simon and Bertha's lives illustrated were themselves an education. Watching Bertha taught her that she would rather not lead a woman's life; there was too much disparity between the rewards a woman could expect and those the world gave to men. It was clear that she believed in the primacy of men's roles and the subordination of women's. Nevertheless, within her family, Gertrude rejected a servile role. She would not work to make her father less of a problem, as Milly had, nor would she take his orders, as Bertha did. She would, instead, try to form a relationship more like Mike's—distant but supportive, principled but flexible. This strategy had two flaws: (1) as a man, Mike could assume an equality she did not have; (2) the contradiction in a set of moral codes that were both principled and flexible trapped Gertrude. If she adopted a value system and then modified it to please her father, only inconsistency could result.

Living her privileged life as "Baby" in the midst of her generally unappreciated brothers and sister Gertrude had learned that ladylike, or childlike, behavior was her only option. She was, indisputably, a daughter. But she was also the youngest and in some respects the brightest of the Stein children; she learned a lot about surviving in her family by watching her older siblings interact, particularly with their father and particularly after the death of their mother. The role she eventually chose—a subtle but consistent withdrawal—was comparatively healthful, at least for a time. She had early recognized that "not any of them [the children] were really important ever" to their father and that Daniel's chief reason for being angry with Milly when she was still alive was that she was doing "things for the children" rather than for him. She did not try to change her father; nor did she try to save her siblings or to improve their situations, leaving to their fates those who allowed themselves to become Daniel's victims.

The motherless Stein household swung crazily on an axis of submission to power. Certain that she would never be equal to her brothers in Daniel's eyes, Gertrude transferred most of her affection to Mike and Leo.

She often played the piano for Mike when he practiced the violin. Like Leo, she studied history for the answers it provided; their shared knowledge was at the root of their compatibility—along with the fact that Gertrude subordinated herself to Leo's dominant role. Being older, Leo did the planning for the two. Gertrude's love for him was partly that of a child for a surrogate parent, and their relationship reinscribed the stability of their early childhood. As she wrote later, "My brother and myself had always been together."

Her sexual identity—determined as female by her early menstrual periods but as masculine through her studious tendencies—was already fluid. Not only did she increasingly ally herself with her brothers, she also liked the things they did better than she liked girls' pastimes. As a child, Gertrude played rough. She mussed her hair, got dresses dirty, and scoffed at admonitions to be ladylike whether they were given in French, German, or English. She never abandoned her female self, however: she used the name *Gertrude* or *Gert* throughout her life and wore dresses, skirts, and waists resignedly. Unlike Willa Cather, who called herself "William Cather, Jr.," during four years of her adolescence, Stein never wore pants or men's jackets, though she did don derby hats, ties, and vests later in life. She also continued to use the nickname *Baby* that her family had given her in infancy. She did not deny either her gender or her place in her family.

And she survived her difficult adolescence, knowing that she wanted an education. She attended Oakland High School until 1889, when the building burned to the ground; she then read daily in the Oakland and San Francisco libraries (the Mercantile and Mechanics Library on Van Ness). The truly significant choice Gertrude made when she left high school was that she did not stay at home and help Bertha. It would not have been considered appropriate—given the family's class—for either of the Stein daughters to have worked outside the home.

Leo would have been better off if he had taken the same drastic action as Gertrude instead of playing the role of angry, self-righteous child. Rather than withdrawing, however, he tried to teach his father. Daniel did not pretend to listen. Leo's insistence was an error; the more tenacious he became, the more stubborn his father grew. Leo never buried his unresolved angers, and his resulting abrasive manner created lifelong problems. As he later wrote, "People commonly considered me conceited and arrogant, whereas I was always troubled by the fact that I didn't know enough about anything, or understand enough of anything, to be really contented." He isolated himself even from his sister: "It was a fact that Gertrude and I despite constant companionship throughout our childhood . . . , in which we talked endlessly about books and people and things, never said a word to each other about our inner life. She knew nothing about mine and I knew nothing about hers." Simon was shut out of the family because of perceptual and intellectual differences, but Leo was shut out by his reluctance to express his emotions.

As in many troubled families, direct communication was the last thing any of the Steins wanted. So long as no one said what was wrong, the pretense that all was well could continue. What the Stein children wanted to forget was so dangerous that written or voiced language avoided the topics. Neighbors reported that Daniel "shuts himself up for days at a time." Gertrude commented in her working notebook for *The Making of Americans:* "Disagreeable condition at home after death of mother and beginning of father's business troubles . . . (loaned money) . . . spiritualists and Cora Moore. . . . Father angry the way pa was with me." Linking financial worry with Daniel's moral disintegration was accurate, but his change from Orthodox Judaism to spiritualism was hard to explain.

Socially, friends and acquaintances abandoned the Steins: "All stopped after death of mother." This exclusion suggests ostracism, perhaps because the Jewish community disapproved of Daniel's behavior. Upper-class Jews were monogamous; a long-suffering wife dying of cancer should have received Daniel's complete devotion. Instead, Gertrude's comments obliquely suggest that her father was courting governesses, governesses' sisters, and other women. One of her notebook entries mentioned Daniel's plan to remarry, until Mike forbade it. Gertrude quoted Milly's early saying that she hoped "to outlive papa for our sakes. Good man as he was he would need a woman to lead him."

This sexual dimension may be one reason for the obscurity in her texts. Her notes suggest that not only was Daniel courting women, but— much more disturbing—he had approached Bertha sexually, "coming in to her one night to come and keep him warm." Writing about an attempted sexual encounter was dangerous for Gertrude, particularly since she had been reared to avoid such topics. She added to the risk by combining her account of that incident with her memory of "my experiences with Uncle Sol [her father's partner in Allegheny, now a New York banker]." She mentioned, too, another "scene like the kind I had with Sol" and later drew the comparison "like me what he tried to do." If the adult men of the Stein family proposed intimacies with their daughters and nieces, the family had indeed broken down—and the children needed help from those neighbors who shunned them. In another note, Gertrude fused the branches of her father's and her uncle's families to implicate both men in this pattern of abuse: "Fathers loving children young girls. Uncle Sol, Amy [one of Sol's daughters], uncle them to them?" Whether or not Gertrude's accounts are accurate, they show her pervasive fears about her relationship to the relatives she loved and trusted. All she wanted was to be a loved child, but as she grew older, the concept of *love* became tainted with the threat of sexual harm.

Gertrude's notebook also sketched skirmishes that showed the reversal of roles between parent and children after Milly's death. The children corrected Daniel for his blustering: "Mike stands up against father's irritability about eating and things when business goes bad [*sic*] You have no right to lose your temper and act peevish like a baby. Not eating your dinner and saying it was because of not being fit to be eaten." One of the areas of disagreement was over the children's staying out later than Daniel approved, and Gertrude notes, "father angry hit her," in reference to either herself or Bertha.

Faced with his children's hostility, Daniel spent less and less time at home, but he usually appeared for breakfast. On a January morning when he had not come downstairs, the children wondered about his absence. Knocking at his locked bedroom door, they called to him, but there was no sound. In the silence, with only their own breathing audible, they agreed that Leo should investigate. He climbed up onto the roof and through his father's bedroom window. The corpulent man lying peacefully on the bed did not seem to be in pain; his expression was natural. He was, however, cold. Leo could believe neither his eyes nor his hands. After a lifetime of wishing his father dead, of leading his life to avoid conflicts with him, Leo got his wish. Not yet sixty, the successful Daniel Stein—of Weigergruben, Baltimore, Allegheny, Vienna, Paris, and Oakland—was dead.

Mike's January 28, 1891, letter to Uncle Meyer described Daniel's death from apoplexy: "He never knew that it was coming. This is shown by the position in which he was found and the expression of his face, which showed no evidence of pain." He mentioned that Daniel had been a "hearty eater" who had "bilious attacks, which usually ended in a spell of diarrhoea." The five children were to share equally in the estate, with Mike serving as Leo and Gertrude's guardian until they were of age. Conducted by M. S. Levy, Daniel's funeral was "attended by many prominent men of San Francisco," homage that would have pleased him. The letter closed with Mike's expression of deep grief.

Quickly moving his siblings to a house on Turk Street in San Francisco, Mike tried to support the family on his income from Omnibus. With Leo a sophomore at the University of California (majoring in history and political science), Simon doing yard work, Gertrude reading, and Bertha running the household, Mike's assessment that he needed to find a way to provide incomes for his brothers and sisters was accurate. For all their father's talk about economy, after his death the children sorted through evidence of extensive debt: Gertrude said wryly that whenever there was profit and loss, most of it was loss. Except for property in Baltimore and Shasta County, their father's chief asset had been imagination. Mike knew from years of listening to Daniel talk about the future of the street railways that his plan to combine the many separate lines was innovative; he also knew that the railway magnate most likely to respond to innovation was the wealthiest, Collis P. Huntington. Mike drew up Daniel's ideas for combining the street railways and sold both that plan and the franchise for Omnibus to Huntington.

Had his maneuver not worked, there would have been no Stein family trust. But it did work. Whether Huntington was impressed with Mike's audacity or with the plan itself is unclear; whatever the case, in 1893 the great consolidation of the cable railroads was effected, and in 1895 Huntington hired Mike to work for him as division superintendent of the Market Street Railway Company. In the interim, Mike invested money from the deal in real estate. Just past the turn of the century, he built a block of duplexes in a new residential area on Lyon Street. Designed by Arthur Matthews, a good local architect, the houses were shingled, comfortable, stylish. The concept was new to San Francisco, and each unit brought a good rental.

Mike could handle being the financial head of the household, but he did not want to be responsible for four brothers and sisters who were—to all appearances—already adults. He was the only one with employment, yet none of the others cared for the house or prepared meals. One night during a fire alarm, none of the four even awoke, and Mike realized that he had become the parent to his siblings. It was a role he did not want.

Arranging with Milly's younger sister in Baltimore for the younger Steins to board in the Bachrach household, Mike allowed Simon—who liked to work occasionally on the cable line—to remain with him in San Francisco. In the spring of 1892, Leo withdrew from Berkeley and, with his two sisters, set off by train for the east coast. Bertha was twenty-two; Leo, twenty; and Gertrude, eighteen. As Gertrude was later to write, "Then our life without a father began [sic] a very pleasant one."

Colleges and Marriages

Living in—and Leaving—Baltimore

Excited as she was to be traveling east, Gertrude knew she would miss the poignant beauty of the Pacific Ocean, the hints of fog early in the day, and the richly varied shore, peopled as it was with African-Americans, Chinese, Italians, Portuguese, Indians. Parts of San Francisco were worlds away from the sedate parlors of Oakland or Baltimore, and she and Leo had done their share of exploring in the exotic—and erotic—underworlds. Although at eighteen and twenty they had never assumed the responsibility they might have at home, Gertrude and her brother were much less sheltered than were most of their peers. Their self-definition included the sense that they were more worldly, more exotic themselves than most college-age Americans were, and in her later writing Gertrude used the words *Western* and *Californian* to suggest their robust, even scamy, life experience.

The five-day train trip erased much of that experience. Gertrude felt as if she were a moth leaving the cocoon of both her worldly adventures—with their predictable guilt—and her orphanhood—with its continual pain—and emerging as a new woman, ready and eager for a different kind of existence. The journey by train became a rite of passage back into a stable family life, a life the three Steins found themselves surprisingly hungry to enter.

When Gertrude, Bertha, and Leo entered their aunt and uncle's Linden Street house in 1892, the spacious living room suggested comfort; the tasteful furnishings, prosperity. Surrounded by the cordiality of her mother's people, a relieved Gertrude settled enthusiastically into the activities of the large extended family. She learned to love the carefully prepared meals and the slow pace of daily life, hours spent playing games and gossiping. She also learned—sometimes to her discomfort—that Baltimore, like San Francisco, had rigid social and gender codes. The outspoken, tomboyish woman was hardly a typical eighteen-year-old urban Jew.

Despite the Bachrachs' welcoming hugs, the Steins felt out of place. They worried about their comparative poverty, their clothes, their manners, although Gertrude scoffed at what she called overly polite Southerners. Still, Leo found agreeable the man-about-to-enter-college pose and liked lording it over his younger cousins. And after the struggle of keeping house for her difficult family, Bertha felt that she never wanted to leave the kindly Bachrach household; she also flourished in the city's art world. She liked her new role as modish Baltimore woman.

Living with their relatives gave the Steins a new conception of what family life could be, and they learned that strong fathers were not necessarily autocrats. David Bachrach, though German born, had been educated in New England and then apprenticed to photographers in Baltimore. A brilliant iconoclast, he wrote essays about photography (he invented the self-toning process, among other things), belonged to both the Har Sinai Reform congregation and the Masonic Lodge, and read John Stuart Mill and Henry George. While a student at Berkeley, Leo had been involved in George's Single Tax movement, and both he and Gertrude were interested in economics: they enjoyed talking with their uncle David. Like him, they, too, worried about escalating anti-Semitism.

Both Gertrude and Leo believed that worrying about world affairs was preferable to worrying about marriage and fashion, the pastime of the Sociables, as the young Baltimore women from the Cone, Gutman, Bamberger, Guggenheimer, Frank, and Federleicht families called themselves. Gertrude found it hard to be interested in fashion after years of living with her father, whose criticisms made her feel, in her words, "homely." She moved a bit awkwardly and had stubby hands, but the youngest Stein's high color, deep-set dark eyes, and thick, lively hair enhanced the attractiveness of her regular, well-defined features. And her personality remained compelling.

Although she was the most amiable of the Steins, Gertrude's informality caused problems. Friends remember her loud voice carrying from one yard to the next as she recited poetry in the garden, legs elevated, feet above her head. Hungry for sunshine, she often stretched out on the lawn, dreaming or reading. Unlike other women of her social class, she took long walks by herself around the city, to Johns Hopkins University, the art galleries, the harbor. The young woman with the earnest expression had the habit of stopping to talk to anyone who looked interesting, her ear for idiom growing sharp from immersion in Southern speech, black as well as white.

Even at their most eccentric, however, Gertrude's habits were easier for the Bachrachs to accept than was Leo's diffident cynicism, the result of years of contention in the Stein household. Left to himself, Leo found a niche at the three-story brownstone of the wealthy Cone family. Sharp-tongued Etta, who was Leo's age, wrote her older sister, Claribel, a physician, that Stein was "quite a flirt," but because he was intelligent and "good company," he was popular. His close relationship with his sister surprised the Baltimoreans, however, and they privately criticized both the younger Steins' sometimes inappropriate laughter, slouching postures, and spirited arguments about art and philosophy. Because Bertha was more conventional, she was more easily accepted.

Pressure to conform in the Bachrach household intensified as Aunt Fanny began playing matchmaker. Bertha was happy in the role of adopted daughter, but Gertrude and Leo were suspicious of adult attention: they had lived too long with little of it. They also were not sure they wanted to be paired off with possible romantic mates. At eighteen and twenty, Gertrude and Leo each saw long years of exploration and adventure ahead. So, in August 1892, Leo left for Harvard, taking a room in a three-story frame boardinghouse at 123 Irving Street, Cambridge. As a special student, he did not worry about how much of his two and a half years of study at Berkeley could be transferred to the Harvard program; what Leo loved was the excitement of new courses, new professors, and new social circles.

Lonely at the Bachrachs' without him, Gertrude decided that going north to school—three hundred miles from Baltimore—was a good alternative to a life dependent on whomever her aunt decided she should marry. Visiting Leo later in the fall, she interviewed with the admissions board of the Harvard Annex, the women's college, dreaming that the next year, while Leo read history and economics, she would study philosophy. Once accepted, she wrote Mike to get her finances in order so she could start school during the fall of 1893. Both she and Leo were anxious about money: with their income set at approximately $100 a month, they could barely afford college. Some suggestion of their intensity is evident in a September letter Leo wrote to Mike demanding that he reply "within 24 hours" about the sale of some stock. Much of this letter described his division of the family's summer allowance among Gertrude, Bertha, and himself: Of the $830 total, Leo received $365; Gertrude, $280; and Bertha, $185. Leo did not explain the inequity, though from the allowance he paid his college expenses (yearly fees at Harvard were $150 for tuition, $25 to $60 for books, $175 for room, and $300 for board). The economic realities of their lives led Gertrude to consider them the poor branch of the Stein-Keyser-Bachrach family.

Gertrude at the Harvard Annex

In early September 1893, when Gertrude arrived at Leo's boardinghouse, where she was also to live, she brought along trunks of books. Her floor-to-ceiling shelves held a collection more like a professor's than a student's. Excited about classes, she was also nervous: it had been nearly five years since she had gone to school. To disguise her anxiety, she threw herself into college life, exploring (the Longfellow house, Concord, and Lexington), playing tennis, and going about with Leo. She was eager to know new people.

Meeting other women was easy: each Annex class had forty regular students and the same number of specials (students not admitted into degree programs). Gertrude, having failed the Latin entrance exam, was a special, which meant she could take whatever courses she wanted. She registered for philosophy with the famous professor George Santayana and for two psychology classes—one a Harvard graduate-level seminar—taught by visiting professor Hugo Münsterberg, a disciple of William James from Freiburg, Germany. Her other courses, in history, economics, and German literature, filled requirements.

The vivacious Stein was initially more interested in social events than in classes. She reveled in the freshman-senior Tally Ho (to Fresh Pond in horse-drawn carriages) and the class trip to Rockport, Maine. She made friends with Adele Oppenheimer, Marian Walker, and Margaret Snyder, who took courses with her; Margaret Lewis, a psychology graduate student who had taught at Smith; Lillian Wing and Mabel Earle, who later boarded with her; Mabel Weeks, who taught in a New York girls' school; Beulah Dix, class writer; and others. The women visited each other in their cavernous boardinghouses, taking along their sewing. Gertrude preferred conversation to handiwork and soon had a reputation for being "a terrific talker, but an elegant listener too; though if you asked her a question she didn't like she just looked through you and went on with what she was saying." Her friends soon came to value Stein's "rare, warm, human quality."

The women talked seriously about careers on their way for ice cream; they also looked for excitement and just plain fun. As one friend recalled, "We were all trackers then—often on a Saturday night Gertrude and I used to take the street car to the terminus and walk out anywhere in the country. Our friends thought we were crazy and sure to get into trouble, but I said if we had any bother with a man she [Gertrude] was going to climb out on the furthest limb of a tree and drop on him. She was not light." In the evenings, groups of women headed through the dimly lit streets for concerts or operas; the "very musical" Gertrude played themes on the piano for her friends beforehand, because she did not want them to miss key motifs.

Other sources of entertainment were dances, sings, and Idler Club plays. Students also went boating, canoeing, and skating, played mandolins and banjos, swam, hiked, played tennis, and bicycled. (Gertrude soon asked Mike for money to buy a bike.) Going into Boston was an adventure, though a slow one, as the horsecar with straw on the floor, heated by a smelly oil stove, bumped along the old bridge road. It was a time for conversation, and friends remember Gertrude's kindly face and eyes as she listened to, and counseled, them. She had the gift of being truly empathetic.

Part of the reason Gertrude was able to form good friendships—with men as well as with women—was that, unlike Leo, she let herself need people. She was not afraid to ask for help, particularly on writing assignments (one friend recalled, "She never wrote good English and grammar meant nothing to her"). She liked to go out; she liked to talk with people. Hardly a fashion plate, her shirtwaists often out of her belt, she wore such deplorable hats that friends stole the most offensive and burned it, forcing her to buy another, which they hoped would be more becoming. Above all, she infused her friends' lives with her immense personal energy: she "knew how to enjoy life and could lead others to enjoy it with her."

Once classes were under way, Gertrude began to see why the Harvard system worked. Most faculty implemented President Eliot's dictum that the college (which included the Annex—Harvard professors also taught the women's classes) was to be "a society of scholars," dominated by small-group student-teacher interaction. The articulate Gertrude thrived in the seminar atmosphere; she reasoned well and liked class discussion, which she called "gossip." A classmate later pictured Stein "sitting monumentally in one corner" as she talked "*very* ably—quite the cleverest person there." Hugo Münsterberg, having taught her in two courses, thought Gertrude was so competent and so project-oriented that she was for him the "ideal student," one who did "model work." In both classes, Münsterberg gave the nineteen-year-old Gertrude As.

George Santayana, too, found her impressive, giving her one of the three As in his class of sixteen. His Philosophy I, a survey of religious thought from Judaism and Catholicism to Eastern belief, was also a language class. Sparking their interest through his unorthodox combination of poetry and intellectualism, Santayana insisted that students discuss ideas. He showed them that all language was discourse, that an understanding of grammar (in the broad sense, of language system) was essential for coherent thought, and that poetry and prose had specific, different characteristics. Through his fascination with the Spanish, especially with Saint Theresa's mysticism, Santayana introduced Gertrude to a culture and a belief system that was to be important to her.

Besides religion and linguistics, Santayana's class taught Gertrude writing. His emphasis on the mot juste went beyond Flaubert's in that, while he valued words, he saw them as only "a stage in the series of formations which constitute language." Words express not simply meaning but attitudes toward meaning, as he wrote: "'bread' is as inadequate a translation of the human intensity of the Spanish 'pan' as 'Dios' is of the awful mystery of the English 'God.' This latter word does not designate an object at all, but a sentiment, a psychosis." He praised English ("No language has so many words specifically poetic") but emphasized that grammatical structures, not single words, underlie the best expression.

The most significant of Santayana's beliefs about writing, for Gertrude, was his theory that the artist made correct choices not through reason but through "contemplation," what he called "the intuition of essences." His belief that writing, like the acquisition of all knowledge, started with mysticism—and that writing was in some ways itself an acquisition of knowledge—set him at odds with most philosophers. Santayana believed that the human mind operated in two modes, one of participation ("the sense of existence") and the other of disengagement ("the intuition of pure being"). While most people lived largely in the participatory mode, the artist needed at times to be disengaged in order to create.

Gertrude took Santayana's yearlong course when she was a freshman. Unfortunately, during the next year, when she took English 22, the required composition course, she found much of that instruction inferior to Santayana's. Although she tried to write as intuitively as she could, the theme-a-day course demanded that students work from models, copying conventional literary styles. By putting Gertrude into this formalist straitjacket, English 22 almost kept her from being an effective writer. But even in her writing from that year, she managed to compose a group of themes that spoke to her personal interests, especially those related to gender. She also wrote an important, and unusual, series of stories about a young woman's developing sexuality.

Her themes show her working in the manner Santayana proposed: turning inward, finding the essence of an experience, and then creating language structures to capture that essence. "Woman," an obvious exercise in irony, depicted feminine flightiness; the male voice criticizing the woman protagonist sounded a great deal like Leo's. Other themes described women as the subjects of laboratory experiments, being observed by male scientists. "The Conference" is an almost existential dialogue between "English Professor" and "Meek girl student," with the real meaning of the language hidden in a gendered subtext. The student defends her use of the imagery of summer in a theme because she was writing about summer; the professor wrongheadedly insists that the season must be spring or fall and that the imagery must be changed accordingly. Other of her themes showed her internal conflicts about being in college; some criticize New Englanders for snobbishness; still others are slice-of-life pieces about frightened children, blacks, and family quarrels. She also wrote paeans to William James, to sleep, and to Baltimore's sensuality.

That spring she wrote a "connected work" about the studious, dark-skinned Hortense Sanger. Leaving "the library where most of her young life had been passed," the woman complained, "'Books, books . . . is there no end to it. Nothing but myself to feed my own eager nature. Nothing given me but musty books.'" Rejecting a bright woman's normal life, Hortense experiences a sexual awakening when a strange man rubs up against her during a crowded church service. Stein's focus is on both the character's acceptance of the situation and her family's censure of her for allowing it. Although Stein received a C, the usual mark in the class of fifty-six students, her grader, the young poet William Vaughn Moody, complimented her on the long story.

Stein's linked stories show her ability to write with both passion and style, yet some of her strategies indicate that she knew the dangers of writing too clearly and of breaking codes of propriety. By temperament, Gertrude saw herself less as a "creative" writer than as a "lover of argument" who wanted to "get argument into every thesis." Enrolling the following year in English C, George Pierce Baker's forensics course, she wrote and argued so well that Baker gave her an A–, one of only six As in the class of thirty-seven. An admirer of Ibsen and Meredith, a playwright and an actor, Baker had his feet firmly planted in the twentieth century. Stein liked that, and she liked him.

Her twenty-page essay remaining from this course, "The Modern Jew Who Has Given Up the Faith of His Fathers Can Reasonably and Consistently Believe in Isolation," shows how good Stein could be when she cared about what she wrote. In standard rhetorical style, she defined terms—*Jew, faith, isolation*—in the context of marriage, writing, "The Jew shall marry only the Jew. He may have business friends among the Gentiles; he may visit with them in their work and in their pleasure, he will go to their schools . . . but in the sacred precincts of the home, in the close union of family and of kinsfolk he must be a Jew with Jews; the Gentile has no place there." Concluding that a person was "a Jew first and an American only afterwards," she emphasized that "race feeling" was "an enlargement of the family tie." She also lamented increasing anti-Semitism. Her well-argued essay convinced Baker, who corrected only a few transitions and marked an occasional "unclear." For the most part, Gertrude's prose was, as Santayana had directed, radiantly clear as it expressed both the argument and the writer's self.

A Radcliffe Woman

Despite community efforts to prevent the Harvard Annex from becoming Radcliffe College, the state legislature approved the name change in 1894. While women had received educations comparable to those of Harvard men, the change allowed them also to be given diplomas—and to feel as if they were engaged in a respectable educational enterprise. Gertrude already knew her enterprise was respectable, and by the close of her first two years, she had compiled a good record. To her substantial number of As in philosophy, psychology, forensics, and history, she added B+s in German literature and philosophy (from Josiah Royce, who kept discussion to a minimum), a B in economics, and the C in composition. She had also seen most of the operas and theater productions in the area, attended every meeting of the Philosophy Club, and taken time for whatever fun classmates could devise.

Her junior year, however, provided the core of her undergraduate education. William James, back from leave, resumed teaching the psychological laboratory. Stein enrolled not only for that but for his yearlong seminar, a study of feelings and emotion and, in the second semester, "Consciousness, Knowledge, the Ego, the Relation of Mind and Body, etc." The engagingly unorthodox James, who had been a painter and an explorer before taking a teaching post, was world-renowned for his 1884 essay "What Is an Emotion?" (With Danish philosopher C. G. Lange, he formulated a theory of emotion that asserted emotion was the effect of organic changes rather than being a primary sensation.) Now a professor of philosophy and chair of both that department and the psychology program, he had made famous his customary blend of theory and practice, research and intuition. His reputation was more than academic: he lectured widely and published in both professional journals and popular ones (*Scribner's, The Nation, The Atlantic Monthly*). Seldom had difficult and provocative material been presented so gracefully; his two-volume *Principles of Psychology* was already a classic text. Yet, most important, no professor at Harvard had a better reputation for caring about students.

Because she had already worked with Santayana, Royce, and Münsterberg, Gertrude knew a great deal about James and his clinically based animal behaviorism. (Münsterberg had used James's *Principles of Psychology* as the text in her freshman course.) To study with James was a validation, a confirmation, of her belief that learning was wholistic: he accepted every part of human experience as valuable. (Stein sometimes felt isolated among college intellectuals and demanded that knowledge include real experience. Basking in the sun, for her, was as meaningful as studying Hegel.) As she later wrote, James was "the important person" in her Radcliffe years and that he simply "delighted her. His personality and his teaching and his way of amusing himself with himself and his students all pleased her. Keep your mind open, he used to say."

The laboratory class, though overenrolled, did not disappoint her; she later recalled, "We were quite a funny lot. . . . McDouglass a man afterwards well known who worked on conversion. William James was interested in that in connection with his Varieties of Religious Experience. . . . William James liked thinking and talking and wondering about what any one was doing." Stein was one of James's favorites. He paired her with Leon Solomons, a California graduate student trained in biology, as a research team and suggested they "do something connected with a tuning fork but as neither one of us had a very good ear for notes that was given up." Solomons, who had come to Harvard purposely to work with James—sharing his interest in the paranormal and the demonic, the less acceptable side of psychological research—also had a number of James's health problems. His insomnia, headaches, and faintness made him a difficult partner, though he was admittedly brilliant. But Gertrude was good balance for him, and together they worked out a study in attention, using themselves as primary subjects.

At James's insistence, the study—published in the September 1896 *Harvard Psychological Review* as "Normal Motor Automatism"—also made use of a planchette to test subjects' ability to move without conscious direction. Never intended to be a study of automatic writing, as it has erroneously been described, the project also tested the limits of a normal person's capability to perform various acts without "thinking" about them. The team concluded that "real automatism, that is, dropping out of consciousness" comes only for very short periods of time—and only when the attention is sufficiently distracted. The results of whatever the subject does during those periods are infinitesimal. In short, there is no such thing as "automatic writing." (Stein later wrote a friend about the term, explaining that her research represented "xamples of a certain amount of distraction of attention" and that she concluded "that there are no real cases of automatic writing, [though] there are automatic movements. . . . Writing for the normal person is too complicated an activity to be indulged in automatically.")

In the laboratory course and project, Stein received an A; in the seminar, however, although James gave her an A for the first term, the grade for the second was a C. Such an anomaly may explain the apocryphal story of her not taking the final examination. As the story is told, Gertrude wrote Professor James a note, "I am so sorry but really I do not feel like an examination paper in philosophy today," and in return, she said, he gave her the highest mark in the class. There is no question that Gertrude remained close to James—they corresponded, he visited her in Paris—but it seems plausible that her not taking the examination brought her mark of A down to C.

Her other grades during that year were also uneven—Bs in zoology, a C in physics, and a B and a C in mathematics. The slide continued during her fourth year: her C– in chemistry was the lowest in the class of fourteen, as were her Bs in small botany and zoology seminars. In psychological laboratory, however, this time with Professor Delabarre, she again starred. Her senior project, investigating responses from fifty women and forty-one men, studied attention during times of rest and fatigue. Published in the May 1898 *Harvard Psychological Review*, "Cultivated Motor Automatism: A Study of Character in Its Relation to Attention" suggested that people could be divided into types on the basis of the way their minds responded to stimuli. Gertrude's first type—"nervous, high strung, very imaginative, has the capacity to be easily roused and intensely interested"—she found in women literature students and men "going in for law." "Type II" people were "more varied" though many of them were pale, blond, and "distinctly phlegmatic." Their ability to concentrate was inferior. In both kinds of people, fatigue adversely affected responses.

Attention to her research did not change Stein's social patterns. To her involvement with theater, the Philosophy Club (of which she was secretary during her junior and senior years), and campus lectures, she added membership in what Arthur Lachman, another California student, called "a small group of earnest young people" who met weekends at the home of a Cambridge family. Including Leon Solomons, the group often attended church services, listening to ministers who spoke as scholars rather than preachers. They then went to the family's home for good food and "vigorous arguments and discussions." Lachman recalled sessions lasting "far into Monday's wee small hours."

During Gertrude's senior year, however, Solomons returned to California to recover his health. She sent him a draft of her senior essay, only to have him scold her for its style. He admired its content, however, and, despite his querulous tone, showed that he cared about her and her work. In her later notebooks, Stein described their friendship as both intellectual and sexual: "long walk in hill country back gives way forced to lie flat and then move on the way I did once with Leon," and, more specifically, "Lying out in the country arrange midnight walk etc. Platonic because neither care to do more. She and he both have their moments but they know each other and it is not worthwhile. She tells her experiences, he never his." There are references to Leon's flirtations (his "semi-flames") and a number of statements that compare Solomons with herself: both Jewish, both from San Francisco, both Californians who wanted to live a "free life in the mountains" and were distressed to come east with the "civilised ones."

One entry suggested that they were intimate enough to disagree: "What right have you to talk like god almighty you never succeeded in doing anything. Perhaps not but I have a fighting chance to do a big thing sometimes and that makes it right for me to feel." In some ways, Leon was like Leo Stein, especially in his lack of humor and in his tendency to close off "a triumphant argument" with "unpleasant rapid utterance and self contemplation." For at least some of her time at Radcliffe, however, Gertrude considered Solomons a possible marriage partner. Years later, she wrote about the "definite mark" the older, experienced man had left on her life. By all accounts, Leon was "widely read, deeply thoughtful, and enormously stimulating." And pressures on young Jewish women to marry had not diminished during Gertrude's four years in Cambridge.

Marriages

While Leo and Gertrude went east and Simon—despite what his brother called his increasing "ponderosity"—worked as a cable car gripman, Mike became engaged to Sarah (Sally) Samuels, daughter of a San Francisco attorney. Valedictorian at fifteen of her high school class, Sally had studied painting and done charity work after graduation. Fascinated by spiritualism and fortune telling, she was eager to meet Mike because a fortune teller had predicted that she would marry a man from Baltimore with an interest in wheels.

After their 1893 wedding, the Steins lived at 1118 O'Farrell Street in San Francisco, and Mike continued working for Omnibus. The address marked them as upwardly mobile though not yet a part of what Sally called "the Jewish money aristocracy." O'Farrell was a German-Jewish neighborhood; the Levys and the Levinsons—Harriet Levy's and Alice Toklas's families—lived nearby. During the summer of 1894, at the end of Gertrude's first and Leo's second year in Cambridge, they traveled west to meet Sally. As if testing her, Gertrude asked her to read aloud from Robert Browning's poetry and then soberly nodded approval. The younger sister regretted losing Mike; he was both brother and father to her.

Sally had to use ingenuity to outwit the protective Stein siblings. She befriended Gertrude and Leo and put up with brother Simon's frequent visits, although dealing with him was frustrating. Buying him an account book, she helped straighten out his finances, but she complained to Gertrude about his girlfriends, his garish clothes, and his limited power to do anything of interest. While she humored Simon, as Gertrude did, Sally wanted nothing to do with Bertha, even though they had not met. One of the first family arguments occurred when Bertha, planning to visit Mike and Sally in California, was told by Sally that her coming would be inconvenient. Months went by. Bertha, in Baltimore, waited for an invitation that never came.

Finally, in 1895, Bertha responded to Sally's inhospitable behavior by demanding her share of her father's estate. Mike was "exceedingly put out" at her request, but the will had been probated, so he gave Bertha a cash settlement. She wanted her money so that she could marry Jacob Raffel, a Baltimore paper manufacturer. While Sally was happy that Bertha was marrying ("she won't get a chance like this again in a hurry"), she was angry that the older sister appeared to mistrust Mike's management of her funds. Perhaps as a result of Bertha's demands, in the fall of 1895 Mike set up bank accounts for Gertrude, Leo, and Simon. He wrote Gertrude that her account had $258 in it, to be augmented soon with $300 from Omnibus bonds and on January 1 "probably $240 as direct from German Bank and I hope some dividends on Market Street."

Sally's animosity toward Bertha in part reflected the family's hostility toward the older sister, which had increased after their parents' deaths. Yet, though Bertha had used the responsibility of running the house as a way to boss her brothers and sister, she was no more stubborn—nor more at fault—than were her siblings. Sally's attitude suggests some of her own troublesome characteristics—a quick temper, a distant manner, and a need to be the center of attention. Early in her marriage, those traits were hidden. Sally was delighted to be Mrs. Michael Stein; to Gertrude, she praised Mike as being "much stronger than I am in every virtue . . . and in his relations to me, very near heroic." She also wrote to her sister-in-law about plays and books—*The Green Carnation, Trilby,* Olive Schreiner's short stories, *Art and Criticism,* by Theodore Child—mentioning as well that she had enjoyed hearing William James lecture in San Francisco. She had also read a selection of James, Royce, and Münsterberg from materials Gertrude sent her.

Between 1893 and 1896 Gertrude's and Sally's letters were affectionate and often intimate; in 1893, for example, Sally wrote that her "dear doctor" had told her about several self-abuse cases he was treating, and she used the topic to point out to her sister-in-law that the doctor felt just as Gertrude did about possible permanent damage from masturbation: "It seems that he has two young girls now under treatment, one of whom he feels sure he can cure; the other he knows to be hopeless. Both are of fine family. He gives . . . very strong medicine to dissipate the sensations . . . but when the habit is particularly abnormal in its method and of very long practice there follows an aversion to the opposite sex, and marriage itself is of no avail." Sally concluded with the horrific note that removing the ovaries was the next step in treatment. Demonstrating typical turn-of-the-century attitudes, Sally also praised a friend's "missionary work" advising men with homosexual leanings to marry early and find happiness in "healthy intercourse."

Sally's views about deviance were the norm; *perverted* or *inverted* were accepted labels for homosexuals, and the attention soon to fall on Oscar Wilde's scandalous sexual practices revealed the depth of social disapproval. While in retrospect the hysteria about "perversion" seems to reflect the growing power of a conservative culture—reinforced by the growing power of the male-dominated and conservative American Medical Association—the fact was that even Sally Stein, a reasonably sophisticated woman, was suspicious of anything her culture labeled *deviant.*

Writing soon from a new address at 707 Pierce Street, during the next years Sally described for Gertrude her gynecological and obstetric problems. All medical treatment had grown dependent on drugs and surgery, and most women's medicine focused on curing the womb problems said to cause many women's illnesses. Dr. S. Weir Mitchell, the American expert on women's medicine, relied on "the idea of experiment" as he developed his rest cures for such neurasthenics as Edith Wharton, Jane Addams, and Charlotte Perkins Stetson [Gilman]. To relieve the fragile female from stress by putting her to bed, feeding her rich foods, and enjoining her to keep her mind clear of thought—no reading, writing, or studying—was to "cure" her, but it was also to infantilize her. Mitchell and his friend William Osler of Johns Hopkins Medical School became so influential in women's medicine that few people knew of any treatments besides theirs. (On January 17, 1896, during Gertrude's junior year at Radcliffe, S. Weir Mitchell spoke to the women students about "the mental training, health, dress, and manners of college women.")

Sally's letters document the practices of gynecology in the late 1800s. Her traumatic medical history began soon after Gertrude and Leo visited; in September 1894 she was "curetted." She spent two weeks in bed, partly because of long nausea after the chloroform, and was subjected to what she called "diabolical" uterine massage every day; because she was constipated, she also received abdominal massage. Her gynecological condition improved enough for her to conceive. By March 1895 she was having morning sickness, and an October 28 letter spoke of awaiting the baby after "the longest seven months of my life."

Sally's five-day labor began at 4 A.M. Sunday, with the doctor spending the entire time with her and finally taking out the baby at noon on Thursday. The labor was dry; there was an attached placenta. Allan safely delivered, Sally prepared for the operation to repair her cervix. On March 27, 1896, she wrote that the surgery would be in three weeks and said bluntly that Gertrude should not come for the summer. In compensation, Sally invited her for the following year, closing "My head aches, and my back aches, and my legs ache, and my hands are swollen, and I suppose I had better spare you for the present any further expression of my condition."

Despite her medical problems, an underlying theme of Sally's letters was that Gertrude should marry and have children: bright Jewish women became the wives of smart Jewish businessmen. Sally reminded Stein that she had to recognize that, as a college woman, she threatened prospective suitors. As the years passed and Gertrude moved further from the idea of marriage and closer to understanding her own homosexual preferences, the friendship between the women cooled.

Sally Stein as married woman worked to keep her independence; Bertha Stein Raffel, however, chose a different kind of relationship. Jacob Raffel, younger than Bertha by several years, was the inventor of a process for making corrugated paper boxes that provided him a substantial living. After their courtship, nurtured carefully by Aunt Fanny Bachrach, they were married in September 1897. Because he was an Orthodox Jew, Bertha learned to prepare kosher food. As her daughter Gertrude later wrote, Bertha "wasn't accustomed to religion but she had to learn. . . . She personally did her own shopping for the house, even after she could have telephoned her orders. She went to market on Tuesday and Friday, and on Thursday she went in her car to get fresh vegetables, fruit and eggs from the farmers outside Baltimore." In any case, Bertha no longer had to question her role in life; she was a wife, soon to become a mother, and her home would be the center of her existence. She would never be one of those single women who were, in Jewish law, "liable to suspicion."

Leo Abroad

While Mike and Sally and Bertha and Jacob married, Leo's lifelong dream— to travel the world—was becoming a reality. In August 1895, Uncle Sol invited Leo to accompany his cousin Fred on his round-the-world tour. Sol would pay expenses beyond what living in Cambridge cost, so Leo accepted. Like many educated, middle-class people of the late nineteenth century, Leo loved travel—thinking about it, planning it, doing it. The fascination of being well traveled stemmed from the myth that the educated man— whether Boswell, Stendhal, Darwin, or Lawrence—knew the world and the important things in it. Some of this spirit of wonder is clear in Leo's comment to Gertrude that Antwerp is "a different world. You feel it and see it all about you." Of the world, in his limited experience of summers abroad, Leo preferred Germany. Except for its art, Paris was a disappointment, although Leo referred to the Salle Carrée of the Louvre as his schoolroom. He wrote Gertrude frequently about his tastes: "For color and composition I swear by Rubens. I haven't grown enthusiastic about any of the Italians though except Leonardo. He has here the Mona Lisa and another portrait of a woman also wonderfully subtle." Leo was soon to experience much more than the limited Western culture of France, Germany, and Italy.

In late summer 1895 Leo met Fred Stein in New York, and they traveled to California, where they took the *Coptic* to Kyoto, Japan. There they lived for a month in "a 7-room Japanese house with cook boy interpreter . . . and waiting girl." Their party now included Hutchins Hapgood, a Harvard graduate whom they had met on board ship. Leo wrote, "We sleep on and under futons, i.e. mats [*sic*] we eat off of little stands about eight inches high with supplementary stands about three inches high for salt cellars glasses etc. We wear kimonas [*sic*] and sit on the floor." The men learned to eat with chopsticks, but they did not appreciate such traditional Japanese "chow" as "birds broiled in their own feathers . . . sour fish chowder . . . the vilest lot of tastes and smells imaginable." Leo found Japan "surprising in its continual unreality."

Leo's letters to Gertrude are the chief source of information about both his travels and his college years, yet those letters are strangely impersonal, filled with commands that she rent out his rooms or pay his bills. Faced with a year's separation from her, he never acknowledged that his trip would deprive Gertrude of family—she would be alone in Cambridge—or that he would miss her. Instead, Leo grieved about his books: "How I hate to leave my books for a whole year. I have a feeling of sadness that is very kin to pain. . . . For goodness sakes see that they are all there again on my return." (His absence led to Gertrude's friendship with Leo Friedman, an Ohio student who also boarded at 123 Irving Street. Sharing her love of music, Friedman went to concerts and the opera with her. His June letter as she was leaving for the summer—"Weeks ago I felt how lonesome it would be here without you"—suggests that they had become close.) Her brother's impersonality in letters is surprising, too, because Gertrude was his confidante; he complained to her about his boredom with Fred and with other friends. He told her to share his letters with the Baltimore Keyser/Bachrach families and then send them on to the California Steins. Perhaps his arbitrariness was an attempt at humor; in an apparently scolding letter, for instance, he criticized Gertrude's friends, what he called her "scurrilous scrawl," and her "psychology bemuddled intellect" but closed by making her the deal that if she got his Cambridge room rent reduced, she could have half the reduction as a "bonus." Perhaps Gertrude understood that affection lurked under Leo's gruffness. Friends recalled that "the love between the brother and sister then was very beautiful."

In contrast, Leo's letters to Mike and Sally were irritably defensive. In a December letter from Kyoto, he compared the "Japs" to Shylock, calling them "the most infernally irresponsible people I ever saw." From Hong Kong, he described China as filled with dirt, bad government, and enough corruption to make Japan seem charming. His skirmishes with Sally suggested that he was being misunderstood over sexual innuendoes or gifts that might be offensive, such as an undraped madonna figurine and a much-discussed white elephant; in return, Sally wrote that one of his friends was serving a two-year jail term "for sending indecent matter through the mails." In these family letters, Jewishness remained a bond, as when Leo wrote about a train conductor's complaining that Jewish passengers never bought goods from him because "them Jews—all have friends in business."

In Leo's memoirs, however, these months abroad take on a romantic radiance. He recalled

> the first view of Fujiyama after nine days of storm at sea with all hatches closed; the wonder ride . . . through the paper-lantern-lighted streets of Yokohama . . . months of fascinating life in Kioto [*sic*], which was out of bounds and where there were no foreigners. . . . Canton with its mysterious, keenly, almost ferociously intelligent-looking crowds; Ceylon, where I sat under a upas tree and survived; . . . Egypt, where more fascinating than the monuments were the gallops in the desert; Italy and the first taste of Naples, Rome, Florence, Venice; the trip through Vienna to Carlsbad.

As his year with Fred neared its end, Leo invited Gertrude to tour Europe with him during the summer:

> If you came over on the Red Star . . . you would strike Europe at perhaps the most favorable spot [Antwerp] for getting a really satisfactory impression. . . . We could go through a number of delightful old places, Bruges, Liege [*sic*], Mechlin, etc., and then into Holland, with the Hague, Amsterdam, Rotterdam, Scheveningen and others. . . . We could go to Cologne take the steamer up the Rhine to Mainz and then via Heidelberg or Frankfurt & Strassburg to Rheims & Paris. . . . Opportunities are infinite.

Leo's confidence that his sister would particularly love Paris reflected the excitement that then suffused the city. Sometimes called "the banquet years," the late nineteenth and early twentieth centuries in Paris produced an avant-garde that was a way of daily life rather than simply an aesthetic movement. Leo also knew that Gertrude was as open to experience as he was and thought either Paris or Florence the perfect setting for adventure.

Both Leo's and Gertrude's memoirs suggest that traveling gave them not only information but also the idea that they might adopt European lifestyles. Their summers abroad—beginning in 1896—prepared them to consider expatriation as a way of living graciously on their comparatively small incomes. Despite Gertrude's clamorous enthusiasm for being American, she was practical enough to see that living well in the States would require more money than she had or was likely to have. And as Leo grew more and more fascinated with the study of art, Italy became his lodestar.

The Sexual Century

Leo and Gertrude at Johns Hopkins

For a time, however, their educations kept them in the States. Gertrude finished her senior year at Radcliffe, though she could not graduate with her class because she had never passed the Latin entrance exam. Feeling debilitated after his year abroad, Leo spent 1896–97 living quietly in Cambridge. During the summer of 1897 he and Gertrude—with her classmate Margaret Lewis—went to Cape Cod for the Woods Hole marine biological course, which consisted of individualized laboratory research. Leo studied invertebrates, while Gertrude took embryology. With Margaret as tutor, she also studied the necessary Latin.

Late in the summer, after attending cousin Bird Stein's wedding in New York, Leo and Gertrude settled into a three-story row house at 215 East Biddle Street in Baltimore. After years of boarding out, they enjoyed living in their own place, decorated with Leo's Japanese prints and etchings he and Gertrude bought together. Mike complained about their spending money to furnish the house, but they also hired Lena Lebender, a German cook-housekeeper. Worried about Leo's continual lethargy and indigestion, Gertrude wrote Sally that their living together was part of her plan to "keep house and nurse him [Leo] according to all the latest medical school theories."

In Baltimore, cousin Helen Keyser, too, coached Gertrude for the September Latin exam. Her acceptance to medical school was conditional on her passing it, which she did. She then began her medical studies at Johns Hopkins and the following May, in 1898, graduated magna cum laude in philosophy from Radcliffe.

In retrospect, Gertrude was not sure why she had wanted to go to medical school. William James had advised her to get an M.D. in order to become a psychologist; as James's pupil, she was accepted at Johns Hopkins. She had not, however, investigated the program there and found to her dismay that "hard" science dominated laboratory work; at Harvard, James's experiments were human-centered, or "soft." In Baltimore, she reminisced nostalgically about Radcliffe and Harvard. While the world grew more anti-Semitic, as Alfred Dreyfus's conviction for treason and his imprisonment on Devil's Island showed, Harvard opened the country's first Jewish museum. And even though one Harvard professor patronized women students by saying that they "ought to be playing," the rest of the faculty had encouraged her—and other women students—to excel.

Radcliffe's supportive atmosphere was worlds away from the keen competition at Hopkins, where many male medical students disliked having women in the program. Of the sixty-three students in the class of 1901, eleven were female. Many professors were sexist, as were textbooks and jokes: women students recorded being hit by "missiles of paper, tinfoil, [and] tobacco quids." When she learned that a visiting German anatomist had said disdainfully that the models of brain tracts that women students made were suitable work "for women and Chinamen," Gertrude became politicized. She knew that Franklin Mall, the anatomy professor who urged women students to make such tracts, did not ask male students to do so. She began calling herself a *woman* medical student, taking on the challenge of the influential professor William Osler, who often remarked, "Human beings may be divided into three groups, men, women and women physicians."

The Johns Hopkins Medical School—the first American program to meet high German standards—had admitted women since 1882. By 1890 there were forty-five hundred practicing women physicians in the United States; most of them, however, like Claribel Cone, sister of Leo's friend Etta, had been trained in women's medical schools. The American Medical Association discouraged women doctors from applying for licenses; it accepted no women as AMA members until 1915. Society's reaction, too, was often hostile, and many women physicians never practiced or did so only in small towns.

Part of the professional animosity against women physicians was the fear that they represented not only feminism but also what the AMA called "irregular" medicine, practices promoted by the Popular Health movement, which stressed diet-based treatment. In contrast, the AMA urged the use of surgery in all areas of medicine but particularly in the treatment of women's illnesses. In 1860s America, because so many women suffered from an indefinite malady called "hysteria," clitoris removal was in vogue. Later, ovariotomy, the removal of both ovaries, was popular; by 1906, over 150,000 American women had had this operation. The AMA had already accumulated a bleak record in its treatment of women's illnesses: it regularly condoned the use of opium, cocaine, and alcohol to treat women's pain and "nerves," thereby addicting thousands of female patients. AMA physicians also treated many women for a malady they called "disease of the womb." Historian Ann Douglas Wood describes "senseless injections" of milk, water, linseed tea, and "decoction of marshmellow [sic]" into the uterus, as well as "leeching . . . placing the leeches right on the vulva or on the neck of the uterus, although Bennet [a widely read English gynecologist] cautioned the doctor to count them as they dropped off when satiated lest he 'lost' some. Bennet had known adventurous leeches to advance into the cervical cavity of the uterus itself, and he noted, 'I think I have scarcely ever seen more acute pain than that experienced by several of my patients under these circumstances.'"

Although not all women had gender-based reasons for studying medicine, Gertrude did. Her mother's long painful illness and death and, more recently, her sister-in-law's obstetrical experiences made her care passionately about women's medicine. Treatment of women was flawed in part because so little was known about women's sexuality—or any sexuality. The 1897 publication of the first of Havelock Ellis's six-volume *Studies in the Psychology of Sex* shocked the polite world by defending male homosexuality. In 1899 Ellis's second book, *Auto-Eroticism,* explained both female and male masturbation. That sex could be enjoyable—and that it could exist in something other than heterosexual pairings—contradicted the usual medical view. Ellis's work also introduced readers to the notion that women's sexuality need not be passive, nor need it be unhealthy.

Along with a developing discourse about sexuality, which had clear implications for medical treatment, Ellis's work and current events provided Gertrude with information about public reaction to homosexuality. Society's view was best illustrated by the 1895 trial and imprisonment of the brilliant English writer Oscar Wilde. That this complex, talented artist was trapped by a rigidly circumspect society and punished for the freedom art itself advocated was an irony Gertrude found difficult to understand. In 1898 when she read *The Ballad of Reading Gaol,* Wilde's long poem about his two-year imprisonment for homosexuality, Gertrude awoke to the dangers of admitting sympathy for homosexuals or expressing those tendencies in her own life. As a woman who thought she might be able to love other women, Gertrude realized she needed to be silent about her private erotic life.

The presence of women students in medical school classrooms had little effect on subject matter—male professors saw their field as scientifically pure, though there were some who would not teach anatomy to women— but Gertrude was glad there were other women in her class. Studying at Johns Hopkins were Marion Walker from Radcliffe and other women from Smith, Wellesley, the University of Wisconsin, and Stanford; along with these students, several physicians—Claribel Cone among them—took courses. A bonus for Gertrude in the move back to Baltimore was her friendship with Claribel. Not only had she received her medical degree a decade earlier, the older Cone sister was independent and acerbic, a feisty role model for the frustrated Gertrude, who saw some friends marrying and others content to live at home while she was still deciding what she wanted from life. Some of Gertrude's friends were teaching, but others had given up careers. One Radcliffe classmate wrote her that working was too strenuous:

"A 'career' is the last thing on earth from my desires. . . . A sheltered life, domestic tastes, maternity, and faith are all I could ask for myself or you or the great mass of womankind. I overworked and overreached—too much ambition, too little faith in traditional ideals." Sally's letters to Gertrude also continued praising marriage and motherhood as woman's greatest happiness: "Therefore my dear and beloved sister in law go and get married, for there is nothing in this whole wide world like babies."

Claribel Cone's view that most women's lives were boring provided a corrective. On the streetcar ride to the university each morning, she and Gertrude swapped stories about patients, friends, and school experiences. A good storyteller, Claribel often spun a tale from the streetcar through the six-block walk to campus, continuing it the next day. Gertrude's intimacy with the older Cone sister showed her that a woman could lead her own life, despite familial and social pressures.

Early in their friendship, Claribel asked Gertrude to speak to a Baltimore women's group about the advantage of college educations for women. Gertrude's remarks were admonitory; she referred to Charlotte Perkins Stetson's [later Gilman] 1898 book *Women and Economics* to emphasize that, without educations, women were only pawns in the economic system and that they were, in fact, overpaid for the strictly domestic tasks they performed in their households. She described the roles women were asked to play in "this hopelessly complex period in which we live" and contrasted the human life cycle with that of animals, calling the human species "over sexed" because it allows sex to determine male and female behaviors throughout life rather than only during child-bearing years. As sex objects, Gertrude said, women are disadvantaged. Prevented from developing, they are unhealthily dressed and fed and forced—physically and mentally— to be passive. Discussing the greatest objections to higher education for women—that it is unfeminine, that it makes women ill and/or desexes them—Gertrude argued that it is the finishing school graduate (who spends all her life thinking about the sex role) who is troubled. Women who marry for love and not out of financial need, she asserted, are more satisfying sex partners because they do not feel coerced into giving their husbands pleasure.

Instead of argument for her controversial statements, Stein relied on humor, as when she contrasted the life of the modern woman with the lives of her predecessors: "We do not have to spin and weave and knit and make worsted work in endlessly ugly patterns and most of us do not even have to, as Thackeray says, make puddens with our own hands." When she described a dozen women medical students on a crab boil, she stressed that "they were not selected with respect to their picnic qualifications but were an haphazard collection." These capable women could row boats, build fires, cook crabs, and have fun—without men.

Gertrude's remarks about child rearing showed her reliance on William James's beliefs: "We must study the nature of the individual child. . . . We must realise the effect of health and nervous conditions and where the old time mother stood the child in the corner we give it a rest cure or a physic." She emphasized, too, every woman's duty to the poor, to the so-called fallen woman, and scoffed at "charity in the good old fashioned lady bountiful method. We cannot go around with a basket full of things to eat and feed the first deserving poor we run across." She told her listeners instead to train their eyes to see into the darkness of existing social conditions, to assume "the awful sense of responsibility for our neighbors' suffering. . . . In the hands of women must to a great extent lie the amelioration of the condition of women." In an age when fashionable women prided themselves on their moral superiority, her comments bordered on the offensive.

She concluded by stressing that it was a valuable experience for a woman to be away from home for four years "with no one to protect you or be fond of you unless you earn it." Gertrude did not claim that all women would benefit from college, but she did present the experience from a number of perspectives, always grounded in the life choices her listeners would understand. It was clear that she saw her Radcliffe years as valuable and herself as a healthy, educated woman well prepared for a useful future.

Her confidence crumbled, however, as she faced Johns Hopkins's intimidating atmosphere; most days she dreaded going to class. She sometimes took refuge in her old Baltimore friendships, spending time with the Bachrachs, the Steins, and the Sociables, although she avoided the newly married Bertha. Both Etta and Claribel were pleased to have Leo and Gertrude living in north Baltimore. When Gertrude returned home to Biddle Street, however, she had to study; Leo, on the other hand, was more likely to spend his evenings at concerts at the Peabody Institute, at lectures and openings, and at the William T. Walters private gallery, where he studied Chinese porcelains and the work of the Barbizon painters. (After a decade of study abroad, uncle Eph Keyser had returned to Baltimore to teach, giving the Steins—including Bertha—entry to more circles of the art world.)

At Johns Hopkins, Leo was receiving the highest grades of his career. During what was his final year for the bachelor of science degree (after more than two years at the University of California, two years at Harvard, and a year at Harvard Law), Leo received 1s in chemistry, geology, osteology, and biology. Math still troubled him: in solid and analytic geometry and trigonometry, his grades were only high Cs. After he graduated in 1898, Leo entered an advanced program in zoology, with minors in physiology and physics. His first year of doctoral study was Gertrude's second of medical school. Both did reasonably well, but Leo disliked laboratory work so much that he knew he would never complete the degree. The high point of his week was the meeting of the zoological journal club, and he spent more and more time in art galleries.

As he had in Cambridge, Leo lived a selective life. He chose the people he wanted as friends and the role he played in friendships. He liked being a moral and an intellectual guide, so his friends were often younger than he. Little about Leo was spontaneous: a Harvard acquaintance remembered that in Cambridge, Leo, often ill with digestive upsets, had lived so privately that he seemed neurotic. It was not uncommon for him to follow diets that were more like fasts, staying on them several weeks (he records one fast that lasted thirty days). Leo demanded order and control in whatever he did.

Gertrude continued to be the more outgoing of the two. One of the men from medical school recalled, "Almost every week we went to the Holiday Street Theatre. Gertie was excited by those old melodramas. She was such fun and I always found her very bright." As it had in both San Francisco and Cambridge, theater occupied a special place in her existence. During her second year at Johns Hopkins, Gertrude also befriended some of the women in the first-year class, among them two Bostonians who were to figure prominently in her life: Emma Lootz, from Smith, was to share a house with her for several years; Mabel Haynes, an 1898 Bryn Mawr A.B., became a romantic rival.

In her second-year course, Gertrude took anatomy, receiving a 1; pathology and bacteriology, a 1.5; and pharmacology and toxicology, a 2. Her ungraded short courses that year were auscultation (diagnosis through listening to sounds within organs) and physics. Compared with her first-year marks, which ranged from a 1 in anatomy to a 2.5 in physiological chemistry, her grades were slightly better, but she was hardly the brilliant student of William James's predictions.

Medical School and Its Denouement

As a student at Radcliffe and Harvard, Gertrude had been respected; at Johns Hopkins, she sensed ridicule. She was particularly upset over sexist faculty. Ironically, many of her problems were with William Osler and John Whitridge Williams, teachers in women's medicine, the field she considered her special interest. In his memoirs, Williams called his course "anecdotal midwifery," noting that he told tales of delivery with Rabelaisian detail, even though many students—men as well as women—found the stories offensive. Gertrude told him what she thought of his anecdotes, his teaching methods, and his course and stated that she would no longer attend class. "Dr. Williams replied that since his lectures were a part of the curriculum and since he was free to teach as he wished, he was forced to require her presence or ask her to withdraw from the school. She chose to withdraw." Legendary as this story has become, it oversimplifies the conflicts between Stein and Williams. But it shows two of Gertrude's qualities: she knew prejudice when she experienced it, and she never pretended to accept behavior she disliked.

Osler's sexism was more subtle. A disciple of S. Weir Mitchell, whose "cures" for women were already world-famous, and considered a stellar physician himself, although he did no research, Osler adopted Mitchell's paternalistic style, claiming that doctors healed best women who were devoted to the idea of being cured. In his words, "If a poor lass, paralyzed apparently, helpless, bed-ridden for years, comes to me, having worn out in mind, body, and estate a devoted family; if she in a few weeks or less by faith in me, and faith alone, takes up her bed and walks, the saints of old could not have done more." Gertrude wanted as little as possible to do with Osler and his glib answers for women's illness. She boycotted some of his classes, too.

Throughout Gertrude's years in medical school, she tested her learning by counseling her women friends, a practice she had begun when she lived in Baltimore surrounded by the Cone-Guggenheimer set. She continued her counseling at Radcliffe, where many women struggled with the conflict between being like their mothers—who were protected Victorian women, cared for by loving and economically powerful husbands—and being intelligent, wage-earning women who could still be feminine. The choices educated women had to make were difficult, as the increase in women's eating disorders and nervous ailments late in the century suggests; for women in medical school, choices became even more complex.

Gertrude also sensed that part of the hostility toward her at Johns Hopkins was anti-Semitic. Coming from Cambridge, a location she described as the place "where to be a Jew is the least burden . . . of any spot on earth," she was not used to thinking of Jewishness as a handicap. Yet during the 1890s, in her words, the world saw "a new wave of the old prejudices . . . the spirit prevalent in Germany . . . and the not so very distant exodus in Russia." Dorothy Reed, one of Stein's older classmates, called Professor Williams "an aristocrat and a snob" and said that he "couldn't stand her [Stein's] sloppy work . . . or her marked Hebrew looks." The Steins' friend Hutch Hapgood recalled Gertrude's seriousness about her need to marry a Jew: "She talked to me a long time about how impossible it was for a Jewish woman to marry a Gentile. It was one of the most striking examples that I have seen of the deep-seated feeling of the Jews about their race." Intensely self- and race-conscious, Gertrude resented being singled out because of her ethnicity.

She thought often of Leon Solomons. After receiving his Ph.D. from Harvard in the spring of 1898, he had taken a teaching position at the University of Wisconsin. His health deteriorated, however, and on February 2, 1900, one day before Gertrude's twenty-eighth birthday, he died in the midst of, or shortly following, an operation for cancer. That autumn William James wrote Gertrude expressing sorrow over Leon's "untimely and never too much to be regretted death," saying, "Exactly what he would have done had he lived, it is impossible to say, but it would have been absolutely original . . . and it might have been very important. . . . His eagerness, daring, honesty, good spirits, and scorn of all that was nonsensical and mendacious in life were glorious." As Gertrude grew more and more isolated, more and more aware that as a well-educated Jewish woman she would meet few men who would be acceptable marriage choices, she grew unremittingly lonely.

Leo, too, was gone, having moved to New York after dropping out of graduate school near the close of his first year. Gertrude moved to a brick house on East Eager Street with Emma Lootz. There, so depressed that she decided something was physically wrong with her, she hired a boxer to spar with her for exercise; from her room below, Emma could hear Stein ordering the fighter to give her one to the jaw, one to the kidneys. Gertrude kept up her social life, going to most of the plays produced in the city, but friends saw that she was unhappy. Except for her casework, delivering babies in Baltimore's black quarter, she was still doing assignments she disliked and still taking orders from authoritarian teachers.

Reared to be winning, Gertrude worked best in supportive situations; she bloomed under Münsterberg's and James's appreciation. Disapproval, however, reminded her of her father's criticism. What happened to her at Johns Hopkins was simple: without being challenged in a friendly way to do well, Gertrude did little. Disguising the anger she felt at the sexism and racism evident during her years at medical school, Gertrude pretended to be apathetic. As she later wrote, "They would ask her questions . . . from time to time and as she said, what could she do, she did not know the answers and they did not believe that she did not know them, they thought that she did not answer because she did not consider the professors worth answering. . . . It was impossible to apologise and explain to them that she was so bored she could not remember the things that of course the dullest medical student could not forget." In her third year, her grades slipped to a 2 in medicine, a 2.5 in surgery, and 3s—barely passing marks—in neurology, obstetrics, and clinical microscopy.

This pattern continued into 1900–1901, when she failed (receiving grades of 5) both Professor Williams's obstetrics course and laryngology, a class taught by J. N. MacKenzie, who was also known for his sexism. In pediatrics and medicine, she received 3s. Her higher grades during her senior year were a 2 in gynecology (from Osler) and a 2.5 in surgery. On her birthday in 1901, Leo wrote from Italy questioning her dissatisfaction with school and urging her to finish: "It would be too bad if the first person in the family who had gone so far as to get the adequate preparation for anything should go back on it."

On June 5, 1901, however, at a meeting of seven medical school faculty, Dr. William Osler moved that Gertrude Stein "be not recommended for the degree of Doctor of Medicine" with the rest of her class. Afterward, Dr. Williams told her that, of course, she would finish; she need only take a summer school course. To this comment, Gertrude reportedly answered that she was, in fact, grateful for the failure: "I have so much inertia and so little initiative that very possibly if you had not kept me from taking my degree I would have, well, not taken to the practice of medicine, but at any rate to pathological psychology and you don't know how little I like pathological psychology and how all medicine bores me."

Gertrude's record suggests that her grades fell, in part, as she learned what knowledge meant to conventional (male) physicians. Like other women in the program, she was subject to what today would be called sexual harassment: all women were made to feel out of place. At the turn of the century, however, Gertrude had no way to complain about offensive classroom behaviors, and her personality was such that she could not simply overlook them. She would not play the games required of women in order to get a degree. As her housemate, Emma Lootz, said, "Of course she didn't get it [the medical degree]. Do you think I'd have got mine if I hadn't worn my best hat? It had roses on it."

Characteristically, while Gertrude cut classes during her third and fourth years of medical school, she continued to work hard as a research assistant to Llewellys F. Barker, a former professor of anatomy at Johns Hopkins who had taken a post at the University of Chicago. (He would later return to Johns Hopkins as William Osler's successor.) Barker's classic 1899 book *The Nervous System and Its Constituent Neurones* contains three references to the studies of "Miss Gertrude Stein." Despite some faculty members' doubts about Gertrude's ability to do satisfactory work in medical school, she was recognized as superior by a leading researcher.

There is a further chapter in the story of the Stein-Barker relationship. Two years after her work with him and a term after she had finished her fourth year of medical school without graduating, Gertrude spent the 1901–02 year registered at Johns Hopkins as a special student, doing a series of models of the brain and a related essay for Barker. On January 30, 1902, Barker wrote her from Chicago about the second part of her essay, suggesting changes and approving the sixty-three drawings she had done. That spring he sent the complete manuscript to H. McE. Knower, a faculty member at Johns Hopkins who was secretary of the *American Journal of Anatomy*. On April 7, Knower rejected the paper, returning it to Barker with a note saying that it was too long—publishing it would take twenty-five pages of the journal—and commenting that the paper, in need of revision, was not very original.

Barker's April 9 reply both questioned Knower's decision and defended Gertrude's work: "I am convinced of the great value of the material, and am somewhat surprised to learn from your letter that so much of it has already been published. I am certainly not familiar with publications which cover the embryological series. I should be glad to have references to them." No specialist in this field, Knower had relied on the support of other faculty, who had agreed with his decision to reject the essay. Barker was right, however: there was no such material in print.

Before leaving on a long trip, Barker sent the essay back to Stein with a letter explaining the editor's reservations. She then replied, firmly, that she had done the study as she had to fill gaps in existing research: "The embryological series . . . enabled me to understand the adult series that I finally made. The whole point of the adult series . . . is not so much that there is very definite new material although there is some of that but . . . I have endeavored to express a very clear image . . . of a region which the existing literature leaves in a hopeless mess." She closed without apology, saying she had accomplished what she had intended. She also told Barker that Knower was incapable of judging the essay "because he does not know the region and its confusion. My object has been to save the next man from a long preliminary work." She thanked Barker for his help, regretting that she could do no more because she was going abroad. She hoped that her work, which she gave him for his own use, might be "of some service" but said that she did not plan to do anything more in neurology "for some time to come." Gertrude's thoroughly professional letter suggested that it was no accident that the Johns Hopkins faculty had rejected her work but that she had only disdain for their opinion.

On April 15, Knower apologized to Barker for his criticism of Stein's essay. He agreed that nothing like it was in print and said that the journal would accept a revised version. His initial rejection, however, cut Gertrude loose from a research career and confirmed her decision to have no part of the world of medicine.

As a coda to the impasse, on October 23, 1903, Barker again sent Stein's paper to Johns Hopkins, this time to Professor Mall. His cryptic note—that the paper "ought to be published as it is in the *Journal of Anatomy*" but might also be sent to the *Journal of Comparative Neurology*—stated an imperative that Mall did not honor. Despite Barker's enthusiasm, Gertrude's paper did not appear in either journal.

Gertrude's Explorations

One of the most important reasons for Stein's lack of interest in her third and fourth years of medical study had nothing to do with academics. During her junior year, living with Emma Lootz, Gertrude met—and found herself in love with—Bryn Mawr graduate May Bookstaver. Somewhat to Gertrude's surprise, the affair, which began in 1900, both consumed and disoriented her and made her question all the plans she had formerly made. The most frustrating part of the passionate relationship was that it had to exist in silence: no Jewish woman of her class—and few women anywhere—could admit to lesbianism.

Even though Gertrude saw herself as a worldly and progressive bluestocking, she knew full well that she would meet with family disapproval if any rumor of her affection for May reached the Bachrachs or the Steins. The daughter of a New York judge, May (Mary Abletta)—born October 12, 1875, to the Henry Bookstavers—prepared at Miss Baldwin's and took college entrance exams in the summers of both 1893 and 1894. Admitted to Bryn Mawr in 1894, she majored in history and political science with above-average grades and did some writing. After her 1898 graduation, she moved with friends to Baltimore, where she tutored in history and was active in the woman's suffrage and birth control movements. The tall, attractive May impressed people with her wit and her wide understanding of social and business issues, and she respected intellect: both Gertrude and Mabel Haynes, May's lover, were medical students. The women of their social set were all educated and competent, and they all aimed to be influential.

Gertrude had flirted with women before. Her notebooks record a conversation with Leon Solomons in Cambridge in which she admitted having been interested in a woman friend of Etta Cone's only to have Solomons reply that she should forget "all that" and marry Jack Preiss, a mutual San Francisco friend, "now she has the chance." At Johns Hopkins, she had become friends with women in Emma Lootz's Smith–Bryn Mawr circle. The Smith group consisted of such women as Florence Sabin, Rose Fairbank, Dorothy Reed, and Alice Tallant; the Bryn Mawr group, Mabel Haynes, Grace Lounsbery, and Bookstaver. Gertrude, who tended to be idealistic and naive, did not understand that these women were familiar with same-sex relationships through the "smashings" (lesbian courtship) common at women's colleges. When she told the circle of Smith and Bryn Mawr women that their trouble was "raw virginity," they laughed at her.

Gertrude's attraction for May tormented her for months, and eventually for years. She initially pretended to play her by-now customary role of counselor, saying she wanted to wean May away from Mabel's mundane circle. The more experienced May understood that Gertrude's feelings were erotic, and to some extent she seemed to share those feelings. But, finally, May remained enigmatic. Despite their intimacy, Gertrude never knew whether May returned her love, and the fact that their letters were destroyed prevents any reconstruction of the relationship. As the affair continued, Gertrude was faced with the realization that—for all her study of psychology and her experiments with the human mind—she was failing in her efforts to understand another person. Perhaps most serious for Stein's sense of self, she had never before known the power of passion.

Although her love for May is the subject of much of her earliest fiction, which she began writing in 1902, Gertrude did not mention the relationship in letters or memoirs. Like other women of her social set, including Mabel Haynes, May Bookstaver later married well, so her homoerotic years were disguised by what appeared to be consistently heterosexual preferences. A veil of circumspect silence thus covers the relationship that was, in many ways, pivotal to Gertrude's entire life. The passion she felt for May kept her from caring about her medical studies; the grief she felt for the loss of her beloved led her to take up writing as a means of charting and describing her pain, as well as of questioning what had gone wrong in a relationship she valued beyond anything else in her life.

During 1900–1901 she and May evidently carried on their flirtation under Mabel's scrutiny, though it was disguised as friendship. In one of the dialogues Gertrude transferred to her novella about the affair, *Q.E.D. (Things as They Are)*, Adele—the Gertrude character—confesses to Helen—the May character—that she fears "passion in its many disguised forms." Helen's reply is that Adele's ignorance is obvious. When Adele says that she could be an efficient pupil if she had a good teacher, Helen says nothing. In real life, May laughed outright at Gertrude's innocence.

Gertrude used the prospect of summer travel to keep herself functioning during the frustrating winter and spring months. But even after some glorious weeks in the Mediterranean sun of Granada and Tangiers—Gertrude basking while Leo toured the Spanish art collections—the return to Baltimore was frightening for her. If anything, she loved May more than she had in the spring. Accordingly, she delayed her return by spending nearly a month in New York with Mabel Weeks. Once back in the East Eager house with Emma Lootz, working on the brain study for Professor Barker, she led a somewhat aimless existence. Her description of the liaison in *Q.E.D.* suggests that 1901–1902 was the year of her deepest sexual involvement with Bookstaver. Years later May admitted that the dialogue in the novel is based on actual conversations:

> Adele [Gertrude] was in Helen's [May's] room the eve of her departure. They had been together a long time. Adele was sitting on the floor her head resting against Helen's knee. She looked up at Helen and then broke the silence with some effort. "Before I go" she said "I want to tell you myself what I suppose you know already, that Mabel has told me of the relationship existing between you." Helen's arms dropped away. "No I didn't know." She was very still. "Mabel didn't tell you then?" Adele asked. "No" replied Helen. There was a sombre silence. "If you were not wholly selfish, you would have exercised self-restraint enough to spare me this," Helen said. Adele hardly heard the words.

This scene exemplifies the pattern of reversing reader expectations that Gertrude creates in *Q.E.D.*: when Adele expects Helen to be remorseful or guilty, in this case because she has lied about the sexual nature of her relationship with Mabel, Helen turns the tables so that Adele feels guilt. Stein's dramatic shifting of reader expectations shows how different the women characters are and suggests the impossibility of their relationship continuing.

The scene also evokes the sexuality of the affair, using a strategy of ellipsis. There is no overt description of anything sexual; rather, the time that passes in lovemaking is described from within Adele's consciousness as "their long sessions in Helen's room," "the state of perfect happiness," "a very real oblivion," "losing herself again with Helen," "the habit of silent intimacy," "the complete joy of simply being together." Within the text, the women's physical contact is limited to some isolated kisses and a few erotic touches as they lie on a sunny ship deck. When the novella does make clear that the couple found ways to be intimate, it also shows that Adele "lost herself in the full tide of her fierce disgust." Abandonment to a fully erotic love was difficult for the fearful Stein daughter.

So occupied was Gertrude with her love affair that she had no energy left for study. Her pretended boredom was a mask for sexual frustration. She pretended that she did not care to finish her medical degree, though she easily could have. When friends insisted that she must finish in order to further the cause of women, Gertrude replied that they did not know what it was to be bored. (A later notebook entry, however, describing her feelings of "despair" in the Johns Hopkins gardens when she "got sick and faced flunking [her] exams," shows more complex reactions to that failure.) She pretended that she did not care to take up any practical work but was content to travel in Europe with Leo. In reality, all she could think of, and yearn for, was her beloved. Years after studying William James's writing on passion (defined as a kind of "monomania," second only to the fury of rage), Gertrude was caught in a maelstrom of feeling that drained her energy and her ambition. It was one of the only times in her life when she was in the grip of something stronger than her own will.

Leo's Explorations

It is stretching the biographer's role to conjecture that Gertrude might never have fallen so terribly in love with May if she had not been lonely. Had Leo continued to live with her in Baltimore, his presence might have provided some balance or some useful distraction. But after living for a while in New York, in 1900 Leo made the dramatic decision to move to Italy to study art. The decision to leave the States represented a careful renunciation of the American dream that his father had valued and his uncles and his brother Mike were following. Being tied to one location and routine and a social life dependent on occupation had never appealed to Leo.

His knowledge and brilliance served him well in his new life; acquaintances were hard-pressed to find subjects he did not know something about. His steady acquisition of information about art gave him an occupation searching for avant-garde paintings in private holdings and galleries. He mused about aesthetic questions related to both art and philosophy, the latter of which he had studied at Harvard along with his various majors in government and economics, law and history. Although he learned a great deal about Italian art during his two years in Florence, he continued to read philosophy; he later said ironically that he had "discovered pragmatism." Since both Charles Peirce and William James had already coined the term, Leo applied it to what he called "the mysteries of metaphysics." During his years in Italy, Leo studied Schopenhauer, Berkeley, Nietzsche, Leibniz, and Kant, work that gave him a basis for his later career as art critic.

Leo's first letters from Italy mentioned that, through Hutch Hapgood, he had met Bernard Berenson, the young Harvard aesthetician. Leo was impressed with his knowledge, with his house "filled with beautiful old Italian furniture and hangings," and with "his really magnificent art library." But when he again met Berenson and his British companion, Mary, the sister of Logan Pearsall Smith, he was bothered by "that tremendous excess of the I." Attracted by erudition and wealth, Leo was often critical of people's pride in their achievements. He himself remained dissatisfied with his own accomplishments, even after years of education, as he admitted to Gertrude: "I have numerous and varied interests: scientific, philosophical, literary, artistic with . . . no very decisive convictions." Defensive about his weaknesses, Leo said that life in Florence suited him because the city's "limited range of activity" kept him from intellectual game playing.

Unless introductions were carefully arranged, however, living in Florence—as in Europe as a whole—was isolated. Leo appreciated his acquaintance with Bernard Berenson; the expatriate colony in Italy was not welcoming. Historian John Rewald describes the "strange atmosphere of suspicion, intellectual snobbery, bruised scholarship, and stubborn grudges that engulfed the small Anglo-American colony of Florence and its surroundings." Though Leo adopted the colony's habit of reading the London *Times* every morning, he missed news about America and his friends there. Once more, he felt himself the outsider.

Correspondence between Leo and Gertrude shows how different the siblings were. Leo stated and restated his thoughts, discussing topics in June and again in October; as Berenson said, he was forever inventing the umbrella. Gertrude wrote short letters about immediate events, avoiding introspection. Concerned about Leo's recurring dyspepsia and diarrhea, she asked him about these matters but said little about her boredom with medical school. She wrote Leo that Mike, trying to maintain their allowances at a hundred dollars monthly, had invested the family money in gilt-edged stocks and bonds that paid between four and a half and five percent. Gertrude also wrote Leo with news about Simon, whose idea of fun was to buy cheap cigars and give them to unsuspecting friends. He had apprenticed in a foundry, but he seldom worked; he preferred visiting Mike and Sally at mealtimes. But she mentioned Bertha only briefly and her children—the first two having been born in 1898 (Daniel) and 1900 (Gertrude, her namesake)—not at all. (Bertha and Mike continued to wrangle over finances; she owed Mike nearly $500 for her share of their parents' gravesites and upkeep.)

Despite his living in Italy, Gertrude still saw Leo as an integral part of the family and an integral part of her existence. The first summer after his move abroad—1901—they had spent together in Spain; by early spring of 1902, Leo had tired of Italy, and, after Gertrude joined him in Florence for a while, they decided to try living in London, where they rented a flat at 20 Bloomsbury Square, very near the British Museum. The brother

and sister next went to the Lake Country (Gertrude loved, and often recited, Wordsworth's poetry) and liked it so much that they briefly rented
Greenhill, a cottage near the Berensons' home. During the season, people
commented about the "very American" Steins: both Leo and Gertrude enthusiastically praised the United States. Bertrand Russell, the Berensons'
brother-in-law, thought this curious because most other Americans came to
Europe in order to escape their provincial country.

Late in the autumn of 1902, the Steins returned to London, where
Gertrude read daily in the British Museum. Winter in England was depressing, however, and Gertrude was unnerved by the visible poor—especially
the children—she saw on the streets. On Christmas Eve, Leo abruptly left
for France, partly because he wanted to avoid holiday social engagements.
Gertrude stayed in England, alone, for another six weeks before sailing back
to New York to live with her friends Mabel Weeks, Harriet Clark, and sculptor Estelle Rumbold in their "little White House," a colonial building with a
rose garden. From New York she traveled to Baltimore to see May and occasionally Bertha and her children. Her visits to the Raffels were so uncommon, however, that her young niece, Gertrude, did not remember who her
aunt was when she came to the door, and Bertha's maid described her as "a
lady who looks like a gypsy." Art historian Georgiana King, another college
friend, recalled Gertrude's restlessness during the spring of 1903; she often
visited King's bohemian Fifty-seventh Street flat, where she would "cram
herself out of the window" to look at the river as she talked "at length about
anything from art to psychology."

More importantly, that spring Gertrude began keeping a notebook,
recording scenes and ideas for the long novel that would become *The Making of Americans* and working on both the start of that book and the con-
clusion of *Q.E.D.* When she once again returned to Europe during the summer of 1903 to accept Leo's invitation to make a home with him in Paris, it
was with a sense of relinquishment. She had accepted the fact that her affair
with May would never be resolved; even if May admitted that she loved
Gertrude, she was still in a kind of financial and emotional bondage to Mabel
Haynes, her companion of many years.

Leo and his sister toured Florence, Siena, and Rome, where Gertrude
spent some uncomfortable days with the vacationing May and Mabel. Then,
living at rue de Fleurus in Paris, Gertrude finished *Q.E.D.* The stability of
knowing that she once again had a home, that she was a part of a loving family, gave her the tranquillity to complete her first long prose work. For her,
living abroad meant escaping the conventions of an American woman's life
at the turn of the century and being accepted—either as herself, the incipient writer, or as Leo's younger sister—by a cosmopolitan culture. For Leo,
being abroad meant simplifying, carving out the leisure to live well and
affordably, and Gertrude's presence would double the income for the house-

hold. For both Steins, living in Europe was the way to lead a more private, even an anonymous, existence.

Living and traveling with Leo was, in other ways, a kind of panacea. His need to take practical control of their lives was comforting, particularly in Gertrude's state of depressed confusion. His ability to be completely absorbed in both natural and artistic beauty was also helpful, because his enthusiasm drew her into more intense appreciation. Learning about the art world replaced her emptiness whenever she thought about her wearying relationship with May, and for a time she found a stable base for her life with her brother.

PART 2

Americans Abroad

(1903–1919)

Literally at the threshold of a new life, Leo, Gertrude, and Michael pose together in 1904 near the entrance of Michael's rue Madame apartment. Mike and Sally, with their only child, Allan, had moved to Paris late in 1903, joining Leo and Gertrude. Michael was thirty-nine; Leo, thirty-two; and Gertrude, thirty.

In 1904 few people knew more about contemporary Italian, French, and Spanish painting than did Leo. After graduating from Johns Hopkins University in 1897—as Michael had a decade earlier—Leo located in Italy to study art. Several years later, in 1902, he moved to Paris and invited Gertrude to live with him. She had graduated from Radcliffe in 1897 and attended Johns Hopkins Medical School for four years, leaving without taking a degree; "Baby," as she was still known to her family, was at loose ends: she was thinking of becoming a writer. By moving to Paris and living with Leo, Gertrude became as involved in the New Art as he and saw in the techniques of Cézanne and Matisse, and later of Picasso, Gris, and other cubists, styles that would affect her writing.

"The Stein Corporation," as the four Steins were soon named, purchased several dozen paintings and countless drawings by Cézanne, Matisse, Picasso, Toulouse-Lautrec, Derain, Manguin, and Renoir each year. They lived modestly on $150 a month each, spending most of their income on art. Both Leo and Gertrude, who shared a flat at 27, rue de Fleurus, and Mike and Sally, living at 58, rue Madame, were gracious about showing their collections; by 1905, they had instituted the Saturday evening salons that were to immortalize them in the history of modernism.

(The Baltimore Museum of Art, Cone Archives)

The Steins in Paris

27, rue de Fleurus

When Leo rented the rue de Fleurus flat in 1903, he outfitted himself for the life of painter rather than that of aesthetician: the separate atelier cried out to be a studio. Arranging his etchings and prints on the stark white walls, he was as pleased with the artistic effect as he was with the apartment's Left Bank location near the Luxembourg Garden. An interior garden separated the atelier—which became the center of activity—from the two-story main building. On the first floor of the main building were the kitchen, a small dining room, and Leo's study; upstairs, two bedrooms and a bath. In April 1903 Leo wrote Mabel Weeks, "I've got my house, my atelier, and my fencing school all engaged for the summer." Like many Americans, he also enrolled at the Académie Julian, a traditional art school like the Ecole des Beaux-Arts.

Leo wrote often to Gertrude, but he did not tell her about his moment of revelation soon after he arrived in Paris, during a supper with Pablo Casals. Telling Casals that he felt himself "growing into an artist," Leo went back to his hotel, built a fire, took off his clothes, and sketched his own body. During the spring he drew statues in the Louvre. Returning to his childhood interest in drawing was liberating, as was his first purchase of a painting: "To have bought an oil painting may not seem like a remarkable thing to have done, but it was remarkable forty-odd years ago for one who was not rich. I had already bought etchings and Japanese prints, but when I bought that picture by Wilson Steer I felt a bit like a desperado. Oil paintings were for the rich." Once Leo began collecting, his passion for new art became intense: "I didn't have so much money that I couldn't spend it all without buying pictures—perhaps a hundred and fifty dollars a month on the average—so that my real search was for contemporary art." His next purchase was a late impressionist study by Du Gardier of a woman in white with a white dog, standing against a lush green lawn.

Leo was painting, studying painting, and buying paintings. Satisfied with his impressionist landscapes, he was discouraged by his drawings of the human figure. He was also discouraged in his search for the new, until Bernard Berenson sent him to Ambroise Vollard's gallery to see Cézanne's work. In the spring of 1903, Leo purchased his first Cézanne, *Landscape with Spring House*. That was the painting—unlike anything she had ever seen—that greeted Gertrude when she arrived in Paris. She felt as if the flat were Leo's, and she began to fit her activities into the corners of their life. Being abroad was difficult at first for Gertrude, still mourning the loss of May, still unsettled from the debacle of medical school.

Though she did not admit it to Leo, the idea of permanent expatriation frightened her (she later said that her "conversion to Francophilia" was never "wholehearted"). Because she and Leo pooled their incomes, she insisted that funds be budgeted for her to return to the States once a year. Homesick, she wrote to friends that she yearned for American food—cornbread with molasses, apple pie, especially with cheese. Even the news that Mike, Sally, and Allan were moving to Paris later in 1903 helped only slightly.

Gertrude was also unsettled because Leo made it clear he did not approve of her writing. When she showed him parts of *Q.E.D.*, his response was chilling. To avoid his observation and advice, she began writing in the atelier late at night, and soon she had finished the novella. Much of her interest in 1903 was in the notes she made toward what she called her "American" novel, fragmented jottings such as "Jewish parents do not like children's minds to wander beyond their keeping," or "Writing books is like washing hair you got to soap it a lot of times before you start to rinse it." A few passages show her questioning the suitability of marriage for some women: "It is dangerous to take to wife loyal and affectionate daughters and sisters of strong considerate men. Their family feeling and pure affection for their early home are certain to be stumbling blocks in the path of marital happiness. . . . Have you ever known a young sister brought up by an older brother she deeply loved." Some notes suggest that she was searching for answers to her personal dilemmas. In them she began defining herself as a writer, a viewer who lives at the margins of life, "only a chronicler" watching "all my generation into marriage and into middle class life." As a lonely female observer, Gertrude asked repeatedly, what happens to "passionate women"? Her cryptic answer was, "Sometimes they marry well. . . . More often their marriage is a failure and then they rush about miserable seeking to escape."

So dedicated to her writing was Gertrude that her outgoing personality changed for a time: the forthright woman became known in Europe as Leo's sphinxlike younger sister. Alfred Stieglitz said that she was the most silent person he had ever met. Photographs show that she had gained weight, as if she were filling an emotional void with food. In her notebooks, she wrote again that the passionate woman was the mother of the world, even though passion was admittedly an "affliction." She justified her own need to be full by equating physical emptiness with an inability to feel: "The stomach overloaded is always very sick but then it can discharge itself upon the world. The empty starving stomach can only weaken, sadden [sic] grow more helpless."

Happily, her spirits improved, and she learned to spend time playing tennis, bicycling, and talking for hours in cafés. She continued her practice of taking long walks, from the rue de Fleurus through the Luxembourg Garden on her way to the Tuileries, the Cluny and Carnavalet museums, Notre Dame, and the Arc de Triomphe. At times she went by train to the country, to walk in the Saint-Germain forest or the Versailles gardens.

But early in 1904 the allure of seeing May Bookstaver once more drew Gertrude to the States. For four months, she lived in New York with Mabel Weeks, continuing to work on the early draft of what would become *The Making of Americans*—her study of marriage in the States—and visiting Baltimore several times. In June, with Etta Cone, she sailed back to Paris— to remain in Europe for the next thirty years. Much of Gertrude's nomadic life between 1900 and 1904 resulted from her need either to encounter or to avoid May Bookstaver.

Her traumatic romance made Gertrude see that her earlier concept of a person's "type" or "bottom nature" had to be expanded to include the quality she now called "sexual base." Thinking about the sexual qualities of people she knew, Gertrude diagrammed them in relation to one another. Her notebooks include statements about relative masculinity and femininity: she listed Mabel Haynes as "masculine," for instance, but described her own nature as "pure servant female. I like insolence [sic] I find it difficult to work up energy enough to dominate." She concluded, "All people . . . are mundane who have not a kind of muggy sexuality."

Some of Gertrude's friendships during this period remind us that at the turn of the century, women frequently pledged themselves to same-sex erotic relationships. Even if the relationship was not sexually intimate, the verbal re-creation of it might be, as in letters between Gertrude and Dolene Guggenheimer, one of the Cones' younger cousins. The correspondence began during 1901, when Dolene traveled to the Bahamas with the Solomon Steins, and from then on her letters are filled with endearments, wishes that Gertrude were with her, pleas that she write. In closing her letters, she sent love, describing herself as "a naughty little girl" to send such a big share of her love to "the cousin who has taken such a strong hold upon her heart." Once Gertrude moved to Paris, Dolene wrote often about her plans to visit, but she did so only years later.

Gertrude's relationship with Dolene paralleled that with Etta Cone. The Cones and the Steins had been friends since 1892, and they often traveled together; after Leo and Gertrude moved to Paris, the Cones visited them frequently. Biographer Brenda Richardson makes the point that Etta's

1901 journal about a return trip from Europe with Gertrude suggests possible intimacy; if such a relationship existed, then the shipboard scenes in *Q.E.D.* might be drawn from a Stein-Cone liaison rather than from the Stein-Bookstaver affair.

Writing as self-exploration can be as painful as the life lived, however, and so being in Paris was good for Gertrude in many ways. For one thing, she could submerge her problems in the busy day-to-day life of art collecting. Leo was rapacious about being first on any scene, avidly spending their joint income to build an amazing collection of avant-garde paintings, and Gertrude usually accompanied him on his treks. While she did not study the whole process of collecting as diligently as he, she found it all "interesting."

In studying Cézanne, Leo decided that twentieth-century art differed from the traditional in its emphasis on "construction." He concluded that any painting that does not integrate construction and composition becomes only "illustration or decoration"; his collecting depended on that aesthetic principle. Linking Cézanne with the impressionists and Renoir, Leo began to search for art in that vein throughout Montmartre. There, he found Seurat and Gauguin and, at the 1903 Autumn Salon, in his words, "Bonnard and Vuillard and Maurice Denis and Van Gogh, Dufrenoy, Laprade, Girieud, Matisse, Marquet, Vallotton, Baltat, Rouault." Although he bought nothing, he learned an immense amount. The following spring, at the 1904 Indépendants' Salon, Leo did purchase paintings by Vallotton and Manguin. Meeting these painters led to his knowing other artists, and he learned to listen to them as well as to study their work. When the Autumn Salon of 1905 opened, Matisse's *La Femme au chapeau* (*Woman with the Hat*) caused riots. When Leo purchased the notorious work—"the nastiest smear of paint I had ever seen . . . what I was unknowingly waiting for"—he became as notorious as the painting.

Leo enjoyed his "adventure" in the Paris art world; he enjoyed his reputation as the rich American who had paid the asking price for Matisse's scandalous painting. And he thoroughly enjoyed knowing Henri Matisse, whom he described as "really intelligent. He was also witty, and capable of saying exactly what he meant when talking about art . . . a rare thing with painters." No wonder Leo kept dealing. As Gertrude wrote in her comic folksy idiom, "We is doin business too we are selling Jap prints to buy a Cézanne at least we are that is, Leo is trying. He don't like it a bit and makes a awful fuss about asking enough money but I guess we'll get the Cézanne." The painting was the large *La Femme à l'éventail* (*Portrait of Mme Cézanne*).

Although later he did not recall the encounter, in May 1905 the model Nina Auzias—his future lover and eventually his wife—discovered Leo. She described him as "like an Egyptian statue of a handsome giant. . . . His hat and golden beard hid from me his features, but I was certain that he was the mate of my desires." When she told friends she would marry him, they laughingly told her that Leo was "the great American Maecenas." Whenever she was near him, she was debilitated by shyness: "I hardly dared look at him. He always seemed completely to ignore me. I was so overcome that I heard and understood nothing." Nina of Montparnasse, as she was known, a singer who had run away to Paris at age fifteen, was the child of a mathematics professor. Notorious after several love affairs, she also enjoyed a reputation for her marvelous laugh and her beauty. It would be four more years before she modeled for Stein.

Leo's memoirs are silent about early encounters with Nina and less than trustworthy about his art purchases. Correspondence and photographs of the atelier walls show that he owned many paintings before the 1905 salon. Many of his acquisitions date from early in 1904, in fact, when Mike found a surplus of 8,000 francs in Gertrude and Leo's account. With this windfall, the two bought Gauguin's *Sunflowers* and *Three Tahitians,* two small Cézanne *Bathers,* and two paintings by Renoir, Leo's favorite. Grateful for their patronage, the dealer Vollard threw in a small Maurice Denis painting of a mother and child, the mother's bare breast shockingly visible against a black dress. Photographs of the atelier walls show that by early 1906 these paintings occupied places of prominence. Added to the Cézanne portrait of his wife and Matisse's *Woman with the Hat* are Renoir's *Two Women,* Manguin's *Standing Nude,* Daumier's *Head of an Old Woman,* Toulouse-Lautrec's *The Sofa,* Bonnard's *The Siesta* (perhaps the most vivid presentation of nudity), Vallotton's *Reclining Nude,* Picasso's *Young Girl with a Basket of Flowers,* Cézanne's *Bathers,* Delacroix's *Perseus and Andromeda,* and other paintings of either human figures or landscapes. The atelier walls also display Leo's paintings, several of a bare-chested Mike. It was clear that Leo's fascination with the nude influenced his choice of art.

Leo's recollections also mislead by suggesting that his collecting was a solitary activity, when between 1903 and 1906 he was often accompanied by Gertrude, as well as by Mike and Sally. Long before moving to Paris, Gertrude had bought etchings and in 1902, for six hundred dollars, an oil by Alexander Schilling ("I wanted it because it looked like any piece of American country . . . like something in movement"). She had traveled enough, and spent enough time with the Cones as well as with her own family, to understand the possible appreciation of paintings' value. Her biography contradicts Leo's claim that she learned everything she knew about art from him. Mike had taken courses and tried painting himself, and Sally—to whose judgment he usually deferred—was well trained and interested in collecting. In San Francisco they had acquired some good Chinese pieces, and they were experienced enough to recognize what was truly new. Their interest in art was, in fact, one of the primary reasons for their move to Paris.

58, rue Madame

When, during the 1902 San Francisco streetcar operators' strike, Mike found himself on the side of workers rather than of management, he realized that he should change occupations or perhaps even do what he had long dreamed of doing—leave the world of business. Careful planning enabled him to invest so that the resulting income, augmented by rents from the duplexes, would provide a modest living for his family and for Gertrude, Simon, and Leo. Sally, who worried that Mike worked too hard, envisioned the family's leading something other than a staid middle-class life; like Gertrude, Sally coveted "gloire." In December 1903, then, Mike, Sally, Allan, and Therese Jelenko, a teenage neighbor who taught Allan piano, arrived in Cherbourg. They were met by Leo, who regaled them with news of the Paris art world.

Invigorated by Leo's enthusiasm and Sally's imaginative ideas, Mike led a radically different life. Staying first in the modest Hôtel Fôyot, near the Luxembourg Garden, they soon moved to what Sally thought the perfect living space, a large loft apartment at 58, rue Madame, in a building that had once housed a Protestant church. The enormous combination living-dining room—forty by forty-five feet—had large windows facing west over a garden, and there were two large bedrooms. The street ran at right angles to the rue de Fleurus, so they lived scarcely four blocks away from Leo and Gertrude; the households often took tea and meals together, at either one home or the other. The four Steins also frequently ate at neighborhood cafés, enjoying the leisurely atmosphere and long evenings of conversation. More important, they frequented exhibitions, galleries, and salons, learning daily about the great expansion of art, music, and literature in France: living in Paris was sheer excitement. To experience these times was to learn to value the new or to be shut out forever from the twentieth century.

Once settled in the rue Madame flat, Sally and Mike went junking, scouring antique shops and secondhand stores for Italian furniture that could be rebuilt and refinished; they had brought Persian rugs and decorative objects with them. One of the reasons Sally liked the rue Madame apartment was that the high ceilings resulted in immense wall space, a wonderful setting for paintings. So that they would have money for art, they lived—in Therese Jelenko's words—"meagerly." On outings, they carried treats rather than going to tea rooms; sometimes they bought "a delicious hot crisp croissant with a piece of chocolate" to eat as they walked. Therese recalled Mike's scolding Leo for spending too much money on Japanese prints.

But despite their differing views of economy, Mike and Leo both loved music and art, and both were fascinated by eating fads. While Leo dieted intensely, Mike's approach to eating was more intellectual. His enthusiasm for the Haig diet, which he claimed solved female nervousness, is clear from his letter about a friend's wife "who had hysteria induced by womb trouble, and migraines" and had recovered because of the Haig. Sally, too, Mike felt, had become "as tough as a trooper without a sign of nervousness."

Mike's Paris lifestyle entailed family outings, long walks, afternoons in cafés, searches for art, jewelry, and furnishings, and the continuous reading of newspapers and magazines. These were not new habits. Pablo Casals recalled staying with the Steins in San Francisco, thinking Mike "a highly cultured man, a patron of the arts, wonderfully hospitable. His house was full of paintings, books and magazines in various languages—everyone seemed to be always reading and making voluminous notes—and the conversation constantly turned to art." In California, Casals had also met Gertrude, whom he recalled as "a sturdy young woman . . . with a strong handsome face. She had a brilliant mind and a vivid way of expressing herself." Like other of the Steins' friends, Casals also visited them in Paris, where he attended both Stein salons. He described what he called "Gertrude's flat": "I would find her reading and Leo drawing. The walls of the flat were crowded with paintings. 'These pictures,' she would tell me, 'are by young painters that nobody wants to pay any attention to.'"

When relatives and friends came to France, even though Eph Keyser was sculpting there, it was steady, solicitous Mike who hosted them: he made hotel reservations, took time to plan activities, and arranged gallery visits, making sure the Americans "were properly respectful and appreciative of what they were privileged to see." He hoarded cards from the Durand-Ruel gallery for their monthly private showings and delighted in taking visitors to see the Renoirs, Manets, Monets, and Cézannes. Like the other Steins, Mike cherished art. For him, buying paintings was never simply investing.

Although Leo actually purchased the Steins' first Matisse, it may have been Sally who discovered the painter. Therese Jelenko recalled that Leo took Mike, Sally, and herself to see *Woman with the Hat* before he bought it: "I still can see Frenchmen doubled up with laughter before it, and Sarah saying 'it's superb' and Mike couldn't tear himself away." Memoirs written by Leo, Gertrude, and Sally disagree about the circumstances of the purchase; Gertrude said that she found the painting, and Sally said that she would have bought it but Leo wanted the work in his atelier in order to study it. Because the Steins often traded pictures, the agreement may have been that Mike and Sally would later buy the painting, as they eventually did. The important fact about the purchase is that of all the critics in Paris in 1905, only the Steins were sure enough of Matisse's art in the new mode to buy. So controversial was the work that the critic Vauxcelles named Matisse and his friends the "fauves," the wild beasts of the art world. Alfred Barr, the foremost biographer of both Matisse and Picasso, observed that between 1905 and 1907 Leo Stein "was possibly the most discerning connoisseur and collector of 20th century painting in the world."

After the Autumn Salon purchase, Leo took Mike and Sally with him to visit the painter. Their warm rapport with Matisse led to countless visits, meals, and—inevitably—purchases. Despite limited funds, Mike and Sally made buying Matisse's work a priority, and he in turn tried to price his paintings so that they could afford them. Within the next two years, Mike and Sally bought all his major pieces: his seascapes, several studies for *Joy of Life* (the large oil that Leo bought in 1906), and *Young Sailor I, Pink Onions, The Gypsy, Self-Portrait* (which Gertrude thought was too intimate to be shown), *Nude before a Screen, Woman with a Branch of Ivy, Marguerite* (Leo owned *Marguerite in a Veiled Hat*), *Blue Still Life,* and the bold *Mme Matisse* (known as "The Green Line"). The last was Matisse's answer to the outraged painters who had in 1905 sent him a mocking painting of a woman's face striped with chrome oxide green from forehead to chin. The Steins also bought prime examples of Matisse's bronze sculpture—*The Serf, The Woman Leaning on Her Hands, Small Crouching Nude without an Arm, Portrait of Pierre Matisse,* and other pieces. And Sally became his publicist. She bought, hung, and talked about his art; she took visitors to meet him and encouraged them to buy. She also convinced Matisse that his work was of primary importance. He later recalled that, of the Steins, "Madame Michel Stein was the really intelligently sensitive member of the family. Leo Stein thought very highly of her because she possessed a sensibility which awakened the same thing in himself." The friendship between Sally and Matisse lasted till their deaths.

Although Sally knew less about modern art than Leo did, she made it her business to learn, partly because she needed to feel superior to Leo and Gertrude. The volatility of her temperament had grown more noticeable with time, and the line between enthusiasm and imbalance sometimes blurred. Her family and friends knew well that Sally, even more than Gertrude, was given to outbursts of temper. One late July morning, Mike planned a surprise breakfast for her birthday. As the guests, most of them family members, entered her room, Sally became enraged—partly because her privacy had been invaded but largely because Mike had mistaken the date. The guests tried to escape her insults, putting their presents behind their backs and looking longingly at the bedroom door, but interrupting one of Sally's rages was difficult. For Matisse, however, her directness—coupled with her seemingly boundless enthusiasm for his work—made her the answer to an artist's prayer. He would often appear at rue Madame, carrying "bundles of pictures under each arm, and [she] would tell him what she thought of things, sometimes rather bluntly. He'd seem to always listen and always argue about it."

Having a difficult personality might have been Sally's entry into the Stein family. Mike was used to playing mediator; both Gertrude and Leo were known for stating opinions directly. Gertrude's intense interest in people balanced the sharpness of her temperament, however; for all her tendency to pride, friends remembered her "remarkable" rapport with others. Lee Simonson, the stage designer who was a longtime friend of the Steins, described her fondly: "Gertrude like an amiable giant breaks a person open with her hands as one might a fruit to see if there is a pit or how many." In contrast, for all Leo's intellectual power, he appeared to have little compassion for people. As Hapgood wrote, "He was almost always mentally irritated. The slightest flaw, real or imaginary, in his companion's statements, caused in him intellectual indignation of the most intense kind. . . . Whenever I think of Leo Stein, I like him better than when I am with him."

Both Stein households had acquired controversial paintings so rapidly that Leo, Gertrude, Mike, and Sally came to be known as "The Stein Corporation." The two couples owned more contemporary art than the Paris galleries did. Leo and Gertrude bought more paintings by Cézanne than did the Luxembourg Museum—and the museum had none of his watercolors at all. As a result, everyone who knew the international art scene, both the French and the visiting Americans, British, Europeans, and Russians wanted to see the Steins' collections. Bothered day and night with calls and notes from visitors, the two households began to hold Saturday salons. Sally and Mike's gatherings—thoughtful discussions, with Matisse and other artists present— began at 9 P.M. Gertrude and Leo's visitors came later, some directly from the first Stein salon. At 27, rue de Fleurus the crowd was larger and the atmosphere, freer; Gertrude sat smiling, and Leo lectured to whoever would listen, sometimes until "almost dawn." At both salons, curious viewers found themselves surrounded with canvases and sculpture so unusual as to be indescribable. The surprised and sometimes disapproving visitors came away, talking. They returned, talking. And they brought more of the curious with them.

Collecting Modestly

Between 1904 and 1908, the Steins bought many paintings, seldom spending more than $200 for any work except Cézanne's. Leo told the story of a woman who refused to buy a good painting by Raffaelli from a Paris dealer because it was priced at $160 and she wanted to spend at least $1000; the dealer sent her to a more costly gallery, where she paid five times as much for a painting of the same value. Price was no indication of quality in the rapidly changing Paris market.

After Leo bought Matisse's *Woman with the Hat* in 1905 and the Steins became known as collectors, celebrity followed them. In March 1907 Mike took Allan and the visiting Annette Rosenshine to the Viau collection auction and paid $200 for Cézanne's *Portrait of the Artist's Son, Paul.* Again newspapers called Stein a "crazy American" for buying what they thought was overpriced art.

The Steins were unique as collectors because they made their own choices. In the world of art patronage, most collectors relied on mentors who were artists or critics—the Henry Havemeyers on Mary Cassatt, Isabella Stewart Gardner on Berenson. That the Steins assumed they knew enough to make their own decisions seemed audacious, and some of Mary Cassatt's animosity toward them stemmed from this social impropriety. She wrote to Adolphe Borie: "As to the Steins, they are Jews and clever, they saw they had no chance unless they could astonish, having not enough money to buy good things so they set up as apostles of Matisse and pose as the only ones who know, and it has succeeded! . . . It is very amusing but cannot last long. . . . Those who have the money buy Manets." The American collector John Quinn declined an invitation to the Steins' salons, although he noted in his journal that it was "wonderful how the Jews collect art. Two in Paris have a fine coln. of nothing but new men." Another of the Steins' improprieties was that they entertained painters along with collectors, friends, and writers: in the world of art collecting, wealthy patrons were accustomed to moving in only the most fashionable circles.

Part of the fame of the two Stein salons arose from the siblings' varied personalities. Gertrude and Leo, both distinctive, mesmerized people; they were sometimes taken for husband and wife. Mike and Sally's "At Homes," as they called their salons, were modest, except on the nights when they dressed formally. Mike's steady predictability balanced Sally's whimsies. Ambroise Vollard, recalling the early salons, described Mike as the kindest man in Paris. Collectors usually did not show their purchases, yet the rue Madame collection "was virtually open, in particular to any fellow countryman passing through or living in Paris, and to many others too, such as . . . the English critics Roger Fry, Clive Bell, C. Lewis Hind, and Frank Rutter, or such Russian fellow collectors as Sergei Shchukin and Ivan Morosov." So gracious was Mike that, Vollard noted, "people who came there out of snobbery soon felt a sort of discomfort at being allowed so much liberty in another man's house." Sally, dressed originally and wearing antique jewelry, played the gracious hostess as she spoke intently about the brilliance of Matisse's work. And Matisse himself was an attraction; as Gertrude said, "When Matisse comes into a room he brings with him a force and a virility."

Discourse among visitors was the model at Mike and Sally's salon, where the ideal guests were the critics Matthew Stewart Pritchard and Georges Duthuit, but lecture was the style at Leo and Gertrude's. Most memories of the rue de Fleurus salon are of Leo, "always standing up before the canvases, his eyeglasses shining and with an obstinate look on his face," as Mabel Dodge remembered him. Lee Simonson recalled the way Gertrude's quiet amusement contrasted with Leo's intensity "expounding with Socratic patience the esthetic importance of the pictures on the walls while reaching for heated nuts in a small brazier—a regime he was experimenting with at the moment." Leo was an oracle to young artists: "A trained and profoundly analytic mind, Leo could, if he chose, discuss theories of esthetics and the history of painting by the hour. But he was also contemplative to a degree that very few connoisseurs of fine art are capable of being." For journalist Agnes Meyer, later a cofounder of Stieglitz's "291" gallery, "Leo's brilliant conversation on modern French art and the remarkable collection" were the reason people visited the salon; "most of the visitors . . . paid little attention to Gertrude." For sculptor Jo Davidson, however, Gertrude, who watched the crowd "like a Cambodian caryatid, wearing a smile of patience, looking as if she knew something that nobody else did," was amusing, whereas Leo was known to have twisted "a button of his listener's waistcoat until it became a straitjacket. One could not get a word in edgewise."

The art also had its detractors. So long as people could concentrate on painting by Renoir and Cézanne, they viewed their visits to the salon as an education. But once the walls were filled with Matisse's oddly colored *Woman with the Hat* and the Picassos, Braques, and other Cubist canvases that followed, many visitors thought the avant-garde had become a joke. Nina Auzias recalled several who "laughed out loud in the hall and loudly ridiculed the paintings that they had admired inside." The success of the art collections was a mixed blessing: while the Steins entered varied social and artistic circles, many of which would otherwise have been closed to them, they also were tainted by their association with the demimonde. The new art was considered degenerate; the Mauve Decade and fin-de-siècle eroticism had long been associated with experimental art, music, and literature, and patrons of those modes were often suspect. Visiting 27, rue de Fleurus late at night may have been an exciting part of a glamorous trip abroad, but it was not the way visitors lived back in America.

Among the paintings on the walls were several of Leo's, just as Sally's and Mike's paintings hung on the walls of 58, rue Madame. In the attention given the Steins as collectors, it is easy to dismiss their activity as painters. Harriet Levy recalled that Sally painted in Matisse's atelier from eight in the morning till five. In 1906 the New York artist George Of asked Leo to send him photographs of his recent work, having seen some of Mabel Weeks's. Leo frequently worked at the Académie Julian; Morrill Cody, a young American student there, recalled the amiability of the older Stein "with whom I used to drink and talk for hours on the terrace of the Dôme or the Closerie des Lilas. Leo was a keen-minded romantic, a warm personality . . . not a doer, but a delightful dreamer with a fine intellectual background."

Mike and Sally's salon during 1905 and 1906 was dominated by Matisse; the Steins' acquaintance with that other giant of the avant-garde, Pablo Picasso, had not yet begun. But toward the end of 1905, attracted by rumors of their wealth, Picasso saw Leo and Gertrude in Clovis Sagot's gallery and spoke to the dealer about the possibility of painting Gertrude. When Sagot approached her, she agreed: having one's portrait painted was fashionable.

Another version of the encounter attributes the meeting with Picasso to the fact that Leo and Gertrude had recently purchased his gouache *The Acrobat's Family with a Monkey* and his large oil *Young Girl with a Basket of Flowers*. Despite his sister's feelings—Gertrude thought the girl's legs and feet were monkeylike (Sagot suggested cutting down the canvas)—Leo bought the work, one of the most important paintings from Picasso's Rose Period, for $30. Once Leo owned a painting, he wanted to meet the artist, so Henri-Pierre Roché took Gertrude and Leo to Picasso's studio. During their visit, the Steins bought paintings worth 800 francs ($150), including *Two Women at the Bar* ($40), and Leo then invited Picasso and his lover, Fernande, to dinner. Later, at table, Gertrude took a piece of bread lying near Picasso's place, and Picasso snatched it back. In that crude but forceful interchange began their friendship. After the meal, when Leo showed Picasso his Japanese prints, the painter was bored and suggested that he paint Gertrude. However the invitation was conveyed, during the winter of 1905–1906 Gertrude sat for Picasso between eighty and ninety times. They became close friends, and she—and, for a time, Leo—grew more interested in Picasso's work than in Matisse's.

From the time of her first sitting in Picasso's cold, cluttered studio, Gertrude's life changed. Seeing her hours with him as a chance to learn about the art world as well as about Picasso and Fernande—a more likely interest for the woman who was ever in search of people's "bottom natures"—she traveled several times a week to the flat in the Bateau Lavoir, called the "laundry boat" because of its misshapen structure. Sometimes she walked the four miles, going down the rue des Saints Pères, crossing the Seine near the Louvre and continuing down the rue de Richelieu past the Bibliothèque Nationale; at Boulevard Clichy, the cobbled streets ascended toward Montmartre. On other occasions, she took the horse-drawn omnibus across Paris from the Odéon up to the Place Blanche and then continued up hill to the little square that adjoined Picasso's studio, one of the clustered ateliers without either electricity or water. Picasso at twenty-four was handsome and sexy (one of Gertrude's friends called him "a good-looking bootblack"). He was also motivated: the son of a professor of painting, he had been successful in Spain and was learning to attach himself to the right people in Paris. His conquest of the Steins was his first move into quasi-fashionable currents of Paris collecting. Although he later ridiculed her egotism, Picasso did not know enough buyers in Paris to be other than gracious to Gertrude.

Fernande sometimes read aloud as Gertrude posed, calming the sitter with her beautiful voice. She later described Stein as "Fat, short, massive, a fine head with noble features, clear-cut and regular, the eyes amused and intelligent. The mind clear and lucid. Masculine in her voice and her entire bearing." Gertrude enjoyed quietly thinking about her own work—"Melanctha," the last fiction to be written for *Three Lives,* was in process—although hearing Fernande recite the La Fontaine fables may have changed the way she listened to the rhythms of spoken language. A deep bond developed between Gertrude and Picasso, and as his biographer John Richardson claimed, next to his mother and Fernande, Gertrude became the most important woman in his life.

Picasso had been painting a number of women—*Woman with a Fan, Woman with Bangs, Seated Woman with Hood,* as well as nudes—but he had seldom drawn so large a female figure, although the woman in his 1905 *Nude with Hair Pulled Back* was ample. Picasso's figuration of Gertrude also resembled that in his *Seated Female Nude with Crossed Legs* (1906). It could be that Gertrude, in size and manner, suggested the imposing models of the Cézanne and Matisse paintings of wives, but Picasso took care to avoid direct comparisons: he did not have Gertrude hold a fan, as had the models for those paintings. Instead, he arranged her somewhat ungainly hands like those in Cézanne's *Woman with a Coffeepot* or in Ingres's portrait of Louis-François Bertin, a painting he had studied in the Louvre. Richardson suggests that Gertrude represented the "nouvelle femme," an androgyne. In many of Picasso's sketches done after Gertrude's portrait, large females appear in pairs, arms around each other's waist.

Because Picasso found Gertrude enigmatic and his own style somehow inadequate for the vision he had of her portrait, he could not finish the work. Telling Gertrude he could no longer "see" her, he painted out the head, leaving the canvas unfinished while he went to Spain for the summer. That autumn he painted in a new head and face, drawing on techniques of Ingres, Cézanne, and African sculpture to give the face the unmatched eyes and surreal angle that distort its otherwise realistic effect. When Picasso invited the Steins to see the painting, Gertrude was pleased: it was of the new. It expressed the same kind of difference she aimed for in her writing. Although at first she had protested that it didn't look like her, Picasso assured her that it would . . . that she would come to look like the portrait. Gertrude was finally so happy with the painting that it became the one piece of art she protected throughout her life, taking it with her wherever she went and finally—at her death—bequeathing it to the most prestigious museum in the States, the Metropolitan. Picasso's painting of Gertrude became the icon of both her and his own "gloire." As she said, "For me it is I . . . and it is the only reproduction of me, which is always I."

Soon after completing Gertrude's portrait, Picasso did a small but perfect likeness of Leo on a "random bit of painting-board late one evening when he, Leo, and Gertrude had returned from Montmartre," in the style of Lautrec he sometimes adopted.

Between 1905 and 1911 the Steins devoted their lives to art—learning about it, learning to do it, learning to know the painters who created it, and, in Gertrude's case, learning to know the way painting related to writing. All descriptions of this fruitful period sound exaggerated. Years later, Gertrude and Picasso in conversation reminisced "but all that couldn't have happened in that one year, oh said the other, my dear you forget we were young then and we did a great deal in a year."

Their salons were one reason the Steins became central to art circles in Paris and, by extension, in the world. Another was that they each took their passion for art outside the salons. For Sally, it was part of her discourse with American visitors, as well as with her fellow painters in Paris. Leo could be heard talking about art and aesthetics in the Montparnasse cafés, to both strangers and friends. For Gertrude, it was both a part of her engaged life as expatriate and the entry to innovative writing. For all three, and for Mike, still managing the family income, collecting and showing art was also a way to earn money. Profit from collecting was significant given that it increased the Steins' fixed, comparatively small principal, whose income supported only severely middle-class existences. Mary Cassatt's acerbic comment about the Steins' economic position was accurate, but in the middle-class American ethic, to succeed in acquiring fortunes (even small ones) was to capture the American dream. Some of the Steins, during some of their years collecting, were not disdainful of that ambition.

Writing Modestly

Any separation between avant-garde art and literature in Paris early in the twentieth century is artificial. Friendships among the artists Picasso, Georges Braque, André Derain and writers Paul Fort, Paul Claudel, Pierre Mac Orlan, Alfred Jarry, André Salmon, Guillaume Apollinaire, Max Jacob, Paul Moréas, Maurice Cremnitz, Maurice Raynal, Blaise Cendrars, and others are evidence of the great reciprocity that existed between innovative painting and writing. In 1905 the advance man for the new arts, Guillaume Apollinaire, began publishing art criticism in *La Plume* and *Je Dis Tout* (he also wrote a gossip column, "La Vie anecdotique," for *Le Mercure de France*). Until his death from influenza in 1918, he was a clearinghouse of information for the worlds of both art and literature. Given his "Rabelasian" personality, provocative and often comic, whether he was urging people to see exhibits or writing pornography, Apollinaire enacted in life the same kind of "surprise" he demanded for art.

During 1903, after the demise of the literary magazine *Revue Blanche*, *La Plume* sponsored weekly poetry gatherings to which came Apollinaire, Max Jacob, André Salmon, Alfred Jarry, Pierre Reverdy, Charles Vildrac, Georges Duhamel, and others. The Montmartre café Lapin Agile (the Dancing Rabbit) became the headquarters for these artists who shared admiration for Rimbaud and other symbolist poets, a blatant anticlericalism, and beliefs in occult powers. Maurice de Vlaminck and André Derain, former athletes, brought a less elite group of Parisians to another vortex of activity, Paul Fort's Tuesday night soirees at the Closerie des Lilas. Fort believed in living life to the full; he planned special evenings to honor artists, and when the cafe closed at 2 A.M., he and Apollinaire, Picasso, Jacob, and others "nactambulised" through the streets till dawn. These forays—marked by sexual encounters of various kinds, drugs and alcohol, and fortune telling—resembled the adventures of the younger "Picasso gang." Fernande Olivier described these younger men as "frequently drunk, shouting and declaiming." Noting that Picasso "always carried a Browning," she reported that his waking up the neighbors with revolver shots was not uncommon.

Once a week the artists—fascinated with the possibilities of moving images—went to the local cinema; other nights were spent at the circus, the Cirque Medrano. Friends with the clowns Footit and Chocolat and other performers, the men were attracted by the unconventional lifestyles and the mixture of daring and sorrow in the clowns' performances. The Steins sometimes went along. Gertrude recalled, "The clowns had commenced dressing up in misfit clothes instead of the old classic costume and these clothes later so well known on Charlie Chaplin were the delight of Picasso and all his friends." As part of this attention to costuming, Picasso and Max Jacob searched Paris for what would appear to be laborers' clothes, buying sweaters in one of the city's most expensive wool shops. Leo and Gertrude's brown corduroy and strap sandals were also seen as costume.

Picasso brought many of these artists and writers to Leo and Gertrude's salon; by early 1906 Gertrude knew them and liked their aesthetics, motivated as they were by the desire for fame rather than money. However, seeing them in the cafés and entertaining them in the salon led the Steins to adopt distancing techniques: intimacy with people so bent on the unconventional could be dangerous. Issues of class also surfaced. As Matisse asked, when the Steins introduced him to Picasso, what did Gertrude, a woman of quality, have in common with such a man? The sedate atmosphere of Sally and Mike's salon, which ended with late tea, was meant to curb guests' possible high spirits. In contrast, Gertrude, undisturbed by rowdiness, listed Picasso, Max Jacob, and Apollinaire as her favorites. She wrote about the last, "Nobody but Guillaume . . . could make fun of his hosts, make fun of their guests, make fun of their food and spur them to always greater and greater effort." She also wrote Mabel Dodge that Apollinaire "is so suave you can never tell what he is doing."

As for Max Jacob, he had an appealing history, something like Gertrude's own. He had first prepared for a career in foreign service and then finished a law degree without ever practicing law. Brilliantly interested in language and its function in society, he was "a compulsive punster," managing to introduce a surreal dimension into every conversation. One of his hobbies was classifying people into his own thirty-six astrologically defined categories, complete with files of detailed histories about them. Gertrude liked his manipulation of language, his sense of fun, and his irreverence for custom. She also liked his rapport with Picasso, who had been his best friend since 1903 when Picasso had drawn Max a comic strip in eight parts, "The Plain and Simple Story of Max Jacob and His Glory, or, Virtue's Reward."

When Gertrude posed for a painting by Felix Vallotton in 1906, she added to the knowledge she had gained from posing for Picasso. She saw that the painters were working like their writer friends to incorporate fragments of modern life into art, hoping to create effects that evoked the mysterious "fourth dimension." Apollinaire, who coined the literary use of that phrase, explored new techniques in the poems he wrote from early in the century. One of the first changes in the new spirit of literature was to use street speech in poems; as Apollinaire wrote in "Palace": "Lady of my thoughts with ass of fine pearl / Neither pearl nor ass can the Orient rival." Mixing vulgarity with lyricism was meant to create both humor and sensuality. Words were also intended to be suggestive; at times the literal meaning of lines was intentionally obscured. From the same poem, the image of the rose merges with that of the body and the sun: "Flogged flesh or roses from the rose garden. . . . / And the sun mirror of roses is broken." The poem also juxtaposes unexpected and unpleasant images: "We entered the dining room nostrils / Sniffed an odor of grease and burnt fat phlegm / We had twenty soups three were color of urine / And the king had two poached eggs in bouillon."

In his search for new sources of imagery, Apollinaire turned to the symbolists. Foreshadowing surrealism, he laced his work with dream imagery, insisting that the real drew from both observable life and an often-hidden interior life. The subjects of Apollinaire's poems were similar to those of Picasso's Blue Period paintings: drawn from the common, the bent and wizened figures, wasted by hard work and poverty, nevertheless suggested transcendence. Picasso and Apollinaire also saw themselves as Nietzschean supermen, able to excel through a combination of artistic genius and sheer physical strength. They agreed to create at least one new work each day and by means of this series production to transform the existing art world.

Gertrude's writing also became a daily event, and it, too, drew on both extended consciousness and reality. As she described her life with Leo: "We were settled in Paris together and we were always together and I was writing. . . . I was writing." In 1905 she wrote friends that she was "working tremendously." The steadiness of her writing paralleled the production of the painters; Matisse, she noted reverently, was always working. (As Henry Peyre explained, Matisse believed in "constant labor in order to reach spontaneousness"—the goal of the avant garde.)

After Gertrude had finished *Q.E.D.,* she started two other novels. *The Making of Americans* in its first comparatively short version is the story of Julia Dehning's life shaped by her poor marital choice. Like Henry James's *The Wings of the Dove,* Gertrude's fiction showed the ways society disenfranchised unmarried women. Ironically, this first version of what was to become a monumental work seemed to be a complex response to what she saw as Bryn Mawr cynicism and May's unfaithfulness: the text stated repeatedly that being "middle class" is good, "the only thing always healthy, human, vital and from which has always sprung the best the world can know." Stressing that a "normal" family life is strengthening, Gertrude implies that sexual deviance is dangerous and tempers her praise of individuality by warning that it must be governed by "conventional respectability."

Fernhurst, the second novella she completed, retold the true story of Alfred Hodder, a brilliant Harvard philosopher who took a post at Bryn Mawr and once there began an affair with Mary Gwinn, an English professor. Gwinn was already involved with Helen Carey Thomas, soon to be president of the college. In real life, Hodder and Gwinn eloped; in *Fernhurst,* he leaves the college for a disappointing career, without Gwinn, who resumes her liaison with Thomas. Gertrude's version of the narrative further probed the theme of sexual betrayal though the introduction of a new character, Hodder's wife, Nancy, to make what she called an "interesting quartet" of people. Like Gertrude, Nancy is an "eager, anxious and moral" Westerner. She consistently denies her husband's adultery; only when Helen Thomas confronts her with the affair does she admit its existence. Stein describes Nancy as bound by "her straight Western morality," terribly hurt by her husband's infidelity.

In case readers missed the sympathy with which Nancy was drawn, Gertrude as author announced that *Fernhurst* was an American story and that American values differed from French. "It is the French habit to consider that in the usual grouping of two and an extra . . . it is the two . . . who are of importance." She pointed out that, in contrast, the American reader "finds morality more important than ecstasy and the lonely extra of more value than the happy two." While her implied defense of lesbian love might seem contrived, Stein's emphasis on the power of sincere caring—and its frequent betrayal—was stated almost too didactically.

By 1906, steeped in naturalist novels and with these works of her own behind her, Gertrude began writing about common people. The subjects of her next writings—"The Good Anna," "The Gentle Lena," and "Melanctha," composed in that order for their inclusion in *Three Lives*—differ appreciably from the educated, white middle-class characters of *Q.E.D.* and *Fernhurst.* The radical aspect of these early fictions was her exploration of sexual power, both heterosexual and lesbian, though the latter was not shocking in Paris, where "discreet homosexuality was fashionable for both sexes." The radicalism in *Three Lives* was Gertrude's choice of inarticulate, lower-class characters as protagonists and the harshly objective style she used to present them.

Critics have cited as important influences on *Three Lives* the painting of Mme Cézanne hanging above Gertrude as she wrote and her reading—and planning to translate—Flaubert's lyric story about the servant Félicité, "Un Coeur simple" from his *Trois Contes.* The unhappiness of the three women characters in Stein's portraits also echoed the author's life in 1905, still shadowed by her love for May Bookstaver. About this time, Emma Lootz Erving had written her that May was reading aloud at dinner parties excerpts from Gertrude's letters to her; Emma warned her not to write anything she did not want others to hear. Chagrined, Gertrude accepted the fact that her relationship with May was over.

Using her art to disguise her continuing pain, Stein observed her subjects scientifically. Her choice of Anna Federner, the German house servant, as protagonist distanced her from her own life. To draw the good-hearted martyr, she used a vocabulary so repetitious it seemed simple: the reader knew Anna through her "arduous and troubled life," her "strong, strained, worn-out body," and her lesbian love for Mrs. Lehntman, her "only romance."

As Anna's name suggests, the character was based on Lena Lebender, the woman who ran Gertrude and Leo's household in Baltimore. In Stein's telling, however, Anna became complex, partly through the emphasis on her love for women. Her aim in life was—supposedly—to serve, but the text showed that Anna was happy only when she controlled the people for whom she worked. Dedicated to wiping out sensual pleasure in life, Anna exhausted herself into an early grave. Gertrude's ironic emphasis on Anna's "good" life, with its core of self-abnegating service, was the beginning of her characteristic double meaning in fiction. Contrasted with Anna's tight-lipped insistence on propriety was the relaxed acceptance of Miss Mathilda, her slovenly but generous mistress, a humorous self-portrait of Gertrude.

In the second story of *Three Lives,* that of the victimized Lena Mainz, Gertrude focused on wider social and gender issues. When Lena, a naive, uneducated German immigrant, is brought to the States by her aunt, the powerful Mrs. Haydon, she becomes a puppet. Her aunt finds work for her and decides whom and when (as well as whether) she will marry. The debacle of Lena's marriage ends with her death during her fourth childbirth. The story is an admonitory narrative about power within marriage, the power of heterosexual culture (the fact that Mrs. Haydon is always referred to by her title as married woman underscores the values of the culture). The implications of Lena's story are frightening: that women deserve to make their own choices about sexuality, marriage, and motherhood and that when those choices are taken away, the will to live may also vanish.

The last of the three lives was that of the inscrutable Melanctha, a young mulatto whose chief occupation is "wandering," expressing her passionate, uncalculating nature through liaisons of various kinds. Melanctha, in Gertrude's words, "always loved too hard and much too often." Influenced in part by her Paris friends' fascination with African art, Stein moved from her portraits of German women—led through their ineffectual modesty and their culture's mandates to miserable deaths—to that of a black woman. If "Negro" art was fashionable, she felt that no one knew black culture better than she. During her teen years in Oakland, California, she had listened to and watched blacks in Fruitvale; during her practical training at medical school, she had known black women as patients in Baltimore.

Melanctha Herbert's understanding, Gertrude suggested, stemmed from her bisexuality. In adolescence, Melanctha explored heterosexual relationships with dockworkers, but later she became intimate with Jane Harden. Stein says clearly, "It was not from the men that Melanctha learned her wisdom." The two years of their relationship pass quietly, with no "wandering" for either of them; Melanctha spends "long hours with Jane in her room," a description that echoes scenes from *Q.E.D.* Melanctha's later liaison with Rose, the narrative of which opens the novella, adds to the lesbian strand of the story.

After thirty-five pages of Melanctha's bisexual history, Gertrude introduces Jeff Campbell, the black doctor who grows to love Melanctha while he attends her dying mother. The story then becomes an extended dialogue between the arbitrarily rational Campbell and the purposefully inarticulate Melanctha, a tour de force of voiced dialogue unlike anything in literature of the time. During the lengthy Jeff-Melanctha interchanges, Stein draws Jeff as the rational speaker who wants permanence, exclusivity, security. His polemical insistence is shown to be absurd when contrasted with Melanctha's silences. She loves through action; she gives Jeff what she has to give and does not talk about it. While he accepts her love, he verbalizes all parts of their relationship and forces her into language that becomes destructive. Whatever she says, he argues against. By the end of the dialogue, the reader sees that Gertrude has constructed a classic philosophical discourse between reason and emotion.

Her fiction continued what was becoming her life process, melding the knowledge she had acquired from her studies of philosophy, psychology, and medicine with the new insights gained from literature and painting. Gertrude's main interest was presenting the person: her fascination with the portrait was a culmination of years of formal study as well as the result of the contemporary artistic excitement over portraiture. Some of Cézanne's best paintings are portraits; Picasso's work is largely portraiture; Matisse's most effective distortions are of representations of the human figure and face. In "Melanctha" Gertrude created a double portrait—or, rather, the fictional portrait of the author as deeply divided person. Although the dialogue between Jeff and Melanctha has been described as typical of conversations between Gertrude and May Bookstaver, with Stein represented by Jeff Campbell and Bookstaver by Melanctha, Gertrude portrayed herself, too, in the character of Melanctha. Born of very different—and irreconcilable—parents, isolated from family and friends, the maturing Melanctha—like Gertrude—tried to escape her feelings of difference and looked to sexual love for self-knowledge. Jeff and Melanctha's impasse mirrors Gertrude's sense of her conflicted emotional loyalties to both self and beloved.

In 1905, at thirty-one, Gertrude remained confused about what direction her life should take. Still toying with more than friendship with May, Etta Cone, and Dolene Guggenheimer, she saw no way to align emotional and sexual understanding with intellect. The affair with Jeff is only one segment of Melanctha's portrait; Melanctha as protagonist exists past her involvement with Campbell and loses her will to live more because of her failed relationship with Rose than from the disappointment of other lost loves. But her death in *Three Lives* parallels the deaths of Anna and Lena, all three women victims in some way of prescriptive heterosexual culture.

Gertrude's identification with the character of Melanctha mitigates what seems to be racism in the text. In her notebooks, she repeated that her own sensual nature was "dirty": "the Rabelaisian, nigger abandonment . . . daddy side. bitter taste fond of it." She may have been reacting to Leo's comment that "mysticism and sexual abandonment have it in common that they deny the intellect," and, in that context, Jeff Campbell's rationality may mirror Leo's attitudes as well as those of Gertrude as intellectual. But here locating herself in the camp of the sensual, she used the stereotype of the sexual black woman (and of Melanctha's black father) as a kind of self-portrait. When she used the phrase "the simple, promiscuous unmorality of the black people," she was writing about herself: *she* wanted a simple erotic relationship, but her society censured that pleasure, calling *her* relationship promiscuous and "unmoral." In some ways, the language of "Melanctha" works to create the same effect that the ironic stereotyping of the good Anna and the sadly gentle Lena does. The reader of Gertrude's *Three Lives* comes to understand that, in any society that imposes its rule over women's lives, misreading and misunderstanding can result.

Stein first gave her narratives of women's lives—titled "Three Histories" at this time—to her sister-in-law to read. After Sally approved the stories, Etta Cone typed the manuscript, and Gertrude then sent it to Hutch Hapgood in New York. Though he warned her that some readers might think her writing "superfically irritating and difficult," he wrote that he found the stories "extremely good—full of reality, truth, unconventionality. I am struck with their deep humanity, and with the really remarkable way you have of getting deep into human psychology. . . . The Negro story seemed to me wonderfully strong and true." Most important, Hapgood sent the stories on to Pitts Duffield, a prospective publisher. Gertrude, relieved that someone as well-read as Hutch liked her work, said little about her project to Leo, whose criticism about anything she wrote was consistent—and all too predictable. But after having put *Q.E.D.* and *Fernhurst* away and questioning whether she could indeed write a major novel, she was excited to know that somewhere in New York City her recent work was being read.

CHAPTER 6

Tremors of Change

At dawn on April 18, 1906, a major earthquake devastated San Francisco, killing seven hundred people. The first shock damaged the water system, so that when fires broke out, they raged unchecked. On the third day, with the city a veritable inferno, more than five hundred blocks of buildings were dynamited to create a fire wall. The entire business district and many residential areas were in ruins, but the plan saved at least parts of the city.

Feeling responsible not only for investments but also for Sally's family and his brother Simon, Mike felt compelled to go back. He booked passage immediately, and in a few weeks Sally, Allan, and he, with three of their prized Matisse paintings, arrived in Baltimore. They visited with family and friends before going by train to California. From the coast, Mike and Sally wrote that although Simon's house had burned, he was all right and everything else was fine: damage to the rental duplexes was slight. Sally chuckled that the Matisse paintings were upsetting a lot of people and that both her art and her Parisian clothes created "a sensation."

Perhaps more important to the later configuration of the extended Stein family, Sally resumed her pivotal role in the lives of her California women friends, a group of unmarried, artistic, German-Jewish women of at least middle-class status. These women had long envied Sally her marriage and motherhood; now their friend was also privy to glamorous Parisian ways. She urged them to visit France. Among her frequent visitors were Harriet Levy, now an aspiring writer and the drama critic for *The Wave*, a local weekly; Annette Rosenshine, an art student; and Alice Toklas, Annette's cousin and Harriet's O'Farrell Street neighbor, who had studied piano at the University of Washington Conservatory. After her mother's death from cancer, Alice had begun running her grandfather's household, which now included her father and her only sibling, Clarence. Unlike Harriet, Alice had never been abroad; yet when Sally asked her to return with them to France, she refused. The reason she gave was that leaving home abruptly would be difficult, but she also was not sure she wanted to be indebted to the persuasive

Sally (it was well-known that Sally liked to arrange her friends' lives). Annette Rosenshine was invited in her place.

In Paris, Leo and Gertrude enjoyed caring for Mike and Sally's paintings. They asked the concierge to rearrange their atelier walls, a practice they continued whenever they made new purchases. Then they entertained their painter friends, seating them in the atelier, surrounded by their work, rather than the dining room. Gertrude recalled placing "each one opposite his own picture . . . they were happy so happy that we had to send out twice for more bread." In her personal social world, Gertrude occupied herself with the artists because she felt change coming. She heard less and less often from Dolene Guggenheimer—and not at all from May Bookstaver. Although Etta Cone had rented rooms on the rue Madame, just above Mike and Sally's flat, Gertrude spent more time with the lively Mildred Aldrich, an older Boston journalist who had settled in Paris to write and work as a theatrical agent. Admiring Gertrude, Aldrich described her "deep and understanding interest in art" and her "brilliant mind, delightfully tolerant—a clean straight thinker and an amusing talker." She called Stein "the greatest reader I had ever known and the most catholic."

After years of intimacy, Gertrude seemed to be renegotiating her friendship with Etta Cone, who talked and wrote openly to Gertrude about her lesbian liaisons. Their friendship had survived both secrecy and argument (Etta remembered fondly their being drunk together in Fiesole, as well as talks that lasted much of the night during their travels). Gertrude's comments about the "spinster" Etta in notebooks at this time, however, suggest that she did not find the younger Cone sister attractive; in her notebook taxonomy, Etta's kind of woman was marked by "lack of generosity. . . . Conceive themselves heroic but do nothing. . . . Etta Cone perfect type with all her splendor and richness." But Gertrude's criticism here was new; in 1904, before Etta and she had sailed from New York, Claribel had playfully written her sister: "I sincerely trust your ocean trip may be a comfortable one . . . that you may enjoy it to the utmost—Also Gertrude (this may be taken in both ways)."

The friendship now centered on the art world. When Leo bought Matisse's *Woman with the Hat,* Etta, too, began collecting. Her diary listed her purchase of a Nicholas Tarkhoff oil—perhaps *Woman Reading*—for 125 francs and "1 picture 1 etching" from Picasso for 120 francs. Later, for 175 francs, she and Claribel bought eighteen Picasso etchings and drawings. Through Sally, Etta bought drawings, watercolors, and oils from Matisse, as well as Manet etchings and lithographs by both Renoir and Cézanne. Gertrude urged both Etta and Claribel to buy from painters who were in need of cash, but she did not regularly include the sisters in social events. According to one biographer, "The Steins introduced the Cones to their friends when it suited them, and, as Gertrude Stein used to say, when not, not. This kind of compartmentalized living was very pleasant for the Steins. Friends would turn up from Harvard days, from Baltimore days. . . . All this delighted Gertrude, she liked a variegated stream of new and old." Etta's relationship with the Steins in the spring of 1906, despite her willingness to type the manuscript of *Three Lives,* was limited to taking walks, visiting galleries, and shopping at the Bon Marché. American painter Maurice Sterne recalled going with Etta, Leo, and Gertrude to visit Picasso, only to find on his door a note with a drawing of a Picasso-like man "in a crouching position, with his pants down." Sterne remembered, "Leo looked angry and Miss Cone was embarrassed, but Gertrude, with the sudden eruptive laugh that had become famous in Montparnasse said 'Isn't he cute!'"

If Etta and Gertrude were not involved romantically in 1906, Stein may have thought about encouraging a liaison. Particularly with Mike, Sally, and Allan in the States, she was lonely. She had angered some of her New York relatives by writing her cousin Bird Stein a letter that a friend described as "shocking . . . unnecessary and harsh." It was becoming clear that the American branch of the Stein family was casting aspersions on the taste, and perhaps on the morality, of the Paris Steins, and Gertrude, who considered herself uprightly American, was hurt by such behavior. She felt that her family no longer understood her, and when a number of relatives visited France during the summer, she left Paris to spend the season at Bagni de Lucca with the Hapgoods. As in her early years, Gertrude did not respond well to criticism.

During the Italian summer, while she was working hard to expand *The Making of Americans,* Gertrude heard from Emma Lootz Erving that May Bookstaver had married Charles Knoblauch, a New York broker. It seemed incomprehensible. Gertrude found herself staring at blank sheets of paper, feeling her usual drive to write drain off into still pools of memory. And the news about May's marriage echoed that of a few months earlier that in Baltimore Dolene Guggenheimer had quietly married Simon Stein, Gertrude's cousin. Trying to be philosophical about these startling changes, Gertrude reminded herself that as women grew older, they looked for companionship, stability, and acceptable lifestyles. As she wrote in *The Making of Americans,* "Sometimes it is very puzzling that so many are certain that they are really loving some one. . . . They have ways of beginning loving and ways of ending loving . . . and ways of marrying and not marrying that certainly are puzzling." She then added ironically, "Some say not very many kinds of loving are right loving. . . . I like loving. I like mostly all the ways any one can have of having loving feeling in them."

Change and the Worlds of Painting

When Sally, Mike, Allan, and Annette Rosenshine arrived at the Gare St. Lazare on November 17, 1906, after their crossing from the States on the Dutch ship *Ryndam,* Leo and Gertrude met them. On Annette's second day in Paris, Leo took her to the Louvre; from then on, she was as fascinated by art as were the Steins. Living in a room on the floor above Mike and Sally, she wrote often to Harriet Levy and Alice Toklas, who were feverishly making plans to come to Paris. She also learned that, in France, aesthetics sometimes had a sexual text. When she accepted Picasso's offer to trade some of his drawings for her Chinese silk gown, which he wanted as a gift for Fernande, she wondered why Sally and Gertrude went along to his studio. Picasso's exchange consisted of two drawings of female nudes and a watercolor titled *Cocks.*

Besides her involvement in the art world, Annette spent much time with both Sally and Gertrude. Born with a harelip and a cleft palate, Annette was talented but shy; both the Steins encouraged her to be more outgoing, to use her gifts more fully. Although Gertrude could be frightening, Annette remembered her as a woman of "dynamic magnetism, an inner distinction which, while quite sensible, remained indefinable. There was power in the beauty of her splendid head with its heavy coil of brown hair. . . . An intellectual luminous quality shone in her face. . . . Her infectious chuckle and low guffaw seemed delightful, though the latter, I found, could be disconcerting when directed against me." Usually, however, Gertrude was a good friend. In her notebooks, she called Annette a "striking contrast" to Etta: "Annette never interprets smally though she sees smallness by instinct." In their almost daily talks, the young Californian learned from Stein how to use her creativity to reduce anxiety. Intimate as they were, however, when Annette broached the topic of sexuality, Gertrude ended the conversation, saying that "sex was an individual problem that each one had to solve for him or her self." Because Gertrude had decided that "in most cases intellect goes with sexual quality not with the temperament," she was fascinated by the sexual, but her practice was not to give specific personal advice.

In the midst of rewriting *The Making of Americans,* Gertrude continued developing her teleology of personalities. Labeled "The Book of Diagrams," one of her notebooks was filled with schemata of people she knew arranged by personality traits. The chart of the sexual qualities of men, whom Gertrude divided into the "Jewish group" and the "Anglo-Saxon" group, is representative.

Jewish group

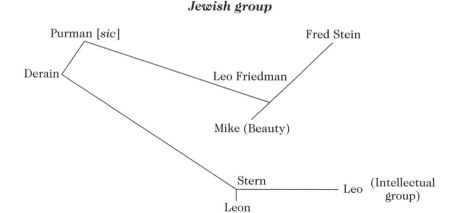

Notes surrounding this chart show her need to compare and contrast and her tendency to privilege her oldest brother, Mike: "Leo F. [Friedman] is more practical. . . . His sexual base is nearer Mike's it has less turgidness than in the others who are much nearer Leo [Stein]. . . . Mike has a certain judicialness of the highest type—he introduces a pagan sensibility to beauty and so tolerance." Praise is rare in Gertrude's charts.

The dominant impression of her "Book of Diagrams" is that she was curious about people's behavior and their motivation for that behavior. Hungry for characters to build into her various systems, she began collecting people's letters. In 1906 she asked Annette if she might see the letters she received; Gertrude therefore read most of Alice Toklas's correspondence with her cousin. In 1907, when Toklas arrived in Paris, Annette confessed that she had allowed Gertrude to read her letters. Alice's reply was noncommittal but wary.

Resuming their Paris life after the six months in the States, Sally and Mike followed Matisse's work with increased interest: George Of had commissioned Sally to buy him a Matisse. She chose *Nude in a Wood* as the first of Matisse's paintings to be purchased by an American collector; for themselves, Sally and Mike bought *Pink Onions* and *Self-Portrait.* The 1906 Autumn Salon was filled with paintings by the fauves, particularly interesting to viewers in the aftermath of the controversial spring Salon des Indépendants, when fiery discussion had centered on Matisse's *The Joy of Life,* an oversized painting of nudes that Leo Stein purchased. Paul Signac, vice president of the Indépendants, was so incensed over the painting that he picked a fistfight with Matisse. Within six months, two paintings by Matisse—*Woman with the Hat* and *The Joy of Life*—had, in their respective exhibits, polarized the art world. And Leo had bought both. In the spring 1907 exhibit, he again purchased the most controversial piece—another Matisse painting, *The Blue Nude, Tableau No. III.*

The furor Matisse's work created as he struggled to use color and form in new ways influenced Picasso, who envied the older painter, though he tried to avoid imitating him. His incorporation of various styles of art and his distortion of human figures was, however, similar. Picasso agreed with Matisse that the painter is *"representing* the model, or any other subject, not copying it." In 1907 Picasso began his own large study of female nudes, the painting later known as *Les Demoiselles d'Avignon* (named for Barcelona's Avignon Street, the city's red-light district). Finished within the year, it was not exhibited for thirty years although Derain, Braque, Salmon, Apollinaire, and others studied it in Picasso's studio. (Both Félix Fenelon and Apollinaire were at first bewildered by the "indescribable" painting.) For twelve years the rolled-up canvas leaned casually against a wall. Even without a showing, "The Philosophic Brothel," as Picasso's friends called it, became the centerpiece of cubism, revered for its geometric patterning of women's bodies and its use of incalculable differences in perspective. Derain and Vlaminck were delighted with its resemblance to the African sculpture they had found in curiosity shops and taken to show both Picasso and Matisse. A companion work to *Les Demoiselles d'Avignon* was Picasso's massive red-brown *Three Women,* which the Steins bought.

By the fall of 1907, when Picasso returned from Spain and Matisse from visiting the Steins in Italy, the Paris art scene was already changing. Admiration for the work of Cézanne, which had earlier marked the avant-garde, was becoming the norm. Painting during the next few years changed rapidly: Apollinaire raved through columns of newsprint about cubism, defining its greatness as an "analytic tendency which reconstructed the world of nature according to rigid rules of geometry," leading to effects of "surprise and spontaneity." He wrote often about the painters he called cubists—Picasso, Gleizes, Braque, Picabia, Gris, Metzinger, and Marie Laurencin, his lover. Memoirs and diaries suggest that these cubist painters and writers were frequent visitors to the Stein salons, as were hundreds of the curious, among them Maurice Sterne, Kees Van Dongen, Max Weber, Maurice de Vlaminck, Alfred Maurer, Infanta Eulalia, Emilio F. T. Marinetti, Lady Ottoline Morrell, James Stephens, Nina Hamnet, Stanton Macdonald-Wright, Wilhelm Uhde and Sonia (later Delaunay), Arthur B. Davies, Clive Bell, Harry Phelan Gibb, Henry McBride, Katherine Dreier, Jo and Yvonne Davidson, Elmer Harden, Abraham Walkowitz, Agnes Ernst (Meyer), Lee Simonson, Elie Nadelman, Paul Fort, Duncan Grant, Roger Fry, Edward Steichen, Mary Cassatt, Maud Hunt Squire and Ethel Mars, Raymond and Phoebe Duncan, Alfred Stieglitz, Henri-Pierre Roché, Emily Dawson, Thomas Whittemore, Florence Blood, Walter Pach, and a stream of family members. As a result of the celebrity of the Steins' Matisse collections, visitors included artists and tourists from Sweden, Germany, Hungary, Spain, Poland, France, and Russia, particularly the collectors Sergei Shchukin and Ivan A. Morosov.

The Stein collections were admittedly impressive, but Leo's many purchases had depleted his and Gertrude's coffers. He continued to buy paintings, but Gertrude tried, unsuccessfully, to sell her etchings in the New York market. Late in 1906, Etta Cone offered her money, admonishing her, "Don't hesitate and you needn't luxuriate in the feeling of poverty, for it's no use to." The next summer, Etta was pleased when her sister-in-law bought a Picasso drawing from Gertrude's own collection. The Steins were more than willing to sell from their private holdings.

Much of the Steins' family correspondence from this period concerns financial affairs, with a number of informational letters going from Mike to Gertrude. Leo liked spending the household income; Gertrude saw herself as the responsible sibling. A friend was to comment years later that "Gertrude, about money, did not joke." Evidently, all the Stein children found living within their means difficult; the few existing letters from Simon are cajoling notes, hopefully suggesting to Mike that there might be a "surplice" in his account.

Gertrude knew that at least some writers made money, so she continued trying to place *Three Lives*. After rejections from publishers and agents, she had in exasperation sent the manuscript to Mabel Weeks in New York. Weeks in turn had given it to May Bookstaver Knoblauch, now prominent in New York society. May interested the Grafton Press, a self-publisher, in bringing out the book for a cost of $660. When Gertrude heard from Grafton in 1909, she was grateful to have the book accepted anywhere, though she tried to avoid paying the fee herself (it was nearly half of her year's income). She approached Etta Cone, suggesting that because she had typed the work, she would be interested in its publication, but Etta declined the privilege. Grafton meanwhile sent an editor to Paris to inquire if Miss Stein needed grammatical help. Gertrude informed the man that the book was just as she wanted it to be, telling him, "I am not uneducated. I have had more education and experience than they or you."

Most rejections of the manuscript had spoken of its difficult style, but Gertrude's friends found that style more interesting than troublesome. Ralph Church recalled that Gertrude never intended her work to be "esoteric." When asked if *Three Lives* was a novel, she replied in her plainspoken way, "I hate labels. It's just a book, a book about different characters, three different people I knew long ago." But for all her lack of pretension about her writing, she began to claim an affinity between Picasso's art and her own: when he said that his imagination was masculine, she noted, "Pablo and Matisse have a maleness that belongs to genius. *Moi aussi* perhaps." Gertrude usually placed herself in male company while assigning other women to such classifications as the "indolent" "earth group" or the "Maddalena," women with "no important feeling of themselves inside them. . . . Their intellectual life is not connected with their nature." Because she admired so few women, she had difficulty identifying herself as female.

While Gertrude championed the new art, particularly Picasso's, Leo was having second thoughts. Still playing the role of explainer at the Saturday salons, he was unnerved by *Les Demoiselles d'Avignon*. He began to travel, often without Gertrude, finding in absence from the rapidly changing Paris art scene a kind of insulation from what he saw as chaos. In May he joined Mabel Weeks for a bicycle trip through Italy; later, for some weeks, he visited friends in England. After buying Matisse's *The Blue Nude* in 1907 and a sketch of the painter's large work *Music*, Leo stopped buying from either Matisse or Picasso. He remained visible in Paris, however, and several people recalled his intentionally cantankerous poses: "Mr. Stein's phrase, 'Define what you mean by—' is most famous. It is well known wherever he appears. . . . He strode into view, sandals on his feet, a bundle over his shoulder, and carrying an alpenstock . . . [and] asked me, in response to an invitation, to define what I meant by 'cocktail.'"

As Picasso went further into cubism, Leo called the mode "utter abomination. Somebody asked me whether I didn't think it mad. I said sadly, 'No, it isn't as interesting as that; it's only stupid.'" Leo took little pleasure in distortion or parody; he preferred Renoir's use of color and form to create mimetic art, especially that of the human figure. As he later wrote, "When my interest in Cézanne declined, when Matisse was temporarily in eclipse, when Picasso turned to foolishness, I began to withdraw." An observer of the art scene described Leo's real interest as "the painters of the 'third dimension,' the painters of atmosphere, and the space between objects, for thus he describes the impressionists, and he includes Peter Paul Rubens in this group." Both Matisse and Picasso still attended the Stein salons, but Leo was too truthful to pretend to admire work he disliked; his disapproving silence blanketed the atelier. For Gertrude, who admired the painters' new directions, it was the beginning of a vast change in the household.

Alice B. Toklas

Harriet's and Alice's September arrival in Paris provided a useful distraction. Not only were they close friends of Sally's and Annette's, they were educated, middle class, Jewish, and Californian. On the day they arrived, the two went immediately to Mike and Sally's. Harriet wore a fashionable "fur-lined steamer coat"; Alice was more modestly dressed, though she sometimes imitated the actress Lillian Russell and tried to play the femme fatale. She had some money to spend on clothes because Harriet had lent her a thousand dollars to make the trip. When they reached the Steins' flat, they found Mike, Sally, Allan, Annette, and also Gertrude, "a golden brown presence," her dark corduroy waist set off by a large coral brooch. Mesmerized, Alice recalled that Gertrude's voice was "unlike anyone else's . . . deep, full, velvety like a great contralto's, like two voices."

Already privy to information about Alice through having read her letters to Annette, Gertrude invited Toklas to walk in the Luxembourg Garden the next afternoon. Planning a late lunch, Alice sent a *petit bleu* telegram saying she might be late (Mike had a telephone, but Leo and Gertrude did not). When Alice appeared half an hour late, the amiable Gertrude had become a furious "vengeful goddess." Alice's account of this meeting stops abruptly with Stein's anger; the scene resumes with Gertrude saying, "Now you understand. It is over." She changed her clothes; they took their walk, stopping for cake and praline ices; and Gertrude invited Alice and Harriet to come for Saturday dinner. Alice, bothered by Gertrude's calling them by their first names, said stiffly and ironically that she "did not propose to reciprocate the familiarity." When Gertrude told the story in *The Autobiography of Alice B. Toklas,* she included the legend that when Toklas saw Gertrude, she heard a bell within her ring ("only three times in my life have I met a genius . . . Stein, Pablo Picasso and Alfred Whitehead"). In her own later memoir, Alice called her meeting with Gertrude the beginning of her "new full life."

The first dinner at rue de Fleurus was also memorable. Harriet recalled being puzzled when Leo asked whether they were monists. Given the surroundings—walls hung with incomprehensible art, and Picasso and his lover sitting next to them—philosophy seemed remote. Because the women were introduced as friends of the Steins who had survived the earthquake, most guests wanted to talk about their part in the San Francisco disaster. After a few weeks of being so described, Harriet told Alice that they needed to add something to their stories to keep people's interest. Alice replied drily, "We may even have to be burned with the house."

Alice remembered vividly the first dinner at Gertrude's because there she began to learn about the new art, the kinds of people Gertrude found interesting, and the magnificent Gertrude herself. Picasso and Fernande's lateness that evening was blamed on their waiting for the delivery of a dress; Alice wondered if Gertrude planned an angry explosion for them too, but none occurred. A quixotic mix of energy, order, and passion, Gertrude intrigued the younger Californian beyond mere curiosity. When Mike wrote Alice a week later, scolding her for not immediately visiting the Louvre and saying he would soon take her, Alice replied matter-of-factly that, in Paris, pictures were not her "major interest."

Matisse and Picasso

As Alice and Harriet settled into Paris routines, they were drawn in to the growing excitement over the opening of the Académie Matisse in January 1908. After Sally returned from the States in 1906, she grew so serious about her painting that Matisse allowed her, and Hans Purrmann, a serious young German artist, to paint with him. At their urging, he then agreed to conduct a school, provided he did not have to do anything except critique student work on Saturdays. Sally, Hans, Annette Rosenshine, Max Weber, Patrick Henry Bruce, Oskar and Greta Moll, and others constituted the first class; Maurice Sterne, Harriet Levy, Walter Pach, Leo Stein, and others visited. Students were from Central Europe, Scandinavia, and the States, though hostile reporters said everyone came from Massachusetts. Despite the autumn stock market crash, Mike helped rent space for the school in the former Convent des Oiseaux.

Max Weber thought Matisse a good, if shy, teacher. Knowing there were no shortcuts to excellence, he sometimes took the group to the Louvre; he also showed them work by Cézanne, "the father of us all," and invited them to his own studio. Weber recalled, "During those veritably festive afternoon hours, he showed us many of his early drawings and paintings, and spoke freely and intimately about them. . . . Along with his own work, he showed us with great pride and loving care examples of the work of his colleagues . . . Maillol . . . and four large ink drawings by van Gogh. With great modesty and deep inner pride, he showed us his painting of Bathers by Cézanne. His silence before it was more evocative and eloquent than words."

Matisse cared about students' work, so much so that by the end of 1909 he had decided to cut back his involvement in the school to save his energy for his own work. The school continued for another two years, housed in the Hôtel Biron; as many as 120 students attended for at least part of its four-year existence. During the first months, Sally Stein transcribed Matisse's comments, and she and Mike were financial backers until they returned to the States in the summer of 1910. Her support for Matisse's work remained so vehement that Harriet was afraid to antagonize her by purchasing work by Picasso, buying Matisse's *Girl with Green Eyes* instead.

In the other camp of new art, "the Picasso gang," with Apollinaire heading its literary wing, also united. But whereas the Mike Steins were central to activities around Matisse (and the painter often took meals with them), Leo and Gertrude remained peripheral to the Picasso gang's Lapin Agile soirees, although they heard stories about them. In 1908, however, they were included in the banquet for "Le Douanier" Rousseau, the primitivist who had exhibited his paintings—without sales—for years; in fact, one participant said the feast was an elaborate practical joke intended to "scandalise the [Steins'] American puritanism."

Discovered by poet Alfred Jarry, who called him "the miraculous," the mild-mannered Rousseau lived in poverty, pining for a distant love, seeing ghosts, and working at his art. Picasso and Fernande's banquet for him was in the Paul Fort tradition of Tuesday night soirees. The evening started at Fauvet's Bar, with the guests—Braque, Apollinaire and Marie Laurencin, Max Jacob, André Salmon, and others, some with lady friends; three collectors from Germany and the States; and the Stein party—then climbing the rue Ravignan to Picasso's studio. After more than two hours, the food that had been ordered had not come; the improvised menu finally included sardines, Spanish rice, and fifty bottles of good wine. Rousseau played waltzes on his child's violin, and people danced.

Whatever the impetus for the party, most accounts describe it as a "Picasso gang" orgy. Guest-of-honor Rousseau was sent home early by cab. Alice remembered that Apollinaire slapped the drunk Marie Laurencin so she could walk; Picasso sang; Apollinaire recited poems. The women's coats and hats had been stored in Salmon's studio; later, he was found asleep in the midst of their finery, a partly eaten yellow feather from Alice's elegant hat nearby. Fernande Olivier's account credits the proprietor of the Lapin Agile with bringing along his donkey, Lolo, no doubt the villain responsible for destroying Toklas's hat.

Although participating in such an event was not expected behavior for middle-class Americans, much of the Steins' life was still spent acquiring art. Even Leo, despite his withdrawal from the salon, prided himself on managing their income in a way that supported the habit of collecting; as he explained, "Sometimes people who knew our circumstances wanted to know how we managed. We not only had the pictures, but also thousands of books; we traveled as we wanted to and entertained a great deal. . . . We never kept any accounts and never had any debts. The dealers often wanted to sell me things which I could pay for later, but I would have none of this. We spent all the money we had and no more, and so we were free." Others, however, remembered Leo less as a good manager than as an oblivious one. Mabel Weeks, touring Italy with the Steins, recalled not only listening to Gertrude's fantastic conversations but trying to repay Leo for expenses. When she handed him the amount of money she thought was fair, Leo "looked at the money vaguely and asked, 'Why this amount more than any other?'"

Weininger's Contribution

A comparison of Leo's and Gertrude's purchases and travels during the years after Gertrude came to Paris in 1903 suggests that his being "free" cost more than hers. There is no question that his sister felt the lack of ready cash. It was hard to have nothing to wear; she knew that friends were laughing about her studentlike costumes. As Mary Berenson wrote in 1906, she saw Gertrude and Leo, the latter dressed in corduroy clothes "made with wide trousers and fly-away jacket, like the typical Parisian 'art student.' They simply hurt one's eyes." Yet when Leo dressed in corduroy and sandals, he was less noticeable than Gertrude was when she did so.

The woman's dressing as man, or as nonwoman, confirmed their painter friends' belief that the Steins were tolerant of sexual difference, and the macho Picasso and his buddies liked to test what they considered the Americans' puzzling attitudes. The banquet for Rousseau may well have been one of those challenges; another was Picasso's repeated comment that, sexually, American men and women were the same. Another instance was Picasso's squeezing Alice's hand under the dinner table; Gertrude spoke at some length about what his behavior might mean. During her early years in Paris, Alice was considered a siren; her large somber eyes and small frame added to her seeming fragility and her exoticism. When Gertrude took her to meet the Berensons, however, Mary—who liked nothing about Alice—described her as "an awful Jewess, dressed in a window curtain, with her hair completely hiding her forehead and even her eyebrows."

While Gertrude's notebooks continued documenting her taxonomy of friends' "bottom natures" and "sexual bases," her notes about Alice during the first months of their liaison show great ambivalence. She described Toklas as sexually unaware and yet "low"—that is, having the potential for sexual enjoyment—in Gertrude's lexicon, a positive characteristic. She suggested that Alice was "somehow mixed up in San Francisco with Annette and Sally." In another passage, she called her "crooked, a liar," "unimaginative prostitute type, coward, ungenerous, conscienceless, mean, vulgarly triumphant and remorseless, caddish." That the course of the liaison was rocky seems clear from Stein's choice of unusually strong phrasing, connecting Alice with "charlatanism," a "melodramatic imagination," and being "decidedly weak." She even said that Alice dressed in "whore clothes."

Elsewhere, in contrast, she wrote that Toklas had an appetite only for "tasting" and was therefore "not dangerous," that she had, in fact, "an exquisite and keen moral sensibility." Gertrude also observed that Alice—whom she compared with Sally and her sister Bertha in this respect—got her way through flattery: "She listens, she is docile, stupid but she owns you. . . . Gradually she gets superior." Describing Alice as a social climber, Gertrude wrote that she would "have to do miracle to win her, the worldly side of her, the appeal to her admiration of success."

Evidently, some of Gertrude's ambivalence was hidden because Alice later recalled only that during these months, Gertrude teased her that she had the soul of an "elderly spinster mermaid," a mild comment considering the extensive notebook material.

Most of Alice's time with Gertrude was quiet. Inseparable, they took daily walks, attended concerts and the theater, and included Alice's California friend Nellie Jacot and her husband in their lives. Alice came to the apartment early each morning to type Gertrude's writing in the French notebooks written the night before and then stayed most of the day. At Gertrude's suggestion, Alice and Harriet studied French with Fernande. Harriet spent time with Mike and Sally, often taking her meals with them and listening to Sally proselytize about Christian Science. This new interest in that belief led to her friendship with David Edstrom, a handsome Swedish sculptor and painter for whom she posed. Although Edstrom was married, he and his wife lived apart. Alice recalled hearing divorce rumors about the Edstroms and noted that Harriet ordered many clothes from a stylish dressmaker, but the sculptor remained elusive.

Hints of Gertrude's torment over her love for Alice appear in much of her writing from this time. In "Americans," a text that pretends to be a group portrait, she sets the tone by juxtaposing the sentences "Two together, two together" with "There is no sign of sin." Filled with "songs," "words," and the sexually suggestive "gaps" and "holes," her meandering soliloquy talks about the "lovely life in the center," a kind of "sweet" excellence, which her "resolution of today" will accomplish. The prose poem (a clear foreshadowing of her enigmatic style in *Tender Buttons*) ends with the admonition "Put a sun in sunday. Sunday." Gertrude Stein wanted to love Alice Toklas. After years of being Leo's sister and Mike and Sally's charge, she wanted her own place, her own family, her own independence, her own sexual identity. And she wanted Alice.

Judging from what she had read in Annette's letters and what she had learned from Alice herself, Gertrude felt—correctly—that Alice would be amenable to a same-sex relationship. Although Alice told people she had been engaged twice (first to a young sailor who died; a second time to an older music professor she had not liked), she also had been in love with several women (Nellie Jacot among them). After the loss of her mother during her college years, Alice had found herself surrounded by men for whom she had the responsibility of caring—her grandfather, father, brother, uncles—and so she defined *vacation* as escaping from that role. Once a year, she put away the modest gray clothes she usually wore, donned a red shawl, and spent a week or two in Monterey at a pension called Sherman's Rose. Fragments of Gertrude's later writing suggest that, like herself, Alice had had unpleasant sexual experiences as a child. All this coercive male definition of her life role may have fostered an empathy with other women. In any case, Gertrude was reasonably sure that she and Alice had a great deal in common—educationally, emotionally, and, perhaps, physically.

In the midst of her personal turmoil over her relationship with Toklas, Gertrude, browsing in a bookstore with Leo, found a copy of Otto Weininger's *Sex and Character*. Translated into English after its initial German publication in 1904, the book put forth theories of sexuality reminiscent of those of Havelock Ellis and Edward Carpenter, especially the latter's *Love's Coming of Age*. Weininger, however, capitalized on the prevailing interest in hard science by creating mathematical formulas to represent what he called "Laws of Sexual Attraction." The anti-Semitic and anti-female Weininger believed that all people were bisexual. Each sexual nature, he claimed, is comprised of maleness and femaleness in differing proportions, and the best sexual matches are between people with complementary sexual natures. He discounted the importance of what he called female traits, whether they occurred in women or men, but he privileged homosexuality, calling it a higher kind of love. He insisted that a lesbian love, for any woman, is the "outcome of her masculinity, and presupposes a higher degree of development" than would participation in a heterosexual relationship.

Leo and his crowd discussed the book; British novelist Ford Madox Ford wrote essays about its hold on intellectuals; and Gertrude sent copies to American friends. Much of her writing in *The Making of Americans,* as well as the three fictions she started next—*A Long Gay Book, Many Many Women,* and *Two*—shows Weininger's influence, in that her descriptions of character are based on her protagonists' erotic practices. Her long later version of *The Making of Americans* is almost pure Weininger. Although the novel is structured around marriages, its final narrative is that of young David Hersland's death. His "choice," a word Gertrude repeated often, was to die rather than to commit to an erotic love (although Hersland married in the novel, his relationship was convenient rather than passionate). Unable to sort through elements of male and female character within himself, David (modeled partly on Leon Solomons and partly on Gertrude) chose the conventional role of husband—and mysteriously died.

Like her fiction, Gertrude's life was voicing the story of herself as sexual being, a woman who took the chance of committing to a lesbian love and therefore saved her life. Gertrude's decision to make that commitment was the most significant result of her reading Weininger. During the summer of 1908, with Mike and Sally renting the large Villa Bardi in Fiesole so that Leo and Gertrude could live with them, leaving the smaller Casa Ricci for Harriet and Alice, Gertrude openly courted Alice. She took her on visits to friends—Florence Blood and the Princess Ghyka at the Villa Gamberaia, the Cone sisters, the Berensons—and on countless walks and hikes. (When overcome by the heat, Gertrude lay down on the ground and reveled in the warmth. Never a walker, Alice disliked both the exercise and the sun; on one occasion, she stepped behind a shrub and took off her silk undergarments and stockings.) Late in the summer, Gertrude and Alice walked the long pilgrimage route from northern Italy to Venice, with Harriet traveling by train to join them there.

In Florence, the extended Stein family shopped for old jewelry and furniture. Mike and Sally worked hard at their jewelry making, and Sally and Harriet read Mary Baker Eddy together, as well as the mystical poet Rabindranath Tagore. According to Harriet's somewhat cynical memoir, however, the most dramatic part of the summer was Gertrude's coming to the Casa Ricci every day, professing her love for Alice. According to Harriet's memoir:

> Alice wept and she wept.
> Every day she wept because of the new love that had come into her life.
> Alice used thirty handkerchiefs a day.

Despite Harriet's (and Sally Stein's) lack of sympathy with the relationship, the results of the virtual marriage between Gertrude and Alice were far-reaching. Among them was a visible change of lifestyle for both, which involved keeping their love a secret from their American families. A minor result was Leo's psychoanalysis of, and flirtation with, Nellie Jacot, Alice's friend and former lover. Jealousy flared everywhere, but the important partnership between Gertrude and Alice was launched. Less visible than the San Francisco earthquake, Gertrude's profession of a humbling, sincere love for Alice Toklas was nonetheless dramatic for both of them, changing the path of their lives forever. And Gertrude felt that she had, indeed, achieved her miracle.

Portraits

Changing Alliances: Gertrude and Alice

Returning to Paris in the fall, Alice and Harriet rented a flat on the rue Notre Dame des Champs, furnishing it partly with pieces Alice had bought in Italy. Alice's daily life, however, revolved around Gertrude and Leo's rue de Fleurus apartment, and she often spent the day and evening there, walking home alone, late at night, a practice that worried Harriet. Gertrude, however, blossomed as a writer at least partly because of Alice's support: Alice learned to type, she read proof, she praised Gertrude's work to whoever would listen, and she found ways to meet publishers and other writers.

In 1908 Gertrude began focusing her creative energy on what she called "portraits"—prose poems, plays, and essays, all marked by innovative styles and structures. The portraits grew from her aim to characterize "kinds in men and women." As a student, trained to observe, she had tried to draw categories of human personality. The process now was the same, but an element in her life was new: she had someone to share—and approve— her notions. As she and Alice grew closer, Gertrude became more confident about both her vision and her writing; it was appropriate that among her earliest portraits was a study of her beloved.

On Sunday, the cook's day off, Alice prepared American food—"fricasseed chicken, corn bread, apple and lemon pie." (Although she had never cooked for her grandfather's household, she had long been interested in recipes.) On one of these evenings, Gertrude demanded that Alice listen to her read "Ada," a new portrait. When Alice demurred, saying she had to attend to dinner, Stein was hurt, so Alice took the food off the stove and listened. Less esoteric than some of Gertrude's writing, the portrait of Ada [Alice] and her brother, their previous California life, and Ada's happiness in her current love for "some one" included a description of their lovemaking: "Trembling was all living, living was all loving. . . . And certainly Ada all her living then was happier in living than any one else who ever could, who was, who is, who ever will be living." The portrait led to a number of other short word pictures, all characterized by indirect, almost obscure, word use. It was as if Gertrude were posing riddles about her subjects, and part of the reader's work was to figure out the meaning of the abstracted language she chose.

Both in painting and photography, the art world was privileging portraiture; Alfred Stieglitz's photography magazine *Camera Work* dated from 1903. Interest in portraits in the new realistic style was high. Matisse himself tried to define the mode as he reflected on his own series of crayon self-portraits: "Are these drawings portraits or not? What is a portrait? Is it not an interpretation of the sensibility of the person represented?" Intimate with the art world as she was, Gertrude knew the value of portraits: Picasso had painted not only hers but those of Leo and her nephew Allan. Matisse had also painted Allan (*The Boy with a Butterfly Net*) and would later paint both Mike and Sally.

Responsive to what her friends found interesting, Gertrude wrote and then assembled collections of portraits. She later explained, "I had to find out what it was inside any one . . . that was intrinsically exciting and I had to find out not by what they said . . . but by the intensity of movement that there was inside." More than re-creations of characters' voices, her portraits stemmed from her study of psychology. Already able to ferret out a person's bottom nature and sexual base, now she could refashion that self for others: she wrote portraits of nearly everyone she knew. "Harriet Fear" drew the timid side of Harriet Levy; the double portrait "Miss Furr and Miss Skeene" depicted Ethel Mars and Maude Hunt Squire, early visitors to the salon. The picture of the women's good-humored dependence on each other featured a sly repetition of the word *gay,* used with sexual intent for one of the first times in linguistic history. Eyeing the market, she then did Matisse, Picasso, Pach, Manguin, Roché, Chalfin, Purrmann, Russell, and other painters. She continued to use the technique of juxtaposing individual portraits within such long works as *Two Women* (about Etta and Claribel Cone) and *Two* (about Leo and either Sally or herself).

During these years, Gertrude wrote about Leo as often as she did Alice, but her comments about him were largely negative. Living with Leo was becoming more difficult; as the family explainer, he felt bound to tell Gertrude why he disliked her writing, just as he told Picasso why he disliked his current work. Alice remembered Leo's taking Picasso into his study, and the painter coming out "furious saying, He does not leave me alone. It was he who said my drawings were more important than Raphael's. Why can he not leave me alone then with what I am doing now?" The angry Picasso left the house; the angry Leo slammed the door to his room. Later, when Leo went to Gertrude's room to explain his actions, "she dropped books on the floor to interrupt him." Grateful for Gertrude's support, at Christmas Picasso gave her *Homage to Gertrude,* a small tempera painting of statuesque nude angels.

Toklas thought Leo's dislike of Picasso's painting and Gertrude's writing brought on the siblings' larger troubles, but there had been signs for several years that they were unhappy with each other. In Gertrude's recreation of Leo's persona in *Two*, she described his unfortunate tendency to harangue: "Why did he always begin. . . . Beginning arranging he was arranging beginning arranging everything and telling. . . . He said everything." In contrast, to show that "he was different from her," Gertrude described the less-talkative woman character by saying, simply, "She works."

The welcome that Leo had often found at the Berensons' I Tatti in Fiesole also cooled because of his impolitic honesty. Dining with Bernard in 1907, Leo had given him an "unflattering" lecture about his character. Before this, the Berensons had enjoyed the Steins, talking books and art while they smoked cigars, and Leo and Gertrude were sometimes included in Mary's select swimming parties. (At a "ladies only" swim, Gertrude went in "clad in nothing but her Fat." Mary commented that she "really didn't know such enormities existed.") At dinner in 1908, Berenson returned Leo's insults, saying things "so horribly inapropos that one shivered." Perhaps he couldn't bear Leo's Fletcherizing (chewing each mouthful thirty-two times); perhaps he was angry about Gertrude's borrowing valuable books and returning them in bad condition. When Isabella Stewart Gardner asked Berenson who the new collectors (the Steins) were, he replied, "[a] tribe of queer, conceited, unworldly, bookish, rude, touchy, brutal, hypersensitive people [who] come often to forage in the library." Describing Sally as "quivering, fat . . . but magnetic, bold, and genuine," he called Gertrude "a sort of Semitic primitive female straight off the desert."

Changing Alliances: Leo and Nina

After Gertrude's *Three Lives* appeared in July 1909, Leo found keeping silent even more difficult. He did not believe Gertrude had talent, yet some of the reviews were very good: the *Boston Morning Herald* called *Three Lives* "an extraordinary book," and many critics praised the work's innovative language. Reviews appeared in *The Nation, The International,* and a number of city newspapers, and besides the Hapgoods' comments on the dust jacket, Gertrude had collected praise from H. G. Wells. Leo was bewildered: life at home was echoing the absurdity of the art world. That his hearing had deteriorated at least kept him from having to listen to Alice and Gertrude discussing the book's reception over their interminable cigarettes.

The frustration of feeling that his home had been invaded led Leo to spend more time on his own painting, and he sometimes rented a studio outside the house. He enjoyed being with other painters at both the Julian and the Matisse academies, where he was occasionally joined by Mike. In spring 1909 Nina Auzias made an overture to Leo, asking him how to spell a word. Leo answered quickly, "You know it yourself," and, in Nina's account, "we both burst out laughing." Leo then asked her to pose for him, but when she did, he was hostile. He said that her body was not "inspiring"; when she kissed him, he "spat on the floor." Nina ran out and did not see him for six months. It would have been easy for Leo to find her; she lived in a "little air-tight room at the end of the courtyard in the rue Dulin" and crossed the Luxembourg Garden several times a day. Eventually Leo admitted that he was interested in Nina and hired her as what he called a psychological model, for which service he paid four times the usual modeling fee. So, "like a modern Scheherazade," she spent hours in Leo's studio telling her "fantastic adventures." The two were soon sexually involved.

Leo wrote Mabel Weeks about the affair, enclosing a note Nina had sent him and emphasizing his lover's talent for juggling simultaneous affairs:

> There are three men that I know who would give their all if she would marry them (they have all been her lovers at one time or another). One is an Englishman of 48, another an American of 27, the other 24. . . . No. 3 swears that he'll kill me and himself if she leaves him, and he's both hotheaded and desperate enough to do it. . . . As she is in love with nobody except me you can see that at my present staid period of life I'm in a perfect whirlpool of tragicomic romance.

He then said that he had never been in love before and that he could not predict what was going to happen: Nina, he thought, could not sustain passion for long.

What Leo knew about either passion or himself, sexually, was minimal. Maurice Sterne described him, at thirty, as erotically naive; Leo admitted that he preferred sex with prostitutes because of his neurotic shyness around respectable women. (In 1901 he had written Gertrude that he had spent 150 francs on "a perfect devil of a time . . . for champagne, eats and the lady between twelve midnight and six o'clock but it was more than worth the price of admission.") Sterne recalled that most of Leo's women friends were "intellectuals with fine minds and dull bodies, . . . [who] were awed by Leo's keen intellect. Leo was, himself, more interested in ideas than in earthy experience." Leo had friendships with many women throughout his life, often psychoanalyzing them, a process that depended on an intimacy of knowledge that he found erotic.

In contrast to Leo's intellectual friends and Gertrude, Nina Auzias played the simple, passionate woman, but her writing showed a deep understanding of Leo's complexities. Although in 1909 she was involved with Morgan Russell, one of Leo's young American friends, and during the next years with the wealthy Paris Singer, who tried to leave Isadora Duncan for her, Nina never broke her bond with Leo. His cruelty during these years was his unwillingness to commit his love to her, even as he responded to her passion. By playing contradictory roles—father-confessor and lover—Leo tested Nina. Feigning indifference, he asked her to tell him the details of her sexual life, an interest she thought perverse. But whenever she was in obvious emotional pain and asked for reassurance, he retreated.

He also wrote Gertrude about the affair, again enclosing Nina's notes to him. For his sister, however, happily paired with Alice, Leo's liaison was embarrassing, as her devastating portrait of Nina shows. In "Elise Surville," a name that suggests servility and slipperiness as well as survival, Gertrude described Nina's salient qualities: "This one was one who had been a young one and certainly then had been one who was laughing very often . . . and knowing very many men then and knowing some women." By describing Nina's aging, bisexuality, and promiscuity, the portrait rebuked Leo for his tasteless choice of a lover, a women both infamous and poor (he supported Nina from early in the relationship). Gertrude believed that education and class were more important than beauty, and her impatience with what she saw as Leo's unsuitable romance led to problems he never anticipated. Whether or not his passion for Nina was a response to Gertrude's for Alice, Leo was comforted by the fact that his romance, however inappropriate in terms of class, was at least heterosexual.

Alice in Residence

While Gertrude and Alice returned to Italy for the summer of 1909, Sally wrote them from Paris that life was dull. So distant had the Steins become from Harriet Levy that Sally had not seen her and had heard only "that she took tea at Chalfin's studio." Despite excitement over the Diaghilev ballet with Vaslav Nijinsky and over Louis Blériot's flying the Channel, there was no news. Later, Mike, Sally, Annette, and Allan went to Le Trayas for a "delightful" month of swimming and walking. By autumn Harriet again toured galleries with them, often accompanied by the Russian dealer Shchukin, who wanted to buy *Girl with Green Eyes* from her.

Harriet continued living with Alice, although it was clear she was angry over her friend's liaison with Gertrude. Now past forty, Harriet—accustomed to having romances herself—did not enjoy being companionless. From the time of their crossing, when Alice had allowed herself to be courted by an old military man who later wrote to her suggestively, Harriet had been embarrassed by Alice's liaisons. She invited Caroline Helbing, a California friend, to visit Paris for the winter. The four women went to galleries and restaurants and were entertained in the homes of Marie Laurencin and Mildred Aldrich. Before Helbing returned to the States, Alice told her that she had been invited to live with Gertrude but that she did not want to hurt Harriet's feelings. She asked Caroline to make sure that when Harriet returned to California for a visit, she stayed.

Caroline's visit was marred by the great January flood, the worst natural disaster of the century: sewers burst, fifty thousand people were homeless, the metro was inoperable (water stood five meters deep in the Quai d'Orsay station). In this year of Halley's comet, intellectuals were talking

about Fokine's ballet of Stravinsky's *The Firebird* with its outlandish costumes, about Bertrand Russell's and Alfred North Whitehead's *Principia
Mathematica,* about the cinema, and about the "simultaneous poetry" of
Apollinaire, Blaise Cendrars, and the Delaunays. Most people didn't understand the *Futurist Manifesto of Destructive Incendiary Violence,* with its
glorification of militarism, its "beautiful ideas which kill, and contempt of
women," and its agenda to "destroy museums, libraries, to combat moral-
ism, feminism." Like Gertrude, most admirers of the avant-garde were content with cubism's logical designs and surrealism's mysticism.

Enthusiasm for the work of Matisse and the cubists suffused Paris.
With the Galerie Bernheim-Jeune showing Matisse, Vollard's gallery showing
Vlaminck, and Daniel-Henry Kahnweiler handling both Picasso and Juan
Gris, Paris art circles had finally recognized the painters whose work was related to Einstein, Bergson, and other space-time theorists. Apollinaire wrote,
"There has never been as systematic an art and as great a number of artistic
systems." Despite the attention cubism received, however, viewers at the
Autumn Salon were once again stunned by Matisse's work. This time his huge
paintings *Music* and *The Dance,* which had been commissioned as staircase
decorations for Shchukin's Moscow home, were attacked for their explicit
representations of nudity.

Late in 1909 a letter from Simon Stein in San Francisco made the
three Paris siblings realize how cosmopolitan they had become. Simon
wrote about managing a small cigar counter in a grocery store: "I came
around Saturday morning at 5 o'clock and took posession and took Stock
Since I have somthing on My mind my leg's are better I sleep like a babby
and my time does not drag at all. . . . Well Mike I see a custermur coming
across the street, so I will close, sending my love to you all." Leo, Gertrude,
and Mike often told stories about Simon's inability to learn; when Gertrude
was eleven, she asked him each morning and evening when Columbus discovered America, but he could never remember the date. Seeing his crudely
expressed sentiments now made them realize their brother was hardly literate. He was as warm-hearted as ever, reminding them of "Our Dear Mama"
and sending his nephew Allan "a few dollars."

One of the patterns of family relations that had shifted by 1909 was
Gertrude's view of Mike as the exemplary older brother. When she watched
his relationship with his son, she sometimes wondered where the wise,
moderate Mike had gone. Behaving all too often like their quixotic father,
Mike gave Allan mixed messages. One such episode involved his first urging
the boy to collect butterflies, only to question the pastime subsequently:
"Son you are certain this is not a cruel thing that you are wanting to be doing, killing things to make collections of them. . . . The son was very disturbed then . . . he said he would not do it." The next morning, however,
Mike himself caught a butterfly, pinned it, and proudly took it to show Allan.
As Gertrude pointed out, "The boy was all mixed up inside him." When she
asked Mike why he treated his son more arbitrarily than he had Leo or her

when they were his wards, Mike explained that being a father was difficult: "a son irritates you differently from any other irritation and when a son irritates you you are irritated." It was also clear that Sally and Mike often disagreed over disciplining Allan.

Gertrude, Leo, and Mike were a close family unit; during their first years in Paris they were generally satisfied with their relationships with one another. They agreed on all manner of things, including the fact that they were content to ignore the existence of both Bertha and Simon. (One of Gertrude's notebook comments about her sister—"kind of nasty as only she can be"—is typical.) In this regard, too, the Steins replicated the pattern of a number of other Jewish families divided between the States and Europe in their search for contentment, security, and position. It also seems clear that the bond between Leo and Gertrude was truly intimate; Hutchins Hapgood wrote of the near-reverence she had for Leo, who filled the role of "beloved" in her life.

Given this, there is little question that the presence of Alice in Gertrude's life would create dissension among the siblings. During the summer of 1910 they vacationed separately. Gertrude and Alice rented the Casa Ricci and spent afternoons shopping for old jewelry and visiting Muriel and Paul Draper, Mina Loy and Stephen Haweis, Florence Blood, and others. With the excuse that he wanted to improve his painting (he and Mike had exhibited watercolors at the Bernheim-Jeune's Cézanne retrospective), Leo spent the summer in Berlin, London, Venice, Florence, and Rome, arranging liaisons with Nina throughout Europe. From Berlin he criticized the "disgusting . . . Germans and their beer guzzling," illustrating his comment with a line of distended belly shapes; from London he wrote that he had regained his tranquillity through his "splendid isolation." Looking ahead to the fall in Paris, Leo first demanded that lunch be served at one, because that would fit his study schedule better; later he suggested that he dine out, so that Gertrude and Alice could plan meals for themselves.

Called back to San Francisco because of the illness of Sally's father, on July 16 Mike, Sally, and Allan once more sailed for America. Rather than be alone in Paris, Harriet Levy went with them; happily for Alice, once in the States, she decided to stay there. She wrote that Alice could cancel the apartment lease, asking only that she send Harriet the Matisse and the small landscape by Harry Phelan Gibb. The testiness of the letter stemmed from the fact that Alice had not yet repaid the thousand-dollar loan with which Harriet had financed Alice's trip to Paris. Its tone went unnoticed: Gertrude and Alice were happily making plans to move Toklas's things into the rue de Fleurus flat.

Sally's father died of cancer on November 10, but the Steins stayed in California another year, seeing to business and dental needs. Mike wrote that he had invested part of the family fortune in four-and-a-half-percent bonds but that cash was scarce; Gertrude should spend carefully. Although he was trying to sell the duplexes, the overbuilt San Francisco market made the task difficult. Mike also reported on their brother's love life, saying, "I have to protect Simon against himself and see that he does nothing foolish, while under her [his landlady's] hypnotic influence. It may become necessary to make some kind of trust." As he kept the families in touch, connecting San Francisco and Paris with checks and good cheer, Mike asked for snapshots of "Leo's new room" and furniture. To make room for Alice, Leo had taken his second-floor bedroom as his living space; the first-floor study then became Alice's bedroom. As one visitor wrote, "Leo lives alone, mostly in his room . . . very beautiful."

After Alice moved in, Gertrude faced life with a new assertiveness: she was no longer her brothers' satellite. The two women attended concerts, plays, and films; listened to music on their phonograph (often exchanging records with Mike and Sally); window-shopped; and visited Mildred Aldrich, who kept American and British visitors—many of them theater people—in touch with Paris life (through her, Gertrude met Henry McBride, who publicized her writing in New York; playwright Avery Hopwood; and Roger Fry, British aesthetician). They also visited Alice Ullman, becoming friends with the Infanta Eulalia of Spain, and Grace Lounsbery, Mabel Haynes's former housemate in Baltimore who was now a playwright. (Alice thought Grace amusing, but Gertrude called her "a false alarm.") Socially, they stayed within accepted circles of American expatriates or high-born Europeans, but they tried increasingly to choose their friends from among people not already close to Sally and Mike or Leo. They still enjoyed friendships with Picasso and his circle, however. Kahnweiler, Picasso's dealer, wrote that even though he had first known Mike and Sally, "All my fellow-feeling was for Gertrude, in whom . . . I found the 'great man' of the family. Her calm certitude impressed me far more than Leo's trenchant affirmations, for the latter often changed, bearing witness to a basic instability. A little later I became acquainted with Alice Toklas, whose intelligence and culture I gradually discovered in spite of an extraordinary modesty."

As Gertrude developed self-confidence, she began expressing her resentments about the gendered world. Among these was the fact that men in her circle—painters, writers, and now Leo—began and ended love affairs—sometimes even homosexual relationships—with impunity. She, on the other hand, knew how objectionable her affair with Alice was (or would be) to some friends and relatives. Living together meant that neither she nor Toklas could maintain an honest correspondence with their families; one of Sally Stein's missions while she was in California was to see Alice's father, Ferdinand, and cheer him up about his daughter's decision to remain permanently in France.

Even in Paris, lesbians were less accepted than male gays, and the recent arrival of Natalie Clifford Barney, a wealthy Ohio lesbian, had crystallized the feeling that such women should be avoided: poet Paul Valéry referred to Barney's teas as "the hazardous Fridays." Gertrude's reticence about her life with Alice eventually led to separations from such friends as

Cousin Miriam Sutro Price, who remained one of Leo's favorite relatives. Separating from the family was difficult; middle-class Jewish families were clannish. They were also well traveled: living abroad would not ensure privacy. Gertrude continued to worry about what people would think about her life with Alice.

The proper balance was hard to find. Aunt Rachel Keyser wrote urging Gertrude to correspond with Bertha. According to Rachel, Bertha Raffel—who had problems with illness among her three children and with servants—"feels the neglect so keenly" (there is no evidence that Gertrude ever wrote). Gertrude and Alice did look forward to letters from some of their American friends, especially those who understood their liaison. One of their favorites was Harriet Levy's married sister, Polly Jacobs, who consistently encouraged them to stay abroad in order to maintain their lifestyle: "Lots and lots of congratulations and good wishes for 1911. My best wish is that you may always stay in Paris."

That spring Polly wrote that Mike and Sally had come for supper but, enigmatically, "the conversation was strained and limited." The intimacy between Sally and Harriet Levy, both now so dedicated to Christian Science that they wore black armbands when Mary Baker Eddy died, may have threatened the Steins' marriage; Polly observed that she didn't see much of her sister Harriet, who was "inseparable" from Sally. Calling Alice and Gertrude "selfish happy irresponsible devils," Polly sometimes sent them the long Jewish jokes that Gertrude loved. She also kept them in touch with California mores, reporting that the "all-absorbing" subjects of the day in San Francisco were "Science—Suffrage—Sex" and that "every Jew these days who is of any consequence has an auto . . . plays bridge . . . and goes to her summer home." Gertrude and Alice didn't play bridge, but they soon acquired both a car and a summer place.

By 1912 several patterns had clarified in the lives of the Paris Steins. When Mike and Sally returned in the fall, after what Mike described as an idyllic summer riding and "camping" in Marin County, Sally transferred her energy from painting and touting Matisse's work to Christian Science. She spent a great deal of time at the little Second Church of Christ, Scientist, on the Left Bank, attending services in both French and English. Although she stayed married to Mike, she grew more and more involved in the lives of women who came to her for advice, and the rue Madame household became a haven for Annette Rosenshine, Therese Jelenko, Harriet Levy, Rachel Miller, Sylvia Salinger, and others. As Salinger wrote on arriving in Paris in 1912, "Sarah is so wonderful that any place she was in would seem homelike." Countless afternoon visits, tasty suppers, packages of homebaked cookies, invitations to church, and general spiritual support were hallmarks of the kind of attention Sally loved to give.

Gertrude and Alice, however, no longer needed—or wanted—Sally's help. Although the families continued to share evening meals on occasion, they gradually grew apart. (Sally also made it clear that she worried about

Alice and Gertrude's attentions to her young women friends.) What Gertrude and Alice wanted in life was their love, their privacy, and success for Stein's writing. Alice helped Gertrude decide what she wanted to write; she also devised strategies for marketing her work. A surprising number of letters (most of them typed by Alice on their new Smith Premier) related to finding publishers and reviewers.

Gertrude's continuing frustration with her lack of literary success colored a 1912 letter to Henri-Pierre Roché, who had criticized her portrait style. Midway through the reply, she discussed what happens to women who do not fill traditional roles:

> Construction is a man's business. Being beautiful is a woman's business but there are a great many women who are not beautiful and they act stupidly the ones that are not beautiful if they act as if they were. . . . Now to take the instance of yourself and myself. You are a man and I am a woman but I have a much more constructive mind than you have. I am a genuinely creative artist and being such my personality determines my art just as Matisse's or Picasso's or Wagner's or anyone else. Now you if I were a man would not write me such a letter because you would respect the inevitable character of my art. It would be very much (if I were a man) as if Bruce were to advise Matisse. You would not do it however you might wish my art other than it is. But being a man and believing that a man's business is to be constructive you forget the much greater constructive power of my mind and the absolute nature of my art which if I were a man you would respect.
>
> Do you see why I think your letter unimportant and stupid. I have often felt much pleasure and much encouragement . . . from your appreciation but that is as far as any outsider can be of assistance to any one genuinely creative.

While Gertrude was willing to end bothersome friendships, she also cultivated new ones. During salon evenings, she liked talking with such artists as Sonia and Robert Delaunay, whose home was the site of dress-up parties—known as costume "reform"—on Thursdays and Saturdays, as well as with American painters Charles Demuth, Patrick Henry Bruce, and Charles Sheeler and German visitors Karl von Freyburg and Arnold Rönnebeck and their good friend, the American Marsden Hartley. This last recalled Gertrude's kindly, probing inquiries about his work. Admiring Picasso, Hartley had abandoned representational art and was painting in a quasi-cubist mode. At one point he arranged twenty of his new canvases on the floor of his room and invited Gertrude and Alice for tea. Already impressed with his conversation and his interest in mysticism, Gertrude was astonished at the quality of his painting (though Hartley had had several showings at Stieglitz's "291" gallery). She asked if she could come back again, saying she needed time to think about his work. She then bought one of his paintings and also wrote to Stieglitz praising Hartley's innovative uses of color.

To separate Gertrude and Alice's involvement in literature and art from the interests of the other Paris Steins suggests, unfairly, that they were the only ones following international trends. Mike often wrote Gertrude about new books and new developments in the art world: "There is a new book by Kandinsky published in Munich a bit along your lines . . . called *Klänge.* Faschbacher has it here." He wrote that such new journals in English as *New Age, Rhythm,* and *Freewoman* might be interested in her writing, and he also tried to focus attention on her work, as when two art editors touring Europe wanted to see his collection and he instead referred them to Gertrude, "as there might be something in it for you [Gertrude] in the newspaper line." Mike also watched the values of their art collections and, as prices for Cézannes and Matisses soared, reported to Gertrude, "The academicians must be shitting in their boots." Leo, of course, also knew a great deal about both art and literature, but the information he gave Gertrude only irritated her.

Part of Gertrude's awareness of the politics of gender stemmed from her financial situation. She wanted to buy art that interested her, but she had very little cash. Since moving in with Leo ten years before, she had saved nothing. Even though they lived modestly, Leo had spent their joint income on paintings. While Gertrude recognized the value in collecting, she also saw that she owned very little. Should she want to return to the States, her wardrobe would be entirely unsuitable, and few people besides Alice valued her writing. Gertrude described herself as "reasonably poor," but, even so, she was rich enough to have to pay French taxes. Alice's remarks about Gertrude's "small" income suggest that she herself had more money—though in those years she was drawing on the principal of her mother's estate, and when that was gone, she would have nothing. That she was now living at 27, rue de Fleurus helped the Steins' financial situation; more importantly, her residence there helped Gertrude see how valuable her insights as a woman were and how important her gendered subject matter and perspective were to twentieth-century letters.

The Mabel Dodge Years

As Gertrude and Alice created their life together, they spent less time with Leo, though they still lived as a family. Always critical of his sister's writing, Leo satirized her "portraits"; when he was traveling, however, he wrote her long letters. Many chronicled his liaison with Nina; others were travelogues; still others shared his feelings about mutual friends. In August 1910, he wrote with genuine sorrow about the death of William James. James had visited them several years earlier, marveling at their art collection; he had more recently written to thank Gertrude for a copy of *Three Lives,* sending wishes that she be "sufficiently happy."

Whether or not Leo was home, Alice arranged the household to support Gertrude's writing. The Saturday salons became more welcoming, their tone set by Gertrude's "intellectual silvery giggle" rather than by Leo's lectures. Hartley called her studio "that quiet yet always lively place," where "a fund of good humour [was] thrust at you." Gertrude and Alice gave dinner parties where people gossiped and laughed their way through Hélène's good food, nursing one modest glass of wine apiece; after dinner, there was conversation rather than alcohol. If Leo was there, he was quiet; his language had become more abstract as he shifted his interest to aesthetics and literary criticism. The man who had felt so attuned to life that he danced joyously, Isadora Duncan–style, or argued that sexuality was another of the dimensions of space-time exploration, had grown dour.

The truth was that Leo was uncomfortable with Gertrude's sexuality. Time and again he reminded Alice and her that "any manifestation of homosexuality of any kind annoyed him and he asked them to refrain . . . as they were *accustomed* to being rather careless in their affection before him." While he wanted Gertrude to be happy, he worried that she was becoming so dependent on Toklas that she might never be able to exist without her.

Even if Leo and Gertrude had wanted to distance themselves from each other's lives, doing so was difficult. After ten years of living together, they were connected through their circles of friends and circles of friends of friends. One of these connections was Mabel Dodge, the vivacious American who had come to their salon with her husband, architect Edwin Dodge. In the spring of 1911 Mabel took back to her Italian villa part of *The Making of Americans.* (Gertrude had given other parts of the manuscript to Alice Woods Ullman and Stephen and Mina Loy Haweis.) Like Alice and Mina, Mabel was impressed with both Gertrude's style—she commented, "It is almost frightening to come up against reality in language in this way"—and her subjects—"things hammered out of consciousness into black and white that have never been expressed before." She called the work "as new and strange and big as the post-impressionists" and predicted that it would change literature.

Mabel also liked Gertrude as a person: "[She] gloried in her fat. She had none of the funny embarrassment Anglo-Saxons have about flesh. . . . I seemed to amuse her and she was always laughing her great, hearty laugh at me." She liked the way Gertrude polished off huge portions of food and the way she walked to the Dodge villa, arriving "all in a sweat, and as she sat there, fanning herself with her hat, she seemed positively to steam." Besides Mabel's lavish table, Gertrude liked her stories—wicked anecdotes about the Berensons' notion of "a really gay evening," spent identifying famous paintings from pieces of cut-up photos, or about Florence Blood's tearing off her clothes as she declared her love for Hutch Hapgood and the wry letter Neith Hapgood then wrote to friends admonishing them to wear at least a chemise during their liaisons.

Instead of summering in Italy where they could visit Mabel, however, Alice and Gertrude went to Spain on what was, in effect, a honeymoon. On her first visit to that country, Alice insisted on exploring a bevy of cities, churches, and nightclubs: she and Gertrude saw Burgos, Valladolid, Toledo, Cuenca, Cordova, Seville, Gibraltar, Tangier, Granada with its Gypsies (Alice fancied herself a Gypsy), and Madrid. Both women loved seeing paintings by Goya, Velásquez, and El Greco at the Prado and going to the bullfights; Gertrude told Alice when not to watch, particularly when horses were gored. Their discovery of the Spanish dancer La Argentina, whose performance Alice called "more thrilling than the Russian ballet," kept them in Madrid longer than they had planned. Gertrude's portrait of her, "Susie Asado," was replete with sexual terms, the name *Susie* itself a reference to sexual effluvia. Another of their Madrid enthusiasms was the café singer Preciosilla. Gertrude put up with the extensive travel so long as she could carve out hours in the sunshine for herself.

They also spent several weeks in Avila, St. Theresa's birthplace. A gorgeous Mass for a visiting bishop, complete with a full orchestra and sixteenth-century vestments, rivaled the town's pastry shop and the modest inn for charm. It was here that Gertrude, dressed in her corduroy robe, was taken to be a visiting religious and had to discourage petitioners from following her and kissing her ring. Enamored of the mysticism and beauty of Spanish life, Gertrude read everything she could about Saint Theresa. The only worry during the trip was Gertrude's painful colitis attack, a not-uncommon occurrence; as early as 1907, Gertrude had written to Etta about her digestive troubles.

After Spain, they visited the Dodge villa. Mabel was questioning the stability of her marriage to Edwin Dodge, though Gertrude assured her that he would make "a delightful companion to be old along with—he has such a sense of the ludicrous." (Some of Mabel's attempts to befriend men were efforts to attract future husbands: her letters to Leo Stein suggest that she may have seen him in that role. But the madcap ghost-haunted life that attracted such guests as Mrs. Stanford White, Gabriele D'Annunzio, André Gide, the Haweises, and others was not Leo's style.) When Gertrude and Alice arrived in October, a number of guests had left, afraid of strange sounds and mysteriously moving furniture. Constance Fletcher, the playwright-novelist who had been friends with both Henry James and Oscar Wilde, won Alice's admiration by saying that she had talked all night with a ghost who had materialized from the closet. The more pressing intrigue in the fall of 1912, however, was Mabel's liaison with her son's young tutor ("football player of 22," as she described him).

Gertrude's room was next to Mabel's, and because Stein wrote late at night, she was able to hear the tutor's comings and goings. In Mabel's account, one night she became aware of Gertrude's listening. The next day at lunch, Gertrude gave her a "strong" look, making her own sexual intentions clear. When Alice saw the look, she bolted from the table. Gertrude followed and then returned to explain that Alice was prostrate with heat and would not rejoin them. Gertrude and Alice soon left for Paris, but Mabel wrote Stein begging her to return and also warning her to burn their letters: "Gertrude—if you love me you'll come back. I can't do without you—especially now. . . . I'll send you and Alice nice round trip tickets for its not fair otherwise—but just this once won't you brave Leo and come back? Dam everything." The letter closed with a postscript suggestive of Mabel's brand of intrigue: "Pleeaaasse say yes. If absolutely not you've got to catch E. [Edwin] on the boat train from Savoie as he arrives to talk to him to tell him he's got to leave me alone over here to decide this and not to tear me to pieces with his magnanimity. Please." After this crisis, to which Gertrude did not return, Mabel suggested that she live in Paris with them, but Stein did not agree to her plan.

Although their friendship cooled, Mabel was partly responsible for the American reputation of Gertrude's writing. Constance Fletcher insisted that Gertrude's "Portrait of Mabel Dodge at the Villa Curonia" (which began, "The days are wonderful and the nights are wonderful and the life is pleasant") be printed. Three hundred copies were bound in Florentine wallpaper and given to Mabel's friends, both in Europe and New York. Through this visibility in the world of the avant-garde, Mabel joined Arthur Davies and Walter Pach in a project to collect new French, German, and Spanish art for the International Exhibition of Modern Art, to be held from February 17 to March 15, 1913, in New York's Sixty-ninth Regiment Armory building. When Mike and Leo were asked to lend paintings for the show, Leo offered Matisse's *Blue Nude* and two Picasso still lifes, and Mike and Sally agreed to send Matisse's *La Coiffeuse* and *Madras Rouge*.

As advance publicity for the exhibition, Mabel wrote an essay on Gertrude's writing. "Speculations, or Post-Impressionists in Prose" appeared in *Arts and Decoration* in March 1913, and Gertrude wrote that she was "as proud as punch" when a copy reached her. In the essay Dodge compared Stein's writing to Picasso's painting and, more importantly, discussed the unique way Gertrude saw words: as counters valued for "inherent quality" rather than for their "accepted meaning." Her advice was that people read Stein's work aloud. She also described the way Gertrude wrote: "Concentrating upon the impression she has received and which she wishes to transmit, she suspends her selective faculty, waiting for the word . . . that will perfectly interpret her meaning, to rise from her sub-consciousness to the surface of her mind. Then and then only does she bring her reason to bear." Mabel's essay also appeared in the June issue of *Camera Work,* along with Stein's portrait of her.

United States reaction to the thirteen hundred works by three hundred artists in the Armory show was extreme. Ten thousand people a day visited the exhibition. Students at the University of Chicago burned an effigy of Matisse and a copy of his *Blue Nude* in protest, and the media was filled with satires. One focus of attention was Duchamp's *Nude Descending a Staircase,* which was called "a dynamited suit of Japanese armor," "a lot of disused golf clubs and bags," and "an explosion in a shingle factory." Though Leo was listed as owner of three of the controversial paintings, his sister's became the name used in publicity, jokes, and such quatrains as this from the February 8, 1913, *Chicago Tribune:*

> I called the canvas Cow with Cud
> And hung it on the line,
> Altho' to me 'twas vague as mud,
> 'Twas clear to Gertrude Stein.

The media thought the large woman with her strange language was news; Carl Van Vechten interviewed Mabel Dodge about Gertrude and later, as a result of his *New York Times* story, met Stein in Paris.

Part of the interest in Gertrude's writing preceded the Armory show and occurred because of another contact she and Leo shared—that with Alfred Stieglitz. An early visitor to the rue de Fleurus, he occasionally corresponded with Leo. It was May Bookstaver, however, acting as agent for Gertrude, who took "a portfolio bursting with manuscripts" to Stieglitz (he later recalled the comedy of this "huge woman, leading a huge Boston bull-dog," struggling with loose manuscripts in the fifteen-foot square room that housed the "291" gallery). May explained that she had taken the work to many publishers. "Invariably I was told by everyone [*sic*] of these publishers that there was only one man crazy enough in this country . . . to be interested in anything like these." She responded to Stieglitz's refusal to look at the work by handing him Gertrude's portrait of Matisse. After reading a few words, he said, "Show me the one on Picasso." Again he read a little and then, because he was planning a special issue on the two painters, replied, "I don't know the meaning of all this. But it sounds good to me. I think I can use both manuscripts." Only after his acceptance did May tell him that the author was Gertrude Stein, but at that time her name meant nothing to him. Once she was identified as Leo's sister, however, Stieglitz exclaimed, "The woman who was half reclining on a chaise-longue . . . wreathed in a sort of semi–Mona Lisa smile."

The two portraits differed dramatically in language and emphasis. "Matisse" stressed the painter's worry over his studious approach to art and repeated the words *struggling, certain,* and *clearly expressing.* In contrast, "Picasso" moved quickly, its pace exuding the confidence and sensuality of its subject: "One whom some were certainly following was one who was completely charming." Stein called Picasso's work his essence, describing it as "a solid thing . . . a complicated thing, an interesting thing, a disturbing thing, a repellant thing, a very pretty thing."

When Stieglitz wrote Gertrude for permission to use her work, Leo was amazed that a man he admired valued her writing. "Matisse" and "Picasso" appeared in the August 1912 *Camera Work,* to acclaim as well as to con-troversy. After reading Gertrude's work, John Galsworthy asked that the publication of his essay on pluralism in art, scheduled for the next issue, be canceled.

Ever alert for ways to circulate her writing, Gertrude mailed copies of *Camera Work* to friends. Responding to the controversy over her work, she explained it was "simply"—one of her favorite words—continuing the method of "insistence" she had used in *The Making of Americans:* "I was doing what the cinema was doing, I was making a continuous succession of the statement of what that person was until I had not many things but one thing." She reminded readers, "Any one is of one's period and this our pe-riod was undoubtedly the period of the cinema and series production."

During this flurry of interest of her work, Gertrude, with Alice, decided to visit England in search of publishers; she wrote excitedly to Dodge, "Don't be surprised Mabel but I may be going over to England to see if I can find a publisher. I don't know very well what I am to do when I get there. . . . If you know anyone who knows a publisher and can tell me how to meet him, will you let me know." Encouraged by a California friend, Alice and Gertrude spent several weeks at the Knightsbridge Hotel in London, visiting in the country for a weekend and spending a day with Roger Fry. They went to two of John Lane's open houses and were promised by his wife, who had read *Three Lives,* that she would urge him to reissue it.

Learning about the English countryside and its flowers supplied a pas-time they both enjoyed. They also ordered chintz-covered furniture and tried to arrange a visit with their idol Henry James at Rye. Unfortunately, James refused, telling their friend Alvin Langdon Coburn that he was not then receiving anyone.

Attending a performance of Richard Strauss's *Elektra* and the opening night of the Russian ballet, Gertrude and Alice saw their friend Muriel Draper, splendid in a tall turban. The Drapers invited them to dinner with novelist May Sinclair and others. Even when she sat quietly in the Drapers' home, Gertrude was a presence. When some topic moved her, "she would talk for hours, a steady flow of ideas in an almost boring logical sequence, some of them profound and others merely . . . brilliant dialectic."

Gertrude and Alice also dined with Ethel Sands, at whose home they met novelist George Moore and biographer Lytton Strachey. Stein's interest in people made her a congenial guest, and she and Alice were thoroughly ap-preciated in England. But despite their social contacts and the good offices of Duncan Grant, Logan Pearsall Smith, and Coburn, nothing was published. Al-though Oliver St. John Gogarty asked for a copy of Mabel Dodge's portrait for his friend James Joyce, and Mitchell Kennerley—publisher of the important Modern Drama series—was interested in *Many Many Women,* it was clear that fame in the States aroused little attention in Britain.

The Armory show brought Gertrude a kind of mocking fame. But her

The Daniel Stein family in Europe. *Left to right:* Simon, Daniel, Michael, Amelia, Leo, Bertha; *foreground,* Gertrude, with doll. *(Gertrude Stein Collection, Yale Collection of American Literature, Beinecke Rare Book and Manuscript Library, Yale University)*

The Tubbs' Hotel in Oakland, California, where the Stein family lived for several months when they moved west in 1880. *(Used by permission of the Oakland Municipal Offices, Oakland, Calif.)*

Gertrude's great-grandmother Keyser, whom she was thought to resemble. *(The Bancroft Library, University of California at Berkeley)*

The imposing Oakland, California, high school. *(Used by permission of the Oakland Municipal Offices, Oakland, Calif.)*

Leo and Gertrude's Irving Street boardinghouse in Cambridge, Massachusetts. *(Author photo)*

Gertrude and Leo on the tennis court, Cambridge, Massachusetts, 1893–94. Leo attended Harvard, and Gertrude, the Harvard Annex (later Radcliffe). *(Yale)*

Leo and Gertrude on a Woods Hole marine biological course expedition, Cape Cod, 1897; Leo is holding a specimen. *(Yale)*

Gertrude at Radcliffe. *(Yale)*

Gertrude and friends during undergraduate years at Radcliffe (1893–1897). *(Yale)*

Gertrude about to enter the Johns Hopkins medical program, visiting in California with her nephew Allan Stein, 1897. *(Yale)*

Leo and Gertrude's house in Baltimore, 215 East Biddle Street, 1897–1899. While living here, Leo finished his B.A. and did a year of graduate work in sciences at Johns Hopkins; Gertrude completed two years of medical school. *(Author photo)*

A corseted Gertrude during medical school years. *(Yale)*

Gertrude with the Samuels family in California. *Upper left,* Gertrude; *upper right,* Mike and Sally (Samuels) Stein. *(Yale)*

Leo newly settled in Paris, 1904–5, with the beginnings of his art collection. *(The Baltimore Museum of Art, Cone Archives)*

The entrance to 27, rue de Fleurus, where Gertrude and Leo introduced friends to contemporary painting. *(Author photo)*

Gertrude on a summer tour of Italy with the Cone sisters, Etta and Dr. Claribel, from Baltimore. *(Yale)*

Late in 1903, Sally, Mike, and Allan moved to Paris, bringing San Francisco friend Therese Jelenko with them, *Back left*, Leo and Gertrude. *(Yale)*

The Michael Steins' apartment (which became a Matisse salon) at 58, rue Madame. *(Author photo)*

The Michael Steins (*far left*) with Henri Matisse, a frequent visitor, and Hans Purrmann (*far right*), their collection of Matisse paintings in background. *(The Baltimore Museum of Art, Cone Archives)*

Paintings hung at 27, rue de Fleurus, Leo and Gertrude's salon, circa 1907–8. Works by Pierre Bonnard, Pablo Picasso, Maurice Denis, Jean-Edouard Vuillard, Renoir, and Cézanne made the salon a showplace of contemporary art. Leo, in particular, admired studies of the nude. *(The Baltimore Museum of Art, Cone Archives)*

Center: The Steins as a family unit in Paris (Leo now bearded). *Top:* Picasso's drawing of Leo (1906). *Left:* Arnold Genthe's 1906 photo of the glamorous Alice Toklas, who arrived in Paris—and in Gertrude's life—the following year. *(Yale; The Baltimore Museum of Art, The Cone Collection, formed by Dr. Claribel Cone and Miss Etta Cone of Baltimore, Maryland, BMA 1950.276; The Bancroft Library, University of California at Berkeley)*

Picasso's painting of Gertrude. *(The Metropolitan Museum of Art, Bequest of Gertrude Stein, 1946 [47.106])*

During 1916, when Mike and Sally lived near Matisse in the south of France, he painted these loving portraits of his close friends. *(San Francisco Museum of Modern Art, Sarah and Michael Stein Memorial Collection, Gift of Nathan Cummings)*

Gertrude as driver for the American Friends of the French Wounded during World War I, with her Ford, and Alice as organizer and supply deputy in front of the Hôpital Violet Père. *(Yale)*

The young Hemingways when they met Gertrude and Alice in 1924. *(The Hemingway Archive, John F. Kennedy Library, Boston)*

Gertrude and Alice later in the 1920s in Bilignin. *(Yale)*

The summer home in Bilignin, Belley, where Alice grew her amazing flowers and vegetables, near Lucey's church in the beautiful Ain. (*Author photo*)

After Stein's *Autobiography of Alice B. Toklas* was published in 1933, she and Alice toured the USA (1934–35), wearing fashionable clothes. (*Yale*)

Gertrude and her poodle, Basket, with the Picasso family. Gertrude was godmother to Paolo Picasso (*center*). *At right,* Alice Toklas. (*Yale*)

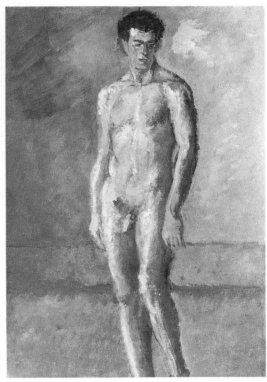

Leo with his wife, Nina (Auzias) Stein, in Italy. Some of her winsomeness shows in the photo fragment below. *(Yale)*

From 1903 until his death in 1947 Leo Stein painted. More than seventy of his oils are housed at Yale. *(Yale)*

Gertrude and Alice's manor house in Culoz during WWII. *(Author photo)*

Gertrude and Alice with Bravig Imbs in Aix-les-Bains before WWII. *(Yale)*

Basket performing. *(Yale)*

Gertrude Stein's postwar friendships with the men of the U.S. forces in Europe are well known. She met as often with women in the armed forces. *(Yale)*

Living in Paris at the rue Christine apartment (which had less wall space for her beloved paintings), Gertrude grew old—and small. *(Yale)*

friendship with the woman largely responsible for her notoriety had come to an end. The last meeting was dinner at the rue de Fleurus in the fall of 1913, when Gertrude and Alice entertained Mabel along with Picasso, Berenson, Leo (clean-shaven after a decade of wearing a beard), and Arnold Rönnebeck. Berenson again thought Gertrude looked handsome but admitted he could not read her *Camera Work* portraits. Leo sat in disapproving silence. Whether relationships crumbled over aesthetic differences or sexual ones, Gertrude and Leo's household was disintegrating.

Ruptures: A Portrait of Leo

"Certainly he was different from her. . . . He had sound coming out of him. He had sound coming out of him." As Gertrude's portrait *Two* insisted, Leo led a talkative life. So did she, for a time, until she was made to feel that her role as woman was to listen. Finding her voice again in Paris, through her writing, Gertrude decided there was more to life than subordinating herself to her brother. If nothing more, she wanted her own silences.

Leo and Gertrude had long impressed friends with their hard-won compatibility. Sterne said after years of knowing both, "Gertrude's tempo was not like Leo's adagio; it was vivace allegro. Her mind moved rapidly and the quicker her thoughts, the greater her physical speed. Although she was stout, her spirit . . . was alive, keen, and active." In their roles as listener (Gertrude) and "mentor, dictionary, and encyclopedia, supplying on demand any information she required" (Leo), the Steins had worked out a balance; what was changing now was Gertrude's tolerance for Leo's constant, vocal presence. *Two* describes the breaking, the rupturing, of the power of Leo's voice as Gertrude changed from thinking him "charming" to finding him an angry— even "terrifying"—brother. She recalled that Leo continued to talk, but "then I was not listening. This had never happened to me before. . . . I had always been listening sometimes arguing very often just being interested."

For Gertrude, personality differences were less important than power inequities. As the older brother, the smart male in the Jewish family, Leo also assumed he was head of the household. He had invited the younger (failed) Gertrude to live with him, understanding that she needed a family home but also knowing that he would benefit from her income. Friends noted that Leo bought whatever paintings he chose, though she supposedly had the chance to disapprove his purchases. Leo also assumed he was the center of the family; from boyhood on, he "was cheerful as long as he was . . . the chief speaker." Mabel Dodge recalled Leo's need for a listener: "He would linger for hours, talking very close into any ear he could secure. . . . I remember being stretched out in a chaise lounge hot summer nights . . . Leo draping himself over the back of it, breathing close . . . uttering his puzzling intellectual profundities down one's neck, scarcely noticing whether one listened or not or answered him."

Gertrude and Leo had shared a flat for ten years. Leo's deafness made living with him difficult; Gertrude's own hearing loss had also begun. The excitement of finding and buying paintings had diminished, and Gertrude now thought of herself as a writer, working daily on projects Leo found dismaying. To friends, Leo called her writing "sheer nonsense." Gertrude, in turn, felt betrayed by her brother—and disillusioned. Her notebook entries suggest that she, too, had accepted Leo's belief that his intellect was superior to hers: "Jews mostly run themselves by their minds, now they have good minds but not great minds." She felt that Leo might not succeed because of his lack of "resolution and singleness of purpose."

Their artistic lives, too, were changing. Leo, surrounded by conservative young painters, feared cubism and futurism, as his own paintings showed. By contrast, Gertrude—guided by Picasso and Apollinaire—moved increasingly toward the surreal. As she became eclectic, Leo grew predictable. She enjoyed Marsden Hartley, Marcel Duchamp, Kandinsky, Arnold Rönnebeck, and Francis Picabia, whose grandfather, with Daguerre, had invented photography; Leo disliked them all. Gertrude also had become the subject of some of the art that surrounded them. While Leo painted Mike and various female models, she had been sculpted by Elie Nadelman (1907) and painted by Felix Vallotton (1906) and Picasso; in May 1913 Alvin Coburn photographed her.

Most important of all, Gertrude had become a sexual person, a lesbian and Alice's partner, not just Leo's younger sister. Alice wrote later of "the miserable time" Leo gave Gertrude, adding, "he made me suffer" as well. In turn, although Leo's romance with Nina seemed impermanent, its existence irritated Gertrude, who "was offended by such unconventional behavior on his part." She objected to the visibility of the liaison and was embarrassed when Leo accepted Florence Blood's offer of her Italian cottage, provided he not marry, only to live there with Nina long before they married. Although Nina recalled Gertrude's kindness to her when she first attended the Saturday salons, being a visitor was different from being a sister-in-law.

Power within the household had also shifted, and one friend noted that "Leo did not accept the position of an also-ran." Letters show that conflicts occurred over what pictures hung in Gertrude's room or who left lights burning or who opened whose door or who paid which bills. Alice later said that although Leo tried to be agreeable, he was often upset over trifles.

His irritation stemmed from financial worries as well as from his discomfort over his sister's lesbianism. Sure that he had been paying more than his share of expenses since Alice had moved in, Leo thought he could live more cheaply alone. Evidence that their joint account was now being divided includes Gertrude's purchase of cubist paintings Leo would not have approved, "a couple of new Picassos" in 1910 and 1912 and, the following year, Picasso's *The Man in Black,* the oil and wax collage also known as *Man with a Guitar.* (For this last work, she traded three other Picassos, *Young*

Acrobat on a Ball, Three Women, and *Nude with Drapery.*) In the autumn of 1913, as part of this exchange, Kahnweiler paid Gertrude 20,000 francs, with which she and Alice added a covered walkway to the atelier, replaced the iron stove with a fireplace, and installed electricity. Leo's only purchase during those same years was one Renoir.

The break between Leo and Gertrude surprised acquaintances, but correspondence suggests that it was years in the making. Art patrons were disappointed that part of the fallout of the separation was the sale of paintings; Sally Stein found it difficult to speak to either of them for a time and used the situation to distance herself from Leo. Gertrude and Leo also had periods of silence, when Alice served as their go-between.

As Toklas remembered the division of the art collection, Leo was given Matisse's *Blue Nude,* which had long hung over the sofa. He exchanged it "(with other pictures) for a Renoir. Leo's portrait was a gift from Picasso to Leo. At the division he (Leo) didn't want it (he was bitter even about that) so it remained . . . until Gertrude sold it to the Cones." To begin the process, Leo wrote Gertrude with his rationale for division, ironically allowing her "the Picasso oeuvre [which he thought of little value] as you left me the Renoir." Leo wanted Cézanne's *Still Life with Apples* and the Cézanne and Picasso drawings he owned. *Still Life with Apples,* one of Gertrude's favorite paintings, became a sore point. Leo kept it, saying glibly, "I'm afraid you'll have to look upon the loss of the apples as an act of God." So distressed was Gertrude about that loss that on Christmas 1914 Picasso brought her *Apple,* a watercolor. He had promised, "I will paint you one apple and it will be as fine as all of Cézanne's apples."

In October 1913 Leo wrote Lee Simonson that he was leaving for Settignano, where he would raise cabbages "and wait for cubism and futurism and the other inanities that grow from the confused brains of clever young persons, to die valid and natural deaths. . . . I expect . . . to survive them." He was tired, he said, of living with Gertrude's "unspeakable canvases." Hungry for privacy, he saw the large villa and its several gardens as ideal: "I don't know which I'm tiredest of—hearing others talk foolishness or hearing myself being wise. . . . I loves my fellow man but I hates to hear him talk." To Mabel Weeks he admitted: "The presence of Alice was a godsend, as it enabled . . . the fairly definite 'disaggregation' of Gertrude and myself to happen without any explosion. As we have come to maturity, we have come to find that there is practically nothing under the heavens that we don't either disagree about, or at least regard with different sympathies. The crucial thing of course is our work." He put it with his customary bluntness: "I can't abide her stuff and think it abominable." The situation was complicated, he said, because Gertrude "hungers and thirsts for gloire."

Undated notes in the Yale collection attest to angry interchanges. In one scrap of writing, Leo wrote that Gertrude could "tell Pablo that I regard my new Renoir as a little testimonial from what the art-conscious world would call the Spanish School of Painting. Voila Espana!" Such a comment suggests that the break was hardly amicable, but what is left unsaid and un-written provides a kind of palimpsest of the emotional dependency that had existed between the two for most of their lifetimes. Separating from Leo was to occupy much of Gertrude's next decade. Separating from Gertrude was to become a near-fixation for Leo for all of his remaining years.

Wars

Writing the Separation

In the process of establishing separate households, Gertrude voiced her discomfort—and her often-unspoken replies to Leo's lectures—in her writing. One of the reasons her brother objected to her work was that he correctly read its criticism of male power. Gertrude's themes were changing: she emphasized women's lives and language (one key phrase was "grand mutter grand mutter shell, real core," a comic insistence on creating a matriarchal heritage for speech). In *Many Many Women* she announced she would write about "how women are lived and what they are. Alice, Nellie, Marion, Bird, Hélène, Mabel Dodge, Emma, Harriet Levy, Germaine, Fernande, Marie Matisse, Olga." She later added the names of Mabel Weeks and the Keyser aunts to this list of lovers, friends, relatives, and cooks.

Women's voices make up the dialogue in Gertrude's fiction and plays. One of the early short plays is titled *Ladies' Voices*—"Ladies' voices give pleasure"—and another, *White Wines,* features interaction among five women characters. Her 1913 play *Thank You* recalls the comment of suffrage leader Sylvia Pankhurst who, when released from prison on condition that she return for trial, said "Thank you, I'll be there." Later, when she did not appear, she explained that by *there* she had not meant the trial. Gertrude knew women's history as well as women's lives.

In her love poem "Sacred Emily," she privileged women's place and language, saying that she would "Compose compose beds" about the theme of women's "tenderness." In this narrative, the narrator explains that after "Apples went"—the Cézanne painting—so, too, did "extra stress." Then the female persona is "able able able" to resume both her writing and the sexual fulfillment implied in "Rose is a rose is a rose is a rose. Loveliness extreme . . . Sweetest ice-cream." Other segments of the poem include such clitoral representations as pearls, buttons, and berries, building to the line, "Cow come out cow come out and out and smell a little." Gertrude's use of cows (and sometimes Caesars) as objects suggestive of orgasm was a staple of her coded writing during the next thirty years. Other examples of her sexual punning occur in "A Sweet Tail" (a description of the female body, subtitled "Gypsies," a reference to Alice) and *Tender Buttons.*

For all her attempts to write her life as female, however, Gertrude often wrote about Leo. He appears in "He Didn't Light the Light," subtitled (in Alice's handwriting) "This One Is Serious," a piece that includes the speaker's admission that "I am often angry. Sometimes I cry. . . . I love to be right." Leo's voice dominates "He Said It, A Monologue": "Spoken./ In English./ Always spoken./ Between them . . . I consider it very healthy to eat sugared figs not pressed figs." A draft of "Publishers, the Portrait Gallery and the Manuscripts in the British Museum" includes her arguments with Leo over leaving on the hall light, as well as her private declaration of independence: "So to measure every daughter and to lessen every sister . . . and to sever every brother . . . and to beam upon a lover so to sing and so to talk and so to change the line together." By cutting ties with Leo, Gertrude relinquished the dependent role of younger sister. Now, in the private world of their home, she and Alice sang and talked and created their own poetry. As she wrote in "France": "Laugh, to laugh . . . What a change from any yesterday."

Gertrude's writing began to reflect the steady tranquillity of her life with Alice. Some evenings they told stories and gossiped; on others, they read from the New York edition of Henry James's fiction, which they had purchased volume by volume between 1907 and 1910. (They did not read to each other; Gertrude could not "hear" words aloud.) Listening to phonograph recordings filled many hours. They regularly entertained Alice's friends from the States, as well as the bevy of Stein and Keyser relatives and friends that frequented Europe. Picasso, with his new love, Eva Groul, visited often to read the adventures of Little Jimmy and the Katzenjammer Kids from the Baltimore papers (many of Picasso's sketches of friends were designed as comic strips).

They continued to meet new people through their salons and through musical and dance events. At the second performance of Nijinsky's ballet of Stravinsky's *Rite of Spring,* they noticed a young American with a fashionable pleated shirtfront. Fascinated by the shirt, Gertrude wrote the portrait "One," unaware that the subject was the Carl Van Vechten who had touted her work during the Armory show. Theater critic for the *New York Press* and former music critic for the *New York Times,* Van Vechten hoped to visit Gertrude and Alice soon. As coincidence would have it, his estranged wife had been a dinner guest a few evenings before, but Gertrude and Alice preferred "Carlo" to the then–Mrs. Van Vechten, and friendship among the three flourished until their deaths. For Gertrude, Carlo was both friend and agent. Sympathetic with her pique at being so seldom in print, he urged Donald Evans to publish her work at Claire Marie, Evans's new press.

Gertrude's sending Evans the segments of prose and poetry that became *Tender Buttons,* a three-part prose poem, led to her final break with

Mabel Dodge, who had warned her not to publish with a press known for its "decadence." Evans brought out Gertrude's experimental work in an edition of one thousand copies, selling for a dollar, and thereby placed a new voice among America's avant-garde poets. While Ezra Pound championed the concrete and William Carlos Williams described the objects of his world, Gertrude drew her immediate reality through "portraits" of household items and foods. Hardly the subjects of either traditional or avant-garde literature, her domestic writings became known less for their unorthodoxy than for their unexpected linguistic difficulty.

Tender Buttons was divided into three sections, "Objects," "Food," and "Rooms." Judging from the manuscript versions of the materials, the assembly of the parts into one long prose poem was itself whimsical. In a letter to "my dear Miss Claire," Gertrude wrote in what sounded like the imperative case: "Tender Buttons, will be the title . . . and after it the three short titles, Food, Rooms, Objects." Perhaps the arrangement did not matter: when *Tender Buttons* appeared, with no context, it was often treated as a joke.

Gertrude tried to give Evans helpful information for marketing. In a biographical note accompanying her letter she wrote that as a student at Harvard, she "specialized in psychology, did research work on automatic action and fatigue and color sensation . . . published in psychological review. Knew William James very well. Then went to Johns Hopkins medical school to comp out psychological work. Did research work in Anatomy of Nervous system. Did not like study of medicine and pathology so did not take degree." She continued that, living in Paris, she had come to know Matisse and Picasso and that there existed a "particularly strong sympathy between Picasso and myself as to modern direction." The profile suggests that she assumed readers would relate her writing to both her study in psychology and her knowledge of the postimpressionist art world.

What baffled readers was the apparent meaninglessness of the text. The short descriptions of "Objects" such as "A Table" or "Shoes" are unrecognizable; word choice seems random. "Shoes" begins, "To be a wall with a damper a stream of pounding way and nearly enough choice makes a steady midnight. It is pus." The section "Objects" includes descriptions of "A Box," "A Seltzer Bottle," "A Red Hat," "A Piano," and other things, but it also includes such nonobjects as "More" and "A Time to Eat" and segments that question both the precision of language and the utility of naming ("A Piece of Coffee," "Peeled Pencil, Choke," and "Careless Water"). The reader discovers quickly that Gertrude's portraits are playful rather than realistic.

Her portraiture reappears in the "Foods" section (notebook evidence suggests that many of the "foods" were the first portraits written), where entries range from "Roastbeef" at nearly two thousand words to "Oranges," for which the portrait entire is "Build is all right." Some of the food passages are slyly referential, even sexual. Others tease the reader by including a predictable word or two, as in the entry for "Milk": "Climb up in sight climb in the whole utter needles and a guess a whole guess is hanging. Hanging hanging." The section "Rooms" is a single long text that describes peacefulness in a home after a difficult person has moved out; then "No song is sad. . . . There is quiet, there certainly is," and "nothing is hidden." Despite the section's title, Gertrude's focus throughout is on people rather than places: "Rooms" includes the lines "The sister was not a mister. Was this a surprise. It was" and "Replacing a casual acquaintance with an ordinary daughter does not make a son." The persona also discusses education and religion, sometimes in straightforward sentences such as "Why is there so much useless suffering. Why is there" and "Almost very likely there is no seduction." Without context, however, even such simple sentences become riddles.

Gertrude's focus on the parts of a viewer's world in its immediate, daily existence makes the reader's problem one of reading that life, and that persona, with only slight authorial help. Gertrude as author did not say that a woman's world was confined, domestic, and fragmented; instead, she showed both its confinement and its fragmentation. Published a decade before *The Waste Land*, T. S. Eliot's 1922 montage poem about the terrors of contemporary life, *Tender Buttons* suggested those terrors, as well as the impossibility of any reader's knowing another's intimate life.

The sexual flavor of the work, introduced by its title, came from her admiration for Apollinaire's sexualized double meanings (besides his graphic poems, he and Blaise Cendrars were writing pornographic novels during these years), as well as from themes in her earlier writings. Her "Americans," for instance, included this direction, "Press juice from a button, press it carelessly, press it with care, press it in a storm. . . . The point of it is that there is a strange strawberry in any strange ice cream." In "A Long Gay Book," she had meditated, "What is a bud. A bud is a sample. A bud is not that piece of room and more, a bud is ancient." Whether *button* was a code word for brussels sprouts or the clitoris, or suggested *bud* with its connotations of flowering, or referred literally to buttons, Gertrude's combining it with the adjective *tender* opened the noun to a number of associations. Patterns of words throughout the text continued its sexual innuendo. Even the commentary, which was apparently about Gertrude's break with Leo, assumed sexual dimensions.

Difficult and allusive as *Tender Buttons* is, or perhaps because of those qualities, the work became a key force in American modernity. Sherwood Anderson praised her virtuosity with language, describing the book's publication as "a good deal of fuss and fun." By introducing American readers to the surprising uses of words then current in French and German avantgarde circles, Gertrude became known as a literary cubist, like those European poets who tried to re-create the worlds of dream and the surreal using techniques from cinema, though most of their poems began with "an everyday event." In "The New Book, Book about the Artists," her playlike text about Matisse, Derain, Manguin, and Picasso, Gertrude used words nonreferentially, much as Kandinsky did in his prose-poems. (Rönnebeck had sent her these from Germany, calling her attention to words used as "pure interior sound.")

Tender Buttons was like much of Gertrude's other writing of this period, pieces such as "Miguel (Collusion). Guimpe. Candle," which she subtitled "a still life" and "Bee Time Vine," a study of sexuality. Her focus on the objects, food, and rooms of the implied subject—a living space, a house—connected Tender Buttons with the metaphor of the house that she had used earlier to connote sexual satisfaction. Several years later, in "A Very Good House," she wrote more explicitly about the connections among body, house, and church and about the role of nuns in the last, emphasizing that nuns were sisters, a common metaphor for lesbian love. Sexual punning underlies many of Gertrude's domestic and religious references, as in her later novel, Lucy Church Amiably.

Gertrude was not mistaken in letting Evans publish Tender Buttons. She may have erred in refusing him her plays, his first choice of her work, but she was in that decision influenced by Mildred Aldrich's knowledge of experimental theater in the States. Gertrude herself knew the Hapgoods, Maurice Sterne, Mary Foote, and Mabel Dodge, all founders of the Provincetown Players, and she and Mildred both were sure Stein's plays would become important to American drama. If the new theater was to be self-consciously theatrical, letting stage production replace meaningful language, as it did to a moderate extent in Synge's Playboy of the Western World and O'Neill's The Hairy Ape and The Emperor Jones—and as it had more radically in Europe in Alfred Jarry's Ubu Roi, Apollinaire's The Breasts of Tiresias, and Kandinsky's Yellow Sound—then Gertrude's plays were appropriately innovative. Through Henry McBride, she angled—unsuccessfully—for production of her plays at the San Francisco Fair in 1914. And Marsden Hartley later wrote to Stieglitz that when Gertrude's plays were produced in an "ultra-modern theatre in New York," he might be asked to design the curtain.

The plays were closest in some ways to Yellow Sound, which relied on colors and shapes presented onstage rather than on dialogue. In his 1912 essay "On Stage Composition," Kandinsky wrote that "drama consists here of the complex of inner experiences (spiritual vibrations) of the spectator," using color and music, defined as "bodily spiritual sound," for "their inner value." Words in such drama, although used sparingly, help create "a particular 'mood,' which makes the ground of the soul receptive. The sound of the human voice has also been used purely, i.e., without being obscured by . . . the sense of the words." Most of Gertrude's early plays simultaneously break existing stage conventions and insist that language help to form a new theatrical experience based on the viewer's reception of what is performed.

Tender Buttons and Stein's experimental prose in general received a good deal of attention. As a result of the number of reviews published during 1914 and 1915, columnist Don Marquis mentioned, or parodied, Stein half a dozen times each year in the *New York Sun*. In his 1913 *Sun* column, McBride had published excerpts from Gertrude's catalogue copy for Marsden Hartley's exhibit. In 1915, after Gertrude had supplied McBride with her portrait of Ambroise Vollard, he ran that sketch in his October 10 column; earlier, he had commented that the first issue of the little magazine *Rogue* had published Stein's "Aux Galeries Lafayette." H. L. Mencken also wrote two columns about her influence on American prose, and Alfred Kreymborg and Carl Van Vechten each wrote about her writing. Visibility was not the issue.

Living the Separation

A well-educated and spirited American who liked good food, drink, tobacco, and stories, Mildred combined stability with adventurousness. Gertrude and Alice's friendship with her substituted for their diminishing family ties. In a sense, Gertrude and Alice were orphans. After Alice left the States in 1907, she never saw her father again, although he lived until 1924; she dutifully wrote him each week, often going to the Closerie des Lilas to do so for privacy. It was only from a California cousin that she heard that her brother, Clarence, had moved to New York in 1910 but had later returned to California where, in 1916, he married well. Alice's close relationship with Mike Stein, and the correspondence they shared when traveling, may have replaced ties with her brother and father. For Gertrude, too, her close association with Mike replaced the slight contact she had had with Bertha and her family in Baltimore and with her brother Simon in San Francisco. When Gertrude's cousin Simon—who was her age—died suddenly in August 1913, she began several portraits of him, but they went unfinished. In her notebook, she described herself as "very nervous like Simon"; otherwise, until "A Bouquet, Their Wills.," she did not mention either cousin or brother.

In 1914 Mike and Sally summered in Agay on the French Riviera. They had vacationed there before and loved the inexpensive pension (full meals and room were 7 francs a day, less than $1.50). The family all swam ("The bathing is wonderful . . . the walks are superb"), and Mike and Allan cycled, rode horseback, played tennis, and learned to dive. Before they had left Paris, they had chosen not to sell a number of their Matisse paintings to Scandinavian collectors, instead loaning nineteen to the Gurlitt Gallery in Berlin for a retrospective Matisse show. The Steins were always generous with their art, though they tended to undervalue their collection.

Free from having to justify her tastes to Sally, Gertrude grew more and more enthusiastic about the cubist paintings of Juan Gris. In June she bought both *Glass and Bottle* and *Book and Glasses* from Kahnweiler; the next month she purchased a third painting, *Flowers*. She continued praising Picasso's and Gris's cubism, as well as Hartley's paintings and Rönnebeck's sculpture.

Otherwise, Mike, Sally, and Allan's absence didn't affect Gertrude and Alice much; they had gradually broken away from the family circle, largely because of Sally's obsession with Christian Science. Trained as she was in medicine, Gertrude could accept neither Sally's belief in Christian Science's healing power nor the secrecy that shrouded worship of Mary Baker Eddy's texts. David Edstrom recalled discussions at the rue de Fleurus salon marked by "great merriment and disparaging criticism" of Sally's belief; Leo referred to it as a common American phenomenon.

Leo's letters to Gertrude suggest he believed his move to Italy was healthful for them both. Early in 1914 he wrote cheerily about his isolated life in the Villa di Doccia in Settignano, where he had moved on April 3. He mentioned, however, that he was hurt that Berenson was telling people that Leo's "favorite authors were Weininger and Freud and from that one could judge what" he was; had he known how much Mary Berenson disliked him and his family, he would have considered the comment friendly.

Set on a gentle hill, Leo's villa was surrounded by tuberoses, lush azaleas, and black-eyed Susans as well as garden plots, and he had added a number of tomato plants, squash, and zucchini to the regular plantings. A scrawny black cat had joined his household as soon as he arrived, and now young replicas of their mother scattered across the sunbaked courtyard, sometimes playing with the laundry as it hung from the line. Leo spent hours reading at the back of the lawn, delighting in the shy two-inch lizards that scuttled in and out of the sun and the colorful birds that learned quickly to find the crumbs after his meals. When he left the villa for his daily walk, he could turn north and take a steep winding route, or he could go south through a number of villages and pick up supplies for the cook on his return. His day was entirely his own. He went to bed very early and rose with the hazy sun, thinking himself truly fortunate.

Nina was soon to join him. In the five years since their affair had begun, they had weathered her various liaisons with other men and his shades of disinterest. Part of the motivation for Leo's setting up housekeeping in Italy was her willingness to live with him there. Although he missed Paris, he was happy living with Nina and supporting her as she studied voice; except for letters to women friends, Leo's attention to Nina was exclusive. Their lengthy correspondence shows that, although it took Leo years to speak of marriage, he knew that he needed Nina. In 1914 he wrote, "You are for me a kind of reality, more real than myself, full of a richer life and grander human value." During this long period of courtship, Leo spoke of his feelings of "fatherliness" toward Nina; both sensual and motherly, she accepted this unconventional relationship that allowed him to vacillate about his love as his emotional needs changed. In 1914 the forty-two-year-old Leo was still sampling romance.

Writing to Mabel Weeks, he described the relationship as one of "absolute confidence, perfect candor, complete toleration and unlimited goodwill"; unfortunately, he often reminded Nina that she was his intellectual inferior: "I cherish you enormously as a person who is close to me in a poignant way, but intellectually speaking, in a simple way. I do not mean that I consider you stupid. Quite the contrary; but your mental processes . . . are not subtle or complicated." Maurice Sterne recalled friends' asking "how anyone of Leo's intellectual powers and breeding" could be involved with "a person like Nina." Sterne replied that, after one knew her, there was no mystery: "Although Nina seemed completely immoral from a conventional point of view, she had a strict sense of morality of her own. Love was sacred to her. . . . To understand what Leo was, and what he was not, one had only to see Nina. She was the living being of the abstraction he longed for." Sterne knew that Leo created fantasy worlds based on his idealization of female beauty.

Nina's love also reassured Leo of his own value after he realized that Alice and Gertrude—and, later, Sally and Mike—were happier without him. But unfortunately for Nina, Leo's model for marriage was his father's domination of a wife who seldom contradicted him. One of the reasons Leo avoided commitment for so long may have been his worry over copying Daniel Stein in any way; once involved with Nina, however, Leo found that he wanted a classic male-dominated marriage.

In contrast, Gertrude had found a balance of power in her relationship with Alice, a union based on mutuality and sharing. In the women's liaison, both partners worked toward what Milan Kundera was later to call "co-feeling," a sharing of similar states. Neither demanded power from the other; each led in some part of the marriage. There was frequent discussion and argument, stemming from both partners' "ability to share feelings and intentions without demanding control." For Gertrude and Alice, there was no need for any division between "powerful and helpless, active or passive."

Gertrude and Alice in War

Planning another visit to England, Gertrude and Alice were not deterred by the assassinations of the Archduke Francis Ferdinand and his wife in Sarajevo in July 1914. So sure was Gertrude that there would never be war that she argued with her British friends, telling them that they were needlessly concerned. The idea of war—unreasonable and wasteful and violent—was incomprehensible to her. When she thought of conflict, it was the Civil War she imagined, and a pastel version of it at that. She remembered her mother's stories of Baltimore citizens shooting at Yankee soldiers, a memory as remote as most other family tales. Like many citizens of the world in 1914, smug about technological achievements that supposedly ensured human progress, Gertrude had no way to envision the kind of bloodshed World War I would entail: ten million people dead and twenty-two million wounded in the barbed-wire-and-machine-gun nightmare—not to mention the use of exploding bullets, liquid fire, and poison gas.

Staying in England until late in July, because John Lane promised Gertrude a contract for the publication of *Three Lives* when he returned from vacation, she and Alice lived a pleasant literary life. On July 31 Gertrude signed the contract, and then the two women boarded a train for Wiltshire, where they spent a weekend at Lockeridge with the Alfred North Whiteheads and their daughter, Jessie. Having long been intrigued with Whitehead's concept that all life—event, time, character—is interactive, Gertrude longed to talk for hours with her host. She got her wish: Alice and she spent the next eleven weeks with the Whiteheads. On August 4 England declared war on Germany, and the Great War had begun.

Even if they had wanted to, the women could not have returned to France. All assets in French banks were frozen, and the two lived for a time on Alice's letter of credit on a U.S. bank. Finally, through Evelyn Whitehead's influence with Lord Kitchener and their own aggressive petitioning for temporary passports at the American Embassy in London, Gertrude and Alice returned to Paris. In the nearly three months since they had left, they had been kept informed through letters from Mildred Aldrich, whose farmhouse in Huiry, thirty miles from Paris, was in the path of the German offensive.

Having retired to the modest old house in June, Mildred had regaled them with letters about the "perfect peace" of her country life. In August, however, she began writing grimly about the invasion of France: "Since the 4th of August all our crossroads have been guarded, all our railway gates closed, and also guarded—guarded by men whose only sign of being soldiers is a cap and a gun . . . with stern faces and determined eyes." By September 5 there was a picket at her gate, the post office was gone, villages to the north had been evacuated, the English had cut telegraph wires, and bridges across the Marne were being destroyed as she moved her possessions into an underground passage near the stable. Then began Mildred's days of serving tea to French and British officers on her front lawn. Dressed in white, with ribbons in her hair, she tried to provide comfort for the haggard men, while the battle of the Marne—one of the bloodiest actions of the war, engaging several million men from September 6 to 12—took place in full view. During one day of fighting, enemy troops were quartered on her grounds; after another day, she could see the bodies of four thousand dead Germans.

Visiting Mildred was Gertrude and Alice's first priority. Then they returned home. Eva Groul, writing that she and Picasso would return to the city in November, said that she was glad Alice and Gertrude were "happy in Paris" once more. They lived quietly, spending much of their time worrying about friends. German citizens Daniel-Henry Kahnweiler and William Uhde took refuge in neutral countries to escape internment, while their possessions in France were confiscated as enemy property. Duchamp and Picabia had gone to New York. Derain, Braque, and Léger had been drafted and were fighting at the front; Apollinaire applied for French citizenship and joined the artillery; Matisse, at forty-five, tried to enlist but was rejected. Juan Gris, left penniless when Kahnweiler moved to Switzerland, was desperate, and in late October Gertrude sent him two hundred francs.

For Max Jacob, Blaise Cendrars, Pierre Reverdy, Erik Satie, Darius Milhaud, Arthur Honegger, Francis Poulenc, and—before his tour of duty began—Apollinaire, the Salle Huyghens at the Louvre offered a place for readings and concerts throughout the war years. Being in Paris, however, offered
no respite from the omnipresence of war—rumors about attacks were
frightening, shortages were rampant, and officers, nurses, and wounded men
filled the cafés where Gertrude and Alice had once enjoyed leisurely meals.
Alice accepted that she had to stand in the long queues to buy food, but
both women found themselves bewildered and frightened by the changes
that had occurred during their absence. Both were nervous—more nervous
than they admitted—about the possibility of attack. One night after Alice
had gone to bed, when Gertrude was downstairs writing, an alarm sounded.
Gertrude called to Alice that she should put on something warm and come
down; once there, Alice realized her knees were knocking, an event she
thought occurred only in fiction.

The one bright spot in wartime Paris was Mildred Aldrich's successful
book *A Hilltop on the Marne*. Having written to friends, including Gertrude
and Alice, about the battle, she composed a narrative from her letters. Eager
for eyewitness accounts, the public first read excerpts from Aldrich's work
in the *Atlantic Monthly* and then bought out seventeen printings of the
book. Unfortunately, the soothing account of the Boston lady serving officers
tea on the lawn masked the horror of the mutilated, decomposing bodies
strewn across nearby fields. Mildred's prose at times disguised war's brutality: when she described the "long lines of grain-sacks," which, when set on
fire, "stood like a procession of huge torches across my beloved panorama,"
her readers would not necessarily know that the piles being burned were
not grain sacks but rather heaps of the German dead. Mildred's having lived
through the massacre, and profited from it, sent the wrong message to
Gertrude, who sometimes viewed war as adventure rather than devastation.

Mildred was not the only woman who found opportunity in the Great
War. Edith Wharton was involved in establishing both nursing facilities and
orphanages (Gertrude read Wharton's *Fighting France: From Dunkerque to
Belfast* when it was serialized in *Scribner's* magazine). Florence Blood and
Princess Ghyka turned the latter's villa into a hospital, which they ran, and
countless English women acquaintances—Vernon Lee, Radclyffe Hall, May
Sinclair, Mary Rinehart, Sarah MacNaughton, and others—drove ambu-
lances or nursed and wrote about their experiences. In Paris, the novelist
Colette covered the war for the newspapers.

Matisse, lonely living outside Paris, frequently came to the city and
would "go to a late afternoon sketch class to draw from a model for an hour"
and then come to the rue de Fleurus to "have supper with us and return to
Clamart early in the evening." His wife sometimes accompanied him. Alice
and Gertrude admired Amélie Matisse's "unconscious, almost tragic" beauty
and style, and Alice recounted their interest in her pinning on her hat:

"When she would rise to go putting with precision two long coral tipped hatpins into either side of her hat there was something majestic in the gesture. Gertrude Stein once said, 'You are certain of what you are doing but to us it does look as if those pins traversed your brain.' This pleased Matisse and he made an India drawing of his wife placing her hatpins and gave it to Gertrude Stein." Both the Matisses shared with Alice an interest in, and an appreciation for, stylish hats.

When Picasso returned to Paris, Gertrude felt that life resumed some normalcy. Walking down the Boulevard Raspail with her and seeing a convoy of heavy guns painted with zigzag patterns, he exclaimed, "We invented that." Picasso took credit for the idea of camouflage, but he had no interest in fighting and resumed his extensive production of paintings as if it were peacetime.

Once it became clear that the war was not going to be over by Christmas, as so many Europeans had thought, artists who had been handled by Kahnweiler, now in exile, looked for new ways of selling their work. Many turned to Léonce Rosenberg, but making sales in wartime was difficult. Picasso and Matisse were well provided for, but rather than see Juan Gris live in poverty, Gertrude (with the American collector Michael Brenner) offered to send him a small monthly allowance, in exchange for which he would give them paintings. The arrangement led only to arguments, and even though Gris and his wife, Josette, had returned to Paris in November, Gertrude and Alice did not see them. The argument contributed to the malaise the women felt living in wartime Paris. The conditions of their friends, the growing inflation, the disruption of public transportation, fuel and food shortages, and the fear of invasion were all worrisome, and by February 1915 Alice and Gertrude had decided to go to Spain. As they were packing, Paris shook under its first zeppelin raid.

Leo in the States

When war was declared, Leo was living in Settignano, seemingly content. Besides the fact that he and Nina could get no money out of French accounts, they were little inconvenienced by the war. Leo's letters in late August sounded calm, but he worried about Gertrude's and Mike's whereabouts. Several months later, he wrote that Nina's two brothers had been wounded, the younger badly. Her third brother, an aviator, had been killed before the war began. Hearing rumors that Delaunay had deserted and that Picabia and Braque were at the front, Leo asked Gertrude what she knew of their friends and what life in Paris was like. He assumed that Italy was about to enter the war.

In January 1915, worried about her brothers and feeling isolated in Settignano, Nina returned to Paris to continue voice lessons. In April, still in Italy, Leo received a joint letter from Miriam Price and Maurice Sterne telling him of their bet that he would be returning to the States after his dozen years abroad. On an apparent whim, Leo booked passage and then wrote Nina from Genoa as he waited to board the *Dricia d'Aorta* on April 27. Although Leo had always told Nina that if she were to leave him, he would probably "go to America to take refuge among friends, so as not to be frozen in such an isolation," his sailing was unexpected: after all, Nina had not really left him. This disruption of the domestic life Leo had charted for them gave Nina pause, and his erratic letters from America did not assuage her fears. While she lived in Paris, enduring food shortages and zeppelin attacks, Leo visited friends and started psychoanalysis anew in the States.

A bleak September 5, 1915, letter spoke of his thoughts of suicide after what he considered failure in this analysis. Of their love he wrote, "My dear Nina, I wish that it were possible to take up again the project of times gone by, but chance has made us miss the moment . . . only a completely new arrangement can give us a future together." Just two weeks later, however, now radiant about that same analysis, Leo was eager to marry her: "I love you darling, honestly, greatly, deeply, you are for me a major part of my life, body and soul—something real."

Leo's unpredictable behavior was not the only troubling aspect of Nina's life. When she had returned to Paris in 1915, she had tried to contact Gertrude, but Gertrude either chose not to reply or had already left for Spain. Leo had written to her sister, giving her Nina's Paris address and asking her to get in touch "if you'd like to see her and hear the news from down here." Again, Gertrude's response was silence. Now that Leo had returned to the States, and the British *Lusitania* had been sunk by German submarines, killing more than a hundred Americans among its thousand passengers, Nina recognized she had only a slim chance of leaving Europe. As Mike wrote on March 23, 1915, "the traveling to America seems to be getting worse instead of better."

Leo found life in the States "thoroughly agreeable." During the early months of his visit, he stayed in Boston, New York, Washington, Cape Cod, Philadelphia, and Baltimore, socializing with old friends and family. Bertha Raffel's daughter, Gertrude, remembered that her uncle Leo encouraged her to continue painting. In New York, besides such family members as cousins Fred Stein and Bird Stein Gans, whose husband, Howard, was a favorite of Leo's, he was intimate with several artistic and literary circles: Alfred Stieglitz's "291" gallery; Mabel Dodge's Fifth Avenue group, which included a range of visitors from Edwin Arlington Robinson and Bill Haywood to Lincoln Steffens and Margaret Sanger; and the Stettheimer circle of Florine, Ettie, Stella, and Carrie at Alwyn Court, a group that included Carl Van Vechten and Fania Marinoff, Avery Hopwood, Dr. Arnold Genthe, Elizabeth Duncan, Edward Steichen, Marcel Duchamp, Henry McBride, Pavel Tchelitchew, Francis Picabia, the young Willard Huntington Wright (brother of Stanton Macdonald-Wright, Leo's disciple in Paris), and dancer Adolph Bolm.

Stieglitz's "291" became a consistent focus for Leo; a number of his friends and acquaintances exhibited there (Walter Arensberg and Arthur

Davies, besides Sheeler, Hartley, and Nadelman), and Stieglitz respected Leo's convictions even if he and Leo did not often agree. Many of the "291" admirers were also involved with Katherine Dreier and Marius de Zayas's Modern Gallery, founded in 1915, and with either *The New Republic* (with Walter Lippmann and Lewis Mumford as editors) or the pacifist *Seven Arts* (which included Kenneth MacGowan, Floyd Dell, Louis Untermeyer, Robert Frost, Waldo Frank, Randolph Bourne, Paul Rosenfeld, Sherwood Anderson, and Van Wyck Brooks, people more influenced by mystical than political rationales). Attracted by *Seven Arts* and its focus on American art, Leo was also interested in *The New Republic,* because of his fascination with theories of history. When friends suggested that he write about art, Leo began a series on contemporary painters for *The New Republic;* he also wrote for *Seven Arts.*

The Stettheimer crowd usually met in Florine's exotic studio, hung with cellophane curtains and decorated with her paintings. Leo appeared in several of these, and her 1915 *Studio Party,* or *Soirée,* correctly placed him at the group's heart, resting comfortably—earphone in hand—surrounded by Ettie Stettheimer, Maurice Sterne, Gaston and Isabelle Lachaise, Albert Gleizes and his wife, Avery Hopwood, Florine Stettheimer, and a Hindu poet. The large female nude in the background of the painting suggests that the occasion was one of Florine's unveilings, the work representative of the controversial new art that the group admired. To them, Leo was the man who had discovered Matisse and Picasso, both of whose shows had recently hung at Stieglitz's gallery.

To Mabel Dodge, Leo was an old friend from Paris, and she was happy to have him near her: "Leo meant a great deal more to me in America than he had in Europe. More and more nowadays I needed people of solid worth, people with ideas and character instead of those who were 'intriguing.' Oddities of nature had ceased to appeal; reality drew closer. Leo had a genius for thinking." She gave him a standing invitation to live with her at both Provincetown (where he sometimes stayed with the Hapgoods) and at her new acquisition, Finney Farm. There, what Mabel called her "cooperative commonwealth" was comprised of stage designer Bobby Jones, poet Bayard Boyeson, painters Hartley, Dasburg, and O'Keeffe, and writers Willa Cather, Mary Austin, and Jean Toomer. Recently finished with an affair with John Reed, the American writer whose coverage of the Russian revolution would bring him fame, Mabel was currently involved with Leo's old friend the artist Maurice Sterne.

She had become relatively famous herself, after a May 1915 *Vanity Fair* article suggested she was the archetype of the independent, modern woman. Like many New Yorkers, Mabel was interested in hypnosis, psychoanalysis, suggestion, and mental healing. Fascinated with the "talking cure" she was taking with Smith Ely Jelliffe, a New York psychoanalyst, Mabel also knew A. A. Brill, the Austrian analyst who translated Freud's works into English. Soon Leo was working with both analysts. As he wrote Gertrude about New York society, "Everybody is occupied more or less with psycho-analysis and the war and reform and other more or less exciting things."

Leo's analysis—some of which he developed himself after reading all the Freud that had been translated into English—depended on picturing himself as the frustrated child of an uncaring mother and a domineering—if not castrating—father. (Gertrude, by contrast, had found it difficult to rec-ognize herself and her family in Freudian schemata.) By this time, Leo had decided that he suffered from "three major complexes: an inferiority com-plex, a castration complex and a pariah complex." In one of his rare lighter moments, he wondered aloud where the people who had been successful in analysis were: "They must keep them in safe deposit vaults."

It was Brill who convinced Leo that he should be a writer. Seeing that he could not otherwise please his father-figure analyst, Leo finally wrote. His first essay, titled simply "Cézanne," appeared in *The New Republic* on January 22, 1916. Tracing Monet's and Pissarro's influence on Cézanne's work, Leo stressed the younger painter's innovative use of light. While prais-ing Cézanne, Leo also argued that his personality was defective—calling Cézanne phobic, suspicious, paranoid—and quoted Freud's theory that aes-thetic pleasure "is the product of frustrated action." In the next issue, Leo reviewed his friend Willard Huntington Wright's book *Modern Painting*. At-tacking it on the grounds that too much theory obscures an artist's inten-tion, Leo repeated some of what he had said in "Cézanne." Although he praised Wright's discussions of more recent painters, Wright read the review as negative and distanced himself from Stein because of it.

Rather than bringing Leo pleasure, his appearances in print generated controversy. He had not only alienated Wright, but the February 19 issue of *The New Republic* published a letter of protest from Albert Barnes, the wealthy chemist who had patented the antiseptic Argyrol. Barnes had begun collecting art; he had, in fact, just bought one of the Cézanne *Group of Bathers* from Leo for five thousand dollars (as in 1913 he had bought Cézanne's *Spring-House* and a Matisse still life and in 1914 a Renoir from him). Taking offense at Stein's linking of pleasure with frustration, Barnes wrote that Leo didn't understand Freud. When Leo defended his theory in the following issue, he cited work by Hugo Münsterberg and Vernon Lee; Barnes's second letter, published on March 18, used Münsterberg and Lee to refute Leo. The exchange hardly merited Mike's description of it to Ger-trude as an "old fashioned epistolary vituperative quarrel" that "began in a controversy they had in print in the New Republic about aesthetics," but Leo found it difficult to take any criticism from Barnes.

When he had first appeared on the Paris art scene in 1912, fresh from Pennsylvania, Barnes had been the stereotypical know-nothing collector, waving his checkbook and eager to buy anything off the Stein walls. When he offered Mike five thousand dollars for a Matisse, Mike refused him. Leo, however, rather than finding Barnes offensive, tried to educate him and since coming to the States had visited Barnes's collection in Merion, Pennsylvania, several times. Because Leo talked at such length, however, Barnes (who compared him to a vaudeville monologist) finally told him he was not welcome. To have his first essays denounced by a man who knew less than he about art defeated Leo. If psychological health depended on work, and if he defined his work as writing, this foray into public argument was discouraging.

It is likely that Leo's analyst also urged him to become sexually active again. In December 1915 Leo wrote Nina that his analysis, while temporarily successful, was creating anxiety because it awakened him to his need for love; therefore, he said, "I want you to come here. I see no other way to recover from my problem. I have fallen back into a state almost worse than before, and only love can bring me out of it. . . . You must come here, as soon as possible. I want you to take the first boat." Unfortunately, French citizens could no longer obtain passage to America, and the next weeks were taken up with cables and letters about that difficulty: for example, "I have just received a cable in which you say Desperate To Get Papers. That is not exactly English or French and I do not understand"; "I have just received your wire reading Impossible Get Papers." By January 22, 1916, Leo understood: "I am astonished to learn that it is difficult to leave France."

Because Leo's father had been German, he could not return to Europe, so he resigned himself to the separation. (Ironically, he now had the money to bring Nina over.) He turned instead to more casual sexual involvements and to helping to plan and publish *Seven Arts*. Its February 1917 issue included "Meanings," his brief essay equating art with primal needs and saying that art completed human experience, rather than copying it. Continuing some of the ideas from his *New Republic* essays, of which he had published four more during the year, Stein warned against too simple a view of art. He urged readers to avoid the current enthusiasm for "exotic literatures, new points of view, new plastic modes" and instead to give themselves "a sounder education" so that they could respond to the new with "deeper integrity."

In May 1917 Leo published "American Optimism," the longest essay in any of the issues of *Seven Arts*. (The fact that both his essays were reprinted in *The Seven Arts Reader* suggests Stein's prominence within the group.) Here, he warned readers against characteristic American cheerfulness and optimism, which differed sharply from the tragic temper of most nations. That same month, in *The New Republic*, he published "Art and Common Sense," the most personal of his essays. In it, he attacked Picasso (and, by association, Gertrude) for a willingness to create work that was merely new: "There is too much originality that is not original."

During the next two years, Leo published essays on William Chase, Arthur B. Davies, Albert Ryder, Degas, Rembrandt, Renoir, and Rubens, creating a series of articles for *The New Republic*. Flattered by friends' responses to his essays, Leo wrote Nina, "Everything I do has quite a success."

He lamented that he wrote slowly, however, and began to think that teaching might provide some additional income. To see how much of a handicap his limited hearing would be, he spoke at Bird Gans's child study group and Georgiana King's art history course at Bryn Mawr. As he later wrote Mike, his deafness made interaction difficult. On May 5, 1916, he told Nina that he had "a kind of machine with which I hear better, which permits me to attend the theatre," but even with such help, Leo was handicapped. Jo Davidson recalled that when he ran into Leo walking on Fifth Avenue, Stein wore "a conspicuous hearing aid. He greeted me effusively: 'Remember when I used to talk and talk and never would listen. Now I want to hear and can't.'"

In the summer of 1916, after months of digestive disturbances and two operations for "fistula," Leo went to a "Western sanatarium [sic]" to recover. Only as far west as Battle Creek, Michigan, the sanitorium was a health spa operated by the Kelloggs that featured bathing, exercise, and a diet based on healthful dry cereals. After his July in Michigan, Leo spent a few days in Massachusetts at another Kellogg spa. Physical health was thought to be an index of mental health: Dr. Jelliffe pioneered in correlating physical problems with psychological ones. Trying to rid himself of his chronic digestive problems, Leo also wanted to be well so that he could continue psychoanalysis.

When Leo reached Cape Cod late in the summer, everyone was occupied with the first official season of the Provincetown Players—if they couldn't act, people built scenery or wrote publicity. Eugene O'Neill's *Bound East for Cardiff* had been presented at the Wharf Theater, an abandoned fish house on a pier owned by novelist Mary Heaton Vorse, as had *Suppressed Desires* by Susan Glaspell and her husband George Cram Cook and other experimental plays with Freudian titles. Mabel Dodge recalled that Leo, only moderately interested in theater, continued talking about "Art, and about Psychoanalysis, in which he was losing (or finding) himself. . . . He was at present analyzing himself and the strange validity of his relationship with Nina, whom he had left behind in Paris." Provincetown's ambience—"those amazing dunes—shifting with the wind before one's eyes" and the "great rumbling, dramatic" ocean—encouraged introspection.

Despite his sale of the Cézanne to Barnes in December 1915, part of Leo's physical distress was economic. He saw that selling paintings was the only way to live comfortably so long as he stayed in the States while simultaneously maintaining a household in Italy and supporting Nina in Paris. In 1913, when he used the fifteen thousand dollars Barnes had paid him then for Cézanne's *Spring-House* to repay a loan he had taken out to purchase Renoirs, he commented optimistically that the sale of some pictures he had at the Bernheim-Jeune gallery would take care of the rest of his debt. But in both 1914 and 1915 he sold more art. In 1916 he wrote Nina that he did not see how he could fund her indefinitely: "Money is worth relatively half what it was, and for three years I have been spending estate. I have been quite unable to live on my income." Again he summarized that his total income was "about 1,000 francs a month [$171]." He gave Nina 600 francs each month, paid his rent in Italy of 125 francs, and had other set expenses. Living in the States was more expensive than in Europe, and analysis two or three times a week added to his costs. Even so, although at one point he planned to return to Italy in the fall of 1916, he stayed in America, regardless of the expense. His choice did not satisfy him, however: "Most of the time I rather have the sensation of wanting to die, or at least not to live, for it is neither pleasurable nor productive. It might change, but as time goes by I feel less strength to fight."

Leo's view of the war, when he mentioned it, was that it was an inconvenience—keeping Nina from coming to the States, preventing his return to Italy, causing inflation. He seldom mentioned it in his correspondence while in the States; to Mabel Dodge, he wrote that he remained loyal to Finney Farm but that he was "not nationally or locally patriotic." Perhaps his tendency to ignore everything that did not immediately affect him was part of what Sterne called his "split personality: cold, annihilating, analytic toward others and blind as a bat about himself. Eventually he realized that he was unhappy and began his interminable self-analysis. For about 35 years, every time we met or wrote he would proudly announce, 'I have practically finished my analysis.'"

Leo's opinion of his work was, of course, positive. He wrote Nina in 1916, "I continue my analysis always and profit much from it. . . . I do not wish to give it up until having plumbed as deeply as possible into my being." In his later *ABC of Aesthetics,* he answered Sterne's criticism: "If I cannot reach a genuine goal, I would rather remain forever on the way."

World War I and the Steins

Gertrude and Alice in Majorca and Paris

Running from the German zeppelin attacks frightened both Alice and Gertrude. In times of confusion, Alice had noticed, Gertrude lost her resiliency; but once in Majorca, settled in a large furnished house on a hillside at 45 calle de Dos Mayo, she regained confidence. Surrounded with almond, fig, and pomegranate trees, the women walked among the brilliant carnations and tuberoses that bordered their terrace. Two hundred sixty flat stone steps down from the terrace was the sea, and they delighted in walking slowly downhill, taking in the deep blue panorama of sea, hill, and sky as far as they could look. Some days, the scene was hazy and indefinite; at other times, it was edged with a sharp clarity. It was always arresting—and, as Gertrude pointed out, walking up and down the steps was good for them.

Warmed by the Majorcan sun, they decided to stay and sent for Jeanne Poule, their Breton cook, to join them. Alice planned meals around chicken, fish, game, "sardines as big as cartwheels," cakes called angels' tresses, and melons. From Jeanne, Alice learned about village shopping; she recalled one frightening day when Jeanne—insisting that the proper way to kill pigeons was to smother them—demonstrated her system in the marketplace, only to find herself and Alice surrounded by "screaming and gesticulating" women. For her own pleasure, and that of the appreciative Gertrude, Alice spent hours arranging the lush island flowers.

Gertrude established a comfortable pace, sleeping till nine or ten, making friends with Europeans and with the American painter William Cook and his French wife, Jeanne, and buying a deerhound, which she and Alice named Polybe. Untrained, the dog was given to running away, chasing sheep, and, on moonlit nights, dancing with wild dogs on the hillside. After they got rid of their pet, Gertrude and Alice enjoyed living in Majorca, and judging from Gertrude's extensive—and humorous—writing, the year was profitable. (She wrote to Carlo that she was working on "quite a number of funny things.") Like their first trip to Spain, this stay, too, became a sort of honeymoon.

Mabel Dodge and Mary Berenson, who disapproved of Gertrude's liaison with Alice, saw this year of isolation in Majorca as the end of Gertrude's independence: she learned to rely on Alice for everything. Leo had earlier used the analogy of a vine's strangling a tree to describe the way Alice's constant waiting on Gertrude eventually made her the stronger of the two. But, in fact, there was nothing sinister in the relationship: each woman was becoming comfortable with her role in the marriage. Alice got up early, did the housekeeping and marketing, made out book orders for Mudie's in London, and spent hours knitting socks and sweaters for French soldiers, keeping herself busy so that Gertrude had time and privacy to write. Together, they worried about German attacks, fearing that their boat from the mainland had been tracked by submarines. They also walked, read, went on picnics, gathered wildflowers, shopped, made love, listened to music, smoked (and complained about Spanish tobacco), and tried to stay cool. Much as she liked Spain, Alice hated the stifling heat and the omnipresent mosquitoes; she was often in tears on Sundays when, by national policy, there was no electricity to run their fan.

Gertrude's long prose poem "All Sunday" uses Alice's frustration as its tonal base. Filled with mentions of the war ("The war will not be over"), it echoes such other of her pieces as "We Are Nervous Because We Did Not Xpect That There Ever Would Be This War" and "We Have Eaten Heartily and We Were Ashamed, (The War)." "All Sunday" refers to physical discomfort lightened by sexual pleasure and becomes an amalgam of the women's experiences, ranging from smoking cigarettes and being displeased with Mike to refusing to use the German word *Fatherland* and noting—about Leo—that "My brother went to America." Part 5 is written in Alice's voice: "I am going to tell all my feeling. I love and obey. I am very sensible. I am sensitive to distraction. I like . . . to have mosquito netting over my bed. I can estimate the reluctance with which I am hurried. I can understand polish. I like to do my nails. How do I do them. How do you do." The melding of meaning here—from *Polish* as language to the (unnamed) *polish* on Alice's lovingly cared-for nails, for example, and from *how do I do* (with its echoes of "how do I count the ways") to the polite greeting—characterizes more obscure passages in the poem as well.

Gertrude was also writing "Lifting Belly," the fifty-page comic dialogue between lesbian lovers that remained unpublished for the next forty years; the fact that the poem remained in Alice's handwriting rather than being typed showed that both women knew it was unprintable. Part of Gertrude's outspokenness in this Majorcan writing came from her recognition that finding a publisher remained impossible. As she replied to Van Vechten's comment that in the States she was as famous as the Swedish singer Jenny Lind, "Alas about every three months I get sad. I make so much absorbing literature with such attractive titles and even if I could be as popular as Jenny Lind where oh where is the man to publish me in series. . . . I would so like to be done. Alas." Mired in Georgian poetics, excited by the mild imagist manifesto, the American literary avant-garde would have been unable to recognize either the sexual subtext or the formal brilliance of Gertrude's poems.

For the next year, Gertrude and Alice lived a quiet island life, going to Barcelona only occasionally to shop and visit a dentist. With William Cook they went to both Valencia and Inca to see peasant dancing and the bull-fights, where they cheered for Gallo, Gallito, and Belmonte. Stein published prose in Robert Coady's short-lived *The Soil: A Magazine of Art,* dedicated to American writing. In January Picasso wrote Gertrude that his beloved Eva was dead and that he missed having "a friend like you" to talk with. The next month Henry James died in England; Gertrude and Alice lamented their never having met him. War news was remote, and what there was favored Germany. The two women had skirmishes with the German governess next door who hung out her flag whenever her country won a battle. Announcing that she would never again speak to a German, Alice tore up Arnold Rönnebeck's gift of aerial photographs of German cities, which he had sent to them after his return to Berlin. She was sure he was a spy.

From Agay, Mike wrote that he and Sally had planned to return to Paris but had instead sent for Allan's schoolbooks and stayed on at the Grand Hotel. Nearly alone there (the proprietor's son was at the front and her husband in training), they enjoyed good meals, mandarin oranges, and calm. Because she worried about money, and because she and Alice had decided to return to Paris, Gertrude agreed to sell Mike and Sally Matisse's *Woman with the Hat.* On February 12 Mike sent her the first check for two thousand dollars and three weeks later paid the remaining two thousand.

Inez Haynes Irwin, Gertrude's Radcliffe classmate who visited Paris early in 1916 with her husband, Will, recorded in her diary France's desperate sadness after Verdun: the "stricken anguished land" was "in tears," she said, with "three fourths of the women in mourning." She wrote that the wounded men were kept outside Paris, because seeing "human gargoyles, faces screwed out of all normality; faces molded to forms subtly monstrous; faces with wounds that made great purple and wealed caverns in their contours" would have demoralized everyone. Impressed with the strength of the French women who had taken over the physical labor of the city, Irwin wrote that she was delighted to see women "invade the professions, the crafts and the trades," able even to "grapple with machinery."

On June 20, 1916, after a stop in Madrid, Gertrude and Alice reached their home. Borrowed history books, complete with maps, had made inspecting officers think they were spies; only Alice's fast talking won them the freedom to take the train to Paris. There, they found much about the French reaction to war admirable, and they readied themselves for such hardships as cold rooms and inadequate food. Actually experiencing shortages was difficult, however. By midwinter, in desperation, Gertrude asked a corner policeman for coal; luckily, the man, sans uniform, soon appeared regularly at their door, and they did not want for heat the rest of the winter.

Alice and Gertrude sometimes dined with Mary Borden Turner, a wealthy Chicagoan who operated a hospital near the front (an admirer of Gertrude's writing, she also had a pleasantly warm home). They also enjoyed the company of Emily Chadbourne and Ellen LaMotte, and they visited with Picasso and his new loves, as well as his new friends the Princesse de Polignac (the former Winnaretta Singer, known for her sewing-machine fortune and her lesbian exploits) and Erik Satie, who had composed the score for the Diaghilev ballet *Parade,* for which Picasso was designing extravagant costumes and sets—including such ten-feet-tall figures as the "American Manager" in cowboy boots. Picasso had also grown close to writers Blaise Cendrars (who had lost an arm after the Champagne offensive) and Jean Cocteau, a brilliant young playwright whom Gertrude particularly liked. Alice and she also made peace with Juan Gris and took frequent trips to the rue Ravignan. But war and its effects darkened Paris: Braque and Apollinaire were convalescing from head wounds, and friends worried about them. Everyone missed the zany antics of Max Jacob, who had converted to Catholicism in 1909 and was now seriously devout.

There was some comfort for Gertrude and Alice in Paris because, like many of the French, they had become admirers of Philippe Pétain. When he was given command of the Second Army in 1915, few people knew much about him; later, when he took charge of the battle of Verdun, Pétain become a hero. His insistence on the use of increased firepower and artillery cover saved lives (although seventy thousand were lost even so). The city seemed safer under his leadership.

They had been in Paris only a month when Alice saw a uniformed young woman backing a Ford along a curb. Questioning her, Alice learned of the American Fund for the French Wounded, a volunteer organization that distributed supplies to hospitals. She called on its chairperson, Mrs. Isabel Lathrop, who accepted them as "delegates" so long as they could provide a vehicle for Gertrude to drive. Alice immediately began to work at taking inventory; pacing while she smoked, she planned ways to stretch scant supplies. Stein's part of the war effort was to write her cousins Fred Stein and Bird Stein Gans that she needed a car. Bird's husband, Howard, replied that he was contributing $100 of the $550 needed but was having trouble raising the rest; as soon as it was purchased, however, the Ford would be sent over. Gertrude meanwhile learned to drive William Cook's ancient two-cylinder Renault taxicab, practicing on hot afternoons in the outskirts of Paris. Cook, who had found no work in the city except driving, was happy to teach her, but unfortunately Gertrude never mastered the skill of reversing, which was at that time difficult even for experienced drivers. Unruffled by her shortcoming, Gertrude said that she would be like the French army—never in retreat.

In August Gertrude had postal cards made from a photograph of herself taken beside a car. After receiving the card, Mike wrote that he liked seeing her as a "chuffer" and that when he moved to California (his current plan) he would also learn to drive—as Harriet Levy was already doing. But

the American car project dragged on, more difficult to fund than Gans expected; it was February 1917 before Gertrude's Ford arrived in Paris. Converted from car to supply truck, painted with the familiar red cross, and
christened with white wine, the Ford was named "Auntie" for Pauline Stein
("who always behaved admirably in emergencies and behaved fairly well
most times if she was properly flattered"). On its first drive into Paris, the
truck stalled on tram rails and had to be pushed clear. As they drove down
the Champs-Elysées, it again stopped dead, and though Gertrude and others
cranked energetically, it would not start. Someone finally diagnosed that
Auntie was out of gas. Another time, eager for lunch, they parked in the
crowded court of a popular inn, blocking other cars. When an officer asked
Gertrude to back the truck out, she replied, "Oh that I can not do, as if it
were an unpardonable sin he were asking her to commit. Perhaps, he continued, if you come with me we might together be able to do it."

Auntie needed both frequent repairs and frequent cranking; as she
cranked, Gertrude would mutter, "I'm going to scrap this car." She usually
got help from passersby, however, and when Mrs. Lathrop commented on
the fact that people did help her, Gertrude replied that others looked out for
her because she was "democratic"—not too proud to accept help. In contrast, Stein said, Mrs. Lathrop looked efficient, too efficient. For all the fun of
having and driving a car, which was usually a man's privilege, Gertrude felt
that her involvement in the war effort was somewhat spurious; she wrote
slyly to Van Vechten that she was "engaged in good works . . . running a little Ford into the country for the American relief committee. . . . Otherwise I
am working." Even in wartime, writing remained her primary occupation.

As they drove in the French countryside, however, Gertrude began to
see how useful having a car could be: they could visit picturesque villages
and quiet lakes—and begin to understand the complex montage that was
France. Traveling outside the usual tourist areas forced them to speak French
more often than English. Before Gertrude had learned to drive, she and
Alice had been outsiders, visitors who barely sampled French culture; now
they had a means of immersing themselves in it.

The American Fund for French Wounded

In March 1917 their real work for the fund began. Delivering supplies to a
Saint-Cloud hospital was their first assignment. That successfully done, at
their request they were sent to Perpignan, in the Pyrenees near the Spanish
border, where they set up a supply depot with materials shipped in by rail.
Not only was the old walled town beautiful and the site of several military
installations, their friend Yvonne Davidson, wife of sculptor Jo Davidson,
helped run one of the hospitals there.

Alice planned their hours on the road so that they could eat in the best
restaurants, but they were usually late for meals because of Auntie and
Gertrude's unpredictability. Convinced that her sense of direction was more

accurate than maps were, Stein meandered quixotically through France. And on this first long drive, weather handicapped them: they faced snowy narrow roads and slippery inclines that sometimes made Gertrude's usual method—driving straight ahead—impossible. But eventually, even though the Ford's parking-lamp headlights were dim, Gertrude and Alice saw the gigantic plane trees of Perpignan. Chilled to the bone in the open-sided car, with only a light canvas keeping off rain and snow, the women wore layers of warm clothing and fur hats that contrasted strangely with their sandals and woolen hose. When they arrived at the small Hôtel du Nord, a letter from Mildred Aldrich was waiting: "Well I am proud of you. Think of you two rushing through the passes in a snowstorm. Now I feel as if there were nothing you could not do."

Gertrude shared Mildred's confidence. She drove through all kinds of terrain, seldom bothering with other vehicles or with military protocol. One of the rules of driving for the AFFW was that drivers apply for gas rations. Because Gertrude hated red tape, Alice pretended to be the driver and went to the interviews. One day the major to whom she spoke said that his wife admired her writing and would like to invite her to dinner. Toklas admitted she was not Gertrude and took the confused man downstairs to introduce him to Stein. Good humor prevailed as Gertrude explained her dislike of officialdom—and they were still invited to dinner.

Settled in the banquet hall of the small hotel, with a corner screened off as an office, Alice found ways to monitor supplies (in one case building steps out of cartons so that only she could move through the storeroom). Gertrude continued her writing, which she learned to do in the car and at odd times of the day, rather than having to arrange her life around her work. She continued the theme of sexual disguise, charting a range of emotion as she and Alice met the stresses of travel with a changing, often worsening, relationship. During these years Gertrude frequently used the terms *pussy* and *lovely, wife* and *husband.* "There is no such thing as being good to your wife" is a line from "Marry Nettie," a title that disguises its reference to Alice's earlier love for Nellie Jacot with a play on the name of futurist Marinetti. The good-humored passage "We are good. / We are energetic. / We will get the little bowls we saw today" is followed with a prose section describing an argument over behavior: "If you care to talk to the servant do not talk to her while she is serving at table. This does not make me angry or annoy me. I like salad. I am losing my individuality. . . . How can I plan everything." While most of the writing is still relationship-centered, Gertrude also treats war themes, using the voice and language of soldiers.

Perpignan with its nightingales was picturesque, but the summer weather was so hot that even Gertrude complained (and she never again sought out sunshine). Alice was busy taking inventory, distributing supplies, and putting in special requests, irritated by a greedy commander who wanted such luxuries as silk pajamas. It was fairly easy to supply the AFFW's most popular item, an American-made comfort bag, complete with pencil and paper, toothbrush, soap, socks, chocolate, comb, knife or razor, cigarettes or pipe and tobacco, and sometimes a game, sewing kit, mirror, and a letter or donor card. Alice described the soldiers' reactions to the letters: "The next day comes each one in great excitement to have the letter he has found in his bag translated, and may he write and may he send a photograph of himself and will he get an answer and will either his letter or the answer be sunk by a submarine and how long will it take?"

Committed to aiding the Allied cause in whatever way they could and with the hope of earning money for the AFFW, Gertrude and Alice had a photo of themselves and Auntie taken at Riversaltes, the birthplace of Joffre, commander in chief of the French army. The thousand postal cards they sent to friends and sold in the States were the beginning of their financial involvement in the war effort; during these years they gave most of their personal money to needy wounded soldiers. Alice also asked her father for help, and his San Francisco lodge sent both an ambulance and X-ray equipment. Other American friends also sent supplies.

Involved as they were in the war effort, they found Leo's letters from the safety of America hopelessly irrelevant. In spring 1917 he sent Alice a riddle about Napoleon and, to Gertrude, his reaction to the film *The Crisis* ("It is the limit"). In contrast to Leo's irritating letters, Mike's remained useful and interesting. Their years in the south of France had brought Mike and Sally even closer to Matisse and his family, and during 1916 the artist had painted their individual portraits, along with *The Moroccans, The Studio, Quai Saint-Michel,* and *Bathers by a River.* The last was painted with angles much like those in the Oriental-style portrait of Sally. As if to show that his paintings of the Steins were labors of love, Matisse's portrait of Mike was larger than life.

In spring 1917 Mike and Sally returned to live in the Paris suburb of Garches. Allan, graduated from college, had enlisted in the French army and was responsible for all supplies—including AFFW goods—arriving for American charities. Mike wrote Gertrude that their brother Simon had died of the natural consequences of his obesity. Dead, too, was Auntie's namesake, Aunt Pauline Stein, as was Caesar Cone, Etta and Claribel's brother; Claribel, presumably still in Munich, had not been heard from for months. Nina Auzias remained in either Paris or Saint-Tropez; late in 1917 Mike commented that although Leo had asked him to increase Nina's allowance by twenty-five dollars a month, he seldom mentioned her, and Mike thought the romance was over. (Mike's regular reports about Nina satisfied Gertrude about the aspect of Leo's life that she found most troubling.)

During 1917 and 1918, however, Mike's most crucial role in Gertrude and Alice's lives was to provide them with tobacco, oatmeal, maple syrup, and Victor phonograph needles while they worked outside Paris. His letters listed the cigarettes he was sending: once, three boxes of Elegants; on another occasion, a tub of Levants, with a note that her usual shop had no Levants, no Marylands, no five-cent cigars, and no smoking tobacco. English cigarettes were available, but Gertrude and Alice much preferred American. Another role Mike filled for Gertrude was that of reader: in 1919 he commented, "I enjoyed the nigger stories. The dialect flows so smoothly."

Recalled briefly to Paris for reassignment, Alice and Gertrude were asked to talk about the French with newly arrived Marines. Staying only long enough to have Auntie serviced, they missed seeing Picasso, who had been lured to Barcelona and Rome with the Russian ballet company of *Parade.* Even though they read through Max Jacob's *The Dice Cup,* his recently published surrealist prose poems, and heard gossip about filmmaking at Cannes, they identified more closely with war work and soon started for Nîmes, a city of a hundred thousand people, with ten hospitals—more than sixteen hundred beds. With the Hôtel Luxembourg as their headquarters, Alice set up and ran the distribution depot and wrote for the *AFFW Weekly Bulletin.* She used her articles both to ask for supplies (she needed "hundreds and hundreds of socks and handkerchiefs" as well as games and chocolate) and to commend the soldiers: "The wounded have a wonderful spirit—they are so appreciative as are the doctors and staffs." In a November 28, 1917, column, she described Gertrude's careful driving of a wounded soldier who was "so brave in his suffering" back to his hometown, at his request. Now a military vehicle, Auntie was requisitioned to evacuate the wounded from ambulance trains; among the first were two San Francisco boys—the elevator man from a stylish shop ("frightfully wounded," Alice recalled) and the son of the owner of that shop. All the women could do was see that they received care quickly. Gertrude was also ordered to transport a number of soldiers ill with the Spanish grippe, and she took precautions to protect herself and Alice from the often-fatal illness.

In Nîmes, Gertrude and Alice took some time for themselves. Once materials were distributed, they were not required to be on hand at hospitals, though Gertrude, with her medical training, was often asked for advice. She took the opportunity to have dental work done, relying on her quasi-military role to get special rates. On October 31, 1917, Dr. Irving Waldberg billed Gertrude for three platinum crowns, a remake of a porcelain surface, and three root canals, noting that the bill of 640 francs was considerably reduced from his regular rates. Gertrude complained. In November Waldberg reduced the bill by another 100 francs.

Bored with the Ford's thirty-mile-an-hour speed and finding that American servicemen could be interesting, Gertrude began picking up hitchhikers. She reverted to behaving like the psychology student she had once been who had studied people's "bottom natures" and "sexual bases." Unassuming, leaving herself and her interests out of her discourse, she asked the young men where they were from and often called them by the names of their states. She and Alice took these men as their "godsons"; they exchanged letters and sent them food packages.

Two of the American doughboys who spent more time with Gertrude and Alice have written about their experiences. William Rogers, whom they called "Kiddy," was a private from Massachusetts serving with the Amherst ambulance unit. He spent ten days traveling with the women, who delighted in taking him to see "the solid museum stretching for miles around Nimes [sic]: arenas, theaters, churches, aqueducts, Caesarean battlefields." Day trips included Les Baux, Arles, Avignon, and Orange, always concluded before dark because of the Ford's feeble lights. In exchange for the tour, Rogers was mechanic, cranker, and tire changer; he sat on the floor with his feet on the running board. His impression of Stein, about whom he knew only that she wrote, was that she was modest and appreciative: "She never suggested that she was anybody but the (incompetent) driver of a rattling Ford truck with a very hard floor." Dressed in "heavy-duty corduroy of a mannish, army-uniform cut, belted with capacious pockets" and wearing either helmets or felt hats, both women looked eccentric.

Samuel L. M. Barlow, Jr., a U.S. secret service agent who had once questioned Gertrude and Alice about a hotel employee, had similar experiences. Overjoyed because they had extra gasoline, which Alice called "more precious than ointment or jewels," they traveled through Provence with Barlow sitting in the rear of Auntie on a soapbox and cushions. Rushing to take in the many sites of interest, Gertrude—a "portly and plain person of great charm"—would cry, "No insides . . . No time!" Barlow remembered the way the women's comments punctuated the tour. At the top of the tower of Aigues-Mortes, Alice remarked that it was "a basalt sarcophagus. One of the grandest places I know . . . and the saddest." When grape-filled carts passed them on the road, Gertrude said to Alice in their private lexicon, "A mirage rather than a vision." Then, with what Barlow called "her wise gaiety," she told him about pagan times: "If a cat sneezed you had to stay indoors all day, neglect the harvest, and give an obol to the priest. And no kissing on Sundays." At the Roman baths, she coveted a large marble tub; at Les Baux, she commented on the perfect workmanship, evident even in the ruins: "Look at this bit, and the stone-joining . . . put together neatly like a good page of verse or prose, without mortar visible or padding,—just the wanted surface." The tranquil trip was shattered when Gertrude suddenly braked and blew the horn. A young biker, calling to friends over her shoulder, hit the car, landing "astride on the hood of the engine, face to face with Miss Stein and Miss Toklas." Passersby surrounded the child, who was in hysterics—though she was unhurt. "'Come on,' said Miss Toklas, 'Let's get out of this.'"

When Barlow wrote later, gratefully thanking them and saying he wanted to remember "every inch of our day and every moment, every shape . . .

everything you said!" Gertrude replied tersely, "God forbid!" Enjoying her role as AFFW driver, she had seemingly forgotten her interest in "gloire."

Despite her duties, Gertrude kept on writing, although she continued to be discouraged that the war had shut off many publishing opportunities. Henry McBride of the *New York Sun* was so pleased with her portrait of him that he arranged for Frank Crowninshield to publish most of *Have They Attacked Mary. He Giggled. (A Political Caricature)* in the June 1917 *Vanity Fair* (thirty-five lines were omitted for lack of space); McBride then had it— with Jules Pascin's caricature of him—printed and distributed. Ever watchful for ways to publish, Gertrude then sent *Vanity Fair* a poem titled "The Great American Army." Fragmented as was most of her writing during this period, the piece praised the American war contribution and toasted its success. Appearing in the June 1918 issue, it was illustrated by a three-quarter-page lithograph by Lucien Jonas, the official French war painter. More interesting than the poem was the colorful description of its author: "Gertrude Stein has, since the outbreak of the war, been living in France and working in war relief as an ambulance driver. Few American women have taken a more active part in the conflict than she." Whether the prose was *Vanity Fair's*, Henry McBride's, or Alice Toklas's, it gave American readers a new gloss on the image of Gertrude Stein.

The Steins and the End of the War

Some weeks during the winter and spring of 1918 Gertrude and Alice were happy *not* to be in Paris. Mike's letters kept them apprised of the destruction of the zeppelin and Big Bertha raids. January damage in their flat was unrelated to war, however: a small bathroom leak had caused an accumulation of more than two inches of water all over the apartment. Making repairs, Mike had the water main turned off. In February air raids intensified; in March Mike and Sally left Paris. Mike's March 20 letter described the "visible exodus" (more than a million Parisians left); on April 8 he wrote that a German shell had fallen in the Luxembourg Garden. His April 11 letter reported that Sally and he had gone back to Paris to take care of both art collections. At the rue de Fleurus, he took Gertrude's Cézanne portrait out of the frame and put it in an inside clothes closet; in the atelier, he moved things away from the skylight and laid all ornaments flat. Then he packaged a number of paintings, insured them for 40,000 francs, and sent them to Gertrude to store in Nîmes. He told her, too, to have the gas and power shut off to reduce the danger of explosions.

In the next few weeks, Mike and Sally moved from Montigny-sur-Loing to Briare, in Loiret, then to the country near Cahors, and finally to Lot. As people fled Paris, safe areas grew more and more crowded, and Mike and Sally stayed in the outer edge of the refugee belt. Even during this transitory existence, Mike continued his family duties: he paid Gertrude's U.S. income tax, sent her as much sugar as was allowed, and wrote that David Bachrach was sending her a large box of photographs from Boston. Late in 1918, back in Paris, Mike and Sally rented a fifth-floor furnished flat at 248, boulevard Raspail that Mike described as "glorious" even though the city itself was "crowded and unspeakably expensive." Worried about inflation, Mike grieved over the loss of the nineteen Matisse paintings he had sent to the Gurlitt Gallery: When America entered the war in 1917, Gurlitt had declared the Steins' paintings enemy contraband and held a private auction at which he bought their paintings at low prices. Mike and Sally were making plans to claim the art, but their spirits were low.

Mike also wrote that their friend Hortense Guggenheimer had died of Spanish grippe, that Claribel Cone was still incommunicado in Germany, and that Nina was in Algiers, and he reported that Leo was headed to Texas for the winter. But while Mike may have thought that Leo's American Southwest was Texas, it was in fact Mabel Dodge's home in Taos, New Mexico. After Leo's flurry of publication in *The New Republic* and *Seven Arts,* his analysis, and his convalescence from operations, he enacted some of the freedoms he had long idealized. Though he claimed that he was more interested in Freud's theories of dynamism than those of sexuality, he spent his days exploring the erotic. Part of Nina's depression after Leo moved to the States stemmed from his candid—and cruel—letters about his sexual intimacies. While declaring that he loved only Nina, he wrote her about his affairs, admitting that he was seeing a "tremendous number of women. In truth it seems to me at the moment that it is raining women." He mentioned *X,* someone he had previously been sexually involved with, writing that his present nonsexual relationship with her was even "more intimate and more interesting." Yet even as he derogated the physical—a pattern he had used before to deny the importance of his affair with Nina—he privileged his own sexuality. He wrote that "for the moment" he "could compile a classified catalogue of about fifteen women and about an equal number of men who interest me."

Earlier, to Mabel Dodge, Leo had written that he had an answer to "the mystery" of psychoanalysis: "I have circumvented many mysteries, and eroticism, and 'why nature loves the number five' (what a poor innocent Emerson was not to know that the mystic number was not five but sixty-nine. Such are the tragedies of a life that ends before the great enlightenment)." Flaunting his sexual knowledge, Leo said he had found "the truth till now hidden even from the penetrating eye of A. A. B. and S. E. J. [his and Mabel's analysts], great men all, but a little obsessed by their own peculiar insights."

Psychoanalysis gave Leo insights into things beyond the sexual, however, and after a year of hearing excited reports of the sheer beauty of Taos—an oasis in the desert surrounded by a half circle of mountains—he traveled west. At first charmed by the haphazard adobe buildings with their uneven walls, doors, and windows, Leo maintained the intellectual reserve that kept him critical of the primitive. Soon, though, his capitulation to the sunstruck sands and limitless horizon was complete: he called it "the only landscape that can compete with the great painters." He wrote Mike that he had purchased a horse and was "negotiating for an adobe hut for $200," and Mike wrote Gertrude that Leo "seems very happy there studying the Indian pueblos." Mabel encouraged Leo's interest in Indian dances, which were by invitation only and were in the process of being outlawed by the American government. Andrew Dasburg, John Marin, and Marsden Hartley, who lived nearby, encouraged Leo to resume his own painting.

In August Leo suggested that Nina come to Taos ("It is far from the affairs of the world, and very peaceful"); he mentioned that he had explored coming back to France through service to the Red Cross but that his deafness had prevented that. Instead, he spent the autumn and winter in New Mexico, celebrating the armistice there and continuing his search for "the strange and wonderful world" of himself. By the spring of 1919, sleeping bag in tow, he was back in New York. So was Maurice Sterne, and he not only invited Leo to stay with him but offered to buy a couch for him to sleep on: "Leo preferred the sleeping bag. . . . He said that when he crawled inside and was cozily tucked in, he felt that he was back in his mother's womb." Having for years joked about what he called Sterne's mother complex, Leo's admission of his own preferences showed a kind of psychic health. (Sterne recalled that one morning the bag would not open; hours later the still serene Leo worked his way out.)

In 1919 Sterne thought Leo healthier than he had been since they had met fifteen years earlier. Howard Gans, too, wrote Gertrude that he was pleased with Leo's steady production of essays and that Leo was unusually docile. Gans also mentioned Leo's hope to publish in the *Saturday Evening Post* someday. Leo may have attributed that ambition to being interested in readership, but it came close to Gertrude's coveting *gloire*—and trying herself for publication in the *Atlantic Monthly*.

As if to complete the pattern he had begun when he first returned, Leo spent the summer of 1919 in Baltimore with relatives and friends. The four essays he published in *The New Republic* that winter were all on aesthetics, rather than studies of painters: he was finally working toward the book on aesthetics he had long talked of writing. In late fall, after more than four years in the States, he sailed for Italy. He wrote Nina, "I shall be most happy to see you again, and I hope with all my heart that things will work out well for both of us. . . . Naturally, one cannot be sure of things after so many years." The ambivalence Nina had lived with for a decade continued, despite the progress Leo felt he had made in psychoanalysis.

The armistice on November 11 surprised Gertrude and Alice; when Alice broke into tears of relief, Gertrude chastised her: "Compose yourself. You have no right to show a tearful countenance to the French whose sons will no longer be killed." Within days they heard from Mrs. Lathrop that, if they spoke German, they should close the Nîmes post and open a depot for civilian relief in devastated Alsace. Giving their provisions to nuns, the women rushed back to Paris, driving the six hundred kilometers in one long day. To save time, Alice had cooked a chicken, which Gertrude ate in halves as she drove.

Back in Paris they bought a German-French dictionary, fur-lined aviator jackets, and heavy sweaters. There they learned of Apollinaire's death in November from influenza (Gertrude lamented that Paris would never be the same) and of the death of Bertha's husband, Jay Raffel, from pneumonia. (Young to be widowed—her youngest child, Arthur, was only thirteen—Bertha was at least well provided for.) Gertrude and Alice also visited with Mildred Aldrich and with Picasso and his new wife, Olga Koklova, a young ballerina he had met when designing sets for *Parade.*

Then began the nightmare trip to Strasbourg. After what Alice called "a mix-up" with horses from the French army, as a result of which Auntie lost its steering mechanism, a window, and the tool chest, they made it to Nancy late that night, "the car weaving and wandering all over the road." The next day they toured the battlefield while Auntie was being repaired. Afterward, driving on through no-man's-land was a sobering experience, in the midst of which the fan belt broke. A French staff car stopped to help Gertrude, ineffectually at work with a hairpin, and they finally reached Mulhouse. But there the French army occupied the best hotel, and they spent the frigid winter in a small residential inn. Distributing warm clothing and blankets to the returning Alsatians, the women were pleased that Alice, whose German was good, could pass for Prussian. Food was plentiful, as was real coffee, and the Alsatian pastries were good. On one occasion, however, when Alice was tempted to buy some link sausage, Gertrude's irreverence broke through, and she warned her not to make the purchase—it might be Claribel Cone.

The women enjoyed the hospitality of some well-established Alsatians, who lived much as had Jewish families in California during the late nineteenth century. Frequently invited to local homes for Sunday dinners, Gertrude and Alice enjoyed the "great elegance and luxury" of the households; such visits helped them tolerate the relentlessly cold winter. The spring—complete with returning storks—was lovely, but they were happy to be ordered back to Paris. After nearly three years, they were going home.

On April 12 the AFFW headquarters gave a party for the American wounded; by early May 1919 the last of the AFFW depots had closed. Routine as their service had been, both Alice and Gertrude had benefited from the roles World War I had provided them. Besides their new confidence in their abilities and their new physical mobility driving Auntie, they also had somewhat different identities. Alice's great capacity to organize had been officially recognized, and Gertrude was now known as the American woman writer whose service to the Allied war effort had brought her closer to battle than any other American woman. At forty-five, Gertrude had an entirely new sense of her persona and her possibility.

PART 3

Celebrity Circles
(1920–1935)

ROSE IS A
ROSE IS A
ROSE IS A
ROSE
        she is my rose.

In 1928, when Gertrude Stein placed this and other fanciful poems and drawings in what she called her "Love Notebook," she and Alice Babette Toklas had been living as a married couple for twenty years. Inside the cover of the small notepad is Stein's drawing of flowers, with the caption "a vase of flowers for my rosebud." After several sketches of two women together, Gertrude wrote another poem: "I love she / She is adorably we. / When it is she / She is me. / She embroiders / beautifully." Y.D., the signature, is a coded "Your Darling."

The "strong" (one of Gertrude's words for *seductive*) look they exchange in this Carl Van Vechten photograph catches for posterity the passion that inscribed their relationship. Stein spoke directly about most topics, whether in her typically earnest rhetoric—"One thing which I have tried to tell Americans is that there can be no truly great creation without passion"—or in the playful language of her love poems:—"Tongue like a whip. / Dear little tongue. / Red little tongue, / Long little tongue. / Let little be mine. / yes yes yes." Beside this poem is a drawing of a round object, or orifice, labeled "earring." Other poems in the notebook play with the refrain "Does my baby love blue / or who," and at times there are more prosaic lines, such as "I am saying here that she is dear. I am saying / here that she has lovely hair, she is saying here that / she has me where she wants me. She is saying here / that I am dear. I wander and I wander and I do not / wander more any more because I know I love her so. Y.D."

(Carl Van Vechten Collection, Yale Collection of American Literature, Beinecke Rare Book and Manuscript Library, Yale University)

The Twenties Begin

Paris was the place for all such possibility. Overflowing now with people who had never seen Paris, or France, or any of Europe until military service had brought them across the Atlantic, the city was full of new energies. The arrivals were middle-class Americans, not the upper-class tourists of the late nineteenth and early twentieth centuries; steamship lines accommodated postwar demand by creating a cheaper kind of passage, the third class, which before the war no tourist would have admitted to using. As the exchange rate grew more and more favorable to American currency—in 1923 hitting the record high of fifty francs to the dollar—more and more young Americans came to Paris. Parisians found that they could rent any kind of room, any kind of flat, to the eager tourists; and the café business spilled from inside to the sunny outside terraces, as young visitors searched to find their compatriots in the crowded city.

In Montparnasse, Americans congregated at Deux-Magots, partly because of its location and partly because its coffee was pure, without chicory. At times it was possible for the steady customers, the eager English speakers reading *The Chicago Tribune* or *The Herald,* to buy two-pound bags of Deux-Magots coffee for use at home. The Select and the smoky old Café du Dôme, opposite the Rotonde with its paintings of nudes and landscapes from the south of France, attracted even more Americans. Frank Harris, Oscar Wilde's biographer and friend, who looked forty though he was seventy, was often at the Dôme, as were the model Kiki of Montparnasse (Alice Prin), Jules Pascin, Adolph Basler, Leo Stein, and Despiau, the last two "sourly" sipping their glasses of hot milk. Artist George Biddle remembered them as "lone wolves, suffering from chronic indigestion."

When in Paris, Leo stayed at the Hôtel Raspail. From his room, in the early hours of the morning, he could look down on the corner of boulevards Montparnasse and Raspail, where electric lights illuminated the café patrons on the terraces. Someone would be reading Jean Duflex's journal, *Montparnasse, An International and Cosmopolitan Weekly.* More likely, people would be drinking and talking, "gossiping in four or five languages; smugly aware that this was the intellectual, the artistic hub of the civilized universe." At the Café du Dôme, nights were short: at 5:30 A.M., people began coming in for fresh crescent rolls.

Gertrude and Alice in Paris

Newly democratized from their experiences talking with French and American soldiers, Gertrude and Alice relished the city's friendly atmosphere. While they no longer went to the cafés, they did drive through the crowded Paris streets, locating old friends, open to meeting new people. The fear of death—and the experience of so much of it, along with the discomfort of years living as AFFW workers—had increased their need for society: they were on the lookout for sociability. As Alice recalled, "Paris was filled with Allies, the Armies, the Peace Commission and anyone who could get a passport. We lunched and dined with a great many of them, at their messes, headquarters, homes and restaurants." Eyes sparkling, Gertrude engaged passersby in conversation, inevitably stopping traffic as she leaned down from her ramshackle Ford to do so. It was a heady season, a celebration that Paris was intact—"more beautiful, vital and inextinguishable than ever."

Returning to Paris, their AFFW duties over, also meant that Alice and Gertrude could take time for themselves again. For women who had never before worked, the years of service with the AFFW had been uncharacteristically busy, and they looked forward now to "madly running about, to see our friends. . . . It was gay, a little feverish but pleasurably exciting. Auntie Pauline took us to lunch and dinner parties. Our home was filled with people coming and going." For Gertrude, being back in Paris meant she could resume her steady hours of reading and writing, and for a while she read more than her customary book a day. But the women were faced with one major difference in their postwar lives: touched by the needs of various soldiers and their families, they had given away much of their income. Referring to themselves as "the chauffeur and the cook," they lived with only minimal household help. Finding some zest in their new roles, Alice wrote, "We would live like gypsies, go everywhere in left-over finery, with a pot-au-feu for the many friends we should be seeing." In the postwar Paris of 1919, poverty seemed appropriate—even a bit adventurous. Even though Gertrude and Alice enjoyed a full social life, they remained friends with only a few of the people they had known before the war. Gertrude's long friendship with Picasso had diminished; playing the role of bourgeois husband to his new wife, he seemed determined to break with old friends. While she delighted in her made-over Ford, Picasso bought a Rolls Royce. At the height of cubism, Picasso and Braque signed each other's names to their paintings, a mark of their disdain for the responsibility she thought an artist should have toward his or her work. Alice and she still saw the Braques and André Masson, however, and in the spring of 1920 Gertrude sat for sculptor Jacques Lipchitz, whose gossip amused her.

The Matisses had moved permanently to Nîmes. Gertrude and Alice thought that Henri would rather remain intimate with Mike and Sally—from whom they were now comparatively distant—than with themselves. They saw him only once more, at an exhibit, and although he was friendly, it was clear that he had built a different life. What replaced their previously intense friendships with Picasso and the Matisses was their bond with Daniel-Henry Kahnweiler, now returned to Paris after his exile in Switzerland, and with his family, which included his sister-in-law Béro and her husband, the painter Elie Lascaux, as well as Juan Gris.

On some Sundays—as Gertrude revived the American custom of driving out to visit friends—they headed to the Kahnweilers' home in Boulogne. Some of these Sunday gatherings were in honor of Juan Gris. More often, the Kahnweilers dined alone with Gertrude and Alice. The art dealer recalled one occasion when the fireplace was blocked and the dining room filled with smoke. Calling the concierge, Gertrude remained calm, even as firemen and police pushed into the room: "I can still see Gertrude's fine Roman head, impassive in the midst of the tumult, while the pebbles (which had been thrown from the roof down the flue to smother the fire) tumbled down onto the hearth with a sound like hail. At last everything grew quiet, and Gertrude went on talking as if nothing had happened."

Attracted by Gertrude's tranquillity and her innovative yet common-sense approach to both writing and painting, Kahnweiler determined that he would publish her books in his new series of pamphlet-length works printed on beautiful paper with illustrations by significant painters. He planned three. Picasso was to illustrate one, but that was never completed. Gris illustrated Stein's As a Wife Has a Cow, A Love Story, and Elie Lascaux, A Village Are You Ready Yet Not Yet. Kahnweiler later described his confidence in Gertrude's writing and persona:

> I found in her writings a state of mind and aspirations which I had been defending for years. . . . Gertrude's poetry seemed to me very close to the painting of Picasso and Juan Gris, and, in another field, to the music of Schönberg. There was in it for me a manifestation, through language, of the same tendencies which had been made way for in Cubism, in plastic art. There was the same revolution in profundity, the same raising again of the problem of what makes the raw material of each art. . . . The poetry within her comes from an entirely new use of vocabulary, no longer accepting any law and antecedent to the act of creation but freeing this act and leaving it abandoned to its interior logic.

Warmed by Kahnweiler's appreciation, Gertrude maintained her friendship with him and his circle throughout her life. It was satisfying to find someone who could speak eloquently about the similarities between her writing and Picasso's and Gris's painting. With Juan Gris, too, Gertrude felt there was no need to explain herself or her work: like her unspoken rapport with Picasso, her empathy with Gris was deep and sincere. When he became ill, his friendship grew even more precious. From the fall of 1920, when Kahnweiler opened Galerie Simon (his galleries never again carried his name), Gertrude bought Gris's paintings. In April 1921 she purchased *The Table in Front of the Window;* that spring she and Alice drove to Monte Carlo, where Gris was designing for the Ballets Russes, and spent a few days with the Grises at Bandol to discuss their collaborating on a ballet project of their own. (The way to reach one elite strand of Paris society was through innovative theater, dance, and opera, and the way to be staged in Paris was through initial productions at the Théâtre du Casino, which the prince of Monaco leased for Diaghilev's use each May.)

Stein continued to enjoy the freedom of having a car. Though repainted, after hard years on the road, Auntie looked so disreputable that Gertrude and Alice were prevented from parking when they dined at fashionable hotels, and eventually laws prohibited them from driving the Ford in the bois de Boulogne, Gertrude's favorite park. Friends teased Gertrude about her "second class hearse." It was clear that the women needed a new car and that this time they would have to pay for it themselves. They therefore ordered the cheapest open-top Ford available. When the car arrived in December 1920, Alice looked with dismay at the bare dashboard; Stein, however, smiled and named it "Godiva" for the naked horsewoman. The fact that Paris was crowded with cars meant that Gertrude had to concentrate on her driving: people recalled her "stern expression" while she drove, in contrast to "Alice sitting beside her, elegant and detached."

Part of the women's visibility in postwar Paris derived from their contrasting appearances. Alice's wardrobe continued to be quietly distinctive, long brilliant earrings and wildly trimmed hats its chief extravagances. Gertrude's continued to be unpredictable, chosen chiefly for comfort. Friends noted that Stein could be elegant, particularly in long-lined dresses that made her look taller, but that she could also look like a fussy grandmother in brightly flowered blouses and stodgy skirts. And her hats could be nightmares—some elaborately beflowered concoctions with sweeping brims; others, "cut off coal scuttles." Dressing for AFFW duty had introduced her to roomy jackets with pockets (so that she had a place for cigarettes, change, and car keys). She often wore a jacket or coat over a long skirt, a blouse, and sometimes a vest. Both women preferred sandals, wearing them in winter with woolen stockings, but Alice also wore conventional dress shoes with raised heels.

The Steins en Famille

Once Mike and Sally returned to Paris from the south of France, they included in their household the witty Gabrielle Osorio de Monzie, a woman as active in Christian Science as Sally was. Gabrielle, who was divorced from the French politician Anatole de Monzie, lived with her beautiful young ward, Jacqueline, as an integral, expense-sharing part of the Mike Stein household.

During 1919 much of Mike and Sally's energy had gone into retrieving, through Hans Purrmann's negotiations, the Matisse paintings confiscated by the Gurlitt Gallery. When the paintings finally arrived safely in Paris, Mike sold them to Scandinavian collectors Tetzen Lund and Trygne Sagen. While his interest in Matisse's work remained high, Mike kept an eye on world economics; he was sure the dollar was the currency to be invested in. The vicissitudes of currency throughout the war had frightened him. He tried to teach Gertrude about the complicated world financial market, but she was not interested—nor was she amenable to his suggestion that she sell some paintings. Gertrude didn't mind selling to the Cones and other Americans, always at what she saw as a premium, but she did not intend to do any wholesale liquidating. Mike's strategy influenced Leo, however. Worried about money for a decade, Leo had seen his resources depleted when he funded Nina's household, his Italian place, and his travels in the States. When he returned to Europe in the fall of 1919, reuniting with Nina in Algiers, his attempts to get her to understand that his finances were limited became a near-obsession.

Nina's image of Leo and his family as wealthy art collectors, which was the way she had been introduced to them in 1905, was impossible to dislodge. While Leo was in the States, he had written that he could no longer continue her 600-franc monthly allowance. Terribly hurt, Nina had complained, cajoled, threatened. Leo's behavior was unpredictable, she said; he had obviously never loved her. In turn, he accused her of being mercenary. Try as he might to explain his financial position, Leo could not persuade Nina that his small income remained constant: $100 to $150 monthly was all his investments would ever yield. His only means of getting more money was to sell pieces of his art collection (his "principal"), which he had been doing almost from the time of his first liaison with Nina.

As Nina and Leo discussed marriage, his anxieties about money grew. He knew that he wanted to continue psychoanalysis; the costs of that treatment might continue for years. His correspondence with Nina suggests that he preferred to remain single: he spoke of "a future together . . . only on condition of my liberty," assuring her that "I am never going to abandon you." If Nina insisted on marriage, he continued, he would give her all—"marriage, baby, home"—but perhaps not happiness. He admitted to being sulky, reminded her of his feelings for an American lover, and made a veiled reference to pregnancy. On April 13, 1920, he wrote that he could promise her nothing. Finally, after more than a year of this dialogue, Leo agreed to marry Nina, though it had become clear that she would remodel the villa if she lived there and that she would also expect some kind of residence in Paris, not only because of voice lessons but because of her need to see friends. Settignano was a wonderful Italian village, but it was just that—a village. No cosmopolitan Parisian could be expected to live there permanently.

As a result of his coming to understand what would represent a suitable lifestyle for them as a married couple, Leo wrote to Albert Barnes, the collector who had purchased paintings from him throughout the decade. In late December 1920 Leo asked Barnes what he should do about the paintings he had left stored in New York. "Apart from a painfully small property which has been enjoying some shrinks recently," he wrote, the New York paintings were his "principal possession," and, of them, he assumed that the Renoirs were the most valuable. He told Barnes that he didn't know "where to strike the balance between the rise in Renoir prices and the fall in francs. If you don't mind giving me some counsel in the matter as to whether there is a practicable market now or whether one had better wait, whether selling at auction gives a fair return or whether some other method were more judicious . . ."

Had Leo asked Mike, he would have received better advice. Though nervous about the world money market, Mike was never concerned about the market for art: he would have told Leo to hold on to everything. Prosperity, and people's desire to acquire tangible evidence of their wealth, was just around the corner. In 1919, when Mike and Sally bought *Tea*, the painting that was to be their last important Matisse acquisition, it was with the understanding that art could only appreciate. But Barnes wrote Leo a cautionary letter, and on March 8, 1921, Leo asked him if he would go to the New York storage space and look at what was there: the Renoirs, a Delacroix, a Daumier, a Matisse bronze, and the Cézanne watercolors and an oil, *Still Life with Apples*.

Leo's March 8 letter, written just three days after he and Nina finally married, shows that he had become neurotically unsure. Leo Stein, the most important collector in Paris between 1905 and 1908, the man who had taught Barnes how and what to collect, wrote submissively to one who had consistently proved his unfriendliness: "Do about them whatever you think most advisable. I'm afraid that you think of them as more important than they are. Most of them are small and slight, and one very lovely nude I cracked by foolish handling in the old days of my pathological impatience. . . . Anything that you think advisable to do about them would suit me, as I have much more confidence in your judgment than in mine." Leo's letter suggests that his days of "pathological impatience" were hardly over—what was the urgency to get rid of these pieces? Because he still had art in Europe housed with various dealers, he was in no immediate need.

Unfortunately, Barnes said that Leo should sell: it was a good time to do so. But later he wrote that he could find no buyers and so offered to buy some of the pieces himself—not the insignificant Renoirs, however, nor Cézanne's apples. Barnes seemed to be taking the opportunity not only to buy Leo's collection for very little but also to malign his judgments. According to William Schack, Barnes's biographer, mutual friends thought the purchase "a steal, that instead of being generous to an impractical friend Barnes acted on the principle, Never give a sucker a break." But, Schack continued, "If Stein himself was aggrieved, there is no mention of it in his published letters." Indeed, he continued selling: later in 1921, the Durand-Ruel gallery bought his last Cézanne (*Still Life with Apples*) for eight hundred dollars. Leo's modus operandi at this point in his life was to tie up loose details, to separate one part of his life—that of bachelor and art collector—from the next, a life as husband, man of the world, and writer/aesthetician. Completely lacking flexibility in his self-image, Leo operated at odds from Gertrude, who was ready to seize any chance for new self-creation.

Having returned to Italy in the fall of 1919, on December 14 Leo wrote to Gertrude about his analysis and his need to reestablish a relationship with her. He described what he called their "Family Romance," which had disturbed his digestion—and hers—whenever they quarreled, and said he was finally able to deal with conflict: he had simplified his personal contacts and found relationships easier. But his primary reason for writing was that he wanted her to know that most of his adult life had been "a prolonged disease, a kind of mild insanity. I always knew that despite the general opinion to the contrary, I continually acted on impulse, but hardly realized till quite recently that it was not only impulsion but compulsion as well." While he did not apologize, even this admission that he had been somewhat to blame for the household dissension was unusual for Leo. There is no evidence, however, that Gertrude replied.

Despite not having heard from his sister, in the spring of 1920 Leo called on Gertrude and Alice in Paris. It had been more than six years since he had moved out of 27, rue de Fleurus, and they had not seen each other since. When he left their apartment that afternoon, he forgot his notebook, and his next letter to Gertrude asks that she send it to him. (It was either on the table in her study, he wrote, or on a corner table in the American University reading room.) The last piece of Leo's correspondence in the Yale collection is an April 13, 1920, postal card to Alice, thanking her for sending the notebook. No correspondence exists from the last twenty-five years of Leo's and Gertrude's lives.

The rue de Fleurus Once More

No longer limited to Saturday salons, Gertrude and Alice found themselves increasingly surrounded by visitors. Their late afternoon entertaining was often simple: Alice made several kinds of good cookies, which she served with small cups of heavily spiked punch or tea. She poured at a sturdy low table decorated with two elaborate silver candlesticks and a highly wrought silver teapot, bowl, and pitcher. The cups and saucers were white, of classic design, with a heavy gold band. When there was a larger party, Alice covered small tables with beautiful china "heaped with homemade cakes, *marrons glacés,* crystallized cherries and violets, and piles of an Oriental fruit like tiny, yellow, Japanese paper lanterns." Many visitors were curious Americans; others were Paris friends. Alice and Gertrude, however, were more chary about invitations; meeting people as they entered, Alice would ask, "By whose invitation do you come?" From the responses, she learned whether visitors could be trusted and, more important, whether she and Gertrude could entertain as a couple or would need to separate, with Gertrude staying with the male artists and writers and she talking with the "wives."

Many of their postwar visitors were artist friends from the past. Sonia and Robert Delaunay, like Yvonne and Jo Davidson, were welcomed enthusiastically as couples. Gertrude was equally interested in the cloth and clothing design Sonia and Yvonne were involved in and the men's sculpture and painting; Sonia also painted and in 1914 had published a collection of her poems, *Prisms and Discs.* Braque, Marsden Hartley, Nancy Cunard, Djuna Barnes, André Masson, Brian Rhys, Tristan Tzara, art dealer Jean Aron, Marcel Duchamp, Muriel Draper, Carl Van Vechten, Avery Hopwood, Jessie Whitehead (now working in Paris), the Kahnweiler group, and Josette and Juan Gris all visited regularly. En route to Zurich, where she was to undertake psychoanalysis with Carl Jung, Annette Rosenshine also returned for a visit.

Other postwar visitors were writers. The Steins' being important art collectors did not induce young writers in Paris to seek out Gertrude; they wanted to meet her because of her inexplicable portraits, because of *Three Lives* and *Tender Buttons,* because of the fame the Armory show had brought her, because of the hold her work—and her persona and her name—had taken on the American imagination. Her role in this increasingly literary—and increasingly American—expatriate culture was much more important than it had been before the war. Although Alice would label the young writers as people who thought "writing was a contagious craft," they did care what Gertrude thought about writing, and they cared specifically what she thought about *their* writing. The bravest of the visitors brought her their manuscripts.

In little more than a year, Gertrude had gone from being a hearty AFFW driver in Alsace, bundled in fur and eating fiercely through the cold winter, to being "Our Lady," "The Presence," "Le Stein." Leo could hardly believe it, and as he spent afternoons at the Dôme or the Rotonde and overheard young writers talking about Gertrude, he joked with them about her: "What are you afraid of? . . . My God . . . you have no idea how dumb she is! Why when we were in school I used to have to do all her homework for her." He sometimes suggested that his sister did not know what words meant. (Gertrude herself seemed surprised by the attention; in 1921 she wrote Harry Phelan Gibb, "I suppose some day I will be the acknowledged grandmother of the modern movement.")

Those who visited the salon, however, were impressed. Bryher (Winifred Ellerman, whom Stein described as "an ethical Jewess . . . rather a rare type"—although Bryher was not Jewish) recalled the atmosphere in Gertrude's atelier as "full of gold," spun from the energy of both Stein's manner and her talk. Bryher described the conversation there as less a dialogue than a distillation of what Gertrude's visitors were interested in hearing: "At first there was a little general conversation, then she would pick up a phrase and develop it, ranging through a process of continuous association until we seemed to have ascended through the seven Persian heavens and in the process to have turned our personalities inside out. Make no mistake, however, it was not an ego selfishly seizing the stage, it was rhetoric, spare and uncolored by emotion." "How bitterly I regret that there were no tape recorders," Bryher lamented. Other regular visitors remembered the "sparkle" of Stein's "mind and vitality and wit which seemed to be constantly bubbling over and made others feel that they themselves had ideas, but it was always she who said the unexpected and paradoxical thing . . . possibly a quotation from James Joyce or William James which exactly fitted our conversation in a slightly twisted and therefore even more amusing sense." Janet Flanner noted that "Gertrude led everything" and talked "with the greatest sense, coherency, simplicity, and precision." Serious or comic, Stein created maxims about writing, repeating them to her listeners like mantras: "Before you write it must be in your head almost in words, but if it is already in words in your head, it will come out dead."

Alfred Kreymborg, who had self-published a collection of poems at the same time Stein had published *Three Lives,* was pleased that she knew of his work and "found to his surprise that his praise meant a good deal to her." As a mark of her fondness for him and his companion, Harold Loeb, she pulled open "a row of ponderous drawers in a cabinet," disclosing "a pile of huge manuscripts she had been working on for some years. . . . The sight stunned him." Once Gertrude discovered that the younger writers were appalled when they learned how much of her work remained unpublished, she used the disclosure strategically. Most visitors responded with shock or with sympathy; a few tried to help her find publishers. Others, like William Carlos Williams, were callous. When Stein asked him what he would do with such a quantity, Williams replied that he would sort through it, save the best, and "throw the rest into the fire." The shocked silence that greeted his comment was answer enough, but Stein followed it with, "No doubt. But then writing is not, of course, your metier [*sic*]." The two were never friends, but Williams later wrote a key essay about the significance of Gertrude's writing, for which she thanked him.

What Stein tried to convey to her listeners during these postwar salons was the meaning of concentration. She believed that no artist could create fully unless he or she tapped into the essence of being, or soul; her problem was how to describe a process that was inherently without language. She was searching for a way to unlock these writers' deepest consciousness, or unconsciousness, so that they would be able to understand their work without talking about it, just as she, Picasso, Matisse, and Gris understood each other's work. Gertrude was earnest about what she was doing, and ridicule hurt her terribly. With her usual perspicacity, she knew who took her seriously; those who didn't were not invited back to the rue de Fleurus.

Lincoln Steffens, who went often to Gertrude and Alice's with his wife, Ella Winter, liked Stein's earnestness. He described her as "content to be herself, do her own work, but when the young . . . came to her, she gave them all they would take." Her relationships reflected her personal wisdom, Steffens said. "She accepted herself as she was. She was large; she dressed as a large woman. Yvonne Davidson, one of the most creative of the famous French couturieres of the day, made for Gertrude Stein, at her behest, a great flowing fat gown to wear. . . . 'Dress *me*,' ordered the writer, and Yvonne dressed *her*, beautifully." Steffens and Winter responded positively to Stein's ambience, saying that everything fit—her car, her living space, her "perfect little dinners. . . . You felt there her self-contentment and shared her composure, but, best of all, the prophetess gave you glimpses of what a Buddha can see by sitting still and quietly looking."

For poet John Peale Bishop, Stein was "as unmistakably American as Mark Hanna. . . . She might have been an adornment to the McKinley era." Van Wyck Brooks, long a friend of Leo's, saw her popularity as being based in the young "Middle-Western" writers, heavily dependent on her maternal bearing ("the mature Gertrudian bosom") and her ability to give them a sense of community. For Frederic Prokosch, however, coming from a private college culture where students waved copies of *Tender Buttons* "like a banner," meeting Stein was a miracle. "She was smaller than I expected (I had expected a giantess) and her voice was less sonorous, her manner less intimidating. . . . There was something very delicate about her. Her face looked coarse and furrowed . . . [but also] civilized and gently speculative." Of her conversation, he wrote, "Gertrude's style was irresistibly contagious. One lapsed without being aware of it into her conversational cadences. It may have been hypnotic or even a kind of witchery but it was impossible to talk to Gertrude without slipping into her rhythms." Like Steffens, Prokosch attributed this effect to the integrity of her persona: "She created an eerie sense of living totally in the present and of seeing the life around her in a series of instant visions."

Young Dartmouth writer Bravig Imbs appreciated the sense of rightness in Stein but focused more on the great benefit she conferred on anyone brave enough to bring her manuscripts. What Gertrude liked best was to point out "with unerring accuracy . . . the phrases, sentences and paragraphs where the literary intuition had been direct and pure." She would not correct the writing, nor would she later ask about it. Imbs noted that when she did speak about specific works, she did so "rapidly, monotonously . . . with embarrassment." Because writing for her "meant discipline and duty and loyalties," she preferred to talk about pleasant things so she could "laugh and expand and radiate." At the base was her conviction that writing expressed the soul and so was the most serious work possible.

She believed that if the heart of the writer was firmly engaged in the writing, there was no need to revise: "If you have something to say, the words are always there. And they are the exact words and the words that should be used. If the story does not come whole, *tants pis,* it has been spoiled, and that is the most difficult thing in writing, to be true enough to yourself, and to know yourself enough so that there is no obstacle to the story's coming through complete. . . . It is the fundamental problem in writing." For specific criticisms she would mark "with a faint pencil across the sentences or words which displeased her." She assumed writers would be able to understand what correction was needed—if they understood the central method in the first place.

When she used herself and her work to illustrate method, she may have sounded egocentric, but her remarks were set in the larger context of the writer's need to draw from personal consciousness. As Bryher pointed out, Stein was trying to be helpful; she was not telling people to do things the way she did. She would be the first to acknowledge that they were individuals. All she wanted was for them to find their own themes and their own styles in as distinctive a manner as she had found hers. She did, however, have to draw on her own experience for illustrations, and Imbs quotes her saying, "In my own writing, as you know, I have destroyed sentences and rhythms and literary overtones and all the rest of that nonsense, to get to the very core of this problem of the communication of the intuition. If the communication is perfect, the words have life, and that is all there is to writing." Stein took all discussion about writing seriously, and the reason she often built her comments out of phrases and lines from her listeners' statements—as if she were composing an aria to elaborate a simpler line— was so that people would hear what she wanted them to know in their own language.

Unsympathetic portraits of Stein dot the memoirs of visitors who did not understand (or did not care to understand) the seriousness of her comments. When Wambley Bald asked her why her prose was obscure, she replied—with as much hostility as his question posed—that it was difficult only for the lazy-minded. In an interchange with Samuel Putnam about abstraction, Stein insisted that the direction of American writing had been "toward abstractionism . . . an abstraction without mysticism" and that her writing contributed a kind of abstraction "without being mystical. There is no mysticism in my work," she said. When questioned, "No mysticism?" she replied more severely than she would have to a different audience: "None whatever. . . . My work is perfectly natural. It is so natural that it is unnatural to those to whom the unnatural is natural. I reproduce things exactly as they are and that is all there is to it. The outer world becomes the inner world and the inner world becomes the outer, and the outward is no longer outward but inward and the inward is no longer inward but outward and it takes genius to do that and Gertrude Stein *is* a genius."

Morrill Cody went to the rue de Fleurus purposely to dislike Stein and was flip with her, so Gertrude, in turn, disliked him. For all his friendship with Leo, however, Cody was impressed with her:

> Her lips moved, her dark intelligent eyes, piercing yet kindly, moved, but the rest of her body was almost totally inert. All in her company were held by the depth of her eyes, which seemed to be looking at you in whatever part of the room you were standing, like the eyes of the horses in Rosa Bonheur's painting *The Horse Fair.* . . . She pronounced all these "truths" with calm and firm assurance, as though they were established facts known to every, or at least almost every, schoolchild. No one laughed. For the moment, we all believed.

Cody recalled her hearty laughter, which others described as "the easiest, most infectious laugh. Always starting abruptly at a high pitch and cascading down and down into rolls and rolls of unctuous merriment, [it] . . . would fill the room and then, as it gradually dwindled into chuckles and appreciative murmurs, the silence that followed seemed golden with sunlight." Stein at home was difficult to resist, and it was a tribute to both her intelligence and Toklas's entrepreneurial skill that they understood how powerful she was in her own setting.

In contrast, Mahonri Young, a friend of Leo's from earlier years, used the image of a spider to describe Gertrude's social powers: "She spun webs around people and then stung them to death." He cautioned that she was not joking about being a second Shakespeare: "There were no limits to her ego"; she "genuinely thought she was great." Despite her self-congratulation, however, Young conceded that "it is marvelous how people put up with her pretensions and her rudeness. People were fascinated by and genuinely fond of this sacred monster. Overcoming crippling drawbacks, she attained serenity."

Ezra Pound's famed misbehavior, then, is easier to understand when compared with the adulation of most visitors to the rue de Fleurus. Although there were several visits in the Pound-Stein history, most observers tell the story as if it were one interchange. In the midst of his usual long-winded disquisition, Pound lectured on his literary preferences "from Catullus to Provence, interspersing his remarks with comments on Stein's collection of paintings. Stein found Pound's tone unpleasantly aggressive," according to biographer John Tytell, "and responded with an air of stolid indifference, but what she found difficult to tolerate was the way Pound kept leaning back in her favorite antique chair, balancing it on its two back legs until one of them snapped." Contrary to Tytell's description, however, what irritated Gertrude most about Pound's lecture was its similarity to Leo Stein's. Having spent a dozen years of her life listening to her brother discourse about everything from the history of art to her writing, Gertrude was not now holding afternoons so that she could play the role of listener—she invited people who were interested in what *she* had to say.

The later story, that Gertrude said of Ezra Pound that he was a "village explainer . . . excellent if you were a village if not, not," rings true in the context of gender dynamics. By accusing Pound of provincialism (when, with an M.A. in Romance languages, he did know his subject), she faulted him for the very Americanism he claimed to value. Pound, who was from Idaho, talked in what he called "Amurrican," but Stein saw that he was both Anglophile and Francophile and that his ambition was to be thought erudite and, therefore, not particularly American. Again, Pound reminded her of Leo. She saw no need either to listen to him or to educate him.

Art critic George Biddle remembered that, although he did not get along with Gertrude, they parted "not entirely on unfriendly terms" because he stood up to her. He saw her as a person who "sized up people and situations. . . . She might have been a Bethlehem steel magnate, a labor politician, or a Catholic cardinal." In the midst of her litany of praise for Juan Gris, he and his friends began looking through her album of Picasso's early drawings, "playful little pornographic sketches." But she would not relinquish her control of the group—Biddle called the evening Stein's "seance [sic]"—and when she asked him what *he* painted, he replied that he did not think his work would interest her. Then, "Miss Stein broke out in an Old-Testament-prophetic indictment of my attitude toward art and my own limitations. I would never 'understand' or 'realize,' because of my birthplace, my background, my family, my morals, the Quaker, the Puritan in me. . . . We shouted at each other. I argued with her coldly. I think she called me a lawyer." Katherine Anne Porter's experience was similar, and she later wrote bitterly about Gertrude's followers who "made the tactical error of quarreling with her. She enjoyed their discipleship while it lasted, and dismissed them from existence when it ended. . . . It was not that she was opposed to ideas, but that she was not interested in anybody's ideas but her own." Harold Loeb, however, remembered Stein's drilling as being more sympathetic, "a lively cross-examination."

With most visitors, Gertrude was kindly, or at least she listened long enough to know whether she wanted to listen more. She was a devoted friend to Kitty Cannell, whom she had known since Cannell was a schoolgirl in France in 1910, and to Kate Buss, a New England writer whose 1917 *Jevons Block: A Book of Sex Enmity* was a kind of *Spoon River* modernized and gendered. One of Gertrude's best friends, Buss wrote a critical study of Stein's writing—which, unfortunately, remains unpublished. To Buss, Stein wrote intimately about the way her intellect worked, stressing that "there was no threshold between her conscious and unconscious mind." During the summer of 1922, Stein asked Kate to interview Gris for a *Little Review* profile; she wanted everyone to understand how important his painting was. Friendship with Gertrude had to be interactive—if you understood her, and she understood you, then interchanges would be mutually beneficial.

Janet Flanner, arriving in Paris in 1921, learned to play a modest role with both Gertrude and Alice. Calling Gertrude "Miss Stein," unlike most visitors to the rue de Fleurus, Janet usually brought the women flowers, which they loved. A young journalist, she was not ambitious about her creative work and sincerely liked being friends with Gertrude and Alice. Observing the interaction in the salon, she saw how seriously Stein took everything she said about writing; as Flanner recalled later, Gertrude "thought she had no personality aside from her writing." Writing was the self, and the soul, and as she instructed one of the eager young men who seemed never to listen well enough, "You must cut out excrescences. Let nothing else get in but that clear vision which you are alone with. If you have an audience it's not art. If anyone hears you it's no longer pure. Remarks are not literature."

Flanner was particularly good at listening to the way Gertrude instructed people; years later she emphasized the nuances in Stein's expressions. Purposefully avoiding spoken French, Gertrude said that she wanted her ears to remain American and that she had been able to hold on to American locutions because so many around her were speaking French. For Gertrude, American English was the only vehicle for discourse. Flanner recorded Stein's breaking into a conversation with an English duchess with an exclamation: "Great Jehoshaphat," she interrupted the woman, who was talking about her writing, "you've got that all wrong."

During the postwar years, Gertrude and Alice went out of their way, socially, to go to others' homes to meet people who sounded interesting, especially royalty, but their own guest list was much more democratic. Sam Putnam tells the story of young "Annie from Chicago" who trekked to Paris to find Stein after *Geography and Plays* was published in the States. She found a way into the salon and then, after talking with Gertrude about writing, felt so accommodated by Stein's attention that she asked her whether she should lose her virginity. (Stein responded so warmly on a one-on-one basis that she frequently heard personal stories and was asked a number of things that some literary mentors would have found disconcerting.) According to the person to whom Annie told the story, Stein then replied, "To be a virgin is to be a virgin and not to be a virgin is not to be a virgin and not to be a virgin may be to be a virgin." Out of context, such language takes on an air of sophistry, but considering the difficulty of deciding what *virginity* as a concept has meant through history, Stein may have given Annie useful information.

Gertrude was particularly fond of Mina Loy. Formerly the wife of Stephen Haweis, Loy was herself a painter and poet; in 1923 she published

Lunar Baedecker, which included a number of poems that impressed Stein, as had her 1915–17 "Love Songs, or Songs to Joannes," modeled on *Tender Buttons.* Living in New York during the war, Loy had played the lead in Kreymborg's play *Lima Beans* at Provincetown; in 1917 she was featured as a "Modern Woman" in the *New York Sun.* During the 1920s she was a regular visitor at the rue de Fleurus, knowing she was welcomed for her understanding of Stein's work as well as for her beauty; she sometimes brought as guests Robert McAlmon, Kay Boyle, Natalie Barney, and others.

Loy's important essay on Stein, published in two issues of *Transatlantic Review,* clarified much about Gertrude's writing: Loy linked her with Henri Bergson, saying her aim was to depict "Being" by creating the very pulse of duration. Stein's repetition works like "the fractional tones in primitive music or the imperceptible modelling of early Egyptian sculpture," and her "power of evocation gives the same lasting substance to her work that is found in the *Book of Job.*" Written with all the understanding of a fellow poet, Loy's essay was one of the most accurate comments Stein's work received, and Gertrude referred to it often.

For those who found warmth in the rue de Fleurus afternoons, admiring Stein's ability to lead and respond to conversation, any description of those interchanges pales beside memories of immense energy, golden language, and unfeigned sympathy.

Shakespeare in Paris

Sylvia Beach's English-language bookstore, Shakespeare and Company, became the symbol for the literary revolt that was soon to sweep the Western world. Opened November 17, 1919, after Beach's return from Red Cross duty in Serbia, the shop combined an excellent collection of books with decorating reminiscent of Greenwich Village panache: beige sackcloth wall coverings, white wool rugs, and the latest issues of *The New Masses, Poetry, The Little Review, Criterion, The Egoist, New English Review, Dial, The Nation, The New Republic, Chapbook,* and *Playboy,* all displayed on open racks. Window lettering announced that Shakespeare and Company was both a "Lending Library" and a "Bookhop," the latter spelling remaining as a mark of Beach's sense of humor.

The daughter of a Presbyterian minister in Princeton, New Jersey, Sylvia funded the shop with a small inheritance from her mother. Irreplaceable was the aid of her French friend and lover, Adrienne Monnier. Monnier's bookstore at 7, rue de l'Odéon, with its unique lending library, Le Maison des Amis des Livres, sold French-language publications and hosted readings by André Gide, Jules Romains, Jean Schlumberger, Valéry Larbaud, Léon-Paul Fargue, Paul Valéry, and other French writers. With the help of Monnier's circle, Beach's shop would have had some success, but the fact that Paris was flooded with Americans searching for the new and the exotic—especially in English—helped her business immensely.

Early in 1920 Gertrude and Alice were ecstatic when they saw the large signboard, a portrait of Shakespeare, hanging from an iron finger above the shop door in the rue Dupuytren. Meeting Sylvia, they liked her gracious American manner. Commenting that, next to Gertrude, Beach was the most American person she had ever known, Toklas nicknamed her "the flagstaff," a reference to the American flag. She and Gertrude liked Beach's "classical American beauty" and her commonsense approach to her work; most of the time, they also liked her taste in books (that she had two copies of *Tender Buttons* on her shelves endeared her to them). Soon after paying her fifty francs for a year's subscription to the library, Gertrude brought Sylvia an autographed copy of *Three Lives* and some of her portraits. She teased her about being a businesswoman and about the shop's not carrying two of her favorite novels, Gene Stratton Porter's *A Girl of the Limberlost* and *The Trail of the Lonesome Pine.*

Soon Gertrude brought Sylvia a portrait she had written for her to use as publicity. Titled "Rich and Poor in English, Sylvia Beach," it began "Not a country nor a door send them away to sit on the floor. / Cakes. This is not the world. Can you remember. . . ." While Stein did not mention Shakespeare and Company by name, she had learned that to be connected with a successful enterprise did no harm: when Americans in Paris found Sylvia Beach, they would also be reminded of Gertrude Stein.

Personally, Beach became a way for visitors to meet Stein. As Gertrude told Fania Marinoff, in Paris it was sometimes difficult to meet people: "Sorry I said I do not know them. But you know who they are, oh yes, I said, vaguely. Then she mentioned others. Some I knew and some I did not. She could not understand, in New York, she said, if I knew you I would know them. Yes yes I said but not in Paris. Not to know the well known in Paris does not argue yourself unknown, because nobody knows anybody whom they do not know." Beach brought Adrienne Monnier, Stephen Vincent Benét, Paul Rosenfeld, Valéry Larbaud (for whom Gertrude and Alice entertained), Glenway Wescott (whose 1927 novel *The Grandmothers, A Family Portrait* showed Stein's influence), George Antheil, Sherwood Anderson, and others to meet Stein. Anderson was to become a useful connection to other younger American writers.

Gertrude Reinvents Herself

The excitement of the new in Paris gave Gertrude an opportunity she had been waiting for. Picasso's ten-foot-tall mannequins for the production of *Parade* capped the Parisian artists' interest in costume and self-invention; larger-than-life identities had become the norm. With her characteristic love of play, Gertrude focused more and more often on a new identity that came as a surprise to her, as well as to many of her friends: she became the oracle of the literary world. Posing as the wise expatriate Jewish American, approaching fifty, Stein created herself as the great, undiscovered American writer. With an insistence on her Americanism paralleling James Joyce's fidelity to his Irish identity, she drew from the reservoir of interest that the young Americans in Paris produced. It was time for her to emphasize—and to inflate—her American identity.

Sherwood Anderson helped with that imaging. He was a great personal favorite with both Stein and Alice, who described him as having "a winning brusquerie, a mordant wit and an all-inclusive heart—the combination was irresistible." In a 1922 essay, he created the metaphor of Gertrude as bountiful American housewife, making literature as if she were baking "sweet and healthy" bread. Anderson visualized Stein in a great room in Paris crowded with "shining pots and pans . . . innumerable jars of fruits, jellies and preserves." He called her "an American woman of the old sort, one who cares for the handmade goodies and . . . in her great kitchen she is making something with her materials, something sweet to the tongue and fragrant to the nostrils." As he wrote in his journal soon after meeting Gertrude, "The woman is the very symbol of health and strength. She laughs, she smokes cigarettes. She tells stories with an American shrewdness in getting the tang and the kick into the telling." In 1922 part of Stein's reason for self-publishing *Geography and Plays* was Anderson's offer to write an introduction for it.

Anderson's American mom image, while useful, underrepresented Stein's eroticism. Her heavy body style was not without its attraction during the early 1920s (in the States, admiration for the buxom Mae West outran that for svelte Gloria Swanson), and Count Bibesco, Ernest Hemingway, Bravig Imbs, Glenway Wescott, Maurice Grosser, Donald Sutherland, and others spoke often about Stein's sensuality. Bibesco recalled Gertrude's "large liquid eyes, strong facial planes" and described her as "sybilline . . . curve on curl, adorable, her ready laughter rippling with warmth." Hemingway commented to his wife Hadley that Gertrude's breasts must have each weighed ten pounds, and Wescott described the eroticism of Stein's penetrating look into her listeners' faces, calling her "a far more beautiful woman than Jo Davidson or others ever made her out to be. She was handsome, in a modernistic way, and had a delectable voice, mannish but velvety, and a marvelous laugh." A decade later, Sutherland described her "alarming" sexual attraction for him at nineteen: "The second time I met her she came too close and my sexual response was both unequivocal and . . . bewildering."

Stein's privileging of the sensual was a part of her insistence on being a complete person. No crabbed intellectual, Gertrude wanted to be known for her hearty appetites of all kinds. And as with many of the points of origin for her writing, she never identified in print one of the most constant sources for her postwar self—the French novelist George Sand. From the time of Stein's move to Paris in 1903, she had heard stories of the flamboyant, titillating Amandine Aurore Dupin, whose sexual activities were as energetic as her literary ones. Stein could not walk in her beloved Luxembourg Garden without passing the imposing statue of the writer, and Alice insisted regularly that

Stein deserved a similar monument. From the beginning of her writing career, Gertrude (like Edith Wharton) admired Flaubert's *Un Coeur simple,* his story of Félicité, knowing that it had been written for Sand. The bad woman of France, in a country where badness often went unremarked, Sand produced 150 volumes of writing, including many novels, and as many scandals—the most memorable being her sexual liaison with the young Frédéric Chopin. Wearing trousers and smoking in public, Sand made outrage the mode of her existence.

More important for the way Gertrude saw her own life, Sand was a champion of the common people of France, claiming that she drew much of her inspiration—and knowledge of life—from them. In an 1853 letter, Sand wrote, "As you like to hear me relate the tales told by the peasants at our *veillées*—I mean the watch-nights of my youth, when I had time to listen to them,—I shall try to recall the story." Proud of being a Berry peasant, she corrected Balzac's portraits of daily French life. Her aim in fiction was to show the essential commonality of the real.

It was also to study gender. A champion of women's rights, Sand spoke out for women's powers when most people were unaware there was even a cause, though she often identified herself, as a creative person, with the male. (Her 1859 novel, *She and He* [*Elle et lui*], treats a man's inability to believe he might be friends with a woman.)

Sand was less popular with the common reader than with other European and English writers, who revered both her work and what they saw as her masculinity: Flaubert called her "this great man" and sobbed at her funeral. Balzac praised her as having "the main characteristics of a man." Henry James spoke of her "feminine nature and her giving it a new dimension," that of the masculine. At her death, Turgenev said, "What a brave man she was, and what a good woman." Sand cultivated this image by resisting stereotyped feminine roles: she created herself, a product of the imagination. Innovating in both style and theme, she produced influential work—and quickly, sometimes writing a book in a week. Believing in the restorative power of nature, she insisted on tranquillity: "I have spent many an hour of my life watching the grass grow, or contemplating the serenity of great stones in the moonlight. . . . I have identified myself so much with this way of being of tranquil things, called inert, that I have come to share their calm beatitude." Meditative, reverent toward a "grave and beautiful" universe, Sand claimed, "Everything we believe full of importance is so fugitive that we need not even think about it." Her writing was, simply, a part of her nature.

Her stone manor in La Châtre (Nohant)—her retreat from Paris—kept her in touch with her meditative side as well as with the French people. She lived there lavishly, with one of several famous portraits of herself dominating the dining room. From her window she could see a bell tower and the spire of a little church. Eventually, so many Paris visitors came to Nohant that she had to find a refuge from that flood of company as well, but for many years Sand loved her country château and the opportunities for friendship it provided. She saw herself as a friend, and just as one of her pervasive themes was the redefinition of friendship between men and women, so one of her writing styles was the author's voice in conversation with countless and varied friends.

Later in her life, Gertrude was to occupy a manor house in the same part of France as Sand's, and she, too, saw her inspiration as coming from her meditations about nature. She learned to revere the French people, defined herself as male in talent and independence, and saw no reason to write slowly, or with revision, when her aim was to write truly. Although she knew that some aspects of her life shocked people, she never changed direction because of someone else's opinion.

What is most interesting about the Sand-Stein affinity is the way details of their lives dovetail, speaking either to coincidence or to a careful patterning on Gertrude's part. Manuscript evidence suggests that as early as 1911–1912, in *G.M.P.*, she created an echo by naming her fictional persona "Jane Sands," a dangerous woman intent on doing something different with her life, a woman with whom everyone had "finished." The ambivalence of this persona leads to an increasingly esoteric meditation on "a lovely love" sitting in bed, with frequent mention of buds, cows, "a wedding glance," and "leaves of hair." When Gertrude first visited Kahnweiler, he lived on the rue George-Sand, and in 1913 she sent Harry Phelan Gibb "two little leaves from the garden of G. Sand and Chopin."

These similarities with Sand may provide one explanation for Alice Toklas's coolness to some of the young men who visited Stein. In order to complete the George Sand legend, Gertrude would at some point have needed to play a heterosexual role. During the 1920s likely choices for the part of a young male lover like Frédéric Chopin were both the charming Spaniard Juan Gris, whose considerable physical attraction was enhanced by his illness, and the vigorous—and talented—young American writer Ernest Hemingway.

Legends of
Hemingway and Others

By 1922 Gertrude and Alice had settled in to a less frantic stage of postwar life. They had each received the Médaille de la reconnaissance française from the French government for service in World War I (Alice's carried the greater distinction, the phrase "without respite"), and their social life buoyed them through the more restless periods of Gertrude's writing. (She wrote play after play, sure that someone would produce her work. But her plays, like her fiction, found few markets.) Among their new visitors were Jean Cocteau; Harold Loeb, a *Broom* editor who was descended from New York Loebs and Guggenheims; Man Ray, the surrealist photographer; Djuna Barnes, already famed for her wit; Ford Madox Ford, his companion Stella Bowen, and their young daughter, Julie; and Robert Coates and other American fiction writers.

Ever watchful of Mildred Aldrich's well-being, Alice and Gertrude nominated her for the Legion of Honor, but a civilian's receiving that award was unlikely; they also worried about her finances. And when they worried too much about anything, Gertrude and Alice went window-shopping. Meandering through the streets of the elite shopping areas of Paris, Gertrude admired the window decorations, especially the large movable figures in the high-fashion shops. The more practical Alice was interested in styles that she might copy in her own dressmaking and in hats and their trimmings. She bought only expensive hats and sometimes chose to remodel those she already owned. A friend recalled that Alice's hats "were all in perfect condition, kept in their original pretty boxes from the most famous milliners. She had superb examples of inlaid feather work by Paul Poiret, huge black-and-gold birds of paradise, and tall tufts of aigrettes and ospreys."

The two also searched for new treasures to enrich the rue de Fleurus apartment. Each table there was crowded with oddities—miniature furniture and silver objects (usually of Alice's choosing), "frail Chinese terracotta pottery," strange objets d'art that pleased Gertrude, including the "junk" that she and Picasso took from their pockets and arranged on whatever surface would accommodate it. The pace of window-shopping, too, suited her: seldom in a hurry, Gertrude found something to look at, or to listen to, wherever she was. The placing of a crimson scarf against an azure jacket, the design of a window filled with shades of gold and brown, the group of Spanish porcelain saints she told Alice she didn't need to buy because she had it "inside"—the two women took these sights home and savored them. They would speak years later about a scene, or a hat, or an elegantly dressed woman glimpsed during these sorties. This kind of memory was part of the dialogue that Sylvia Beach called double-voicedness: "Her [Gertrude's] remarks and those of Alice, which rounded them out, were inseparable. Obviously they saw things from the same angle, as people do when they are perfectly congenial."

After several hours of window-shopping, though Alice would first insist on going into the Bon Marché (with Gertrude waiting outside), they had dessert: chocolate cake at Rumpelmayer's on the rue de Rivoli or a brandy-flavored torte at a corner pastry shop, rich desserts that were blatantly bad for them. They loved eating sinful foods, especially since Alice had put the household on a salt-free diet after Gertrude's abdominal tumor had been diagnosed. Before and during the Great War, Gertrude's weight had increased steadily a few pounds each year. The problem was not lack of exercise—she walked eight or ten miles a day—but consistent overeating.

Accompanying her weight gain was troublesome indigestion and colitis, and it was after their postwar return to Paris that Gertrude finally saw a physician. Though she never wrote about the diagnosis of abdominal tumor, a close friend reported: "Her doctor told her she could either keep it or have it out." Hoping to avoid surgery, she reduced; by the early 1920s she ate comparatively little. The surgery she did have in 1922 was for the excision of a tumor in her left breast. The operation and convalescence took a month, but the effects of the surgery were long-lasting. Fearful of cancer, the disease from which her mother had died, Gertrude insisted that they vacation in the country at least part of every year. She also demanded even more of Alice's attention.

In Paris the two continued their hunt to find publishers for Gertrude's work. To that end Stein corresponded with "Miss Ellen Sedgwick," the editor of *The Atlantic Monthly* (who turned out to be Mr. Ellery Sedgwick), but she could not convince him—as she had the editors of *Life, Vanity Fair, The Little Review,* and *Broom*—that her writing would interest American readers. Through her friend Kate Buss, she negotiated with Edmund Brown of Four Seas Press in Boston to publish a collection of portraits and plays: printing *Geography and Plays* would cost her twenty-five hundred dollars. Gertrude wrote encouragingly to Brown, "I have a large selling public," mentioning as possible reviewers not only Anderson but H. G. Wells, Israel Zangwill, Logan Pearsall Smith, Roger Fry, and, in Paris, "Jean Cocteau and Waldemar George of L'Amour de L'Art, Valerie Larbaud etc." In April and July of 1922 Alice and she read galleys and page proof; in May she sent Brown the latest of her Man Ray photos (this one occasioning a falling-out because the photographer wanted payment instead of the usual barter); and in September she redesigned the book cover Brown had sketched for her. At forty-eight, Gertrude was complacent about her choices in life—she loved Alice, she loved their rue de Fleurus life, and she no longer missed Leo (she had recently written "She Bowed to Her Brother" after a chance encounter with him near the church of Saint-Germain-des-Prés). She was grateful for her recovery from surgery and thought the scar on her breast was growing less noticeable with time. But she remained frustrated that fame of the kind experienced by James Joyce and now Jean Cocteau still eluded her.

Enter the Hemingways

Early in 1922 Ernest Hemingway sent Gertrude his letter of introduction from Sherwood Anderson, asking whether he and his wife, Hadley, might call. To Stein's prompt response inviting them to tea, Hadley wrote cordially that Sherwood had told them many nice things. Arriving in Paris a few weeks earlier, Hemingway had written Anderson, "In a couple of days we'll be settled and then I'll send out the letters of introduction like launching a flock of ships." Through the letters, Hadley and he met Sylvia Beach, Ezra Pound, James Joyce, Matthew Josephson, and Alfred Kreymborg; by being friendly in cafés, Hemingway also met Blaise Cendrars, the poet visible in 1920s theater, and other French writers, as well as Leo Stein, Morrill Cody, and a sea of other would-be artists. And by reading Apollinaire, Gide, Wilde, and Stein at Shakespeare and Company, the couple was beginning to understand literary Paris.

They were clearly impressed with the chance to meet Gertrude. In addition to Anderson's praise of her and the near-reverence with which she was held among some café crowds, Hemingway saw the power she had in the art world. As one American observed, after the war Gertrude "became an unofficial pontiff and she could make or mar an exhibit with little more than a movement of her thumb." The always ambitious Hemingway saw her as a means into the avant-garde art world as well as the literary one. He trusted his boyish good looks to make a favorable initial impression and then— charming her from the start—defined his role in their friendship as that of listener. On March 9 he wrote Anderson, "Gertrude Stein and me are just like brothers and we see a lot of her." Alice and she took the Hemingways along on their monthly visit to Mildred Aldrich, where they picnicked for the day. Mildred was also enthusiastic about the deferential, "extraordinarily good looking" American.

From late March into June Hemingway traveled in Italy and Switzerland, covering the world economic conference for the *Toronto Star,* but during the summer he and Hadley resumed their intimacy with Gertrude and Alice. They grew to appreciate the women's joy in their paintings and to see how serious Gertrude was about her writing. When she offered to read Ernest's work—sitting on the bed in the Hemingways' small apartment—he was ecstatic. True to her method, she gave him little specific criticism but praised his "direct" poems and worried that the beginning of his fiction was prolix ("There is a great deal of description in this . . . not particularly good description. Begin over again and concentrate"). She liked all his stories except "Up in Michigan." Antagonized by the blatant pun of the title, she warned him that writing "inaccrochable" fiction was pointless. Just as a shocking painting could never be hung, this seduction story could not be published. What she failed to tell him, though she probably thought he could figure it out from reading her work, was that writing could be filled with sexuality, so long as it was disguised.

Pleased with what he had written, Gertrude urged Hemingway to give up journalism. Not only did he spend much of his time covering stories for the Toronto paper, but such reporting entailed extensive travel. If he were going to learn to write from the center of his being, he would need permanence—a stable place, tranquil surroundings. To that end Gertrude urged him to buy good paintings, explaining that most expatriates' money went into women's clothing, which had a short life. If he could encourage Hadley to dress comfortably rather than fashionably, as Alice and she did, the Hemingways might then be able to make such purchases.

More important than Gertrude's suggestions for living, however, were her prolegomena about the way a writer's work had to come from, and also absorb, the best part of the psyche. Hemingway could see that Alice arranged the days to support Gertrude's brief period of writing. Her work, then, could flow unimpeded because her mind was not clouded with trivia. That Hemingway began to understand Stein's process of good writing is clear from a summer letter: "I've been working hard and have two things done. I've thought a lot about the things you said about working and am starting that way at the beginning. If you think of anything else I wish you'd write it to me. Am working hard about creating and keeping my mind going about it all the time. Mind seems to be working better." Comparisons between his early newspaper columns and his stories from 1922 and 1923 show dramatic changes.

During the summer of 1922 Gertrude varied her routine by sitting for sculptor Jo Davidson and writing a portrait of him in turn. She continued proselytizing for her own importance in literature even as she wondered at the praise both Joyce's *Ulysses* and Eliot's *The Waste Land* were garnering. (As she said of the latter, "The trouble with Tom Eliot is that he tries too hard to be British. That absurd umbrella he totes about—and why not face the fact that splitting an infinitive is American?") For all their love of meeting new people, however, Gertrude and Alice felt that Paris was wearing thin, and in August they drove south to help their sculptor friend Janet Scudder find a house near St. Rémy in the part of France they thought most beautiful, "between Avignon and Aix-en-Province, Orange and the sea." Locating a good hotel for themselves, the two stayed on through the autumn and into winter; Gertrude later said that the peace made her feel as if she had finally recovered from both the stresses of war and worries about her health.

That fall Hemingway covered the peace conference in Germany, Lausanne, Bulgaria, and Constantinople. He complained to Hadley, "I'm so sick of this—it is so hard. Everybody else has two men or an assistant, and they expect me to cover everything by myself—and all for one of Masons little baby kike salaries." (Disillusioned with reporting, Hemingway wrote his father that he had had "a belly full of travelling . . . nearly 10,000 miles by R.R. this past year. Been to Italy 3 times. Back and forth Switzerland-Paris 6 . . . Constantinople-Germany-Burgundy-The Vendee [sic].") In November Hadley thanked "Miss Stien and Miss Toclaz" (she sometimes spelled the name *Tocraz*) for their gift of an "ambrosiac melon," saying that she and Ernest were leaving for Switzerland and hoped to spend January in Italy.

In February 1923 Gertrude and Alice returned to Paris, excited to find copies of the new book, *Geography and Plays,* and the issue of *Vanity Fair* with the photo of Davidson's sculpture of Stein and Stein's portrait of the sculptor. They were ready to resume a busy social life, enhanced now by Mike's acquisition of his first car, a Packard. So long as Leo and Nina were not in Paris, the women were friendly with Mike, Sally, and Gabrielle, and because the Cones—along with relatives—visited Paris regularly, there were many family social occasions. In addition, Mike and Sally were successful in selling pieces from Gertrude's collection to the Cones, who were willing to pay top dollar.

Friends once more with Picasso, Gertrude wrote "If I Told Him. A Completed Portrait of Picasso." In the summer of 1923 the two visited him and his family (Olga, their young son Paolo—for whom Gertrude, as his godmother, was writing her *Birthday Book*—and Picasso's mother, Señora Maria Ruiz) at Antibes on the Côte d'Azur; there they met Gerald and Sarah Murphy, friends of Picasso's. Gertrude and Alice remembered their conversations with Picasso's mother, who spoke only Spanish, about her son's beauty when he was younger; Murphy recalled the dynamic between Gertrude and Picasso, saying that they "were phenomenal together. . . . Each stimulated the other to such an extent that everyone felt recharged witnessing it." (Just before the visit, Gertrude had written Picasso about the possibility of trading his portrait of her for a painting of his that she had seen at the Rosenberg gallery. "The Murphys were shocked and said so. 'Yes,' Picasso said, 'but I love her so much!'")

It was during 1923 that Gertrude gave Hemingway "the run of the studio": she told him that when they were out, he should have a drink and wait for them. Gertrude and he took long walks and discussed writing and art, with her telling stories about Picasso, Rousseau, Braque, Matisse, and other painters; Hemingway recalled that her conversation was "more about them as people than as painters." As part of his indoctrination into becoming a writer, Hemingway (under orders from both Gertrude and Leo Stein, a café friend of his) read Jane Austen—for her conversation. By reading aloud the first chapter of *Pride and Prejudice,* he learned the same thing he did from reading Gertrude's *The Making of Americans*—that conversation written to be read is not the same as what one hears. A friend quoted Hemingway as saying, "Stein made me see that written conversation is primarily for the eye. It is something that has to be contrived in its own right. . . . Mostly you've got to make out a written conversation so that it will seem natural in the imagination of your reader without benefit of his sense of hearing."

Although he had been doing some work that satisfied him, Hemingway had had a frustrating winter and spring. In January Hadley had packed all his writing—including carbon copies—to bring to him in Austria. When her suitcase was stolen, nothing survived from his first years in Paris but a few stories out in the mail. Hemingway made no secret of his agony over this loss. A few weeks later he was again unhappy because Hadley was pregnant; at the close of a long visit to the rue de Fleurus, he announced sadly to Gertrude that he was too young to be a father. (Although she feigned sympathy, she later told Hadley about his comment—which she thought was "hilarious.") Resentful about the impending changes in his lifestyle, Hemingway took two trips to Spain. On one, he "lived in a bull fighters [sic] pension . . . and then travelled all over the country with a crew of toreros." On the second, with Hadley, he took in "the big Feria at Pamplona." After seeing these twenty bullfights, Hemingway claimed to be an expert and announced that the sport was "a great tragedy—and the most beautiful thing I've ever seen." Far from a brutal pastime, he said, bullfighting "takes more guts and skill and guts again than anything possibly could."

The range of emotions Hemingway experienced during this year contributed to the strength of the fiction he was writing using the methods Gertrude urged him to try. As he learned to go inside himself, to find a key image or scene to convey the feeling that drove the narrative, Hemingway wrote some of his best stories. The purity of the distillation of his emotions into words pleased Gertrude, and she continued to encourage him. But unlike Pound, who gave him high praise, Gertrude played the role of hard-to-please teacher. Janet Flanner remembered her being very critical of Hemingway, and another friend recalled a day when he was leaving the salon and Gertrude kidded him by saying: "I've been trying to persuade Hem to omit that fishing episode he's used twice already, but he maintains that he has no imagination and must use what happened to him." As Hemingway left, Alice interjected, "And what happens to his friends. Well, so far, Lovey, he's kept you out of it." Stein's reply was not complacent: "Oh, I won't escape. I'm not deluding myself. . . . But if only Hem would give up that show-off soldiering, that bogus bull fighting, the lowdown on his friends and forget that phoney grace under pressure and just be himself, he'd turn out a real book."

Gertrude believed in Hemingway's talent, and she was also attracted to him. But Alice, who never hid her animosity toward the young American, was becoming more overt about her dislike. To avoid conflicts with Alice,

Gertrude often saw Hemingway in the Luxembourg Garden rather than at home; some evenings they met at the Brasserie Lipp, where they ate the heavy German food and discussed religion. A friend recalled that Hemingway was fascinated with Catholicism as he had observed it in Spain and impressed with the bullfighters' reverence for it. "Deeply interested in the problem of redemption," Hemingway was searching for what his friend called "a theory of grace."

Problems with Hemingway

On August 17, 1923, the Hemingways sailed for Canada so that their child could be born closer to home. John Hadley Nicanor Hemingway (Bumby) arrived October 11, with Hemingway absent from the birth because he was traveling for the *Toronto Star*. In late November Hadley wrote Gertrude about their "healthy and happy and really dreadfully handsome" son, who is also "a tremendous smiler." She lamented the distance between Paris and Toronto and promised that the family would return to France in January, saying "You've no idea how we miss you two."

In November Gertrude sent Hemingway her review of his *Three Stories and Ten Poems* from the Paris edition of the *Chicago Tribune* and in December a copy of her portrait "He and They, Hemingway" from the little magazine *Ex Libris*. While Stein had meant her review to be positive, she had unfortunately used the word *turgid* to describe his fiction (she preferred his poetry). When Hemingway replied, he assured her that he would "try not to be turgid," saying that he had "some good stories to write." He also showed his nasty side, mentioning: "They [readers in the States] are turning on you and Sherwood both; the young critical guys and their public. I can feel it in the papers etc." Throwing down a seemingly innocent gauntlet, Hemingway was playing his game of exercising power, keeping people beholden to him: his letter suggested further that, because Pound had asked him to work with Ford Madox Ford on the new *Transatlantic Review,* he might be able to shore up the older writers' reputations. Perhaps he did not know that *Geography and Plays* had been widely reviewed, receiving high praise from Edith Sitwell, Ben Hecht, and Van Vechten as well as more moderate reactions from Kenneth Burke in *Dial* and Edmund Wilson in *Vanity Fair.*

Hemingway quit the *Toronto Star* on December 31; by then Hadley, Bumby, and he were back in Paris, reconciled to living on Hadley's trust income until his writing brought in money or he began receiving a salary from Ford Madox Ford. When his poems had appeared in Harriet Monroe's *Poetry,* Hemingway had been described as "a young Chicago poet now abroad," but now his identity had changed to fiction writer. The publication of a single story in *The Little Review* was now augmented with monthly contributions to *Transatlantic Review,* beginning with the April 1924 issue, in which "Indian Camp" (titled "Work in Progress") appeared. For much of 1924 the

"Chroniques" section of the journal featured his brief items about artists, writers, bullfighters, and boxers. In December "The Doctor and the Doctor's Wife" appeared. But other than these, Hemingway in 1924 had no publications besides a few poems published in the German *Querschnitt,* one other story in *The Little Review,* and *in our time,* the pamphlet of prose sketches. He made very little money from his writing. Rather, the satisfaction he found in his new life as writer and editor stemmed from wielding power; in his role at *Transatlantic Review,* he wrote Gertrude that they would use excerpts from *The Making of Americans* at a rate of thirty francs a page.

Hemingway may also have seen his connection with *Transatlantic Review* as a way to counter the influence on Gertrude of Harold Loeb, the editor of *Broom* (where Stein's "If You Had 3 Husbands" had appeared). Hemingway observed with jealousy Gertrude's friendship with Loeb, especially the recent portrait she had written of him; he was also watchful of her affection for Jane Heap, coeditor with Margaret Anderson of *The Little Review.* Heap was both a close personal friend and the agent for Gertrude's work. Her obvious lesbianism and cross-dressing, like that of Romaine Brooks, marked a new trend toward visible sexual markers at the rue de Fleurus, and Ernest—like his close friend Pound—was uncomfortable. For Hemingway, being a self-confident male meant being in charge—sexually, physically, emotionally; he often talked about his boxing and skiing. Elizabeth Anderson—when Sherwood and she visited Paris—ridiculed his poses. She described Hemingway's "bouncing into the room, beating his chest and loudly boasting: 'I can walk like an Olympic marathoner. I just walked all the way over here—fifteen blocks—and I'm not a bit tired.'" Elizabeth had just walked twenty blocks, and she wasn't winded either.

Another way of ingratiating himself with Gertrude was asking her and Alice to be Bumby's godmothers. While the Hemingways may have honestly thought the women's support would be helpful to their baby, there was an element of opportunism in the invitation: it suggested Ernest's jealousy of Picasso, whose young son was already Gertrude's godson. On March 16, 1924, with Chink Dorman-Smith as godfather and Alice and Gertrude as godmothers, the youngest Hemingway was baptized at the Episcopalian chapel of St. Luke's in the Luxembourg Garden. On Bumby's six-month day (April 10), they all celebrated again. Although lukewarm about her role, Alice knit the child a sweater and a chair cover, and Gertrude brought a silver cup and rubber animals for his bath.

Hemingway was satisfied that he had made Gertrude happy by involving her in his family and by helping to publish her writing. For her part, however, she had more to do in life than oversee the Hemingways; as she wrote a friend, the spring had been "very hectic" because of relatives visiting (her nephew Allan had married in February) and "young admirers" dropping in. Of the two groups, she said, she preferred the latter. Hemingway knew he had competition, and he vowed to earn her praise someday by improving his writing. His August letters to her in Belley, which she called the "enchanted" valley, showed his pride in his new long story, "Big Two-Hearted River": "I'm trying to do the country like Cézanne and having a hell of a time and sometime getting it a little bit. It is about 100 pages long and nothing happens and the country is swell, I made it all up, so I see it all and part of it comes out the way it ought to . . . but isn't writing a hard job though?" He praised her tutelage: "It used to be easy before I met you. I certainly was bad, gosh. I'm awfully bad now but it's a different kind of bad."

In other of his August letters, showing his tendency to spread tales, Hemingway rehearsed his version of what was wrong with Ford's *Transatlantic Review*. Originally using his own capital for the journal, Ford soon had to find patrons, and the resulting partnership meant the end of the short-lived magazine. While Hemingway played the innocent bystander, attributing all kinds of misbehavior to Ford and those who bought stock, his version of the muddle didn't fool Gertrude: she was one of the stockholders. She knew that if the journal folded, she would lose her outlet for *The Making of Americans* and her monthly payment. Always cognizant of finances, she wrote: "That little check comes in handy, anything comes in handy." She also reminded him, kindly, to "tell Hadley and Goddy [her nickname for her godson] that we speak of them all the time."

Seeing Hemingway's manipulative comments in the wider context of the Paris literary world, Gertrude was happy to do what she could for him, but she also remained friends with Ford and Stella Bowen, continuing her visits to their afternoons and Christmas parties for the young children of the quarter and inviting Bowen to "drop in after dinner." Stella recalled that the three women "would sit beneath the Picassos and the rest of the collection and discuss methods of dealing with one's concierge, or where to buy linen for sheets, or how to enjoy French provincial life." Gertrude saw no need to choose between Ford and Hemingway.

Financial worries had become a permanent part of life at the rue de Fleurus. Even as the exchange rate benefited Americans, prices rose. Making ends meet was difficult, but for Gertrude and Alice, the greatest worry was Mildred. Now in failing health, she had recently lost the legacy that had provided most of her support. To counter that deficit, Gertrude and Alice, with Janet Scudder and other friends, established a fund of anonymous donations (Etta Cone contributed one hundred dollars, Howard Gans, fifty dollars).

Besides asking for help for Mildred, Gertrude wrote Etta about buying the manuscript of *Three Lives:*

> It seems that the latest passion of the art collectors in America is the buying of manuscripts ever since Quinn [John] made such a success with Conrad and *Ulysses* ms. . . . Some one has suggested my selling the manuscript of Three Lives for a thousand dollars, I don't suppose that you want to pay any such price for a manu-

script but since you had a connection with that manuscript I want to tell you about it before I consider doing anything. I think it's kind of foolish.

As Gertrude expected, Etta did not buy the manuscript: she claimed heavy expenses for the year and said she was saving for a Renoir. But Etta Cone's hurt feelings over being asked to buy "her" typescript lasted the rest of her life.

Although her writing was still not making money, Gertrude knew that she was Paris's most controversial American writer. What she wanted, however, was to be a best-selling, and socially elite, American writer. She wanted the acclaim of that wealthy expatriate Edith Wharton, who lived just a few miles from her on the rue de Varenne. Consequently, when she and Alice were invited to a reception for T. S. Eliot, who moved in some of the same circles as Wharton, they were eager to go. A few days before, as Alice was busily making a gown, Lady Rothermere (Eliot's sponsor for *The Criterion*) brought Eliot to them. He asked Gertrude for her most recent work. After he left, she told Alice to forget about the dress because there was now no need to go to the party. A whimsical Gertrude incorporated the date of the visit in the title of her portrait of the poet, "A Description of the Fifteenth of November. A Portrait of T. S. Eliot," so that there would be no question as to its currency (unfortunately, Eliot did not publish the piece until January 1926).

Avery Hopwood brought California novelist Gertrude Atherton to meet his other favorite Gertrude, and other prewar visitors reappeared, usually with new people in tow. The salon was once more becoming an industry, and while Gertrude saw making good literary contacts as leading to success and celebrity, what Alice saw was the expense, and the time, the visitors cost her. Depressed over the recent death of her father, whom she had not seen for more than fifteen years, Alice had become embroiled in a legal battle with her brother over the estate: it was not easy for her to accept being alienated from her only sibling.

During 1924 Gertrude's hopes for advances died as both Knopf and Liveright rejected *The Making of Americans,* but the appearance of excerpts in *Transatlantic Review* had created interest. Later in the year, when Robert McAlmon offered to do the book as part of his Three Mountains Press series, Gertrude accepted readily. She may even have puffed the amount of attention she thought the book would receive, just as she had exaggerated possible reviewers for *Geography and Plays,* but her point was that there was an audience, though small, for her work, and she would use whatever means she could to take advantage of that interest.

Five hundred copies of *The Making of Americans* appeared in 1925, copublished by McAlmon's Contact Editions and Three Mountains Press. Because sales were small, McAlmon's recriminations were vociferous. Before it was obvious that the book would not sell, Hemingway blamed McAlmon's drinking for the problems. "It's hard to see your editor throw up your royalties," he said on one occasion. In the eventual struggle over who owned the remaining unbound pages, Stein almost succeeded in selling the book to Charles and Albert Boni, but the deal fell through. Her friendship with the volatile McAlmon was over, but as a result of the novel's availability, Gertrude's name began appearing everywhere—and made her a more of a threat to Hemingway's own burgeoning reputation.

Hemingway's chief motive throughout his life was to make himself into a successful writer—no matter what the cost. When critic Edmund Wilson, in a 1924 review of Hemingway's early work, linked him with both Stein and Anderson, he planted the seed of rebellion in Hemingway, who would not accept being called anyone's pupil. It was only another year before he wrote the scurrilous *The Torrents of Spring,* a parody of both Anderson's novel *Dark Laughter* and Gertrude's writing. While Hadley and most of his friends told him that he should not publish this two-week effort because it would hurt Anderson and Stein terribly, Hemingway insisted that *Torrents* was good writing. As Hadley watched her husband's judgment disintegrate, she wondered whether his malice was new or had only been well disguised. She continued to take Bumby to visit Gertrude and Alice, but there was a tense undercurrent to the friendship.

Ernest, however, went on bringing Americans to Gertrude's salon; the connection was eminently useful to him as he stormed the citadel of literary acceptance. With him came John Dos Passos, Archibald and Ada MacLeish, Donald Ogden Stewart, Nathan Asch, Ernest Walsh, Evan Shipman, and F. Scott Fitzgerald, whose earlier books Gertrude admired because they captured the spirit of American youth. Predictably, Hemingway resented the achievement of Fitzgerald's 1925 *The Great Gatsby,* and he became even more jealous when he saw how much Gertrude liked Fitzgerald. She was attracted by his modesty, his handsomeness, and his talent, and he responded—with some disbelief—to her praise of his work.

During the mid-1920s Stein established herself in a great many new relationships with protégés. But as she turned fifty and saw that, despite all her contacts with writers, publishing remained illusive, even *her* confidence ebbed, and she resumed her interest in painters. If Hemingway thought he was the chief attraction in the salon, he was wrong: Gertrude paid as much attention to her friendship with the young Russian Pavlik Tchelitchew, whose exuberant laughter—like his long yellow gloves—seemed freshly innocent. She also held court for Bébé Berard, Kristians Tonny, and musician Allen Tanner, as well as Bravig Imbs, Böske and George Antheil, Eugene Berman, Pierre Charbonnier, Elliot Paul, and the handsome René Crevel. (Crevel, a leading surrealist known for his ability to go into trances, was a favorite with both women.) Although Gertrude was never officially a surrealist, she knew of their manifesto and their experiments and was the only woman (with sixteen men) to have signed the verticalism manifesto in *transition* 21.

Another stream of American visitors to the salon came recommended by Carl Van Vechten—Blanche Knopf, singer Nora Holt, novelist Nella Larsen, and, in the fall of 1925, Paul and Essie Robeson. Gertrude's friendship with Paul was immediate, and she and Toklas entertained for the talented black Americans. Gertrude later wrote Van Vechten that they both liked "niggers" not because of primitivism but "because they have a narrow but a very long civilisation behind them. . . . Their sophistication is complete and so beautifully finished and it is the only one that can resist the United States of America." Also in 1925 Elmer Harden, a long-time Massachusetts friend, brought poet Edith Sitwell to the salon, and the meeting of the two wildly experimental women writers was a success. Sitwell's *Facade*, an operetta with lines spoken through megaphones, had made headlines since its first performance in 1922, and her recent praise of Stein in journals and in her book *Poetry and Criticism* had already endeared her to Gertrude, who never forgot a favorable comment. As friendship with Sitwell broadened to include her brothers and others of their circle and the possibility of Gertrude's lecturing in England was often mentioned, Hemingway felt abandoned.

Angry over Gertrude's fascination with the British and resentful that her friendship toward him was cooling, Hemingway one evening came drunk to the rue de Fleurus. It was almost as if he were delivering a challenge: if Gertrude and Alice were so class-conscious and thought of themselves as superior, let them see what their young American friend was really like. Another visitor to the salon described the scene: "The door opened and Hemingway reeled in, accompanied by two buddies also the worse for drink. 'Hi, Gertie,' he bellowed. 'Ran into a couple of your fans at the Dôme who wouldn't believe I was a friend of yours so I brought them over to prove it.'" Stein's reply, according to the observer, was, "I'm not at home to anyone in your condition and don't call me Gertie. Now get out and what's more, stay out!'"

The sulking Hemingway did not return, but he did frequently walk in the Luxembourg Garden. Happy that he was in disfavor, Alice urged Gertrude not to allow him back. In several weeks, however, admitting her "weakness" for him, Stein appeared with him in tow, and the friendship resumed. The young author knew that he needed Gertrude's help as he rewrote the first draft of his Pamplona novel, *The Sun Also Rises*, which he had finished in September. On their autumn walks, they discussed the Jewish character Robert Cohn and the dialogue in what would be key scenes of the novel. It was at this point, however, that Gertrude let him know that she thought him ninety percent Rotarian and agreed with Alice that, while he seemed to be modern, he did smell of the museums. Years later, Alice explained her objection to Hemingway on the grounds that—unlike Picasso,

Gris, or Fitzgerald—he was never a serious artist: "Neither reading nor writing is a natural inevitable necessity for him."

Sometime later, Hemingway was waiting downstairs at the rue de Fleurus when an argument between the women exploded in the bedroom, and he heard the "terrible things" Toklas said "and Gertrude's pleading." Returning home, he told Hadley that he had never heard such language and that he could never have anything more to do with the women. Whether he was truly shocked, or whether he could not bear having Gertrude reduced to pleading with a woman he so disliked, or whether Alice's tirade included him and his relationship with Gertrude, Hemingway chose to use this event to distance himself from the two. When Hadley next took Bumby to call, she was turned away by the maid. Terribly hurt, Hadley accepted the fact that the two women, realizing what Hemingway had heard, also felt that there was no way to save the friendship. The actual scene, however, with the words Hemingway claimed to have abhorred, is lost to history.

Family Matters

Mike and Sally's energies during the summer of 1924 were devoted to their plans for designing and building a house. Intrigued with Marcel Duchamp's model for a cement house, Mike searched art exhibits for the new. Then he and Gabrielle de Monzie (for the families were building the home together) saw some work by Le Corbusier (Charles-Edouard Jeanneret). The William Cooks, following the lead of sculptor Jacques Lipchitz, had already hired the innovative young Swiss architect to design their home.

Earlier in 1924 Mike dealt with other family needs. During and after Allan's marriage to Yvonne Daunt, an Australian ballerina with the Paris Opéra, Mike handled an onslaught of American visitors, substantial work helping the Cones buy art for their collection, and—later in the year—the news of the death of his sister Bertha. Mike conveyed the news, without detail and without much sense of loss, to both Leo and Gertrude. He had earlier written his sister that Bertha's daughter (Gertrude's namesake) was engaged, giving her the Raffels' Baltimore address; later he wrote that Daniel Raffel, Bertha's oldest son, had married a Russian teacher, whom he described as "the Ruth Elkins type of Jewish girl." His notes suggested that Gertrude and Bertha were no closer than they had been twenty years earlier.

As Mike saw his immediate family diminish, he began to wonder again what would become of Leo and Gertrude when he could no longer file their taxes, suggest investments, and insure and sell their paintings. While Gertrude took much of his time, it was Leo's unpredictability that worried him. Had Mike seen Leo's 1925 letter to Nina saying that he had invested ten thousand dollars of principal in a stock market deal his American friend Ned Bruce had told him about, he would have been even more worried (in Leo's words, "Michael's hair would stand on end if he knew"). In contrast to the plethora of family duties Mike shouldered, planning the house with Le Corbusier was sheer pleasure.

A painter himself, Le Corbusier had come to Paris in 1916–17 and joined Léger, Duchamp, Delaunay, Metzinger, and Gris in their efforts to create "the cult of the machine." When he began working in architecture, he located "type forms" that would allow structures—what he called "machines for living"—to use urban space and contemporary materials. After publishing *Towards a New Architecture* in 1923, he designed Jacques Lipchitz's modest house and studio. In the cubelike Cook house, he placed the living areas and kitchen on the second floor, with bedrooms below, to create space full of light and wonderful views of the bois de Boulogne.

After the Steins and Gabrielle had decided to use him as their architect, the long process of design began. Working with his cousin, Pierre Jeanneret—their office a line of drawing tables in a corridor of an old convent—he first decided that the land the Steins had purchased was not suitable for the structure he called "une maison un palais" ("a house, a palace"). He insisted they find a more suitable location, so they bought a long strip of land on the outskirts of Garches, and plans for Les Terrasses began. The house started as a cubed and flat-roofed structure topped with a roof terrace, but before it was completed, it had sprung symmetrical wings, a south facade of cantilevered terraces, and "an asymmetrical sequence of terraces and open-air rooms." By early 1927 the design had returned to a clean block shape that kept the modernist asymmetry in its open floor plan, ribbon windows, floors cantilevered out from interior exposed posts, and countless terraces.

When the Stein/de Monzie house was completed in 1928, it was a showplace of modern design. Costing close to one million francs, featured in the world press (to both praise and ridicule), it became a central example of the International Style. In 1932 photographs of it—with Walter Gropius's Bauhaus buildings and Mies van der Rohe's Barcelona Pavilion—were exhibited in the Museum of Modern Art. Involved in every detail of the house, Mike visited the site every day. But the Steins and Le Corbusier finally disagreed over furnishings, and the Steins brought with them their old Italian Renaissance pieces rather than using Le Corbusier's "machines for sitting in."

Leo, too, was fascinated with the design process and often lived in his Paris apartment at 42, avenue Parc-Monsouris while the house was being built; in fact, he and Nina spent the winters of both 1926–27 and 1927–28 in Paris, at least partly so they could be involved in the project. Leo was working hard on the essays that would make up most of his 1927 book, *The ABC of Aesthetics,* and Paris—with its galleries as well as its people—provided a better setting for that exploration.

Contrary to the way Gertrude represented his role—or the lack of it—once their lives divided, he was a visible, and respected, part of the Paris scene, and such younger writers as Harold Loeb, Hemingway, Marsden Hartley, John Glassco, Morrill Cody, Robert McAlmon, Bravig Imbs, and Janet Flanner found him a source of information of all kinds. Loeb, who met Leo through Hutch Hapgood, kept up a long correspondence with him about *Broom,* partly because Stein was willing to comment on each selection published in the journal, opinions Loeb found valuable. He recalled talking in cafés with Stein, portrait painter Jerry Bloom, and Hutch Hapgood, being surprised at their candor and humor. "Despite my disapproval of their generation on intellectual grounds, I found the company of my seniors agreeable. They seemed to have a gentleness and a tolerance that the younger man had not yet acquired." John Glassco described a comic interchange between Leo and Adolf Dehn, when the "tall, thin, slow-moving man dressed in black" presented Dehn with a photograph of a long-eared spaniel, saying it reminded him of Dehn's wife.

When Robert McAlmon recalled those years in Paris and Florence, he described Leo as a man obsessed with the ways "his sensibility and his creative strain" differed from Gertrude's, as if she were clearly the more famous of the pair. Unfortunately, when Janet Flanner wrote about Leo's forthcoming book in her *New Yorker* column, she reinforced the rivalry: "Leo Stein, Gertrude Stein's brother, is finishing a book called Aesthetic Responses, and she, after the intellectual success of her The Making of Americans, is at work on Portraits and Prayers. A new verbal picture of Carl Van Vechten is to be included. No American writer is taken more seriously than Miss Stein by the Paris modernists." The balance Flanner tried to achieve here spoke to the problem of anyone's remaining friends with both Leo and Gertrude; as Hapgood analyzed the situation, no one Gertrude thought was friendly with Leo was welcome at her salon. Young writers learned to be wary: just as James Joyce was not to be mentioned to Gertrude, neither was Leo.

Although he was not trying to become a writer, Leo knew a great deal more about contemporary literature than Gertrude did. As his borrowing lists from Beach's Shakespeare and Company show, he regularly read Theodore Dreiser, Eugene O'Neill, Edna St. Vincent Millay, William Carlos Williams, Carl Sandburg, Sherwood Anderson, Upton Sinclair, T. S. Eliot, Dorothy Richardson, William Faulkner, Ernest Hemingway, F. Scott Fitzgerald, Ezra Pound, James Joyce, D. H. Lawrence, Wyndham Lewis, Waldo Frank, H. D., Aldous Huxley, Virginia Woolf, Max Eastman, John Erskine, Ford Madox Ford, Frances Newman, Sacheverell and Osbert Sitwell, Laura Riding, Robert Graves, Conrad Aiken, Jules Romains, Sinclair Lewis, Michael Arlen, Sheila Kaye-Smith, Willa Cather, E. E. Cummings, John Dos Passos, Mabel Dodge, Dame Rose Macaulay, Joseph Conrad, Louis Untermeyer, Frank Harris—and Gertrude Stein. Interested not only in the modern, he also borrowed works by Jane Austen, Fyodor Dostoyevsky, Mark Twain, Charles Dickens, George Meredith, Thomas Hardy, Elizabeth Gaskell, Jonathan Swift, George Bernard Shaw, Francis Trollope, G. K. Chesterton, Sir Walter Scott, John Galsworthy, and others.

He also read widely as an aesthetician and was as likely to borrow a book on philosophy or mathematics as a novel. During the 1920s, he read Paul Rosenfeld, Carl Jung, Henry Adams, A. C. Bradley, George Santayana, William James, George Saintsbury, A. L. Kroeber, Lewis Mumford, Roger

Fry, Benedetto Croce, Livingston Lowes, Mathilde and Mathias Vaerting, Alfred North Whitehead, Julian Huxley, Ludwig Lewisohn, J.B.S. Haldane, Irving Babbitt, Van Wyck Brooks, and others. Leo remained friendly with leading social and aesthetic critics from New York, Harvard, and London.

The Shakespeare and Company lists, although they cover only 1923 to 1932 and only the months Leo lived in Paris, suggest the kind of voracious reading that was habitual for him. While he kept himself informed, living pleasantly at Parc-Monsouris, reading on the porch shaded by trees lining the quiet street, Nina continued her singing, talked with friends, and went to cafés. Leo's correspondence also kept him in touch with current thinking in both the States and Europe: he wrote to Trigant Burrow, John Dewey, Waldo Frank, Norman Douglas, Alfred Stieglitz, Mortimer Adler, Adolph Basler, George Boas, and others, often sparking controversies even with people he liked whose work he admired. Beginning in 1924 he published more essays in *The New Republic, Dial, The Arts,* and (a reminiscence of William James) *American Mercury.* Several of the essays appeared in the book he was readying for publication, but most of them were occasional pieces of aesthetic argument or art history, such as his 1924 essay debunking Picasso's current work, written in the past tense as if the painter were dead and calling Cézanne a squeezed lemon. Such writing bewildered his American readers, who knew him as the discoverer of Cézanne, Matisse, and Picasso some twenty years earlier.

When Boni and Liveright published *The ABC of Aesthetics* late in 1927, reviews were positive. Mortimer Adler (*New York Evening Post*) called it "an extraordinary combination of brilliant naiveté and charming sophistication"; Duncan Phillips (*Yale Review*) said it was "essentially a sound and sincere book" and termed Leo "a man of ripe and seasoned scholarship"; Waldo Frank (*The New Republic*) said the book would be "precious to all lovers of delicious talk"; and H. M. Kallen's *Dial* review called Leo "a thinker of originality." The praise Stein valued most came from Alfred Stieglitz, who wrote that he had bought fifteen copies of the book to give to friends.

Leo's life was never exclusively intellectual, however, and much of his effort between 1925 and 1929 went into traveling. Though Nina and he were happily married, Leo still behaved capriciously. Correspondence between the two shows that they were frequently separated, with Leo in Settignano and Nina in Paris or vice versa. During 1925 Leo joined Maurice Sterne and Ned and Peggy Bruce for a tour of Anticoli, Rome, Venice, and Vienna. They painted and saw such old friends as Adele Wolman, Marion Price, Ezra Pound, and André Derain. In 1927 with the Bruces and Bird and Howard Gans and their daughter, Marion, Leo traveled in Italy and France. He benefited from the New York Stein family's outrage over Gertrude's *The Making of Americans,* which included references to sexual misconduct on the part of the family patriarchs. The Steins found it impossible to believe that family disloyalty was necessary to writing: "they were furious, and one [Fred Stein] never forgave her." Concerned about Howard Gans's health, Leo and Gans motored from Perugia to see painter Othon Coubine and Harvard friends, while Marion brought Bird to stay with Nina.

Nina grew jealous of Leo's friendship with Marion. Finally aware of his wife's unhappiness, understanding that her thoughts of suicide stemmed from jealousy, Leo wrote what he intended to be a reassuring letter. He admitted caressing Marion (only "when she is sad") but wrote that he could not conceive of her "as a life companion." His claims that Nina was subject to "extreme phantasy" while he was "quite well balanced" were less than comforting—particularly when he had arranged a lecture tour in the States to begin late in 1928, during which time he would again be with Marion. Nina was to remain in Paris.

Retrospection

When Gertrude and Alice reflected on the position of the Stein family in both France and the States, it seemed as if Mike and Sally had become famous through the building of their Le Corbusier home and as if Leo, with his book finally published, might be winning the battle for fame in the States. Whereas Gertrude's work had never received an advance from a commercial publisher, Leo's *The ABC of Aesthetics* had, and now he was to go to the States to lecture. His prominence forced Gertrude to think that perhaps she and Alice had given too many tea parties and spent too much time talking with and helping friends. When Marsden Hartley wrote, "I have heard about you through others for you are like a bathing place, and people seem to stop off from every quarter and take a look at you," Gertrude was not pleased.

"The Most Famous Jew in the World"

Gertrude's first dramatic change occurred in January 1926. Admiring the short waved bob worn by her friend Elisabeth de Gramont, the duchesse of Clermont-Tonnerre, Gertrude told Alice to begin cutting—which Alice did for the next two days. Gertrude's long, heavy hair caught up in an unfashionable bun had been one of her distinctive markers, but Sherwood Anderson approved of the cut, saying she looked like a monk. Tchelitchew was less complimentary and never painted her portrait as he had planned, while Picasso worried, in a burst of anger, that the short hair invalidated his portrait of her. Gertrude had long compared her imagination to the male power of Picasso and Matisse and, recently, Juan Gris and Hemingway; now her mannish haircut emphasized what she saw as masculine creativity.

The change in hair style signaled other changes. Whether she began acting with a decisiveness new to her or whether the change in her appearance made people more aware that she could be decisive, rumors about Gertrude's difficult manner began. By the time painter Maurice Grosser met her in the late 1920s, she "was not at all the gracious and ingratiating hostess. . . . To the contrary, she was brusque, self-assured, and jolly"—clearly on the lookout for people who could benefit her and her work.

But Gertrude could still be charmingly persuasive, as she was with Edith Sitwell. Linked by their fascination with the uses of words, the women enjoyed each other. Independent spirits, neither belonged to a literary coterie (Sitwell remembered Stein's poking fun at the Bloomsbury group, which she called "the Young Men's Christian Association—with Christ left out of course"). Gertrude had long battled for acceptance in England; in 1920 John Lane had finally published *Three Lives,* but then momentum slowed again. Through Augustus John, Wyndham Lewis, and the young Harold Acton, Gertrude learned to know British students and heard that students liked her, Ronald Firbank, and the Sitwells, for their high camp and sexual ambivalence. When the Cam, the Cambridge literary society, asked Gertrude to lecture, however, her fear of speaking in public made her refuse. Later, when Sitwell proposed that she speak at Cambridge and Oxford, with parties beforehand in London, Gertrude decided to accept.

The idea of lecturing chilled her; she felt nauseated whenever she remembered the June dates. Much as she liked Edith and her brothers, Gertrude did not feel comfortable being a part of English society. Even with the Sitwells on the platform with her, she had difficulty seeing herself at a lectern. Although her voice was beautifully modulated, she planned to take elocution lessons. Her anxiety led her to buy new clothes; it led her to quarrel with some friends and become closer to others. Above all, it led her to question who Gertrude Stein was and what right she had to lecture in premier educational institutions.

As June 4 and 7 drew closer, however, Gertrude grew confident. Traveling with the Sitwells by car to Oxford, she was nervous, but Osbert recalled that once onstage, "she showed a mastery of her audience, and her address . . . proved a consummate piece of lucidity." Impressed by what he called her "monumental" poise, Sitwell thought she handled even the hecklers in "a most genial, comforting manner." Gertrude wrote to her Baltimore cousins, "It has gone off very well." She told them about the excited welcome by an American student and about staying at Faringdon, Lord Berners's houseful of exquisite needlework and orchids. She closed, "Glory is pleasant, it may not be lucrative but it is pleasant."

The omnipresent anti-Semitism that Gertrude pretended not to notice, however, tainted her visit. After the Sitwells' tea, Virginia Woolf wrote scathingly, "Jews swarmed. It was in honour of Miss Gertrude Stein who was throned on a broken settee (all Edith's furniture is derelict . . .). This resolute old lady inflicted a great damage on all the youth. According to Dadie, she contradicts all you say; insists that she is not only the most intelligible, but also the most popular of living writers; and in particular despises all of English birth. Leonard, being a Jew himself, got on very well with her. But it was an anxious, exacerbating affair." Inexplicably, in light of these comments, whether because of Leonard Woolf's Jewishness or Virginia's anti-Semitism, the Woolfs' Hogarth Press published Gertrude's lecture, *Composition as Explanation,* late in 1926.

Resting in Belley after the British talks, Gertrude recalled a mosaic of anti-Semitic comments. Although life in Paris had been more democratic than her existence in the States, particularly at medical school, she saw that prejudice was growing worse. In her early writing, Gertrude had made puns ("May June and Jew lie"), referring to the Alice persona as "my little jew." But as early as the various drafts of *The Making of Americans,* she had replaced the adjective *Jewish* with *German* and then, at times, with *middle-class.* (By the time she finished, there was scant evidence that the families of that novel were Jewish at all.) Now, in the 1920s, there was Hemingway's abrasive use of the word *kike* when he talked about Harold Loeb, Nathan Asch, Harold Stearns, Horace Liveright, and herself. There was Pound's blatant criticism of Jews; it was he who sent to T. S. Eliot Robert McAlmon's mocking comments about Gertrude, the source of the statement later wrongly attributed to her that "the Jews have produced only three originative geniuses: Christ, Spinoza and myself." With Mina Loy, Djuna Barnes, Natalie Barney, and Gertrude and Alice claiming Jewish blood, much of the recognized machismo in Paris's expatriate culture might also have been a disguised anti-Semitism.

Gertrude also noticed condescension in her personal relationships. Although Tchelitchew pretended to accept her, friends knew he was angry that noble Russians like his sister and himself should be, in his words, "kowtowing to a Jewess." His calling Gertrude "Sitting Bull" and Alice "The Knitting Machine" was part of his hostility. From Tunis, although he brought Gertrude an ostrich egg as a souvenir, Tchelitchew wrote to her: "The Jewish women are so fat that I can't tell you their dimensions; they are specially fed to be fat for otherwise the men would not marry them." A friend who understood Pavlik's prejudice reassured him that "Gertrude is the most un-Jewish person I ever knew. She is so dangerous and tolerant and has such a magnificent brain. Those aren't Jewish traits."

Rather than overlook such comments, Gertrude began making statements that—wryly or seriously—identified Alice and herself with Jewishness: "No Jew ever lays down his last cent" and, perhaps with the intention of dismissing acquaintances, "A Jew is a ghetto surrounded by Christians. What we need this year are some new Christians." In 1928 she agreed to an interview for the *New York Jewish Tribune,* where Blanche London's essay on Gertrude as a Jewish writer had run. That same year, talking with her Baltimore nephew Arthur Raffel when he visited Europe, Gertrude told him pointedly that she was "the most famous Jew in the world."

If it wasn't anti-Semitism that bothered Gertrude, it was the question of class. Never admitted to the circles of Edith Wharton or other wealthy American expatriates, Gertrude and her family continued to live modestly, supplementing their incomes with sales of paintings that had appreciated since their original purchase. But while she and Alice considered themselves well born and certainly well educated, they found the Continental view of class troublesome. When the Dayang Muda of Sarawak visited France, she asked her secretary, writer Kay Boyle, which "drawer" the literary set in Paris belonged to. Her scrutiny bothered Gertrude so much that Stein, invited for tea, was virtually tongue-tied and sat quiet, "smiling, smiling like the shyest of children" while a disapproving maid placed a satin cushion under the soles of her heavy, dirty walking shoes.

Gertrude's repeated avowal that she was an American presumed equality—regardless of class, ethnic and racial origin, sexual preference, or ability. Her friendships with blacks, homosexuals, and bisexuals; her valorization of people on the basis of their work rather than their pedigree; her candor about her own origins—though not about her lesbianism—all testified to her firm belief in the principles of democracy that America espoused. She also had developed the theory that Abraham Lincoln's parentage had "a Jewish strain," and whenever she was with Fania Marinoff, a Russian Jew, she brought the conversation around to her belief that "all men of genius had Jewish blood." While Gertrude assumed that social conditions would improve as the twentieth century wore on, what she was seeing in the aftermath of American expatriation to France was a large dose of separatist attitudes—which she thoroughly disliked. "Patriarchal Poetry," her 1927 poem, clearly expressed her anger.

The Changing Salon

Much of the sense that Stein's salon was a difficult place accrued from Gertrude and Alice's love of what they considered lively conversation. Naturally argumentative, both women would take people on, not to stifle ideas but to challenge easy assumptions. As a college friend reminisced to Stein about their discussions at Radcliffe, "I should like to see you and be sandbagged on the head when I didn't agree with you and sand bag you back again. It was a good life we led, that student life." Alice defined conversation as "being able to disagree and still continue the discussion, and this implies a deep-down basis of agreement no matter how sharp the surface dispute. Today [in 1954] there is too much surface agreement among intellectuals and not enough basic agreement, so discussion either is tepid or becomes poisoned." One of the qualities Alice loved about Gertrude was her passion, her ability to cuss a person out, and, above all, to make up her own mind. Gertrude hated people who wavered, calling them "the Indecision Board"; she usually had opinions. For instance, while she did not appreciate the writing of Baroness Else von Freytag-Loringhoven (even though Jane Heap liked her madcap poetry), neither would Gertrude side with novelist Evelyn Scott's view that the baroness's work was unfit for publication.

In the salon, Gertrude sometimes assumed the role of troublemaker that Guillaume Apollinaire had played so well, innocently "setting people at sixes and sevens," getting "malicious pleasure" from their quarrels, and then escaping without blame. Although Alice enjoyed controversy, she reproved Stein for her deliberate machinations, calling them "temptations." Gertrude's reply was to quote Juan Gris's maxim "One must always yield to temptation." There was a gender bias to Stein's mischief, in that it was seldom directed at women guests: when she invited women to the salon, she genuinely wanted to see them.

Gertrude's and Alice's sensitivity increased after the publication of Hemingway's *The Sun Also Rises* with its scathing undercurrent of anti-Semitism and homophobia. (Had she seen his 1925 letter to Pound complaining that "Le Grand Gertrude Stein" refused to review his *In Our Time*—"What a lot of safe playing kikes"—she would have been even more upset.) The characterization of Robert Cohn, which she had helped him write, turned out to be ridicule of the Jewish magazine editor Harold Loeb. Gertrude felt guilt over her sponsorship of Hemingway: had it not been for her, many doors would have remained closed to him. And the unkindest cut of all was his using the good-humored epigraph about the lost generation, a story she had told him about the hotel keeper in Belley, as a way to denounce her and her generation. So much that she had talked about with Hemingway appeared in the book—the Jake-Brett dialogue sounded a lot like their conversations about writing, the comments about creativity came almost directly from her, and the allusions to the Book of Job were surely a retort to a friend's comparison of Gertrude's writing to that book of the Bible.

Alice had warned her that Hemingway was not to be trusted. Alice had also said, "If that nice Hadley and the kid Bumby get in his way he'll desert them like a shot"—and that, too, had happened. Once Hemingway married Pauline Pfeiffer, none of his Paris friends saw much of him. One closing chapter to the Stein-Hemingway friendship occurred in 1927 with his publication in the *New Yorker* of a Ring Lardner–style piece about his break with several well known people, including Gertrude. There would be another such chapter, a more nearly final one, in the 1930s.

Of those who came to the rue de Fleurus in the later 1920s, which of them was truly a friend? Elliot Paul, the *Chicago Tribune* reporter now editing *transition,* whose mellow irony pleased her and who thought Gertrude one of the great conversationalists of the age. Virgil Thomson, whose wicked wit endangered everyone but whose music conveyed the sense of play, and power, in Gertrude's language. Bernard Faÿ, professor of history at the University of Clermont-Ferrand and later, the Collège de France, whose encouragement and vivacious conversation never lagged. Hart Crane, stunned by her acceptance of his difficult work, and his difficult person. Paul Bowles, the young musician who followed Gertrude's advice and moved to Algiers. And the loyal women friends: Janet Flanner, Bryher, Mildred Aldrich, Jane Heap, Elisabeth de Gramont, Natalie Barney, Dolly Wilde, Anita Loos, and the many who never became even marginally famous. But there were many who were untrustworthy: the beautiful Laura Riding, suicidal and dependent but still harsh in her criticism of Stein's writing—and her tales about Gertrude's sexual interest in Picasso; the pretentious Robert Graves; Maria and Eugene Jolas, whose later anger perplexed Gertrude; Kristians Tonny, whose Dutch forthrightness never salved his criticisms; Georges Hugnet, who refused to be complimented by Gertrude's "free translation" of his poem "Enfances"; and Eugene Berman, whose sexual escapades with their maid offended Gertrude and Alice.

Surrounding herself with young painters and musicians, Gertrude tried to erase the memory of Hemingway's betrayal. She also turned to a group of visitors who were either bisexual or homosexual and therefore seemingly less abrasive than the blatantly (or defensively) heterosexual young American visitors. The heterosexual dominance of the salon had been one reason Alice sat with the "wives." She did not want to talk with a segregated audience any more than Gertrude did; what they liked best was to entertain as a pair, which they did in smaller, more intimate groups. (Then Alice, the wittier storyteller, was more likely to dominate the conversation.) Even when it seemed as if Gertrude was leading a conversation entirely separate from Alice's, she knew where Toklas was and what she was doing. Both Kay Boyle and Bryher remember leaving the atelier with Alice to go to the kitchen in the pavilion, only to be called back by Gertrude: she kept Alice within eyesight. When Gertrude took people driving and Alice preferred to stay on the terrace doing handiwork, Stein would return quickly; when she was away from Alice, she got "low in her mind."

What Gertrude wanted was to entertain people who interested her, those she categorized as real people rather than as pretenders. She suffered some of the pretenders because she believed she could help them, but by this time in her life—she was well past fifty—she was more interested in being comfortable herself. People with whom she could talk and quip and gossip were higher on her list of friends than those who were likely to turn adversarial. With Alix Daniel, a young woman from South Dakota, Gertrude and Alice could gossip and laugh, which they all three did, and sometimes Gertrude would walk Daniel back to her hotel, airing her convictions—that U. S. Grant was superior to both Washington and Lincoln, that adjectives emasculated writing, that relatives should be neither seen nor heard, and that using salt in food was "pernicious." What Alix remembered most about her time with Gertrude and Alice was their wry comments about acquaintances: "That Pound. Neither Alice nor I like him or his poetry and what's more important, he simply doesn't amuse me." In contrast, Ford Madox Ford was welcomed, though Gertrude said laughingly, "Ford and his women! What's the attraction? Have you ever seen him dance? It must be that bumbling air of innocence he has. It gets 'em." Gertrude remained friends with him because of what she called his "genuine love of good writing—not only producing it but encouraging the gift in others."

Many of Gertrude's American visitors perplexed her. They so emphasized gender differences that it was as if American culture had never recovered from those decades of "separate spheres" in the nineteenth century, and the American version of women's freedom relied so heavily on a stereotyped sexual text that Gertrude found it all boring. Now she found herself asking, Why did Americans find sexuality so threatening? What was the matter with American men? As she was later to write, "What is the use of being a little boy if you are going to grow up to be a man?" When Sherwood Anderson, feigning illness, did not attend their party for him, Gertrude understood: even her dear friend was caught in a paroxysm of sexual fear, unable to face either his own crumbling marriage or his friend Hemingway's slights.

Gertrude took most happenings in stride, but Alice and she were growing older—and poorer—as they entertained the young, many of whom seemed to care little about Gertrude's knowledge or her person. In search of peace, the women left Paris earlier each spring and returned later each fall, enjoying to the full their summers in the Ain. And when they were in Paris, they went out more often than they entertained. One of the places they enjoyed was Natalie Barney's salon, which mixed French writers and socialites with expatriates—and included a number of lesbians. In the spring of 1927 Barney designated one Friday a Gertrude Stein celebration, which featured remarks by Ford Madox Ford and Mina Loy and Virgil Thomson singing and playing his compositions of Stein's poetry. Dressed in an elegant gray costume, Gertrude drank champagne, listened to good jazz, and greeted nearly two hundred acquaintances.

Friendships and the Ain

The manner Gertrude assumed in her salon was not the manner of her interaction with Picasso, or the Kahnweilers, or Juan Gris. None of these old friends needed to be "instructed," and her feeling in the salon—at least by the later 1920s—was that people came to hear her and so she needed to perform. With her good friends, Gertrude spoke less. Although she was drawn to what she saw as Gris's mysticism, which required little language to express, she felt that she was only an observer of that part of his life and that she could best support him by buying his paintings. She purchased one each in 1924 (*Seated Woman*), 1925 (*The Green Cloth*), and 1926 (*The Dish of Pears*)—purchases that prompted arguments with Picasso. In return for Gertrude's financial support, Gris designed chair and stool covers for Alice to embroider, gave Gertrude drawings, asked her to read and comment on his lectures, and completed his illustrations for Kahnweiler's publication of her *As a Wife Has a Cow*.

When Gris returned to Paris in February 1927, it was clear that his death was imminent, and both Kahnweiler and Gertrude visited him often. She wrote Van Vechten that she was experiencing "a very great grief as my very very dear friend Juan Gris is dying." When he died on May 11, of uremia, Gertrude wrote the portrait she thought her most moving, "The Life and Death of Juan Gris." Though she repeated the word *perfection* in the text, her major theme was linking Gris with his art, which "he made it very well loving," and to suggest the quality of spiritualism that she found in him. She closed with the image of the young man not yet forty as "he smiled so gently and said I was everything," lending credence to her earlier statement that they had been "intimate."

The day Gris died, Gertrude and Alice were in mourning when Picasso came to the flat. Gertrude said emphatically, "Go away, Pablo. Not today." When Picasso begged to come in, she agreed but made him promise not to mention Juan; she could not forgive his having seen Gris as a competitor rather than as a friend. Their meal was somber, and even though Picasso claimed to be grieving, Gertrude told him, "You have no right to mourn, and he said, you have no right to say that to me. You never realised his meaning because you did not have it, she said angrily. You know very well I did, he replied."

Gertrude's seldom-predictable friendship was warmest in Belley. It was as if the tranquillity of the landscape—the Lombardy poplars giving the sense of an eighteenth-century painting—calmed her. That part of France with its serene light, majestic color, simple fields, and clear, beautiful lakes became her favorite. From her balcony, facing south, at the Hôtel Pernollet, Gertrude spent hours absorbing the changing, but always peaceful, blues and grays—this was the period when her writing reflected "landscape" instead of character.

Besides friendship with the Pernollets, Gertrude and Alice enjoyed Fred Genevrey, the local flower expert; through him they met the baroness Pierlot, whose château was across the valley, near Béon. The gracious widow insisted that Gertrude write in her collier (a tiny seventeeth-century building where wine was made), so Stein spent afternoons there. It was no coincidence that Gertrude wrote well in Belley. She also practiced a daily regimen of meditation. Alice and she tried to avoid guests, although Natalie Barney and Romaine Brooks, Henry McBride, Carl Van Vechten, and Bernard Faÿ visited. The women had a new (unnamed) Ford, small enough to drive on the narrow, unpaved roads. And they brought Basket, their large white poodle. Although he never learned to carry the basket that gave him his name, the pet provided Gertrude with a walking partner and a lap warmer and Alice with more chores.

From the Hôtel Pernollet, the two could just make out the manor house of the nearby hamlet of Bilignin, and living there became Gertrude's dream. This was her landscape; perhaps subliminally, she was searching for her Nohant, a place—like George Sand's—of connection with the French people. Finding the substantial *château-ferme* to rent pleased the two women, and they may have resorted to chicanery to get it (it became available when the military officer who occupied the house was transferred). They also liked the fact that the famous gastronome Jean-Anthelme Brillat-Savarin had been born in Bilignin, another link with the good living that awaited them. Gertrude wrote Baltimore cousins that the property's rent—forty-five hundred francs a year, including furniture—was reason enough for them to stay in France.

Acquiring the house took until the spring of 1929, and moving in was arduous. With no running water, slanting floors, and an ancient kitchen, Alice had her hands full doing the cooking. The grounds had been neglected for years, and in ridding the property of nests of snakes, Gertrude was bitten. When Alice closed her eyes at night, she saw weeds. But eventually, the work was done, and the center of activity became the large grass-covered terrace, approached through French doors. There Gertrude sat in a deck chair, "meditating or writing—in a notebook on her lap—or talking." As she went about her work, Alice could look down from the second-story window and listen to Gertrude. Making the place their own—adding paintings and small pieces of furniture—cultivating raspberries, currants, and strawberries, seeding gardens, and planning new flower plots fascinated both of them. Defining herself as a farmer, Alice grew more than thirty kinds of vegetables, many of them unfamiliar to the area. She recalled, "The first gathering of the garden in May . . . made me feel like a mother about her baby—how could anything so beautiful be mine. And this emotion of wonder filled me for each vegetable as it was gathered every year. There is nothing that is comparable to it, as satisfactory or as thrilling, as gathering the vegetables one has grown."

Besides being beautiful, Belley was an interesting place to walk. On her treks, often with Basket, Gertrude stopped to talk with neighbors—she was proud of her Americanized French, which she did not use much in Paris. The farmers, housewives, and garage keepers with whom she spoke wanted to communicate with the American lady, although they cared nothing about who she was or what she did: they knew only that she and her small friend had chosen to live in their village. That was enough.

The two went out afternoons. They drove to the abbaye d'Hautecombe in Saint-Pierre-de-Curtille, as well as to Béon and Aix-les-Bains. Natalie Barney and Romaine Brooks, who lived nearby, often saw them in Aix looking for new desserts. On one occasion, Natalie bought "one of those long, hose-stemmed lotus flowers of dark pink . . . which I stuck between the spokes of Gertrude's steering wheel, with a card of explanation: 'A wand to lead you on.'" Another afternoon, Barney, Brooks, Elisabeth de Gramont, and Gertrude and Alice celebrated summer under a huge parasol, sitting in gaily striped canvas chairs. Drinking Alice's excellent China tea and eating her coconut layer cake—with white icing edged with pink, to match Basket—Gertrude sat like a Gypsy queen, with moccasined feet, telling the story of arguing with Leo as children over which of them would be the family's "genius." Or Alice and Gertrude might take the day to drive to Orgeval to see Noël Murphy and perhaps lunch with Louis and Mary Bromfield, Djuna Barnes, Janet Flanner and Solita Solano, Georgette LeBlanc, Jane Heap, or the always argumentative Margaret Anderson. Known for its nude sunbathing, Noël's house was a place to keep in touch with Paris friends; it was there they met the young painter Francis Rose.

Happily settled in Bilignin by 1930, Gertrude and Alice recovered from the painful losses of recent years. Besides the death of Gris in 1927, gone were Isadora Duncan, Avery Hopwood, and the baroness von Freytag-Loringhoven. In the States, Nicola Sacco and Bartolomeo Vanzetti were executed in Charlestown prison, sparking protests that circled the world. In 1928 Mildred Aldrich died of a stroke in Huiry, where she was buried.

Gertrude and Alice watched by her bedside and arranged the funeral, but—although Stein was her literary executor—they failed to return later to salvage her extensive correspondence.

Back in Paris the café Lapin Agile closed, and as Wall Street foundered, *The Little Review* folded. Many Americans, shaken from their expatriation by economic woes, returned home. In the fall of 1929 Claribel Cone died suddenly while vacationing in Switzerland, and Gertrude wrote Etta, with more warmth than usual: "[Claribel] made a very important and rather wonderful part of my Baltimore past, and [a medical school friend] and I were talking of it all and of her in it when she was here just a couple of months ago, and so strangely enough Claribel had been very near me this last summer, and now Etta you know how I understand your loss and feel for it, do take my love and my fondest thought of Claribel. Always, Gertrude." She had little comment about the suicides of Harry Crosby and Jules Pascin. People in the arts had no business playing with alcohol or drugs; though saddened and thoroughly conscious of being middle-aged, Alice and Gertrude also felt morally superior.

Plain Edition(s)

During the late 1920s, Gertrude produced an immense quantity of fiction modeled on her earlier portrait method, a bevy of surrealist plays—both long and short—and some new writing about writing that she called grammar. When she used the term, listeners envisioned diagrammed sentences, but what she created was a complete epistemological system. From *Composition as Explanation* and *An Acquaintance with Description* through "Regular Regularly in Narrative," "Finally George A Vocabulary of Thinking," "Sentences," and "Arthur a Grammar" to "More Grammar for a Sentence," "A Grammarian," "Narrative," and "Forensics," Gertrude wrote a treatise for using the American language in new ways. As Hemingway said, she tried to "eliminate imagery altogether" as she worked toward her consistent grammar. Had she not been questioned, even challenged, by her younger visitors, she might never have come to this phase of her work.

Nothing about Gertrude's work in the late 1920s was easy. "Stanzas in Meditation" was as unexpected as "Madame Récamier An Opera" or her meditation on Hugnet's poem, *Before the Flowers of Friendship Faded Friendship Faded*. No one could classify it except the few loyal readers who made the study of Gertrude Stein more than an avocation. All the years of entertaining at the rue de Fleurus had not added to the number of those readers. Taking a hard look at the past decade, Gertrude decided that she had spent her limited time, and limited funds, unwisely. Alice and she were financially and emotionally exhausted. That she consulted a fortune-teller was one index of Gertrude's frustration, although she wrote with amusement to friends that she had now been promised a publisher. (The fortune-teller also warned her to watch Alice's health and to put her to bed occasionally for an entire day.)

In 1929 Gertrude and Alice made plans to start their own publishing house—like Barbara Harrison, Caresse and Harry Crosby, and Laura Riding and Robert Graves. Stein wrote Van Vechten, "Alice is managing director [sic] I am author, and we hope there will be purchasers." To finance what they called the Plain Edition(s), Gertrude—through Mike—sold Picasso's *Woman with Bangs* to Etta Cone. (In 1930 she sold Etta some Picasso drawings, again through Mike, for the same purpose.) By January 1931 the Plain Edition(s) had produced Gertrude's long romance *Lucy Church Amiably*. Drawn from the beloved French countryside, the title suggested numerous things, some of them sexual, but it ostensibly named the tiny Russian orthodox church at Lucey, near their Bilignin home. The church was one of the sights they shared with visitors, often taking along a picnic to enjoy while they viewed the diminutive onion-shaped steeple set against the low mountain behind it. But the incomprehensibility of Gertrude's text, which wound back and forth among landscape, lecture, and narrative, meant that very few bookstores would order even one copy. Sales did not improve with their second publication, *How to Write,* a collection of Stein's essays and lectures about writing and grammar (in March 1931 the Library of Congress wrote that it would not be purchasing any edition of the unpublished works of Gertrude Stein).

Alice corresponded with many, many bookstores, in the States as well as in Paris and London, publicizing her company with dignity and aplomb. One promotion letter to Frances Steloff at the Gotham Book Mart emphasized both Gertrude's fame and her influence: "Out of her early experiments has sprung all modern writing." It then got down to sales: "Copies of HOW TO WRITE are sent on consignment post paid: the book, 395 pages, sells for $3.50, 40% discount, bills to be settled quarterly." Alice's return for the number of hours she spent on the Plain Edition(s) ran to negative numbers. It was, however, her final attempt to wrest fame for Gertrude out of what was becoming an increasingly hostile milieu. Despite the fact that Stein had lectured at both Cambridge and Oxford, despite the publications of her lecture by the Hogarth Press and, more recently, other books by Payson and Clarke and smaller presses, Gertrude remained largely unread.

Frustration with their inability to make Gertrude into a significant modernist led the women to outbursts of abrupt anger against their friends. Installing a telephone made breaking with people easy. In the case of Bravig Imbs, whose wife was moving to the Ain to await the birth of their child, dismissal came by phone. Alice told the young man who had long been one of their favorites that locating his pregnant wife near them was "a colossal impertinence." They could not be responsible for the woman's lying-in: the friendship was over.

Gertrude's tendency to dismiss people was hardly new. Bird Stein, Alice Woods Ullman, Etta Cone, Mabel Dodge, Hutch Hapgood, Hemingway, Mabel Weeks, and others—not to mention Leo—had earlier received notice that their relationships with her were over. For Kristians Tonny, in the midst of painting Gertrude, the rupture came in person. Enraged because he changed her appointments in order to accommodate clients who paid, Stein shouted at him, and he shouted back. "Alice was furious. Doors slammed." Kristians did not return.

For Virgil Thomson, the blow came by mail. Although he had set much of Gertrude's work to music and at his urging she had written *Four Saints in Three Acts,* unfortunately he tried to effect a compromise with Gertrude and Hugnet over the "Enfances" argument. A week later, he opened a note from Gertrude and found himself dismissed. Whether in person or by telephone or on calling cards, Gertrude's message was all too clear: "Miss Gertrude Stein [engraved on her calling card, and written below it] 'Declines further acquaintance with Mr. Virgil Thomson.'"

To such a message, there was no reply.

Alice's Book and "La Gloire"

Gertrude's use of the word *patriarchal* in her writing of the late 1920s showed her increasing sensitivity to the role gender played in society's power structures. In her generation, male dominance (the patriarchy) and heterosexuality were the norms. Just as she and her women friends had been disadvantaged in their educations, so they had usually been given no choice about their life roles: the accepted course of action was to marry and bear children. In her long poem "Patriarchal Poetry," Gertrude describes the woman persona as a younger sister to several brothers: "Does she know how to ask her brother is there any difference between turning it again again and again and again or turning it again and again." Instead of answering, the brothers patronize her, as this segment of the poem suggests:

> Let her try.
> Let her be let her be let her be let her be to be to be let her be let her try.
> To be shy.
> Let her be.
> Let her try. . . .
> Never to be what he said.
> Never to be what he said.
> Let her to be what he said. . . .
> Not to let her to be what he said not to let her to be what he said.

Disdain is never encouraging; the very offhandedness of the male voices diminishes the female role.

Gertrude makes clear here, and in her novel *Lucy Church Amiably* and the play *A Bouquet. Their Wills,* that she knows that the patriarchy establishes all cultural rules. Her immediate difficulty was that Alice and she could not marry: the conjugal rights that all husbands and wives shared were forbidden to a lesbian couple. "It is very difficult to be unalloyed," she comments.

Alice and Gertrude's concern with marital rights surfaced in the late 1920s because Mike urged them to make new wills. In the process of building his million-franc house, he had redone his own will, and, as usual, he gave them advice about the process. After Mike sent Gertrude her will to sign, he received not the original but a copy in handwriting, unsigned. She had evidently misunderstood and thought she was to make a fair copy of the document. Mike returned it with a brotherly note, which opens "You poor Kid." After explaining what he needed and stressing that her effort was to no purpose, he closed, "I can just see you copying with your tongue between your teeth." Relegating his fifty-four-year-old sister to the powerless position of "poor kid"—and, by implication, "dumb kid"—was obviously demeaning. Although Gertrude was used to Mike's condescension, she was frustrated here by the sense that she might remain, always, the baby sister.

Just as Gertrude continued to depend on Mike, so she continued to be surprised at her envy of Leo. After he had moved to Italy in 1913, she thought that he would never again disturb her tranquillity or her work. Particularly after what she considered his inappropriate marriage to Nina, she wanted nothing more to do with him. Yet Leo would not disappear: she saw him walking on the boulevard Raspail, sitting at the Rotonde, striding through the Salon d'Automne, and coming out of Shakespeare and Company (as he later said, "Gertrude and I never saw each other after 1920. It was she that avoided me. When we might have passed each other in Paris she and Alice crossed the street"). The *Dial* finally accepted her work, but, ironically, her submission appeared in an issue with one of Leo's essays.

Not much was happening in publishing. H. D. and Bryher asked Gertrude to write for their new film journal, *Close Up. Pagany* ran her work and the first of William Carlos Williams's enthusiastic essays about her; *Blues* and *transition* accepted whatever she sent them. Virgil Thomson's music for "Capital Capitals" and *Four Saints in Three Acts,* like Lord Berners's for *They Must. Be Wedded. To Their Wife,* was excellent, and after hearing the score for *Four Saints* in 1929, Mabel Dodge wrote Gertrude that she "would finish opera just as Picasso had finished old painting." (That June, *transition* published the libretto.) In 1931 Aaron Copland arranged a concert of American chamber music in Belley, which included "Capital Capitals."

Alice and she continued entertaining. Copland, Alexander Calder, Hart Crane, Cecil Beaton, the Bromfields, Tristan Tzara, Mary Butts, Sherry Mangan, Emily Chadbourne Crane, the Abdys, Allen Tate, Carolyn Gordon, Léonie Adams, F. Scott and Zelda Fitzgerald, Hemingway (occasionally, with his new wife, Pauline), Paul Bowles, Gorham Munson, Elsa Maxwell, and their usual friends visited. More importantly, the women went out more. They spent Halloween at Natalie Barney's annual fete for both her birthday and All Hallows' Eve. The menu was American turkey and dressing, as it was at the rue de Fleurus on Thanksgiving, when Alice served her oyster-mushroom-chestnut stuffing. They went regularly to the duchesse de Clermont-Tonnerre's

Thursdays. Martha Gellhorn met Stein at these last (where the young journalist had gone to eat the "giant sort of feasts" the duchesse provided). Dressed in "her greyish wool uniform of sleeveless jacket, skirt and shirt with tie, [Gertrude] looked very affable." In 1931 Alice and Gertrude took a group to Shakespeare and Company for Edith Sitwell's reading of Stein's work. But Sitwell did not even mention Stein because Gertrude had quarreled with Tchelitchew, her lover.

Joyce was there, but he and Gertrude did not meet. Neither had they met at the Jolases' party for *transition* contributors, where the Joyces sat across the room from Alice and Gertrude, seeming not to notice them—or the young men who "squatted in a half-circle before [Stein's] chair." Finally, at the Davidsons, Sylvia Beach conducted Gertrude to Joyce, and the two shook hands "peacefully." Gertrude commented, "After all these years," and Joyce replied, "Yes and our names always linked together." After the greeting, however, nothing more was said, so Stein walked back across the room. It was to be their only meeting.

Life continued with "lots of pleasant xcitement," as Gertrude liked to say. In 1932 Bernard Faÿ was appointed to a professorship at the Sorbonne; Francis Rose had an important gallery hanging; Gertrude's godson Paolo Picasso made his first communion. Success surrounded friends; approaching sixty, Gertrude wanted to share in it. While she wrote seriously, trying to use the American language in truly modern ways, others were writing with more acclaim. The model Kiki of Montparnasse had written her memoirs, with an introduction by Hemingway; so had Fernande Olivier, *Picasso et ses amis,* serialized in *Le Mercure de France.* Memoirs by friends Lincoln Steffens, Frank Harris, Theodore Dreiser, Muriel Draper, Sherwood Anderson, Ford Madox Ford, Janet Scudder, Isadora Duncan, Emma Goldman, Margaret Anderson, Amelia Earhart, Helen Keller, Gertrude Atherton, Mabel Dodge, and Mary Austin also appeared. Gertrude also read the good reviews of Robert Graves's *Good-Bye to All That,* which he had written in eight weeks during a summer, and of Natalie Barney's *Aventures de l'esprit.* It was clear that what the current literary world admired was not serious literature but gossip.

So it was that in the summer and fall of 1932, enjoying a beautiful autumn in Bilignin, she and Alice stayed on longer than usual. And in those six weeks, Gertrude wrote the book that was to change their lives.

Alice's Book

The legend about Gertrude's wonderful spoof of a memoir taking her voice to tell Alice's story and then changing her voice into Alice's is only part of the book's history. She probably had planned to write her own autobiography, given the publicity that met such works by friends, but an event occurred during the first week of May that upset her carefully balanced world.

Gertrude's problems with Alice before 1932 were nothing to the anger that exploded from Toklas when Gertrude unearthed her first (lost) novella and showed it to Alice and Louis Bromfield. Lovers for twenty-five years, Alice and Gertrude ostensibly had no secrets from each other. The recovered manuscript of *Q.E.D.* proved, however, that Gertrude had kept several secrets—not only about having written the work but about having had an affair with May Bookstaver Knoblauch in the first place. That the liaison was over before Alice met Gertrude was no consolation: since then May Knoblauch had acted as agent for Gertrude's writing and had even visited their Paris home. Alice could not believe that she had been so thoroughly betrayed; as she said later, she was "enraged." She was also "paranoid about the name May," and scholar Ulla Dydo has found that in Gertrude's writing during that summer and autumn, many occurrences of the word *may* were changed to *can,* regardless of meaning.

Alice's anger bewildered Gertrude. While she had long worried about not achieving "gloire" through her writing, she had never seriously questioned the permanence of her marriage. Now the basis for her world was crumbling, and she saw no way to undo acts committed thirty years earlier. Gertrude meditated on the disruption early in *The Autobiography of Alice B. Toklas,* saying ironically—and in Alice's voice—"I myself have no liking for violence." Gertrude coped with Alice's rage by writing not only Toklas's autobiography but her own. The very long poem *Stanzas in Meditation* is Gertrude's alternative autobiography. Written in a voice much more her own, *Stanzas* poses questions about identity, fame, and likeness (and *liking,* being *liked,* being *alike,* etc.). Thrown into her old pattern of feeling inadequate, Gertrude tried to write out her fears about Alice's fury. The underlying question was, would Alice leave her?—"Who is winning why the answer of course is she is."

Intermingled with imagery of the individual and the pair is a strong sense of Gertrude and Alice as one: "I have often thought that she meant what I said." If the voice was to be Alice's, as it had been in such earlier Stein works as "A Third," "I Have No Title to Be Successful," and "Farragut or a Husband's Recompense," then did Gertrude even own a voice any longer? If she did, was it truly her own or rather some amalgam of Stein-Toklas?

Even the peace of Bilignin could not alleviate Alice's anger. Neither could the writing process unite them. For twenty-five years, as Alice had typed Gertrude's handwritten pages, she had found the love notes, the sexual drawings, the comments that were not parts of the manuscript but were rather Gertrude's private, often erotic, remarks to her. She had either answered them or simply appreciated them. But now, in the manuscripts of the 1932 *Stanzas in Meditation* and *The Autobiography of Alice B. Toklas,* Alice began writing for herself. For instance, refrains like these appear in her handwriting, "Where they are alike alike and alike forget it" and "aroused by suspicion—Everything away and aroused by suspicion." There is also a longer addition in her writing about possible "arrangements," necessary now because of the way "the wind can blow does blow," until truth is "suddenly recognized. A question and answer. Where did it come from." Besides writing her own comments and insisting that Gertrude confess her duplicity—*where did it come from?*—Alice also interrupted the text with corrections. The dynamic of the women's familiar dialogue was being seriously tested.

While readers have long known that the *Autobiography* was a mixed, fantastic prose form, meant as much to joke as to enlighten, they have not known that it was only half of a paired work that described the life, and perhaps the death, of the women's marriage. *Stanzas in Meditation* has been virtually lost. Yet, in some ways, Alice's anger inscribed every page of both autobiographies. For Gertrude, the process of writing each was a complicated negotiation through personal minefields, history so subjective that not even the marriage partner could share in its reliving, leading to a final battle between self and consciousness. In the extremities of her emotional chaos, Gertrude the writer asked, What is this book? Who is this writer? and, finally, Who am I?

Writing *The Autobiography of Alice B. Toklas* took longer than the six weeks Gertrude claimed in "The Story of a Book" because she was simultaneously writing *Stanzas in Meditation*, as well as such shorter pieces as "Here. Actualities," which also described the torment of being closed out of Alice's life. But Stein in a 1933 letter to Lindley Hubbell continued creating the fantasy of how the book came to be: "We were a little worried Alice and I because incomes were not what they were." One day on their Bilignin terrace, a cuckoo (here Gertrude reminded Hubbell of the superstition that seeing a cuckoo "means money in your pocket") came flying up "and made one loud emphatic cuckoo right at me. . . . I am very superstitious, naturally, everybody is," and therefore "I was a little scared." But she applied herself to thinking what kind of writing might, indeed, make money. (The tone of this anecdote echoes that of the *Autobiography:* the whimsical recounting is staged so that the reader is never sure whether the narration is ironic.)

Another part of Gertrude's post-publication account was that she had often urged Alice to write her story. Now working with literary agent William Aspenwall Bradley, who also marketed Edith Wharton, Gertrude and Alice better understood what might sell. But when Alice had not begun her project during the summer, because in her anger she was not likely to do anything Stein wanted, Gertrude "as a joke" started the book for her. What she wanted to write was Alice's story. Unfortunately, as early drafts of the manuscript show, the telling of Alice's story began in a voice that sounded very much like Gertrude's.

It is this version that includes the passage about violence, as well as long sentences like "This is not what there is to say but this is what there is and what there has been said as it has been hard to say." Several pages into the text, a new section opens,

How does one begin.
One begins very well.

At no time does one fail in beginning very well and
having indeed beginning begin very well one can and one
does begin very well to have been begun.

Into the incomprehensibility of these passages comes a page of direct, acerbic Toklas-like language. For whatever reason, Gertrude needed help in finding her lover's voice, no matter how reassuring she was trying to be about the start. (Pages in Alice's handwriting, which are housed in the University of Texas collection, if collated with the YALC manuscripts, might explain Toklas's role in writing the book. It might be that whenever Stein needed to "hear" Toklas's voice, Alice wrote some material.)

Once transcribed into the black notebook that was to contain the first volume of the *Autobiography,* the text was close to the published version. There are some marginal observations, some corrections, some intertextual arguments as Toklas does more than comment politely (there are some large *NOs,* in fact, and an occasional *Not again*). There is the deletion of Stein's story of Hemingway, "feeling himself to be the coming man" and wishing "to belittle Gertrude Stein," and of her calling John Dos Passos "nothing but a fat head," but generally this handwritten version is the published text. Inside the cover of the first volume are possible titles: "30 Years with Gertrude Stein," the number *30* crossed out and replaced with *25*; "The Autobiography of Alice B. Toklas/By Gertrude Stein"; "How the Saturday evenings changed gradually, beginning with Roger Fry . . ."; and, most interesting, because it suggests that one of the sources of Toklas's anger was less Stein's affair with Bookstaver than the fact that she had written a book to commemorate that affair: "If you love a woman you find her memory . . . and if you *want* [replaced with *need*] to love a woman you have to wait untill [*sic*] you have memory to give her." Guilty that she had seldom written about Alice, Gertrude was intent on finishing *her* story.

Sent to Bradley in October, the *Autobiography* was published by Harcourt Brace in late summer of 1933; it was also a Book-of-the-Month Club selection. Gertrude Stein's name as author appeared nowhere until the last paragraph of the text, and a few reviews questioned the authorship, wondering whether Alice Toklas even existed—despite the fact that the book made use of well-placed photos of the two women, giving it a collage effect. Knowing that Gertrude was the author was itself a mark of initiation into the secrets of Paris life.

The work also brought Gertrude the realization of her fondest dream: publication in the *Atlantic Monthly.* Prior to the book's appearance, the magazine bought a short version to excerpt in four issues, starting in May. There it was that Leo Stein discovered he did not appear by name in the book, so completely had Gertrude written him out of history, and that Hemingway read about his being "yellow," a slavish pupil of both Anderson and Stein, but—rather than being modern—still smelling of the museums. From that time on, Hemingway waged a vicious battle to discredit Gertrude. (Though unpublished, "The Autobiography of Alice B. Hemingway," his description of his unnamed-till-married-to-him St. Louis wife, who—like Toklas—was "gently bred," manages to insult Stein in every way—ethnically, sexually, and professionally. It is also written in the seemingly casual style of her autobiography.)

The Autobiography of Alice B. Toklas succeeded in the literary world because it re-created Gertrude's friends and their times. Although other writers were fascinated with Stein's ability to achieve a sense of unstudied voice and bemused by the flamboyance of her narrative experiment, the reading public read the book for its gossip. Accurate in tone if not in fact, the Stein-Toklas voice gives wit and dimension to the history of painting and writing in Paris. Many of the comments are acerbic, though the quick pace of the narrative disguises the sharpness; others are hardly the expected. Her relegation of surrealism and dadaism to the past, for example, was one of the things that piqued the *transition* group—Matisse, Braque, André Salmon, Tristan Tzara, and the Jolases. In a special issue of the magazine, titled "Testimony Against Gertrude Stein," they criticized her egocentric view of the art world. Unlike Matisse's comments, which corrected what he saw as errors, most statements were virulent. Tzara called Stein and Toklas "two maiden ladies greedy for fame and publicity," surely in retaliation for Gertrude's comparing him to "a pleasant and not very exciting cousin"; Eugene Jolas called the book "hollow, tinsel bohemianism." Braque saw her preference for Picasso, Gris, and Picabia as reason to say that she never understood cubism. Matisse was hostile because Gertrude compared his wife's beauty to that of a horse; Alice later wrote, "Matisse was very offended and even broke into print on the subject—though he didn't read English. Perhaps he did not consider a horse beautiful."

Except for the *transition* response, nearly everyone who knew Gertrude and Alice described the *Autobiography* as "made up word for word of the stories I have heard Alice tell . . . an exact rendition of Alice's conversation." This similarity convinced Maurice Grosser that Alice wrote the book, but most others were convinced that Gertrude's ear was simply so good that her replication of Alice's speech was infallible. Her primary study, at this point in her life, was people's language.

Many of the more than a hundred reviews the *Autobiography* received were glowing. Critics liked the book's fun, charm, "slick dialogue," "crystalline clarity," and exuberant liveliness. Gertrude was compared with Samuel Johnson, and the *Autobiography* with both Franklin's work and *The Education of Henry Adams;* people predicted it would win the Pulitzer Prize. *New Statesman and Nation* called it "a perfect piece of narrative . . . delightful, and brilliant with sincerity." Negative reviews said it was "foolishness," but the consensus was that *The Autobiography of Alice B. Toklas* was "one of the most important books of the season." It was also "delicious" for its humor.

And humor was what Gertrude achieved, from her tongue-in-cheek description of Alice's "gently bred existence of [her] class and kind" to her seemingly casual comparison of the *Autobiography* with Defoe's *Robinson Crusoe.* Just as Defoe's work had created an angry sensation, catalyzing fierce debates over *truth* and *fiction, author* and *protagonist,* so *The Autobiography of Alice B. Toklas* unloosed critical battles that continue still. Never a hoax in any negative sense, the work was a playful defense of human memory, a privileging of imaginative recall over scrupulous—and, for Gertrude, tedious—fact.

In June 1933 she wrote Hubbell, "I am adoring being successful, completely and entirely adoring it." She also encouraged him about his own work, "Don't be too discouraged that they won't print you, it does make one feed on oneself and that after all is the only real food for us. . . . Nobody knows more of that, Alice B. Toklas can bear witness." Vindicated after years of writing without an audience, Gertrude hoped that the fame (and money) that "Alice's book" had earned would help to erase the memory of that other lover's fiction, *Q.E.D.*

The Stein-Thomson Collaboration

Part of Gertrude's disregard for the genre divisions of writing had grown from her years of immersion in French theater, which often bordered on "performance" or "happening" rather than conventional drama. Just as Paris during the 1920s led in musical productions—concerts, operas, and revues outnumbering London's performances almost two to one—so it was the place people came for the theatrical avant-garde. Diaghilev's fabulous productions for the Ballets Russes, with the music of Stravinsky, Rimsky-Korsakov, Satie, and Poulenc, Darius Milhaud, Arthur Honegger, and the others of "Les Six," set the tone for elegant, and unexpected, performance. Picasso, Braque, Matisse, Derain, Gris, Chirico, Léger, Rouault, Marie Laurencin, Miró, and others designed sets and costumes, and Jean Cocteau's literary burlesques provided scripts for the voices.

From 1916, when Diaghilev's *Parade,* with Cocteau's book and sets by Picasso, caused a fury in Paris, each spring brought more sensational productions; in 1922 Picasso's painting *Two Women Running on the Beach* was enlarged to form the curtain for Cocteau's ballet *Le Train bleu.* In 1923 Rolf de Mare's Swedish Ballet performed Blaise Cendrars's *La Création du monde* to Darius Milhaud's score, with a black cast and striking sets by Léger. Cocteau's *Les Maries de la tour Eiffel,* with music by "Les Six," was produced in 1924.

Beginning that year, Etienne de Beaumont and his countess sponsored extravaganzas in the large Le Cigale theater that spilled in to the de Beaumont home, itself equipped with stationary bars for dancers and a cellar costume shop. The house was also the site of fancy-dress balls for international socialites whose support was needed for the immense theatrical productions. The de Beaumonts, like the princesse de Polignac and Misia Sert, were steady sponsors of new art, and so long as it was financed, experimentation could continue. In 1927 Blaise Cendrars's *Le Pauvre Matelot,* with music by Honegger; Stravinsky's *Oedipus Rex,* with costumes by Picasso and sung text by Cocteau; and Lord Berners's *The Triumph of Neptune,* choreography by George Balanchine, were staged to commemorate twenty years of the Ballets Russes. The year 1928 saw the productions of Erik Satie's *Death of Socrates* and Honegger's *Antigone,* and 1929, that of Cocteau's *Les Enfants terribles.* Closer to Gertrude's nonsequential writing was Antheil and Léger's *Ballet mécanique,* a production set to four player pianos playing simultaneously and discordantly, one running a steel propeller and the other a wooden rattle. The ballet, performed in front of a projection of a film of machinery grinding, evoked the voice of the machine age; the film replicated the effects of Charlie Chaplin's movies, which all Parisians admired. The influence of film, as well as that of the dada performances of the early 1920s, showed clearly in the avant-garde productions.

While Gertrude's experimentation paled in comparison, she often achieved the flavor of Chaplin's humor and Cocteau's outrage, and—dating back to Jarry's *Ubu Roi* and Gide's counterfeit journal-novel—retained an unshaken belief in nonlinear form. Her willingness to deviate from the conventional had already given her a place on the world literary scene. Just as her 1914 *Tender Buttons* had redefined what a book of poems was, and her various portraits had demanded that readers see words themselves as things, so her more than fifty plays and operas erased the line between (literary) play and (staged) event.

Although Donald Evans had wanted to publish her early plays in 1914, Gertrude had refused because she knew even then that her montages of words would be more effective produced (plays are to be played). But nothing happened. Paris (and Monte Carlo) became a blur of craziness of both French theater and surrealist events, yet for the plays and operas Gertrude kept writing, there was no market. For the Plain Edition's publication in 1932 of her four-hundred-page *Operas and Plays*—which included among others *Madame Récamier, Louis XI and Madame Giraud,* and the earlier *Capital Capitals* and *Saints and Singing*—there was neither market nor interest. Yet on February 8, 1934, just days after Gertrude's sixtieth birthday, Virgil Thomson's production of *Four Saints in Three Acts* was hailed in the States as "the most important event of the theatre season."

The opera opened in the newly completed Wadsworth Atheneum in Hartford, Connecticut, and then moved to the Forty-fourth Street Theatre in New York. Atheneum director A. Everett ("Chick") Austin, Jr., had invited the production and helped find backing, something Thomson had been unable to do since finishing the score four years earlier. Designed by Florine Stettheimer, choreographed by Frederick Ashton, and produced by John Houseman, the opera was a labor of love: none of these was paid. Neither was orchestra conductor Alexander Smallens.

Both the opening and the February 7 invitational preview were high-fashion events, with guests from New York, Boston, and Philadelphia coming by plane, special parlor cars on the New Haven Railroad, and Rolls Royce. (Buckminster Fuller arrived in a bubble-shaped Dymaxion car.) Bryher wrote Gertrude that "anyone who counted in the artistic world of New York was on the train"; she said of the performance that it was "one of the most triumphant nights that I ever spent watching a stage." The deep reds, purples, and greens of the costumes set against the blue cellophane cyclorama and pink tarlatan palm trees shocked the eye, just as Gertrude's lyrics shocked the mind. The all-black cast, headed by Beatrice Robinson-Wayne and Edward Matthews, was superb; it was also a touch of Paris, which had been suffused during the 1920s with *le tumulte noir.*

Like much of Gertrude's writing, the delightful and joyous opera is a composite. It is a love poem: "To know to know to love her so." It is a rehearsal of her and Alice's Paris life: "What happened today, a narrative. / We had intended if it were a pleasant day to go to the country." As such, it reproduces the building and furnishing of the Stein/de Monzie house—"a masterpiece"—including plans, spaces, halls, windows and curtains, doors, floors, completion dates, even the characters "Saint Sarah" and "Saint Michael." With the satisfactory completion of the house, which throughout Gertrude's writing symbolizes sexual union, a celebration was in order: "Rejoice saints rejoin saints recommence some reinvite." The ebullient tone of the piece, with its various comic recitatives, stems from the contemplation of this great satisfaction. Stein's emphasis never contradicted what Thomson thought was to be the theme of the opera: "the working artist's working life." As Gertrude presented her daily life, however, it included less art and more gossip. It also reinscribed imagery and themes from her 1922 *Saints and Singing,* with its motif of women's lives as both sexual and spiritual—or spiritual through the sexual.

With Thomson, Gertrude had decided to use baroque Spanish saints, one of her great loves, rather than figures from American history. Saint Therese shares qualities of both Gertrude and Alice (in one of Stein's early notebooks, she noted that "Alice is of the St. Theresa type," governed by the "purity of idolizing emotional passion"). Gertrude represents both their complete union during their honeymoon in Spain, when they stayed longer than planned at Avila, Saint Therese's birthplace, and the larger-than-life figuration of Woman. Positive in her sacrifice and later ennoblement, Therese is yet the common woman, unaware of the male power St. Ignatius represents, a nearly deaf patriarchy that cannot even distinguish among words.

> Saint Therese something like that.
> Saint Therese would and would and would.
> Saint Therese something like that.
> Saint Therese.
> Saint Therese half in doors and half out out of doors.

For all her vagueness, Saint Therese acts—"would and would and would." After this emphasis, Gertrude closes the passage with the key to her attitude about having written a seemingly religious opera: "Any one to tease a saint seriously."

The incremental intensity of Gertrude's long lines gave Thomson an essential rhythmic base for his spirited, often exuberant, music. And as the pace slows at the end of the text, with various saints—"One at a time. One at a time"—falling out of the rushed lives of Saint Therese and "the sisters," the opera ends, spotlighting appropriately not *one* Saint Therese but "Saint Therese and Saint Therese too." The twinning of the female character, a device Gertrude was to use dramatically in her novel *Ida,* was here a metaphor to show the unity between women who were both lovers and, in a larger— and sanctified—sense, "sisters." Had it not been for Maurice Grosser's careful scenario, however, the opera would never have been produced: there was not only too much text, there was too much music, because Thomson had set every word of Gertrude's text to music, even stage directions and speakers' names.

In its produced script, *Four Saints in Three Acts* elicited cheers, calls for the composer, intermittent bursts of excited reaction (as when the last act was announced), and curtain call after curtain call. Gertrude, waiting in Paris, heard about the triumph by cable and letter. Van Vechten wrote her that the opera was "a knockout and a wow" and that he hadn't "seen a crowd more excited since Sacre du Printemps . . . pleasurably excited." After the sold-out New York opening a few weeks later, he wrote that it was "a *wonderful* night. *Your* name in electric lights over the theatre. Cecil Beaton in tears, Jo Davidson saying, 'this is the best thing I have ever seen in N.Y.' Cheers. Everything you can imagine." It ran for fifteen "enchanted weeks," the longest continuous run ever for an American opera. Alfred Harcourt described the "thrilling evening and a really splendid performance" and told Gertrude of Toscanini's vigorous applause. *Variety* reported that *Four Saints* received more coverage than any other opening of the season. While much of that coverage was parodic or vicious (Henry Seidel Canby's *Saturday Review* comment was that *Four Saints* "meant nothing, means nothing, and could mean nothing in itself to anyone but a practicing psychologist"), more of it was a kind of reasoned admiration. Gilbert Seldes commented that he was not sure why *Four Saints* had sparked such interest, but he, too, responded to its "taste and liveliness, humor and feeling, fantasy and vigor. . . . It can be taken as a gigantic piece of mystification and a huge joke; it certainly should not be taken without laughter."

There is less laughter in the financial history of *Four Saints.* Attention has usually focused on Gertrude's holding Thomson to his original fifty-fifty division of profits. In 1927, when she wrote the libretto at Thomson's request, she expected production soon. Never so untalented musically as some people thought, Gertrude knew well what her recitative sections could unleash, what the scenic focus of the "pigeons on the grass" passage—which she designed to represent St. Ignatius's vision, complete with a heavenly chorus—added to the whole. As friends said, it suited Gertrude to pretend she knew little about music; Alice had been trained as a pianist and considered music her province.

With the libretto completed, Thomson's delay in composing the score (though he did it within a year; by July 1928 the work was complete) and his inability to find backers may have been one cause of Gertrude's break with him in 1931. In 1933, then, when he wrote about plans to produce *Four Saints* in Hartford, Gertrude—knowing that the reception of the *Autobiography* would enhance notice of the opera—held to the original terms. After several letters about changing her percentage to one-third, she concluded the discussion: "The important thing is this, the opera was a collaboration, and the proposition made to me in the agreement was in the spirit of that collaboration, 50-50, and the proposition that I accepted was in the spirit of that collaboration 50-50 and the proposition that I continue to accept is the same. . . . Our opera was a collaboration, we own it together and we divide the proceeds 50-50, and we hope that the proceeds will be abundant and we wish each other every possible good luck." Once again, her letter left no opening for any answer except agreement.

At the close of spring 1934, Gertrude had achieved many of her fondest dreams—her name in lights on Broadway, money in her pocket from both Alice's autobiography and her opera (though after its New York opening, the *Four Saints* staff received salaries), and more than a modicum of fame. The name of few other American authors evoked such response, whether of serious appreciation or popular acceptance. On the heels of publicity for both *The Autobiography of Alice B. Toklas* and *Four Saints in Three Acts*, Gertrude's insistence that she was a thoroughly American author led naturally to the plan she had toyed with for years: despite her fear of public speaking, a lecture tour of the States. She would make some money, she and Alice would have a pleasant—even an xciting—vacation, and she could investigate what living in the States would entail (and, not incidentally, what it would cost). She was, therefore, willing to listen when the topic came up, encouraged by Van Vechten, Faÿ, Mike and Sally—who were happy that her work was finally being noticed—Kiddy Rogers (her GI friend), and Bennett Cerf, her new editor at Random House, where her collection *Portraits and Prayers* was scheduled for publication in the fall of 1934.

It was a good time to consider touring because Gertrude, almost from the time of the acceptance of the autobiography, had been unable to work. The grandiloquent calm that was her trademark was shattered by the new activities, both social and professional, just as the peace of both her households was disturbed by the addition of telephones. With her usual honesty, Gertrude worried about her writing block, and numerous questions about her identity as writer haunted much of her work during the 1930s. Who was this Gertrude Stein with her name in lights? Was she the same woman who had lived in Paris for thirty years without appreciation? If so, why had the world finally recognized her? Or, with the kind of reversal common in Gertrude's approach to problems, if she was not, why had the world finally recognized her? Perhaps visiting her native country as a lion would help her sort through these conundrums—and simultaneously strengthen her shaky alliance with Alice.

Lions in America

The short, stocky woman standing in the lounge on board the *Champlain* seemed flustered. Reporters surrounded her, and she swung her large head—the bill of a mannish cap shading her face—as if to butt them out of her way. But her eyes, dark and wide, were kindly, and her cheeks dimpled in a hesitant smile. Surprisingly small in stature and surprisingly clear in what she said, Gertrude Stein had arrived in New York for her lecture tour. Those press people who expected a joke, the "Mama of Dada" or a burlesque of the serious writer, found instead an outspoken but likable woman. Gertrude had come to the States, she said, "to tell very plainly and simply and directly, as is my fashion, what literature is." When asked why she did not write as clearly as she talked, she replied, with twinkling eyes, that she did: "After all, it's all learning how to read it." The journalists came to understand that there was nothing accidental about her current fame: she had chosen her life abroad, and her career, rather than material success in the States, and she impressed on them, with her shy authority, that she was more than just an eccentric.

Gertrude saw her tour as a way to situate herself so that she could continue earning money. *The Autobiography of Alice B. Toklas* may have brought in her first dollars, but Gertrude did not intend for that book to be her only moneymaker. Part of her ability to continue earning would depend on her becoming a personality—she understood this from watching friends, particularly Picasso and Hemingway, manipulate the public. No wonder her eyes sparkled. No wonder she looked carefully, though circumspectly, at the people gathered to meet her (it was a comfort to see Carl Van Vechten and Bennett Cerf there on the dock). And no wonder many of her backward glances were directed at the source of her personal stability, her life companion, Alice, who was even smaller, and much more demure, than she.

It was October 24, 1934, and Gertrude and Alice had spent a pleasant week on board ship, trying out new clothes and new identities. The major worry of this trip, for Toklas, was the way the public would respond to them as lesbians. In 1907, when she had last lived in the States, many of her Jewish friends had censured women who were "that way"; accepting Gertrude's proposal in the summer of 1908 had meant, for her, relinquishing the possibility of returning home. Still afraid of slander, Alice defined her role on this tour as that of Miss Toklas, secretary. Never before, and never afterward, did she play such a part. Gertrude's concern was wider: she was afraid of anti-Semitism. As one friend said, "Gertrude Stein was a Jew. There was a lot more anti-Semitism then than now and Jewish writers were rarer. Her own family had to an extent repudiated her; might not the public do likewise?"

Toklas's craft in playing secretary was superb; few people thought of her as other than Gertrude's secretary and maid. For the seven months of the tour, Alice said nothing that would have given away the real situation—that she and Gertrude were a couple and that much of her own considerable ability had gone into making Stein successful. Dressed more fashionably than Gertrude, Toklas escaped notice by placing herself to the rear and at the periphery of audiences. For all the news coverage of Gertrude, very little mentioned Toklas. (The media's failure to connect the women, even after the publication of the best-selling *Autobiography,* suggests that it, too, was sensitive to the lesbian issues.)

"Gertrude Stein has arrived in New York"

So flashed lights around the *Times* building. Out walking on Broadway, Gertrude was amazed. Alice played her customary role of acerbic deflation, saying "As if we didn't know it." From standing eagerly at the head of the *Champlain* gangplank to being taken back inside for a press conference, grateful that their old friend Kiddy Rogers was among the reporters, to going to her suite at the Algonquin Hotel, where she and Alice were to live for the first month of the tour, Gertrude was awed by New York's welcome. After a quiet meal in their rooms, reading the extensive news coverage of their arrival, the two walked out into the maze of lights that New York had become. The *Times* building took their breath away. So did the fact that people stopped to stare at them and a few asked how they were enjoying their trip. Then they walked back to the hotel and, for the first time in thirty years, slept in American beds.

No lectures were scheduled until November 1, so they had time to learn their way around the city. Gertrude was delighted with the long, interesting walks, on some of which fruit vendors gave her apples and many passersby greeted her; Alice scrutinized store windows. By the time Natalie Barney found them in New York, Gertrude was so skillful in crossing streets that Barney asked her how she achieved such calm. "All these people, including the nice taxi drivers, recognize and are careful of me," Stein said. All except the elevator operator at Random House, that is: when Gertrude and Alice paid their first visit to Cerf, the operator—without asking them their destination—stopped the car at the third floor, where there was an employment agency for domestic help. A "highly-amused" Gertrude told her publisher, "That damn-fool elevator boy thought we were a couple of cooks."

Cerf himself felt like an errand boy. He had told Gertrude he was at her service, and she had taken him at his word, letting him know that there were people she wanted to meet and expecting him to make the necessary arrangements. At the Random House party, she saw Henry McBride and the Knopfs again and met editor Saxe Commins, whose question about her logic in *Four Saints* she dismissed imperiously, saying, "My dear, you simply don't understand." She also met Miriam Hopkins, who became a devoted friend; George Gershwin, who played the score of his new opera *Porgy and Bess* for her; and Mary Pickford and Lewis Gannett. At the request of Alexander Woollcott, Cerf gave a private luncheon so that Woollcott could talk with Stein. After the raconteur had interrupted Gertrude repeatedly, she finally "stopped him cold and said, 'Mr. Woollcott, I am talking.'" As the conversation continued, she several times corrected him. When he impatiently informed her, "People don't dispute Woollcott," she countered, "I'm not people; I'm Gertrude Stein." Like nearly everyone else she met, he, too, became a friend.

The Van Vechtens also entertained for them, inviting the Bromfields one time and Katharine Cornell another, along with groups of theater people and such black intellectuals as James Weldon Johnson and Walter White. (Cornell—Kitty, as Stein called her—invited Gertrude and Alice for lemon pie.) It was during this tour that the Van Vechten–Toklas–Stein friendship reached its "family" state, with Papa Woojums, Mama Woojums (Alice) and Baby Woojums (Gertrude) becoming their private names. Many of Van Vechten's and Alice's letters refer to Baby as "it" or "he" and give it the temperament, and demands, of an infant.

Florine Stettheimer's tea was less cordial. The painter who had designed *Four Saints* was a friend of Leo Stein's, and that may have contributed to the atmosphere of "mutual rejection." Observers recalled, "Not a compliment passed between them." But Gertrude had few unpleasant moments. Favorites at the Harcourt Brace offices, she and Alice spent Thanksgiving with the Harcourts in Connecticut. Staff and residents at the Algonquin also liked Stein's "innocent merriment." When Louis Bromfield checked in, not knowing that Stein and Toklas were there, the management arranged a cocktail party for them. Bromfield brought with him his elderly father, an Ohio farmer who was slightly deaf.

> The elder Bromfield stared a moment at Miss Stein's sheared head and tweed-squared shoulders, and clammed up. But the little party went along well until Miss Stein, with her impeccable manners, leaned forward and asked old Mr. Bromfield how he liked New York.
> The elder Bromfield cupped his ear and shook his head.
> "Louis!" he shouted.

His son hurried across the room and Father Bromfield hooked a horny thumb in Miss Stein's direction.

"What did the gentleman say?" he asked.

To her credit, Gertrude thought the misidentification humorous. She was so thoroughly enjoying the attention and the acclaim—particularly being interviewed for the Pathé newsreel and making a recording at Aeolian Hall—that nothing bothered her those first weeks in New York. As she told William Lundell of NBC, "the people on the street—never could I have imagined the friendly, personal, simple, direct, considerate contact that I have with all of them. They all seem to know me and they all speak to me and I who am easily frightened by anything unexpected find the spontaneous, considerate contact with all and any New York touching and pleasing and I am deeply moved and awfully happy in it." Ironically, Gertrude's welcome from this American city reassured her of the goodness of people, whereas during the past year she had been nervous about living in Belley

Gertrude felt that France during the thirties had been subtly, slowly changing. War rumors underlay the decisions of many of her friends and her brother Mike to leave Europe. The Stein/de Monzie house in Garches was on the market and whenever it sold (*if* ever; Gabrielle liked to point out that the Le Corbusier structure was not to everyone's taste and that those who admired the house often had no money), the family would return to California to live. Added to the increasingly frightening political news was Gertrude's anxiety over the mysterious deaths of two women friends in Belley. Perhaps Madame Pernollet's fall onto the cement courtyard of her hotel was suicide, but if so, why? And no one could think the death of another friend's lesbian lover—caused by two bullets to the head—a suicide. And why were cars tampered with near their Bilignin home? If such things could occur in the peaceful Ain valley, where could she and Alice—two aging women—live safely?

In New York, she forgot such history. Alice arranged for everything—interviews, lectures, meals, travel, so she could sleep late, enjoy room service, walk around the city, see films, and sign books. Frances Steloff at the Gotham Book Mart arranged a stunning window filled with her personal collection of Stein's works and Van Vechten's photographs, which Gertrude walked past frequently. (Unfortunately, Random House had arranged her book signing at Brentano's, and Steloff was upset.) At the signing, too, Gertrude's witty comments won friends. The only thing missing in her triumph was attention from her New York relatives, still angry over her depiction of their family in *The Making of Americans*.

Gertrude as Lecturer

Gertrude's first lecture, on November 1 at the Colony Club, sponsored by the Museum of Modern Art in conjunction with a Picasso show, was attended by New York's fashionable. Although she had refused to lend Picasso's portrait when Alfred Barr asked for it, she liked being part of the occasion. (After Mike and Sally's Matisses were held in Germany, Gertrude never loaned any of her art.)

She dressed with care in a dark silk dress, happy that Alice had forced her to order new shoes—flat-heeled Mary Janes, instead of her usual sandals. She added an ornate diamond brooch, checked the handsome leather case—also new—that held her lecture about painting, and then she and Alice set off for their long walk. (They had refused the limousine the museum wanted to send for them.) As arranged with Marvin Ross, the tour organizer, Gertrude would speak to audiences of no more than five hundred, and she would be onstage alone, with no introduction. Her fee was $100 for colleges and $250 for clubs and other community groups. She would eat meals privately beforehand (and usually chose oysters and honeydew melon). Happily, she had recovered from a bout of laryngitis that a throat specialist had assured her was a nervous condition.

Journalist T. S. Matthews described a typical Stein lecture:

> The first glimpse you get of her, as she trudges resolutely up on the lecture platform, is reassuring. This solid elderly woman, dressed in no-nonsense rough-spun clothes, seems at once smaller and more human than her monumental photographs or J. Davidson's squat image of her. As she looks out over the audience and thanks us, with a quick low hoot of laughter, for "controlling yourselves to 500," we laugh too, in appreciative relief, and settle back in our seats to give her the once-over.

And what the audience sees is "deep black eyes that make her graven face and its archaic smile come alive." What it hears is her "flatly sensible, Middle Western aunt" voice saying "Amorrican." And the listeners

> notice with approval that she indulges in no gestures—except the natural, grandmotherly one of taking her pince-nez off and putting them on; and we soon discover, with mixed feelings, that she is not a very good lecturer: she drops her voice at the end of every sentence, and talks more and more to one side of the room. . . . The total impression we carry away is that of a fundamentally serious, not to say megalomaniac writer—are all really serious people megalomaniacs?—who has come back home for a visit in the happy consciousness that she has triumphed at last.

Aside from a few detractors who left early and sometimes noisily, Matthews's was the response of most of the audience. Ross lost his job over the three Columbia University lectures (more than seventeen hundred people had tickets for one of them), so Alice took over as tour manager. She could not change the formidable schedule, however, and Gertrude found herself traveling from New York to Princeton (where her talk made a disciple of critic Donald Sutherland) to Chicago. As guests of United Airlines, Gertrude and Alice flew in to this last city to attend a performance of *Four Saints*, directed this time by Virgil Thomson in Louis Sullivan's auditorium. Although the women carried Hopi Indian rabbits' feet, they were afraid, but once in the air, Gertrude grew calm.

Met on the airfield by women from the Chicago Arts Club waving roses, Gertrude managed a large press conference and then, as guests of socialite Bobsey Chapman Goodspeed, Alice and she saw the exhilarating *Four Saints in Three Acts* from a private box. Dinner for twenty at the Goodspeeds was an example of what Alice called "perfect *cuisine*," beginning with a clear turtle soup and ending with champagne and a dessert of "nougat and roses, cream and small coloured candles." After sitting beside Gertrude through dinner, John Houseman mentioned to Thomson that her lips "showed dark spots such as his father's had" when he was ill with cancer. But no observer would have thought Gertrude ill: her participation in the weekend was so energetic that she was invited back later to give a two-week series of lectures for University of Chicago students. Both women enjoyed meeting Thornton Wilder and seeing Fanny Butcher, Emily Chadbourne Crane, and other Paris acquaintances.

After flying to New York for a lecture at the New School for Social Research and then traveling by train to Philadelphia for lectures in the city and at Bryn Mawr, Gertrude and Alice were tired but still enthusiastic. As Gertrude wrote, "It is wonderful and a little mad but most delicious, a wonderful thing to have happen to me." To other friends, she wrote, "I want to stay in the US forever," and "I will yet write the opera of the States of the United States, it would make a lovely opera," but she could scarcely find time to prepare the new lectures the two-week stay at the University of Chicago required. And there was Alfred Harcourt taking them to the Yale-Dartmouth football game, with a crowd surrounding Gertrude for her autograph. Then another train trip to Boston, for lectures at the Signet Club at Harvard and in the Agassiz Theatre at Radcliffe. And there was the small accident after one of her three lectures at the Academy of Music in Brooklyn (where she met poet Marianne Moore), when her finger got closed in a door by a rapt listener and she was taken to a drugstore for first aid. Disappointed as she was with five-and-tens, Gertrude fell in love with American drugstores, especially the lunch counters: "I was always going in to buy a detective novel just to watch the people sitting on the stools. It was like a piece of provincial life in a real city. The people sitting on the stools and eating in the drug store all looked and acted as if they lived in a small country town."

Detroit, however, was a different story. Out walking one evening, Gertrude ran into police loudspeakers and searchlights: a murderer was on the loose. Rushing back to the hotel, she told Alice to get them out of town, so Alice phoned their friend Joseph Brewer, a former editor at Payson and Clarke who was now president of Olivet College. He drove in and took them back to the tiny campus. As Gertrude wrote, "We had a quiet but occupied 24 hours as I had to talk to the faculty and more or less individually to the very charming 200 odd students." In her interview with the school paper, she pointed out, wryly, that newspapers thrive on repeating what readers expect—especially in headlines:

> For years they have been saying the same thing about me, repeating in the same words over and over again. Now, while they are beginning to realize that they have been wrong . . . they are beginning to find their way gingerly to a clearer statement of my work. The headlines still say the same thing, because as a general rule, that is all that people read, and people can glance at them and maintain an unshattered calm. The stories underneath are beginning to change, however, and sometime, when the public has been eased into it, the headlines also will change.

On the trip from Olivet to Ann Arbor, where she was to lecture next, Gertrude changed a flat tire and reassured Brewer, "Don't worry, we'll make it on time."

Gertrude's pattern in the Midwest remained constant: she gave a serious lecture, took on questioners with tactful relish, and heartily enjoyed the social life. During the two weeks of her New England schedule, well cared for by the Rogerses, she spoke at Smith, Mount Holyoke, Amherst, Springfield, Wesleyan, and Choate and went sleigh riding, saw Deerfield Village, and had tea with people who were embarrassed when she asked for an apple instead of the cocktail food—and there were no apples. Gertrude also disliked dormitory food and often requested a soft-boiled egg and an orange as her meal. And the snow that had been "xciting" in November was, by now, only a worry. She wrote a friend that New England was "just like Switzerland nothing here but education and snow drifts and inadequate food." She did find it interesting that "the negro waiters everywhere want my Gte Stein signature I guess on account of Hartford."

Her progress through the South was similar. After lecturing at the College of William and Mary, the University of North Carolina, and Sweet Briar and in Charleston—where the camellias already bloomed—she flew further south and met Sherwood Anderson, who brought a bag of sweet oranges and drove them to see the Mississippi River. She celebrated her sixty-first birthday "on the road," and enjoyed a lavish dinner party at Ellen Glasgow's Richmond home. But she found the trip tiring:

> seeing all the places were anybody was born and died and lived in Virginia and an awful lot of people did do those things any one of those things in Virginia. The nicest was the University of Virginia and the Raven Society and they gave me the key of the room of Edgar Allan Poe in the University, it says Raven on one side and

Virginia on the other. . . . We did see Union Prison at least where it was which was a relief from too much Robert E. Lee, Virginia certainly has him on its mind you might think it was yesterday or tomorrow.

Busy as Gertrude's schedule was, her writing never faltered. She wrote regularly to friends in France, as well as these in Massachusetts, New York, and Chicago. She wrote a short essay about Alfred Stieglitz, another that Random House sold to *Cosmopolitan* for fifteen hundred dollars, and a series of six essays for the *New York Herald Tribune* on her impressions of American education, homes, crime, and other subjects. She was thankful she had already written the lectures for the tour. Encouraged by Bernard Faÿ and James Laughlin, the young Harvard student Faÿ had brought to Belley, she had prepared essays on painting, plays, poetry and grammar, portraits and repetition, the way *The Making of Americans* came to be written, and—the most immodest title of all—"What Is English Literature." (Laughlin's task—aside from changing tires when they went driving—was to write abstracts of each lecture, to be used for publicity in the States.) These six talks were published in 1935 as *Lectures in America,* and the four additional lectures she wrote for the University of Chicago appeared the same year as *Narration: Four Lectures by Gertrude Stein,* with an introduction by Thornton Wilder.

She also paid her U.S. taxes. As Mike had explained in February 1935: "About your income tax. You have not made a declaration for years because you did not have enough income above your personal exemption to make you liable for the tax. You were living on capital and selling paintings, which you owned." As she filled out the form, Gertrude smiled to think that she had finally—at sixty-one—made enough money to be a tax-paying American citizen.

The Maker of "Great Books"

As a psychologist who had herself been a college student for eight years, Gertrude had been part of the world of America education long enough to know that all the hoopla about the University of Chicago's "Great Books" program meant little if teachers kept lecturing students. She was not awed by Mortimer Adler or Robert Hutchins, the thirty-five-year-old president of the University of Chicago, who had created the Great Books curriculum. In fact, during the Hutchinses' dinner for her, Gertrude questioned Adler about their choices of texts, pointing out that most were nineteenth-century translations and probably bad prose. Adler replied, "But, Miss Stein, we are concerned not with belles lettres but with the communication of ideas." When he argued with the already flushed Gertrude that "Surely you can see that there are more ideas in one chapter of *The Wealth of Nations* than there are in all of Milton's *Paradise Lost?*" she disagreed, "Not at all! There are more ideas in one *page* of *Paradise Lost.* . . . Government is the least interesting thing in human life . . . creation and the expression of that creation is a damn sight more interesting." Unfortunately, she continued, "Now I don't want to argue this any further. You're narrow. And I can tell by the narrow shape of your head that you're a born arguer. You could prove anything to me but you'd be wrong."

Dinner guests were shocked at the interchange. Although Thornton Wilder admired Gertrude for her fierce return, Mrs. Hutchins was angry and saw to it that her husband never offered Gertrude a position at the university as he had been considering doing. As if they were living a Mack Sennett comedy spot, at the height of the Stein-Adler exchange, the maid announced that the police were at the door. "The police!" Adler said, "very red in the face." Gertrude knew they were only there to pick her up for a promised tour of the city, arranged by a journalist friend. Driving through the rainy, badly lit Chicago streets, both women felt, as they had in Detroit, that some American cities were more dangerous than their Paris. They watched the officers question blacks in the ghetto; they visited a dance marathon that had been in progress for six weeks. When asked if they wanted to be photographed with one of the exhausted pairs, the women replied that they did not want to remember this inhumane part of American life. Much about American life during the Great Depression was horrifying, but Gertrude and Alice were usually insulated from what was already becoming commonplace hardship.

Several days later, Hutchins arranged for Gertrude to meet with a Great Books class. Discussion was so lively that Adler and Hutchins were incredulous. When Gertrude explained that students "always talk. They like to talk," Adler admitted, "Not for us." Gertrude then reminded the men that she "always allowed the young people to formulate their own ideas." Her teaching method went beyond the "Socratic": her aim was to be a responsive listener, to force people to "unpack" their ideas for her. She lost interest in people not because *they* bored her but because their *ideas* bored her, and she loved the young because they still had the promise of having ideas: "Everyone had some genius when young, since then he can really listen, simultaneously listen and speak. When growing older, many people become tired and listen less and less. . . . Only the one who was such an eager listener had also the right to demand that he be listened to."

Gertrude's immersion in young people was a continuing source of pleasure for her, but her real enjoyment during this pause in the hectic tour was her reconciliation with Alice. Having seen how integral she was to Gertrude's life as she planned, and controlled, every detail of their trip, Alice was finally ready to relinquish her anger. With the theatrical flair she sometimes hid, Gertrude's lover was enjoying playing the role of Miss Toklas, secretary.

On Gertrude's return to the University of Chicago, she worked individually with thirty students, most of them handpicked by Wilder, as well as lecturing. She wrote Van Vechten, "Being a really truly college professor is hard work, particularly when you have never been one before, I have had to write four lectures . . . then two hours of class every day and then two hours of meeting individual students and looking at their ms. and telling them how not to go on doing the same, that part is easy, and anyway although I really do not like work I am enjoying it a lot and finding it very interesting."

Ecstatic living in Wilder's Drexel Avenue apartment (he had moved into dormitory housing), Alice thought its efficient kitchenette a dream facility. Gertrude rented a Drive-Yourself car, and although negotiating the Chicago streets in snow was difficult, she and Alice made it to a number of places (Alice's favorite was the Chicago Historical Museum). One day, a policeman pulled Gertrude over after she had made an illegal U-turn; he did not ticket her but predicted that she might not live to leave town. Her usual good luck, however, was with her.

Wilder came often for dinner, cementing what Alice called their "warm friendship. Endless were their discussions, on walks in the country, in crowded city streets." Wilder became the ideal pupil. He could absorb whatever Gertrude gave him (unlike Hemingway, whom she described to Lincoln Steffens as someone who sat at her feet and took "'not much,' she said, but it was all he could use"). The two women mixed academics with social life, seeing Ellen LaMotte and Hadley Hemingway Mowrer and meeting Mary Garden, but they felt that returning to Chicago was anticlimactic. They looked forward to the Texas tour; after Dallas, Austin, Houston, and Fort Worth would come California, a state they were both anticipating.

The End of the Story

Being in California was not the homecoming Gertrude had expected. Just as she could no longer find her Cambridge in Massachusetts, so she did not recognize much about Oakland. Although the Tubbs' Hotel was still there, the Stratton house had been moved, and the other houses her family had rented had been replaced with new construction. "It was frightening quite frightening driving there," she told reporters, after she had struggled to find the Mark Hopkins Hotel at the top of Nob Hill in her Drive-Yourself car. Alice, however, loved California's sheer beauty and was so pleased with the unequaled orchards, gardens, and flowers that she would have been happy to stay. For the first time, she and Gertrude tasted avocados, passion fruit, and abalone; throughout California they "indulged in gastronomic orgies— sand dabs *meuniere* [sic], rainbow trout in aspic, grilled soft-shell crabs, *paupiettes* of roast fillets of pork, eggs Rossini and *tarte Chambord*. . . . At Fisherman's Wharf we waited for two enormous crabs to be cooked in a cauldron on the side-walk, and they were still quite warm when we ate them."

California, too, greeted Gertrude with a media blitz. Interviews, stories, articles by any number of old friends (including sculptor David Edstrom), and a private screening of her Pathé newsreel, which made her feel very strange—especially hearing her voice as she read the "pigeons on the grass" passage from *Four Saints in Three Acts*. Her lectures were well received, and countless people wanted to entertain for them. Gertrude wrote a friend, "It is very lively. I had no idea one could have gone to school with so many people. . . . Those I did not go to school with Alice went to school with."

At this stage of the tour, exhausted after six months of performance, the two turned down more invitations than they accepted. Though Mabel Dodge was insistent, having planned to make poet Robinson Jeffers an intimate of the Stein circle, Gertrude and Alice would not see her. At Van Vechten's urging, novelist Gertrude Atherton arranged several days for them in Los Angeles. They did see Harriet Levy, Upton Sinclair, Lincoln Steffens and Ella Winter, and the young novelist William Saroyan; they dined with the Noel Sullivans and had tea with Senator and Mrs. Crocker. At Berkeley, surrounded by an overflow crowd, Gertrude met Robert Haas, then a young student, who recorded her "calm, commanding presence, the freshness and absolute clarity of her language and intention, her natural presentation and her flow of ideas." Another student described Gertrude's warmth: "She really cares. And when it is time to leave there is no curt nod. . . . She smiles, she smiles beautifully, clutches your hand in her warm chubby hands and really gives you a friendly clasp. And she means it when she says, 'Good night. And I *do* hope I'll see you again. And if I don't you will write to me in Paris, won't you? Fine!'"

The California event that the women remembered best was the dinner party given by Mrs. Lillian May Ehrman, who had asked Gertrude whom she would like to meet in Hollywood. Stein had requested Charlie Chaplin and Dashiell Hammett. Although her hostess did not know either and locating the reclusive Hammett took some coast-to-coast sleuthing, everyone she asked (on very short notice) came. Sitting beside Chaplin and Paulette Goddard, whom Toklas called "an enfant terrible," Gertrude "won his heart" by following suit—when he nervously spilled coffee on his hostess's Belgian lace tablecloth. In talking with Lillian Hellman and Hammett, whom Stein thought an important writer because of his bleak view of American culture, Gertrude asked him why male writers in the nineteenth century "did invent all kinds and a great number of men. The women on the other hand never could invent women." But, she continued, in this century male authors "all write about themselves, they are always themselves as strong or weak or mysterious or passionate or drunk or controlled but always themselves as the women used to do in the nineteenth century. Now you yourself always do it now why is it." Hammett replied that the answer was "simple. In the nineteenth century men were confident, the women were not but in the twentieth century the men have no confidence and so they have to make themselves as you say more beautiful more intriguing more everything and they cannot make any other man because they have to hold on to themselves not

having any confidence. Now I he went on have even thought of doing a father and a son to see if in that way I could make another one." With her
usual candor and warmth, Gertrude made friends of even the most taciturn.

When she talked with Chaplin, they discussed the movement of art,
and he said that he found talking pictures very different from silent films because in the former the actor's voice created a rhythm. Gertrude later wrote
that he "wanted the sentiment of movement invented by himself." She recognized the aim; as she had written in a draft of *The Autobiography of Alice
B. Toklas,* she began each piece with the principle of setting "a sentence for
herself as a kind of metronome."

Looking back on the months of touring, both Gertrude and Alice felt
that the closest they had come to feeling at home was while spending
Christmas with Julian and Rose Ellen Stein. The Baltimore Steins were
Gertrude's favorite cousins: Julian handled some of her finances, as he did
Leo's, and Rose Ellen was translating the *Autobiography* into braille. That
Julian was recovering from a heart attack gave Gertrude and Alice reason to
refuse most other hospitality, and Gertrude asked to see only Aunt Fanny,
some of the other Keyser aunts, and Uncle Eph. Opening the Christmas
morning stockings—filled with cooking utensils for Alice and dime-store
oddities for Gertrude—long remained a favorite memory.

When Etta Cone wrote offering to entertain for them, Gertrude refused
her. Rebuffed, Etta went to North Carolina during the week of Gertrude's
stay. On December 24, the two women did visit the Fitzgeralds, compli-
menting Zelda—home from the hospital—on her paintings. Scott's somewhat embarrassing gratitude for Gertrude's coming showed how much her
friendship meant to him. On December 30, at Eleanor Roosevelt's invitation, they went to the White House for tea. Gertrude wrote friends that the
people she met there were "not a bit cheerful, and very strange almost
weird," so busy were they with the president's message to Congress. Recognizing that the Depression was "the disaster of the U.S.," Gertrude still had
little idea of the momentous change in social policy Roosevelt was engineering. Calling the rushed politicians "provincial," she wrote, "Everybody tells
you so many things that you would imagine nobody ought to tell anybody."
The eminently self-confident Gertrude also enclosed clippings from interviews people had done with her, remarking, "You see although indiscreet I
am very discreet."

Though consistently discreet about her lesbian marriage and her less-
than-upper-class origins, during the seven months of her tour Gertrude had
tested America's acceptance of her person and her work by pretending
forthright camaraderie. She had moved in and through the very highest social and intellectual circles in the States and, unlike her experience a
decade earlier in England, she had seen little anti-Semitism. No matter that
her own prominent New York family had snubbed her: crowds of strangers

were eager to take their place. Somehow, and unexpectedly, by going her own way and, of necessity, challenging family authority, Gertrude Stein had managed to win—and to win big.

The discreet, and beloved, Gertrude returned to New York for a week of parties and good-byes before Alice and she sailed for Le Havre on the *Champlain* on May 4. They went to Princeton to hear Ellen Glasgow lecture and to a garden party at the Van Vechtens'. They coped with Leo Stein's *New Yorker* rebuttal of Eugenio Montale's saying that he hated Gertrude (Leo said that although he had never commended his sister's writing, he felt no "personal hatred"). They shrugged off this bit of family conflict at the Random House farewell party, which lasted until four in the morning. As they left, Cerf recalled that Gertrude "told me how much she loved seeing her writing in print and asked me how I felt about it. I told her that anything she wanted to see in print, we would do." What Gertrude heard was that Random House would bring out a book every year, and her response to Cerf was a quizzical "Just like that," to which he answered, "Just like that."

Satisfied beyond her fondest dreams that her publisher would keep this promise, Gertrude looked back at the months in America with joy. She said of Chicago, "I don't know a place in the world more beautiful. And I lost my heart to Texas." Sorry to be leaving Cerf, the Van Vechtens, the Rogerses, and their many other friends, Alice and she were exhilarated by the success of their tour—what Toklas called "an experience and an adventure which nothing that might follow would ever equal." As Gertrude said when she arrived in Paris on May 12, "I am already homesick for America. I never knew it was so beautiful."

The World in Crisis (1935–1947)

She had worked every day for as long as she could remember. She had devoted her best, most intense, moments to her writing, hoping that at the peak of the day (or night) her writing would be its most skillful, most meaningful—that it would be most itself. She had pursued her art through household arguments with her older brother, through the bliss and struggle of her marriage to Alice Toklas, and through two world wars. Now, at the end of the second of those, she was working her way through a novel (*Brewsie and Willie*), a long play (*The Mother of Us All*), and the play that charted her life in Occupied France, *Yes Is for a Very Young Man*.

It was a horrible experience. "I was terribly frightened. I had been so sure there was not going to be war and here it was, it was war, and I made quite a scene. I said, 'They shouldn't! They shouldn't!' and they [Madame Pierlot and the d'Aiguys] were very sweet, and I apologized and said I was sorry but it was awful, and they comforted me—they, the French, who had so much at stake, and I had nothing at stake comparatively." Alice and she hardly knew what to do in Belley. Were they safer there than in Paris? Had all their friends gone to Italy or Spain or managed to return to the States? She wrote, "Sometimes about 10 o'clock in the evening I get scared about everything." Alice wrote, "In the beginning, like camels, we lived on our past. We had been well nourished." The two women who lived and spoke as one shared the world war in its entirety, living on potatoes and what other vegetables they could grow, reading cookbooks at night, growing smaller and smaller. They made coffee from birdseed, and when Gertrude went for her long, long walks, she bartered for a single egg, or a chunk of firewood for the open hearth, or a bit of news.

The Second Autobiography

America might well have seemed "beautiful" and idyllic to Gertrude and Alice. Insulated from the economic chaos that threatened the country's very existence, they had seen the best of its famed democratic life. The still-wealthy patrons of the arts and the students that constituted Gertrude's usual audience were intent on maintaining normalcy, wearing blinders when they had to mix with the steadily growing mass of the poor. Even as protected as they had been, however, both women had realized that they could never move back to the States. As Gertrude had written to friends, acknowledging that she liked "to be fairly luxurious," living in America "would cost a hell of a lot of money." Ironically, she continued, "God did not make me cautious but then on the other hand he did not make me reckless." By choosing to stay in France during the coming war, she and Alice were extraordinarily reckless. That they survived the decade was nothing short of miraculous.

From the euphoric triumph of the tour, the two returned to a country paralyzed with fear. Paris was deluged with rumors of war: newspapers were filled with stories of Nazi aggression; practice bombing alerts were planned. The bewildered women—who could not believe the dramatic change in their city—stayed only long enough to retrieve Basket and Pépé from the friends who had taken care of them and to say a sad good-bye to Mike, Sally, and Allan's son, Danny, who were moving back to the States, traveling with Gabrielle de Monzie and Etta Cone. Frail and kindly, Mike told Gertrude they would not see each other again; his loss was the bitterest in her life of many losses.

Had they been in France during the latter part of 1934 and early 1935, Gertrude and Alice might have understood why Mike was adamant about leaving Europe. The contrast between their recent secure lives as celebrities in the States cared for almost reverently wherever they went, and the unimaginable terrors that lay ahead for an occupied Europe was so immense that few people could have comprehended it. So the women carried on with their unrealistic plan to last out any conflict in pastoral Belley.

They drove to their beloved Bilignin. On May 21, scarcely ten days after their return to France, Gertrude wrote friends, "The French army is with us, that is the reserves in their 15 days training and we have 28 in the barn with their machine guns." Her matter-of-fact tone masked her real concern; as she wrote later, "For the first time in a hundred years truth is really stranger than fiction. Any truth." Less abstractly, "I suppose there comes the saturation point of worry and then normal life begins again and just goes on being." Despite her aplomb, she found it difficult to understand that political situations had worsened so quickly during seven months.

Gertrude could not believe there would be war: she was sure that no European country would willingly face those terrible losses again. As it had been before World War I, her mode now was denial. It had been denial in 1933, when Hitler, as chancellor of Germany, had removed that country from the League of Nations and begun his persecution of the Jews, control of the press and film, and book burning. Observers tried to discount Hitler by linking him with Mussolini: because both governed through fear—"the terrifying SS"—both would be overthrown internally. Most people were not ignorant; as early as 1933, Janet Flanner had written *New Yorker* columns about German Jewish refugees in Belgium and Switzerland forbidden to look for work so as not to compete in the local labor market.

Formally enacted in 1935, Hitler's anti-Semitic Nuremberg laws had actually been in place since 1933: Jews (defined as those having one [so-called] non-Aryan grandparent) could not be citizens, own land, or hold office. Neither could they marry Aryans or shop in Aryan stores. Jews were forced out of the legal profession, medicine, and the universities, where only 1.5 percent of student enrollment could be Jewish. Being married to a Jew was as dangerous as having been born Jewish. Other "imperfect specimens" in German eyes that were liable to persecution were homosexuals, Gypsies, and anti-Nazi intellectuals; many people from these groups had already been murdered. Along with severe Jewish persecution, by March 1935 Hitler had reinstated conscription and military training. He had also established a national air force, breaking all the disarmament provisions of the Treaty of Versailles. Later, when he saw that England and France offered no resistance to Mussolini's taking Ethiopia, Hitler repudiated the Locarno Pact and invaded the Rhineland, also without reprisals.

In 1935 Janet Flanner's three-part *New Yorker* profile of Hitler, based on *Mein Kampf* and interviews, was denounced as "pro-Fuehrer" by Malcolm Cowley and other liberals. Bewildered, the naive Flanner wrote to Gertrude about her chagrin that readers were "so political." Gertrude replied that class loyalties easily obscured reality. (Both she and Flanner moved among well-established people who—in both England and France—favored at least some of Hitler's reforms over what they saw as the more dangerous threat of communism.) She wrote, "It's funny that all these writers who are successful make lots of money and are snobbish are proletarian, while those of us who do not make money and have not been snobbish are conservative, I suppose it is natural, as Robinson Crusoe's father said to him, you my son were born under the most fashionable conditions, your father was neither rich nor poor, and I suppose if you are neither rich nor poor neither money nor position is on your mind."

Gertrude clearly had no conception of everything that was happening in Germany—but she was far from alone in her imperception. What she knew was that, in economic and political terms, France during the 1930s had seen a bevy of governments and financial policies and that many of her French friends were discontent, afraid that sheer anarchy would destroy their country. Outsiders could see that France's internal affairs were not the problem. In 1934, when their young visitor James Laughlin, heir to American steel interests, tried to discuss the threat of Nazi takeover with their French friends the d'Aiguys at dinner, Bob d'Aiguy reprimanded him: "Hush, young man, you do not know anything about war. Our family has suffered in many ways from wars, so please hush until you know more about what you are talking about." Laughlin excused himself and left the table, but in such a contretemps, Gertrude opted for experiential knowledge over intellectual: that the d'Aiguys had survived the Great War gave them credibility nonparticipants would never have. In this case, however, her reliance on the experiential was mistaken: she was confronting experiences no one had yet had—or was able to envision.

And there was always the fallacy of the rational. Gertrude had been educated—and educated well—in an empirically rationalist system. She was sure she could explain the fascist obsession with the destruction of non-Aryans by taking the reasonable, intellectual line. Accordingly she asked, "How can a nation that feels itself as strong as the Germans do be afraid of a small handful of people like the Jews, why it does seem funny, most strange and very funny, they [the Germans] must be afraid. . . . What can they [the Jews] do to them, after all what can they do to them."

There is little question that Gertrude was also influenced by her close friend Bernard Faÿ. The author of a biography of Benjamin Franklin, Faÿ was now translating *The Autobiography of Alice B. Toklas* into French, and he had lectured and written about her work for years. As an intellectual and academic of a certain conservatism, Faÿ approved of Hitler, and when he visited Gertrude, they would discuss the Führer's qualities of greatness. Even at her most positive, however, Gertrude tempered her enthusiasm. When Lansing Warren interviewed her in spring 1934, he misleadingly headlined her ironic remark that Hitler should receive the Nobel Peace Prize—because by suppressing the Jews and others of difference, he was ending struggle in Germany (Lansing did not understand that the concept of struggle was always positive to Stein). Missing her humor, ill chosen as it was, Lansing also did not see that Gertrude was reprimanding the intellectuals of the world for making judgments about matters they did not understand—the

European power struggles. Throughout the interview, she consistently criticized fascism, saying the Germans knew nothing but how to obey.

But so far as leaving France, Gertrude would not listen to Mike: instead, she blamed her brother's apprehension on his poor health and continued her busy, somewhat oblivious life. Alice and she did not own a radio; in Bilignin, they read few newspapers—and those they did see were not given to in-depth political analysis. In France, it was already unsafe to criticize fascism. American friends urged the two to return to the States, under the guise of making another lecture tour, but no one insisted they return— or offered them shelter—although Van Vechten came close to that imperative. Unfortunately, Gertrude was consistent in maintaining her position from before World War I: that there would be no conflict because war was totally irrational. In retrospect, it was her behavior that was irrational.

The Work of Writing

Life in Belley resumed, despite the twenty-five hundred soldiers encamped in the area, six hundred of those in tiny Bilignin. Alice kept her views to herself and worked furiously in the garden, and Gertrude began learning how to help her; they rewarded themselves with visits to the d'Aiguys, Baronne Pierlot and her sons in Béon, and Madame André Giraud. News from the States was good: Ivan Kahn was trying to place "The Gentle Lena" with a film studio. At Natalie Barney's parties, Alice and Gertrude renewed their friendships with novelist Radclyffe Hall and Lady Troubridge and met Gaston Bergery and his American wife, Bettina Shaw Jones (he would later serve as Vichy ambassador to the Soviet Union and to Turkey), and other French socialites. They had lunches with the duchesse of Clermont-Tonnerre and Sunday brunches at the Louis Bromfields. Amid gossip about Mabel Dodge's current volume of memoirs (there would be four) and walks with the dogs, using her new pedometer, a souvenir from the States, Gertrude read detective novels, mysteries, and James M. Cain's *The Postman Always Rings Twice.*

In the summer of 1935, they (on separate occasions) entertained Bernard Faÿ, James Laughlin, and Thornton Wilder, who was traveling from Germany back to the States. During Wilder's ten-day visit, their friendships deepened: Gertrude and Thornton liked each other's writing, and they liked each other's talk. Although Gertrude was more impassioned about methods of writing, they both agreed that "all writing is a Leap," that rational explanations were inadequate. Gertrude's "meditation" was Wilder's "reflection," and he kept journals as a means of trapping his wary thought processes. There he often quoted Stein: "The difficult thing (in 'thinking') is to hold so many things in one's head at one time." In France, he again saw Gertrude consciously setting aside time to let her mind be, to travel on its own pursuits: "In Bilignin she would sit in her rocking chair facing the valley she has described so often, holding one or the other of the dogs on her lap. Following the practice of a lifetime she would rigorously pursue some subject in thought, taking it up where she had left it on the previous day." This sorting was a way of using the essential components of her knowledge, the daily pieces of experience that formed both the woman and her works.

Gertrude believed that knowledge is incremental: "What we know is formed in our head by thousands of small occasions in the daily life," which "go into our head to form our ideas." "Now if we write, we write; and these things we know flow down our arm and come out on the page. The moment before we wrote them we did not really know we knew them." This is not "inspiration," which "suggests that someone else is blowing that knowledge into you. It is not being blown into you; it is very much your own and was acquired by you in thousands of tiny occasions in your daily life." When the writer reaches this summit of impersonality, he or she can claim, with Gertrude in *Four in America,* "I am not I when I see." For Wilder, her writing was most accurately seen as "a series of spiritual exercises."

Gertrude and Thornton also agreed about narrative, the telling of stories and its essential impersonality. As she said, "Everybody's life is full of stories; your life is full of stories; my life is full of stories. They are very occupying, but they are not really interesting. What is interesting is the way everyone tells their stories." What was truly interesting to Gertrude was the relation of narrative to "knowledge" and the way a person knows—by experiencing, as well as by listening. One reason the U.S. tour was so important to Stein and her later writing was that it provided a core of new voices and new experiences, both those she had heard and those she had heard of—a screen of new impressions against which she could test her assumptions. The process of absorbing this flood of material became the text of both *The Geographical History of America; or, The Relation of Human Nature to the Human Mind,* in which she distinguished between "human nature" and "human mind," and *Everybody's Autobiography.* The two were closely linked: the impersonality of her American experiences as she wrenched "knowledge" from them made her consider "her" autobiography to be "everybody's." In this second memoir, Alice is notable for her absence. Yet she *is* there in both the collective "we," with Gertrude, and the collective concept of "everybody."

Gertrude's autobiography—disguised this time as an impersonal narrative—continued the discussion of the problem of identity and its troubling issues of personality and impersonality. *Everybody's Autobiography* helped Gertrude see what her writing meant in relation to the world of work (her essays on money for the *Saturday Evening Post* fit into this exploration). In a culture that assessed a person's worth on the basis of occupation, Stein as writer had been validated—finally, after thirty years of work (all of which had value, she was sure; that was the reason she had never thrown any of it away, contrary to William Carlos Williams's suggestion). Her second autobiography, the one she would again fail to identify as "hers," was a description of that validation—both the world's opinion and her own. Such a validation enabled her to write during the winter of 1935–36 that Paris was "nice and quiet . . . quite prewar, gentle and unworried."

Stein's inner satisfaction helped her shut out the clamor of the incipient war, but that clamor continued to reverberate in Alice's life. Fearful of war and invasion and further saddened by the suicide of René Crevel, Alice made typing copies of all Gertrude's unpublished work her first priority. For safekeeping, she sent copies of everything to Van Vechten. While Gertrude continued to deny any possibility of war, both women admitted to friends that France might have its own revolution. From California, Mike urged Gertrude to be practical and send him her paintings. She responded in the negative, teasing him by saying that there was such a thing as being "too forethoughtful."

Buoyed by the pleasantness of writing about her memories of the tour and reinforced by frequent letters from such new American friends as Wendell Wilcox, Gilbert Harrison, Donald Sutherland, Robert Haas, and Samuel Steward, Gertrude found herself mothering still another generation of young men—this time by mail rather than over tea. Another reminder of the glories of the U.S. tour was being invited to speak in England. In 1936 Gertrude lectured on "What Are Masterpieces and Why Are There so Few of Them," adding for the French Club at Oxford, "An American and France," an essay that was seminal for her work during the next few years. She later admitted to Van Vechten that returning to France after the tour had been "awful," the visit to England the only bright spot.

In 1936 Gertrude's visible self-confidence impressed everyone who met her. American novelist Mary Ellen Chase invited Gertrude and Alice for tea before her Cambridge lecture and got an oral account of the tour: Gertrude "talked about the United States, her girlhood, her life at Radcliffe, and especially about our confused, many-sided civilization. She actually believed in some stout American dream, massive, like herself, rather than sentimental, but, to her, clearly real and even possible of fulfillment. . . . She knew Pennsylvania, Illinois, and Indiana and was, she said, often homesick for them. She found the Middle West 'beautiful and stirring.'"

Chase remembered Gertrude's "oddly serene and still" face. Rather than the color of her eyes, she remembered "the eagerness in them as she talked." Dressed in what Chase called a "dun gray sweatshirt" and "an ample, quite formless black skirt," Gertrude toasted "numberless slices of bread on a long fork over our English coal fire, turning each critically, buttering all generously." She also drank "several prodigious cups of strong black tea." When Alice remonstrated at the quantity, Stein kept on; this was her evening meal. Chase wrote that Gertrude then "lectured magnificently"—sweatshirt, toast crumbs, and all.

Enduring

Gertrude wrote friends that she was planning another lecture tour; she wrote about the fun it would be to return to California and help make a film. She did not pretend that France was the same as it had been before her tour or that rumors of war did not bother her, although she wrote comfortingly to cousins, "Each country if you read the papers sounds awfully upset but if you live in it you just go on living."

And so they did. But despite a three-day visit from Alex Woollcott and others from Wilder and Lord Berners, Alice and Gertrude worried. They worried about money, watching the small reserve they had saved from the American tour dwindle. They worried about Spain, lamenting the destruction of its people as well as the beautiful places they knew. Trying to keep working, Gertrude admitted, "Creative people have been low in their minds lately, that is true enough." By 1936 many Americans were returning home or seeking what they thought was security in Switzerland or Italy. When Janet Flanner planned to go back to the States, Gertrude wrote her tersely that no matter how many of their friends left, she and Noël Murphy were staying and "England and France could do as they wished." Despite the casualties in Spain, civilian danger seemed remote. After all, Alice and she had survived the First World War very well—and they had certainly been in the thick of that conflict.

An integral part of Bilignin life, Gertrude wrote hard that summer, using her work on *Everybody's Autobiography* and *Autobiography of Rose* as antidotes to worry. Visitors were still treated to Alice's gourmet meals as they risked their lives with the explosive water-heating system and watched a steady procession of villagers and friends come to call, bringing Gertrude news of sicknesses, births, deaths, and divorces—and expecting solutions.

Punctuated with intervals of quiet, Gertrude's life whether in Bilignin or Paris showed the force of her immense vitality, her "obsessive energy." She read voraciously, meditated, wrote at the peak of her readiness, took five- to ten-mile walks with Basket, enjoyed her meals, mail, and visitors, and continued loving Alice. Alice did everything else, rising early to shop for the choicest of foods and then spending her day dusting, giving orders to the cook, caring for the dogs, and, in the evening, typing Gertrude's handwritten pages. In addition, Alice was collecting recipes for the cookbook she planned to write, though her progress on that project was slow. They spent time with Max Jacob, who had moved to the ancient Benedictine monastery at Saint-Benoît-sur-Loire, where he served mass and wrote meditations. Secure as they tried to feel, however, politics affected their lives: in October of 1936 Gertrude wrote a friend about their witnessing a meeting of ten thousand fascists, with fifteen hundred cars, in their neighborhood.

As 1936 became 1937, the women spent New Year's Eve among old friends at the duchesse of Clermont-Tonnerre's. The year began propitiously:

Random House awaited Gertrude's autobiography, to be illustrated with a number of Van Vechten's photographs. Her long poem *Stanzas in Meditation* was being issued in a limited edition by Sir Robert Abdy. James Laughlin's young press, New Directions, was eager for whatever she sent for the annual anthology, and Laughlin was writing a study of her work. Yale University agreed to be the repository for her papers. And Margot Fonteyn and Robert Helpmann were chosen as principal dancers for the Royal Ballet's production of Gertrude's ballet, which they saw on opening night, April 27, in London. It was to be Gertrude's only curtain call, and the memory of it concluded *Everybody's Autobiography,* "And then gradually it was ending and we went out and on to the stage and there where I never had been with everything in front all dark and we bowing and all of them coming and going and bowing, and then again not only bowing but coming again and then as if it was everything, it was all over."

Like a faulty watch, the year ran slowly down: little of Alice's garden grew in the dry heat, and the *Atlantic Monthly* bought only one excerpt of the autobiography for advance publication. Gertrude again faced the fact that most of her writing brought in little income; as she wrote to Francis Rose, because we "have no capital to fall back on," we must "live on what we earn." A pleasant visit from Kiddy Rogers and his wife, Mildred, however, during which the four traced the route of Rogers's travels with Gertrude and Alice during World War I, was followed by the visit of Sam Steward, their Montana correspondent. His memoir recalled brisk morning walks with Gertrude, "as if there were a time limit"; sightseeing drives to Aix-les-Bains, with Stein "hunched over the steering wheel" driving fast but well; and a poignant moment when he read her palm and realized that both her life line and her destiny line "cut off dreadfully and sharply at a year or two past 70." She tried to cheer him up after the reading.

Steward remembered the women's loud laughter and Gertrude's squeaky wicker chair but most of all her terrible directness. When she couldn't hear, she interrupted immediately by saying "What" and waiting for a louder restatement; when she finished a meal, she pushed her chair away from the table. Like a bragging adolescent, when she won at Aix's gambling tables, she was insufferable. She was also intent on being Jewish: when she talked about lecturing in England, she observed, "No one expected me to be anything but a Jew and I could say what I pleased." She identified herself as "a Jew, orthodox background, and I never make any bones about it," and described how different a Jew was from a Catholic (which Steward was): from her "Talmudic" background, she explained, she found the world comprehensible, whereas Catholics expected incomprehensibility. Gertrude's claiming her Jewishness with such pride in the midst of the secrecy and persecution that shrouded most of Europe seemed more brave than foolhardy. Above all, it seemed characteristic.

She was also blunt about the alcoholism that plagued many writers.

Now take Hart Crane when he came to Paris. He was too drunk all the time to call on us except twice when he was half drunk. You can't write of the "furious quest" and be drunk all the time, your quest is not furious then. Take Sherwood, he wrote with genuine melancholy because of it. It is a paradox. Hemingway, Crane, Sherwood, they all believed life turns on passion but they were without passion themselves because physiologically liquor kills all passion. But they all had a sense of power, it is very curious the sense of power that alcohol gives, but it is a false sense.

Loving as the women were to guests, they argued with each other regularly—Gertrude's face flushed, Alice's eyes snapping. Observers felt that their arguments had intensified since the U.S. tour—perhaps because Alice was tired of playing the role of subordinate, perhaps because they were both worried about the imminent war. In Uzès, a friend recalled, Gertrude drove for some time on a paved sidewalk, insisting it was "like a road," intentionally to annoy Alice.

Tragedy united the women once again. In the autumn of 1937 Alice learned of the suicide of her brother. Shaken, she and Gertrude meditated on the loneliness of the human spirit, its essential isolation. They thought about friendship and love and family and were perplexed by the human will to end life. So many young men, so many talented young—all dead. Clarence's death made Gertrude think about her own brothers: she inquired about Leo and wrote often to Mike in California. She had opened *Everybody's Autobiography* with the story of his needing to return to the States: "You don't understand, he said I want to say in English to the man who brings the letters and does the gardening I want to say things to them and have them say it to me in American. . . . I can't help it, I must go and hear them say these things in American, I must go back there to live that is all there is about it I must." Reassured that Mike, despite his deteriorating health, was happy in the sprawling Palo Alto house he and Sally had bought on their return, Gertrude began to wonder more about Leo. Since his brief lecture tour in 1929, he had returned to the States only once, in 1937, and he and Nina now lived most of the year in Settignano. (According to rumor, Ned and Peggy Bruce had purchased the villa in which the Steins continued to live—and also gave them money on occasion.) After losses in the 1930s, keeping the Paris apartment had become too expensive, and Leo's hearing was so poor that he no longer enjoyed café conversations.

A three-way correspondence among Howard Gans, Ned Bruce, and Leo tells some of the story of those losses. In 1932 Leo's art works stored in New York were insured for sixty-three hundred dollars, and his cash account balance was ten thousand dollars. But what must have been a substantial amount of his principal had been lost when Julian Stein's new corporation (funded in part by Leo's assets) failed. Bruce reported that Julian said he had put two thousand dollars into government bonds for Leo (they were being held in his safety deposit box) and that he planned to put a thousand dollars each month into Leo's account. He aimed to "clear the entire matter up" as soon as he could. Bruce's advice was that Leo not make trouble over the loss but ask Julian to send the monthly thousand to Howard Gans for safekeeping. In July Gans wrote Leo that he had received a thousand dollars from Julian, but six months later, instead of Leo's account holding sixteen thousand dollars, Gans reported that the balance was barely eleven thousand. The checks had not come in. These financial worries contributed to Nina's declining health, as they did to that of Julian Stein, who suffered a heart attack the following year.

Leo's brief 1937 trip to the States was an attempt to garner financial support. He proposed giving ten of his friends two of his own paintings each year for five years in exchange for an annual stipend of a hundred dollars from each of them. He would then be assured a thousand dollars annually, on which he and Nina could exist in Italy. A friend wrote to Bruce about the impropriety of "a very important person" like Leo having to go to such lengths: "It is a shame that a man who has never had any money worries should, in his old age, have to face a situation for which he hasn't been equipped." While Leo's plan did not work out, friends were able to sell enough of his paintings for Nina and him to have income for the next few years.

For all Leo's emphasis on control, on knowing thoroughly whatever was to happen in his life, he seemed destined to be buffeted by economic and political chaos. His consistent reaction to Mussolini's fascism was to ignore it but not to antagonize the Fascisti. In the 1920s, when Marsden Hartley lived in Florence, Leo had warned him "never to speak the word *fascismo*—say 'bundle' if you speak of it . . . for they don't know what are you saying of it, and they are very volatile and disagreeable."

Having lived in Settignano since 1913, Leo was a familiar figure there, his presence occasioning little notice. His chief link with the outside world was the Berenson household. With his friend, Hartley visited the Berensons for Sunday tea, walking from Leo's to the elegant villa. The seemingly frail Berenson and Leo were immediately caught up in a violent conversation: "It was not long before there was a perfect volley of words . . . and then I head Mr. Berenson say—No Leo, what you mean is not *experimental* but *experiential* or vice versa, and a battle had begun." Neither took tea, and finally Mary Berenson assured Hartley, "Oh, it's always like that with them. They are fond of each other but they should never get together."

Cut off from most of his former friends, Leo did not bury his head in the sand as world conditions worsened. In the depressed art market, he gave up trying to sell anything but Picasso drawings; the only other income art brought Leo came from Etta Cone's purchases of his own paintings, a charitable gesture that he appreciated. In 1939 Leo asked Gans what living in the States would cost. Howard replied that living in Baltimore or the West would be cheaper but to live in New York on the two thousand a year that Leo had to spend would mean that he and Nina could have a two-room apartment with bath and kitchen, a dollar and a half a day for food, and few luxuries. In a later note Gans questioned whether Nina would be happy in such crowded circumstances, even though she was frantic over the thought of a European war. Like many other Americans, Gans was sure there would be no conflict.

For Gertrude and Alice, 1937 ended with the word that their landlord in Paris wanted their flat for his son, so the women were forced to leave what had been their home for thirty-five years. Luckily, they found a "remarkable seventeenth century Latin Quarter flat on the rue Christine, formerly occupied by Queen Christina of Sweden and still containing her original wall boiseries and her reading cabinet." Although the neighborhood looked like a slum, friends called it "magical," and Gertrude liked the apartment's roof terrace. They redecorated, refinishing the parquet floors and putting "blue pigeon in the grass wall paper" in the bedroom and the boudoir. The process of moving, however, was "frightful." Despite a friend's celebratory dinner for *Everybody's Autobiography* on December 19, 1937, Gertrude and Alice were "pretty dead." In late January 1938 she wrote Van Vechten that they were "not in [the apartment] yet but xhausted."

Their immense art collection complicated the process: the rue Christine wall space was smaller than that in the rue de Fleurus apartment, and some paintings had to be stored in a hallway and a china closet. With the art as with Stein's writing, quantity was the problem. When Janet Flanner brought a pot of flowers as a housewarming gift, Gertrude "gave me a pencil and paper and said, 'Put the pot anywhere and make me an inventory of my art here,' which I did." She counted 131 large canvases, 104 of them by Picasso.

The Death of Michael and American Thoughts

No one had the audacity to pretend that 1938 was an auspicious year. While Gertrude and Alice finished their tiring move, other Americans were leaving Paris as fast as they could make travel plans. By March, when Hitler annexed Austria, many expatriates were gone. Stein didn't mention this near-evacuation when she wrote to friends; instead she told them that Alice and she liked their new home "immensely" and that Mike was recovering well from his recent abdominal operation.

One good aspect of their rue Christine location was its proximity to both Picasso and Natalie Barney. Long convinced that Barney was a bright woman, the two were pleased when she dropped in; she and Gertrude often wandered "in our quiet old quarter where, while exercising her poodle, 'Basket,' we naturally fell into thought and step. Basket, unleashed, ran ahead, a white blur, the ghost of a dog in the moonlit side streets." Barney liked

Gertrude because she was "the most affirmative person I ever met," though never blandly complacent. Capable of great human sympathy—the reason people came in droves to bring her their problems—Gertrude always listened seriously and "helped them out, by changing an *idée fixe* or obsession into a fresh start in a new direction." Barney said this perspicacity was not only accurate but immediate: "She never appeared to hesitate or reflect or take aim, but invariably hit the mark." Along with her sympathy, Stein had a "voice always ready to chuckle."

During this year, Gertrude's friendship with Picasso also deepened. She was writing "Picasso," a long essay about him and their friendship, in French. While it summarized the way his painting had changed, and the process of that change, the book both in its original French and in Toklas's English translation was prosaic. Gertrude wrote about her discomfort in using the French, "I have just written a french book in french about Picasso and it was a frightful struggle it is not natural not at all natural to write french, English is what I write, I kind of feel the English language." Despite its laconic prose, "Picasso" convinced readers of both Stein's authority and the painter's greatness, or, in her terms, his "splendor."

Gertrude and Alice received a brief visit from a less-splendid old friend when Ernest Hemingway brought Martha Gellhorn to meet them. Gellhorn recalled that Hemingway, "very polite and respectful," was showing Stein off to her and vice versa. Gellhorn felt that Gertrude was not pleased to see her ("Her 'young men' were supposed to come and worship alone"), but it may well have been that she was not pleased to see Hemingway. By this time he had used—or parodied—Stein's friends and her ideas in not only *The Sun Also Rises* but also *A Farewell to Arms, Death in the Afternoon,* and particularly *Green Hills of Africa.* Alice was later to say that Gertrude regarded the novels as "essays in tactlessness. She recognized the cleverness but rejected the intention and . . . looked on Hemingway as a regrettable lapse in tact." He had insulted Gertrude—and Alice—in print in his essay on Miró's *The Farm,* when he wrote that pregnancy took nine months but that "a woman who isn't a woman can usually write her autobiography in a third of that time"; in his introduction to James Charters's *This Must Be the Place;* and in his first "Paris Letter" for *Esquire,* all in 1934, all in obvious retaliation for Gertrude's comments about him in *The Autobiography of Alice B. Toklas.* While his visit to the rue Christine was short, his vendetta against Stein lasted long after her death.

Less inclined than ever to be absorbed in the pettiness of outworn friendships, Gertrude responded to war rumors as she ironically explored human evil (in the figure of a German authoritarian, Faust) in her new play, *Doctor Faustus Lights the Lights.* Calling her work "a new and very simple drama," she wrote it to be a mockery of things masculine and patriarchal. Now less guarded about her responses to Hitler, Stein referred to him as "that madman in Germany" and clearly questioned what was happening to the world around her. When Janet Flanner returned from Salzburg, where she had gone for the Vienna Symphony's last concert, she told unbelievable tales of stores—and goods in them—marked either "Aryan" or "non-Aryan" and of an anti-Semitic exhibition called "The Eternal Jew" where displays denounced such "degenerates" as Mendelssohn, Marx, and the beloved Charlie Chaplin.

In April Mike wrote her that he was improving—taking long walks and gaining weight. But he was terribly worried about her staying in France. Their grandson, Danny, was still with Mike and Sally, and now that Allan and his second wife, Roubina, were having a family, plans were that—in case of war—their child would also come to the States. Instead of exploring the possibility of traveling to the States, however, Gertrude and Alice—sure that living in America would be financially impossible—made plans to return to Bilignin.

A quiet summer enabled Gertrude to finish a good deal of writing. With German troops massed along the Czechoslovakian border, it was obviously not the time to travel for pleasure. The evacuation of Paris continued. When Ambassador Bullitt requested that all Americans leave France and said that the American Embassy would help with arrangements, Alice and Gertrude stayed put. Finishing *Doctor Faustus Lights the Lights* in June, Gertrude resumed work on the novel *Ida* and also responded to a publisher's inquiry about her interest in writing a book for children. *The World Is Round* was completed by fall.

Basket's sudden death after chewing a glass thermometer demoralized both Gertrude and Alice. They replaced him with a blue-eyed puppy, known as Basket II, although Picasso remonstrated that people did not replace loved ones. The women knew they needed the continuity—and affection—that a second poodle would supply.

Harder to bear was the dreaded news of Mike's death. A good friend to Alice as well as Gertrude's favorite sibling, Mike had made it back to America in time to settle his family in a comfortable house and then prepare to die; at seventy-three, he had cared well for his extended family as well as his own. Allan wrote that his bereft mother was "unable to write to anyone as yet"; Sally had always known where her strength lay. In October, when she did write, she assured Gertrude that a weary Mike had "smiled his way out." He had been happy in the California house with its beautiful garden, and he had felt safe once more in America.

As the military and political events of the fall of 1938 turned into a mockery of civilized behavior, Gertrude thought often of Mike. There was nothing she and Alice could do, as she wrote friends, but "stay fearfully on." The grotesque minuet among Chamberlain, Daladier, and Hitler dragged on until February 1939, when Barcelona fell. Janet Flanner reported on the hundreds of thousands of refugees in concentration camps near Perpignan on the Spanish border: only people with both money and papers were not incarcerated. In March 1939 Hitler invaded the rest of Czechoslovakia and set up a puppet government in Prague. Another year went by; another winter in Paris turned to another Bilignin summer. Gertrude and Alice were happy to leave behind the city's air-raid sirens and posters about blackouts and gas bombs. Windows were covered at night, candles were sold singly, and there were already shortages of sugar, matches, aspirin, iodine, and soap. All foreigners in France were required to carry identification cards with profile photographs showing the bearer's right ear and sometimes fingerprints.

In Bilignin, working intently on her book about her loyalty to France—called simply *Paris France*—Gertrude felt an apprehension that none of her rational explanations could dispel. In August, when Germany and Russia signed their nonaggression pact, roads out of Paris were flooded with evacuees. Belley instituted a curfew; French soldiers swarmed the countryside. And when Germany invaded Poland on the first of September, Gertrude and Alice gave up all pretense of complacency.

World War II
(1939–1942)

In 1939 Gertrude was sixty-five years old and Alice, sixty-three. Moving vigorously through their carefully ordered lives, they thought they were in good health, but they were not prepared to withstand the physical deprivation and mental and emotional strain a major world war would create. No one was, particularly when their chosen place of refuge was set squarely between Italy to the east and Lyon—and the Atlantic Ocean—to the west. Gertrude admitted, "I was scared, completely scared, and my stomach felt very weak, because—well here we were right in everybody's path; any enemy that wanted to go anywhere might easily come here."

Their first thoughts were on target: within a few days of England and France's declaring war on Germany on September 3, they secured a thirty-six-hour permit to make the long trip back to Paris, ostensibly to get winter clothes and money. What they planned was to bring all their paintings back with them to Bilignin. But arriving in the panicked city upset them; evacuees blocked the highway so that driving was difficult, and once they arrived at the rue Christine, both women were distraught. Looking at the walls lined with large canvases, they realized that very few of them could be taken to Belley by car.

Luckily, Gertrude phoned Daniel-Henry Kahnweiler, and he came quickly. But by the time he arrived, Alice had "one foot on the frame of the portrait of Madame Cézanne, trying to remove the picture." He loosened the canvas and rolled it for her. Then the three began taking pictures down from the walls, working from the lower edge up, and arranging them on the floor. Soon, with the high walls less than half emptied, the floor was filled, so they rehung everything. It was growing dark, and they were hungry and discouraged. With Kahnweiler's help, they got Picasso's portrait of Gertrude and the Cézanne canvas into the Ford, along with clothing, some manuscripts, and Basket's pedigree (unable to locate their passports, Alice did find the dog's papers). When darkness fell, Paris was as black as Bilignin on a moonless night, and as they sat in their beautiful apartment, Gertrude and Alice mourned leaving their beloved paintings and their beloved city.

The next day, after talking with their banker and the concierge, they drove back to Belley, the roads still nearly impassable. Arriving in Bilignin was comforting: surely their quiet countryside would be safer than the city. Gertrude had trouble believing that war had begun or that the conflict would be a major one. Lulled by French friends who claimed that Germany was bluffing, she wrote Van Vechten, the Rogerses, and other American friends, "We have no plans at present we stay here and later I do not know probably back to Paris. . . . We are alright, just staying here, I have had a radio put in and I get America on it." Her big concern was that "there is nothing to do to help." (She communicated with friends, but she was not in touch with relatives. When Leo later wrote Howard Gans asking about Gertrude's whereabouts, Gans replied that he didn't know where she was; nor did he care.)

By October 23, 1939, all mail was being censored, and there was little of it from the States; cable service was stopped. Janet Flanner had returned home. Natalie Barney wrote to remind them to have their passports validated before January 1, a task that would need to be done every six months. Lonely during their first country winter, they divided the duty of listening to the wireless radio, with Alice taking the morning and Gertrude the evening. Alice added to her household responsibilities that of food storage, while Gertrude sawed wood ("it takes an awful lot of wood to keep us well not warm but not too cold"), pruned the box hedges, and walked her usual miles. For a while, they anticipated making another U.S. lecture tour, but plans fell through. Van Vechten warned them that even if they got to America, they would never be able to return to France.

By this time, the American consul at Lyon had phoned them with instructions that they should leave while they could. At first, Gertrude ignored the warning, but after a day, they drove to Lyon to have their papers put in order and to investigate leaving. The offices were so crowded, however, that they left without seeing anyone. Gertrude's view was that by staying, they remained loyal to France: "We love France more than ever and they [the French] are all sweeter and more wonderful." She did not see that in the conflict to come, her affection for the French would be meaningless. The only information that would matter was that Alice and she were American citizens—and Jews.

Being Jewish in Vichy

It was Gertrude's affection for, and loyalty to, the French people that shaped her political alliances throughout the war. Never conventionally political, Gertrude and Alice responded to situations as the human beings they were: the French people who were their friends were those they helped. Soon after war was declared, the manor house in Bilignin became the site of mysterious evening gatherings lasting two or three hours. A year later, the house was visited regularly at lunchtime by "Hubert de R.," a member of the resistance from Savoie, who bicycled eighteen miles to reach them. (Among other things, Alice provided him with the sheets of gelatin used for making false identification papers.)

As Gertrude and Alice grew adept at finding foodstuffs and buying on the black market, their home became a refuge for hungry travelers throughout the Ain—and many of those travelers brought information. Gertrude's endeavors to keep herself and Alice supplied with food fit unobtrusively into her daily routine. Taking her long walks gave her opportunities both to barter for food and to exchange news. She later wrote casually about walking her "usual twelve kilometers" (for the purpose of buying "some bread which is not dark and some cake which is very good, very very good"), but a more explicit comment may relate to her carrying of information: "Everything is dangerous and everybody casually meeting anybody talks to anybody and everybody tells everybody the history of their lives [sic] they are always telling me and I am always telling them and so is everybody."

At first, because Germany was frantically preparing for its major offensive, all was quiet. The French pretended to think Hitler was afraid and called the conflict a "phony war" (sitzkrieg). Some expatriates believed they could survive in Paris; Man Ray took a job there with *Harper's Bazaar,* and Kahnweiler wrote, "Paris does not seem very different from peacetime, now, during the day, but nights are dark and sad. We never go to the theatre etc. at night, but spend our evenings at home." Virgil Thomson said that all telephones were tapped but that—even as they listened to the telltale click—some British, Americans, and even French did not take the war seriously.

On April 9, however, the calm ended: Germany began *blitzkrieg* attacks on Denmark, Norway, Holland, and Belgium. By mid-May German forces had outflanked the Maginot Line, invading France through the Ardennes, and thousands more refugees fled from Paris. Each day brought continuing defeat for the French; as Gertrude wrote, no one discussed the war because it was so painful. In Belley, blackout restrictions intensified, and people stayed in their homes at night (Gertrude, practiced now at walking without a light, regretted giving up her late evening pastime—but even without lights walking was too dangerous). Because of worries about bombings and parachutists, the few men who remained in Belley were issued guns and told to patrol the countryside. Happy with Sam Steward's gift of an electric mixer, Alice baked cakes for every occasion and sent them to soldiers and members of the resistance whenever she could.

Then, on a bright Sunday afternoon, after all the nights spent worrying about bombings, German planes destroyed the railway center of Culoz only ten miles away; one of the planes was downed, and the German crew brought in to town by a French teenager. Word came that two Bilignin men had been killed at the front. Lyon was under attack; then the city fell. With that, Gertrude and Alice realized that they should have gone to the States months before. Remembering the chances they had had—when French friends had persuaded them to stay, because living among friends was easier than wandering the globe—the women planned to leave for Switzerland as soon as the fighting ended.

They regretted not having gone to Bordeaux in May, when Ambassador Bullitt had repeated his earlier message that Americans should leave France immediately; special American ships would attempt to sail from southwestern France, and expatriates would travel "at their own expense." Always afraid of running short of money, Gertrude and Alice had decided they could not pay the passage to the States, where at any rate they had no place to go. Now they had decided that going anywhere would be safer than staying in Belley.

On June 10 the last members of the French government left Paris, now declared an open city; on June 14 Paris fell. According to Virgil Thomson's account, "Paris was empty save for the very old, the very young, and a few, a very few, foreigners." On June 16 Marshal Philippe Pétain, now eighty-five years old, took over the Vichy government that was to rule southern France. His radio speech on June 22, 1940, assured the French that an armistice had been reached and that he was in charge, even though northern France—and Paris—was in German hands. What Pétain did not say was that he was following German mandates: "Laws and dicta against Jews were enacted simultaneously with the forming of the new government in July 1940, well before any German ordinances or prohibitions were published." In October 1940 a Vichy law "allowed for internment of foreigners of Jewish race and the establishment of special camps for Jews in France." A month earlier Germany had published the "Liste Otto" (Works Withdrawn from Sale by Publishers), the opening volley in its plan to exterminate the "defective" Jewish, Gypsy, and homosexual population.

Paul de Man's by-now-notorious essay "The Jews and Contemporary Literature" showed that devaluation: "Jewish writers have always remained in the second rank" and therefore failed to exercise much influence on contemporary European civilization. "One can thus see . . . that a solution to the Jewish problem that would lead to the creation of a Jewish colony isolated from Europe would not have, for the literary life of the West, regrettable consequences. It would lose, in all, some personalities of a mediocre worth and would continue, as in the past, to develop according to its higher laws of evolution." Isolating Jews might be intellectually acceptable, but such isolation was not what Hitler had in mind.

Probably unaware that Jews were in grave danger, Gertrude wrote "The Winner Loses," an essay that appeared in the November *Atlantic Monthly,* to explain the French reaction to Vichy. She began by describing people's omnipresent fear and then the comparative joy with which they greeted the appointment of Marshal Pétain. Having won the people's confidence during the Great War, Pétain was considered a patriot who would save his country from the incredible losses of World War I. After the 1940 armistice, there was a brief period of German occupation, the loss of postal service and electricity, some fear about her hoarding gasoline for the car, and some interchanges with German soldiers, but once the Germans left Belley ("miles and miles of them went away"), people resumed their lives. The French, she explained, considered government "something outside which does not concern them." Stein would write more directly in *Wars I Have Seen,* "Pétain was right to stay in France and he was right to make the armistice and little by little I understood it," but her 1941 essay closed, "So everybody is very busy accommodating themselves to everything," focusing their energies on "the business of daily living." What she did not say was that the business of daily living was often activity subversive of Nazi control.

Gertrude never denied that Vichy was an arm of the German occupation. When Bernard Faÿ wrote that a number of his friends were taking posts in the new government but that he hoped to continue his writing, it was clear which side he had chosen. In the French mind—and Gertrude was right about these attitudes—a complete national disaster had been averted, and thousands—millions?—of lives saved. Though defeated, the French persisted in seeing the Vichy government under Pétain as some kind of victory. They were safe, they had their lives and their lands and a modicum of pride.

But despite their sympathy for the French, Gertrude and Alice were American and Jewish. Passing as older Frenchwomen might have been possible if they had not had to speak. Shopping in Belley or Culoz during the German occupation was frightening, however, because Gertrude's voice was harshly American—and she would never remember to lower it to avoid a soldier's overhearing. Once Germans noticed her, Gertrude's Jewish characteristics were obvious; after all, Aaron Copland had exclaimed when they had first met, "My God, the woman's Jewish!" What kind of disguise could the two use if they decided to leave France? It was one of Alice's recurrent nightmares—along with the image of a floating silver dish bearing three slices of succulent ham. The women did not dwell on their hunger, but it truly haunted them.

In August 1940 the Battle of Britain began, to end less than a year later after the deaths of more than forty thousand English civilians. By now, there was no question about the pain, and the risk, of war. Alice and Gertrude missed another chance to leave France during that summer, but they took a few other precautions. Gertrude wrote Julian Stein that he should abrogate her small trust and send her the remaining three hundred dollars. She wrote Marshall M. Vance, the American consul in Lyon, about protecting the contents of her Paris apartment. Forbidden to correspond with anyone in the occupied zone, she missed news from Paris, though she wrote to Janet Flanner in the States, "Come back to us soon" now that "the darkest days" are past.

Enduring: The Fantasy of Food

The darkest days, however, from the standpoint of human comfort and safety, were only beginning. The "interminable winter" of 1940–41 was unusually cold: the cavernous fireplaces burned wood as fast as Gertrude could gather and saw it, and there was so much snow that people used skis for transport. Vegetables and fruits were plentiful in the region, but rationing limited people to one-quarter pound of meat per week, and there were no eggs or dairy products. Grocery store shelves were empty. Alice wrote, "We didn't feel hungry until some weeks after strict rationing had been enforced." Hunger increased gradually as both of them did more and more physical work and ate fewer and fewer calories. In a statement typical of their willingness to get along as best they could, Alice recalled, "Suddenly we realized that we were hungry but it was not mentioned." When Gertrude wrote friends, she compared their existences to those on the frontier: "Life is interesting, it has all the excitement and invention of pioneering, every day a new day in the way of complications." But while she asked for toothbrushes and toothpaste and soap, she did not mention food.

As the community of Bilignin drew together, people shared what little they had. Alice devised a meatloaf made largely of spices; she raised crayfish, and they ate those and fish often; she canned tomatoes and other produce. They were eventually introduced to more black market merchants, and Gertrude's personality enabled her to deal successfully with them. By the next spring, at least temporarily, food was more plentiful, but the search for it occupied a great many hours of both their days.

Years later, Alice was to observe, "Wars change the way of life, habits, markets and so eventually cooking. For five years and more the French were deprived of most of their foodstuffs. . . . [Even after the Liberation] the population had been hungry too long." Gertrude and Alice's poor meals in Bilignin contrasted starkly with their gourmet living during the Great War, when they had traveled from hotel to hotel working for the AFFW. In reminiscences of the second war, the memorable events were the few times they had a good meal—the black market did help, and there was the rare lunch party.

Being hungry was the silent current in the river of their lives. They were not alone: everyone in France was hungry. Rations in the occupied zone were set at less than half the amount a human being needed to survive. Vichy residents had access to more food, particularly during growing season, but even in the Ain no one had enough. Contrary to Gertrude's analysis of French character in "The Winner Loses," by 1941 people, hungry, were ripe for involvement in the resistance. Or for collaboration. Sisley Huddleston pointed out, with deep irony, that whatever side one chose was termed *collaborationist.* Used to mean cooperation with Germany, "in practice it was a word used by the French in order to resist German coercion," as when Gertrude talked about the "collabos" in the Ain. Huddleston said that the ambiguous use of the word, in fact, "had perhaps served to prevent an open rupture of the armistice."

Surviving the hard winter of 1940–41, the people of the Ain and the Savoie, the French provinces backing up to Switzerland, began forming the earliest Vichy resistance. In those remote areas, hiding was easy; patrolling the immense, hilly terrain was impossible. Madame Matisse and her daughter, Margot, were among the most active members of the resistance; like them, Gertrude and Alice defined patriotism in very practical terms.

Many of Gertrude's comments in her censored letters to America have a calculated ambiguity, as when she wrote Van Vechten that "we are all very active, vegetables and all are xtremely occupying." Snippets of information were often embedded in sentences about other things: "The days seem to be so full of people and events and vegetables, and wood, and eggs and other things. . . . I go as much as 16 kilometers in all directions on foot so I get plenty of variety." Her life was filled with tales of talking to "interesting people," even an American now and then, she said, and random bulletins— "everything is getting most xciting these days," "everybody seems to think that things will hum pretty soon"—occur in every letter.

The Third Autobiography

Her writing during the early war years—like her blatant title "The Winner Loses"—clearly shows her sympathy with the French and her hatred of the Nazis. In her novel *Mrs. Reynolds,* Hitler is drawn as an old-style villain from vaudeville melodrama. In *Wars I Have Seen,* the book she began in the winter of 1943, she made direct comments about the aggressor—"The Germans say that war is natural peace is only an armistice"—and about what Hitler's rapacity meant for the French: "Now in 1943 when there are armies and armies and they come humming in and the air of night, when the moon is bright is full of them going over to Italy to do their bombing . . . then you keep on thinking how quickly anybody can get killed . . . those up there flying and bombing and those down below, houses tumbling, and burning." She spoke often of "this meaningless war."

Sometimes compared with Walt Whitman's *Specimen Days,* that movingly personal account of his life nursing during the Civil War, *Wars I Have Seen* was in no way imitative. It did resemble a diary, so filled was it with small incidents from the women's French life, and it undoubtedly stemmed from an earlier comment to Van Vechten that she should have kept a diary, "such wonderful conversations that I have everyday." But it also grew predictably from Gertrude's fascination with the experiential; here she drew *only* from the experiential, from her daily life as farmer, woodcutter, and walker, distilling general observations about the depravity and discomfort of war from the understated mosaic of her own activity. Segments like this dot the narrative: "Victor, he is nineteen, said I am afraid. And we said and why are you afraid, well he said the reason I am afraid, of course they are not dropping bombs on us. Of course not we said even if they are boches because this is no place to drop bombs. Of course not said Victor, but I am afraid."

This third volume of what Gertrude came to see as her, and Alice's, fused autobiography shared many of the themes she had expressed in *Paris France;* indeed, her writing from the late 1930s through the Second World War, that bridge of years between her glorious return to the States and her postwar celebrity to come, was an exploration of what France was—and, from a personal perspective, what living in France for forty years had meant to Gertrude Stein. Alice, as an integral part of her life, was an integral part of that exploration. But in her earlier war writings—"The Winner Loses," "Picasso," and *Paris France*—Gertrude was sure she had the answers to questions about French identity. As World War II showed her, however, even after living nearly seventy years, she remained naive. The process of trying to understand the human mind, as well as the national character, was endless.

Leo and Nina in Italy

Leo Stein had even fewer financial resources than did Gertrude and Alice, though he had closer friends in the States who might have sheltered him and Nina for a time. Once he had refused Ned Bruce's suggestion that he take up teaching in 1939, Leo made the commitment to last out the war abroad. Because of his experience during World War I, however, when he had been able to sail to America long after war had been declared in Europe, he probably thought he had time left to decide. If he had foreseen that Italy would become a principal theater of war, he would surely have gone to the States.

The early months were bearable: there was no variety in food, but at least there was food. The Fascisti, however, were completely unpredictable, and as the military—both Italian and German forces—terrorized the country, Leo realized that being an American citizen in Italy was not healthy. After several years of living quietly in fear, keeping as low a profile as possible, in 1941 he wrote Hutch Hapgood that Nina and he had secured Portuguese visas and booked passage to the States from Lisbon. Unsure whether they could even get to Portugal, he was also worried about making the dramatic change in lifestyle. Nina did not want to leave their things—the Paris furnishings were still in storage, and the thought of storing the furniture from the villa broke her heart. She also feared that her rheumatism and heart condition would make traveling difficult. Having listened for years to horror stories about accidents in the crush of deportees, she knew that something terrible would happen. It was possible that the two of them would not make it to the States at all. Nina's worries affected Leo's judgment, and a postscript to the letter to Hutch explained that they had given up their passage and would remain in Italy.

When the spring offensives began, Leo knew they had erred in their decision. Whereas the Greek armies drove out the Italians in the fall, by April 1941 Greece had fallen to Hitler. Italy was so demoralized by extensive losses in Africa that Hitler moved more German troops in to keep Italy loyal to the Axis. The war was beginning to look like a clean sweep for the Nazis: as Leo wrote early in 1942, it was hard to see what the "Anglo-Americans" were trying to achieve: "Failure in the East, in the eastern Mediterranean states, in Italy, huge losses of planes over Germany and mere talk of invasion." Recognizing that he was getting only pro-Axis news, however, Leo concluded, "Perhaps it is better than it seems."

The real threat was not the outcome of battle so much as it was Leo's Jewish identity. The changes in Leo's journal between the fall and winter of 1941 are dramatic: it is clear that he had no idea that the Fascisti agreed with the Nazis that Jews could be found and killed. During September he wrote about the same introspective, intellectual topics he had explored during the past twenty years: his autoeroticism, shaped in part by the sexual "foolishness" a maid forced him into when he was a child; his ambivalence toward Bertha and cousin Marion; his pervasive yet unacknowledged conflicts with women—sisters, friends, wife. In that context, Leo described the recent visit of his German friend Rudolph Levy, a Jew escaped from Berlin, who brought with him a beautiful woman. The journal charted Leo's growing fascination with Genia: in their three days together, he was attracted both erotically and intellectually. There is no mention of war at all in this sequence of entries; Leo's attention was absorbed by his erotic response.

Less than three months later, however, partly because of the increased German force in the country, the political climate in Italy had changed: the Fascisti had become exterminators. On December 24 Rudolph Levy was arrested, his property, confiscated. The Italian anti-Semitic edict was announced, including the "concentration" of Jews in the so-named camps and the confiscation of their property, which was to be given to Aryan war victims as reparation. After finding out about Levy's arrest, Leo learned from a friend that his name, too, appeared on a list of Jews whose property was to be confiscated. He kept that news secret from the shaken Nina, who was nervous because she knew that her marriage to a Jew would bring her certain hardship, if not death. In a pathetic gesture of confidence, Leo assured himself that the authorities would not take furniture but only "clothes, linen, bedding." To survive winter in Italy without those items would be difficult, but the much-greater threat was that once his Jewish background was known, Leo would follow Levy to the camps. Even in his private journal, he did not admit that possibility.

It was incomprehensible to him: less than a year after Nina and he relinquished their passage to America, he might well be robbed, imprisoned, even killed. A village official told Leo that the fact that their possessions were in Nina's name would not help; he did not tell him that Nina was also, through her marriage, considered a Jew.

In the journal, Leo admonished himself to delay telling Nina as long as he could. Then, miraculously, on January 10 the same official told Leo that his name had been removed from the list and his goods were safe. The frail

Leo, approaching seventy yet still burning with an intensity that bordered on the neurotic, may have seemed such a poor health risk that the official decided to spare him. Or he might have been considered a compatriot for all his years in Italy. For whatever reason, the Steins were given the gift of existence through the coming years of hardship, years of almost no contact with the world either outside or within Italy.

Gertrude's Double Life

The actualities of war complicated the firmest political stands. In September 1941 Bernard Faÿ wrote Gertrude that he had been appointed head of the Bibliothèque Nationale and that he was having "great fun . . . spending 200 millions to house your future books and to build a musical library, a business library and a geographical library." (The irony of his using the pronoun *your* when Jewish books were already banned is not acknowledged.) Although he visited Pétain monthly, sometimes staying a week, he wrote that he was so busy with his administrative duties—which included overseeing sixty thousand troublesome Freemasons, also on the undesirable list—that he would not get to Bilignin for some time. Stein and Toklas were relieved.

Within the strangely divided country, friendships often endured despite seemingly opposed political loyalties. It was difficult for non-French to understand that a person who had been Far Right and then gradually moved to the Left could still be friends with people from the Right; historian Herbert Lottman gave the example of Jean Paulhan of *La Nouvelle Revue Française* who was arrested by Nazis for resistance "but was not shot as others in the network were" because of intervention by a profascist collaborator in his office. On the other hand, old friends sometimes denounced each other, prompted by that same difference of opinion to assume responsibility for someone's death. As Gertrude said in Bilignin when Alice warned her to speak more quietly, "Nothing counts any more." Life during wartime seemed entirely random.

Gertrude was not surprised at Faÿ's being rewarded with a prize position, and she immediately saw how useful his post could be to her. Saddened at news of the deaths of both Sherwood Anderson and F. Scott Fitzgerald and rapidly shut into the isolated life in Belley because of unpredictable mails, she had nothing to lose by playing her friendship with Faÿ for whatever security it was worth. And they were old friends: the politics of war had not changed that fact.

In May 1941 Gertrude was asked to write "a little thing in french on the french language, for a new review called *Patrie,* an official thing under the patronage of Marshal Pétain," which she did. That autumn she began a new project that also supported Vichy, translating into English and writing an introduction for an American edition of Marshal Pétain's *Paroles aux Français, Messages et écrits, 1934–1941,* which she hoped Random House would publish. Aberrant as the project now seems, Gertrude saw the French people's devotion to Pétain as an important part of their character. She was thinking about the situation in France as she helped Janet Flanner, still in the States, write a long profile of Pétain for the *New Yorker*. Flanner's assessment was as positive, and as innocuous, as Stein's introduction.

In her somewhat vapid essay, Gertrude's main point was that Pétain was a trusted servant of the French. Old and childless, he had only France to care for, and, like George Washington, he gave all that he had for his country. Stein believed what she wrote: her association with the French in the Ain had persuaded her. She also surmised—correctly—that Pétain was literally their protector. According to Faÿ's memoirs, he had asked Pétain to protect Gertrude and Alice, and "Pétain dictated a letter to the *sous-préfet* at Belley, placing in his hands full responsibility for seeing that the two Jewesses were left undisturbed. Faÿ himself regularly telephoned the man to remind him of his special mission."

Even as she wrote the essay, Gertrude may have known that the Old Marshal was being held in more and more suspicion by Hitler's forces: Goebbels's journal shows that most Germans distrusted Pétain from the start, and pro-German Frenchmen in Paris, even more hostile to the marshal than the Germans were, intrigued against him from the time of his appointment. Both Huddleston and Richard Griffiths, Pétain's biographer, contend that the marshal did a good job with his holding action. He delayed for nearly three years that "inevitable moment" when the Reich would demand approval of everything, when all Vichy radio broadcasts would be silenced, and when all the Jews in France would be deported and killed. In 1943 Pétain still insisted on individually examining the case of each Jew before arrest—but thousands were killed nevertheless.

At the same time Gertrude was producing apparent propaganda for Vichy, she was contributing to, and helping, subversive new little magazines, vehicles used both to publish banned Jewish and homosexual writers and to circulate information about their whereabouts. Begun in July 1941 in Lyon, the monthly *Confluences* was one of the most active of these publications. By July 1942 Gertrude—along with Max Jacob, Louis Aragon, Sartre, Malraux, and Gide—had appeared in it, and when it was officially denounced by a collaborationist daily paper in Paris, she was among its targeted contributors: "The literary magazines of the southern zone have always manifested, more or less slyly, the greatest tenderness for the defunct Third Republic, its Jews, pederasts, and Freemasons. Among these magazines, *Confluences*, which is published in Lyon . . . has always distinguished itself by its zeal in opposing new ideas. To write for this magazine it is sufficient to be an American Jewess, without talent, like Gertrude Stein. . . . A writer is interned? At once his name appears in the table of contents of the next issue of *Confluences*." Gertrude's work also appeared in a special issue on the novel, which included contributions by Albert Camus, Claude Moyan, Jacques Debu-Bridel, and Robert Desnos, key members of the intellectual resistance.

It was not long before the young editor of *Confluences,* René Tavernier, was visiting Gertrude and Alice regularly. Such a visible friendship was dangerous for the two American women befriended by Bernard Faÿ, but then, as Gertrude would write, life at war was filled with contradictions. On the one hand, "everybody collaborated"; on the other, as Simone de Beauvoir, who worked for Pétain's Radio Nationale in Paris, insisted, "everybody resisted." Official French resistance is sometimes dated from the visible activities of the maquis in 1943, but, clearly, a large resistance effort was already in place during 1941, and it increased after the United States entered the war in December 1941.

World War II
(1942–1945)

If the winter of 1940–41 was excruciating, the summer of 1942 somehow managed to be worse. Worried about the success of his military campaign, Hitler began moving more rapidly toward his purification of the Aryan race. Beginning in June, Jews in the occupied zone were required to wear yellow stars on their clothing (though many ignored the order). By July 1942 "Jews were barred from all public places, including restaurants, movie theaters, and libraries." Most prominent Jews had already left Paris, heading toward isolated corners of the south of France or abroad; the middle-class Jews who were left now saw livelihoods destroyed as they were forbidden to work on stage, in publishing or printing, or elsewhere.

During the summer months of 1942, according to historian David S. Wyman and others, the Vichy government cooperated in rounding up seventy-five thousand non-French-born Jews in the occupied zone, and on July 16 thirteen thousand Parisian Jews, among them, four thousand children (without papers—Pierre Laval would not provide papers) were killed. If mention of these executions ever appeared in United States papers, they were small items on inside pages and, tragically, were usually thought to be the same kind of anti-German atrocity propaganda common during World War I. The horrors of such murders were, simply, unthinkable. During August and September of 1942 fifty thousand Jews were incarcerated at Auschwitz, fourteen thousand of them taken from Vichy France. By November 1942 Germany had taken outright control of Vichy, and in late November the entire "Final Solution" plan was released—but no one believed it. What was believed was that Jews were being taken to labor camps in Germany. Once deported from France, they were forced to send postal cards to friends, saying that they were fine. Locations of the killing centers were secret. Even though it became common knowledge that, ominously, "nobody returns from the east," it was months before the truth was confirmed. An incredulous populace, unaware that thousands of prisoners were already dead and thousands more poised for assassination, thought Hitler was simply making maniacal threats.

Gertrude's correspondence early in 1942 of necessity revealed little about her fears as she observed the changing political climate. Between January and April, virtually no mail got through; then her letters spoke chiefly about sawing wood, walking, writing, and reading her books of predictions. Having abandoned such earlier sources as Leonardo Blake's *The Last Year of War,* she was now committed to Saint Odile, an Alsatian whose blood supposedly flamed when France was in danger. Like her interest in palmistry and astrology, Stein's fascination with predictions may have been part of her pose as an irrational, idiosyncratic Frenchwoman. Then again, she might have believed that mystic predictions made as much sense as anything she heard on the radio during the war. In none of her letters is there any hint of what Alice was to describe as "a possible danger we refused to face." Like their omnipresent hunger, the two could not discuss a reality that could well mean the end of their lives. That Gertrude had information about the truth of the German atrocities seems clear from her September 20 letter to American consul Vance in Lyon: "In my home in Paris, 5 rue Christine, 6th arrondisement, there are numerous valuable pictures, furniture, manuscripts and a literary and artistic correspondence of 40 years of permanent historical interest. Monsieur Bernard Faÿ, administrator of the Bibliothèque Nationale has been protecting these possessions but he now tells me that there is a threat of sequestration and he is not certain that his authority is sufficient to ensure their safety."

Sometime during this period, Gertrude and Alice ran terribly short of funds. Although French friends provided cash for their living expenses (nothing written changed hands; people were learning to transact business orally), Gertrude would not accept such help indefinitely. Late on a moonless night, Alice and she hid the Cézanne canvas in the Ford and drove carefully along the winding, dark roads into Switzerland, where arrangements had been made to sell the painting. Then, even more carefully, they returned along those treacherous roads to Bilignin. When friends later remonstrated that the women should have remained in the neutral country, neither replied. It well could be that they thought their roles in Belley were more important than their lives; it was more likely that they were still convinced that France was where they belonged. Obviously, they could barely eke out an existence among people who cared for them; what would happen to them, with little money, among strangers?

Beginning in October 1942, France became completely inaccessible by mail, a condition that would last until the summer of 1944. In the grim depths of war, living now in an occupied country, Gertrude and Alice continued barely existing—cutting wood and box hedges, reading Alice's collection of cookbooks to try to assuage their hunger, watching the world grow more and more silent and more and more fearful. When their landlord said that they would have to move because he wanted the house for his son, they protested. They even filed a lawsuit. But finally, in the midst of another intolerable winter (during which the tiny Pépé, who so minded the cold, was put to sleep by the veterinarian), word came that their plea had been rejected, and they were to vacate the house immediately.

With her typical understatement, Alice wrote, "We were broken-hearted to have to leave Bilignin." Friends found them Le Colombier, the manor house in Culoz, complete with two old servants, but the two knew that "at Culoz we should be less favored. We had no acquaintances there. . . . There was no vegetable garden. It would be starting over from scratch." At sixty-eight and sixty-six, the two Americans faced bleak choices: starting over in an unknown community, crossing illegally to Switzerland ("by fraud," as Gertrude said), being sent to a concentration camp, or committing suicide. There is no mention in any of their papers that they considered the last option, but many, many Jews did kill themselves.

Their lawsuit, unfortunately, had attracted attention. On the day they were packing came a command to their lawyer from the *sous-préfet* of Belley: "Tell those ladies that they must leave for Switzerland, to-morrow if possible otherwise they will be put in a concentration camp." The official had arranged safe passage for them to Switzerland, but Gertrude and Alice—stubbornly, perversely—instead moved to Culoz. Much more visible there, living in a large house on a hillside at the edge of the busy railway center and near a German security center, Gertrude and Alice seemed to be taunting fate.

In the silence of the very large rooms in the Culoz house, Alice threw herself into the hard work necessary to make even part of the house habitable. Closing off most of it, the women created a place for themselves and Basket II; and while they did not attempt the kind of garden they had grown in Bilignin, they planted potatoes and other vegetables. It was useful for Gertrude to have reason to work outside regularly; she also raked hay, cared for the goat they bought for milk, and kept up her long treks. German soldiers swarmed in the town, so she walked her daily kilometers headed away from Culoz, often in the direction of Bilignin.

Years later, in a ceremony acknowledging her value to Culoz, Gertrude was praised as one who had aided resistance workers "by collecting and transmitting information to them." Because there are so few written records of resistance activity, however, the chief proof of her role is oral. Historians have long noted that many women—particularly Jewish women—worked successfully for the resistance because the Germans thought so little of women that they seldom suspected them. Judy Grahn recently noted that "at the close of the war members of the resistance gave her [Stein] an award of appreciation." The most obvious evidence of Gertrude's familiarity with the resistance in the Savoie is her moving play *Yes Is for a Very Young Man*.

Though dangerous, living near the railway depot was also useful; people came and went, got off trains for a few minutes and then reboarded. Whereas Gertrude walked into town only occasionally, Alice went regularly into the main streets of Culoz because she shopped daily; she had found two grocers who felt it their patriotic duty to sell forbidden goods. (Alice decided that buying those forbidden goods was, in turn, equally pro-French, especially now that they had money from selling the painting. The two women liked to shock mealtime guests by telling them that they were eating the Cézanne.) Friends from Bilignin cycled over, as did the young Pierre Balmain, one of the "bright spots" of Gertrude's life. The son of an antique dealer in Aix, the novice tailor had made them warm suits, bundling the heavy fabric onto his bicycle and pedaling over during the cold Belley winters. Visitors from Lyon seventy miles away, like René Tavernier and a number of other nameless young people—"All in the Résistance, naturally," Alice recalled—came and went. Somewhat awkwardly, so did Bernard Faÿ. And in the drafty old house Gertrude still played rough games with Basket, snapping a large handkerchief up and down before his nose and ordering him, "Play Hemingway! Be fierce!"

Having given their Ford to the Red Cross, Gertrude and Alice benefited from Culoz's being a rail center, though they occasionally took the wrong train and had more adventures than they wanted. Stein liked the camaraderie of traveling in the second-class compartments—she could even stand the cold in the cars with smashed windows—and justified their trips as a way to stay in touch with the French people.

Leo and Nina in Italy

Less well off in Italy, Leo had to do daily battle—literally—to survive. His life became a campaign to find food; standing in what lines existed for whatever was being distributed, foraging in gardens and at roadsides for edible greens, and seeing that he sustained the weaker Nina. She spent much of her time in bed and remained traumatized from Leo's recent near-death from monoxide poisoning. When she had found him unconscious in his bedroom then, Nina recognized that living without Leo would be impossible for her; the residual fear from the shock stayed with her throughout the war. She could not bear to see Leo leave the villa. She had nightmares that he was arrested, and she seldom left him for any reason, as though her presence were a buffer for the innocent, blustering American who had lived thirty years in Italy without ever understanding the Italians—or any Europeans, she thought.

Suffering from failing health and hunger that bordered on starvation, Leo steadily wrote his days away, recording his thoughts and philosophical observations in journals that, year by year, seemed to repeat themselves. In terms of sheer physical hardship, Leo and Nina had drawn the worse lot, but at the close of 1942 they were still alive—and increasingly optimistic. Germany was being defeated in Russia (and by the summer of 1943 would have lost more than six million men in the Russian campaign); the Allies were dropping blockbuster bombs on Germany (sometimes bombing Italy en route), flying in from both England and French North Africa. In May 1943 Germany was defeated in North Africa, and during that summer the Allies took Sicily. In that battle, as in the conquest of Italy, it was German resistance that held off the Allies: the Italians had given up long before. On July 24, 1943, the Italian Fascist Party demanded Mussolini's resignation. Germany, however, still held Italy, and during the rest of 1943 and all of 1944, the country was the scene of some of the bloodiest fighting of the entire war. And as the Allies moved north from the hard-fought conquest of Rome in June 1944, Leo and Nina lived through intolerable times.

In 1943 Leo began to have spells of unconsciousness, along with severe attacks of colitis and vomiting. He attributed his pain to being severely undernourished—and for that, no remedy was possible. In August 1943 Nina and he slept in the cellar while all around them houses were shelled and neighbors killed. "Batteries have been established above Settignano, and Germans and English are now shooting at each other over our heads. Two houses at Settignano have been struck. I was looking at Settignano when Manuelli's house was hit. There was a huge momentary red blaze. People in the street nearby were killed and wounded." Because of his poor hearing, Leo heard the bombs less clearly than others did, and so he could sometimes sleep.

As the Germans marched through Settignano, a village they were theoretically not going to touch, they blew up "a number of houses so to widen the street." Leo's despair surfaced in his journal: "I didn't suspect that this march through would be so disastrous." He also wondered how, in the case of evacuation, he was supposed to carry Nina and the two heavy suitcases she had packed for them: on most days, Leo could barely walk.

After the armistice on September 8, 1943, the truly horrifying events began. Soon the massacre of Jews around Lago Maggiore was under way. Even though local police gave the arrests of Jews low priority (and sometimes refused to participate in such activity), after December 1, 1943, arrest and internment of Jews became government policy. On January 4, 1944, a decree for the confiscation of Jews' goods (including safety deposit boxes and their contents) was enacted. Leo's 1944 journal, however, remains focused on the personal, as if he didn't know any of this. It mostly records where Nina slept, where she would allow him to sleep (Leo kept returning to his bed in the upstairs room), and the general demoralization of fear: "I have not been interested to write lately. The time has been one of waiting."

Leo's journal may have kept him functioning in the midst of intolerable conditions. The notebooks are filled with his understated descriptions of terrible events. One particularly moving account is of his leaving the villa to go for bread only to see the sky illuminated and, fearing that a shell had struck his house, running back to find that all was well and that Nina was safe, although the roof had indeed been hit. His journals continue to chart his observations about himself: "I have noted with interest perhaps with a bit of surprise that so far I have not felt one thrill of fear." On August 12 he wrote in his familiar cantankerous tone, "I'm beginning to feel annoyed by this war. There they go on Boum Bouming apparently with the same guns in the same places. There is a painful lack of variety and this damned cellar is becoming noisome." Enduring more hardship during his seventies than he had ever imagined might exist, Leo was able somehow to maintain both his spirit and his will. It was no small accomplishment.

Gertrude and Alice in France

During the same years, Gertrude and Alice's Culoz home was requisitioned three times as quarters for enemy soldiers. During the first occupation, two German officers and their orderlies lived with the women for more than two weeks, heating rations in the kitchen and eating in a room adjoining the officers' bedroom in the far wing. The women let the servants deal with the Germans most of the time, but the men had arrived so suddenly that many English-language books were in plain sight throughout the house. Gertrude said wryly that her chief objection to the Germans was their fetish for house keys ("They were always going off with the keys, and then I would have to go to the locksmith again"); another strike against them was their imperiousness when they knocked at the door and demanded "this room and this room and say 'no answers, please—' not that anybody would ever try to answer them."

While they were housing Germans, Gertrude and Alice were passing as Frenchwomen. They had not signed the register of Jews at Culoz. When they had gone to the town hall to register, Justin Hey, the mayor, had stopped them, saying that they were too old to endure concentration camps; he and his Swiss wife would protect them, he said. But Gertrude was observant enough to worry about internal dissension: "Every neighbour is denouncing every neighbour, for black traffic, for theft." Some people sent threats of denunciation ("a little wooden coffin sometimes with a letter inside sometimes with a rope inside to tell themselves to hang themselves . . . sent by post or by railroad and sometimes it is hung up in a tree and sometimes hung up in front of the front door"). Others simply denounced people and waited for the Gestapo to arrest the victims.

And then there was the faux pas by Madame Peycru, the baker in Bilignin, who sent Gertrude and Alice one of her good cakes by bus, addressing the box to "The Two American Ladies in Culoz." As Toklas wrote, she and Gertrude were frightened: "Not one of the two hundred and fifty Germans and their officers stationed at Culoz suspected our nationality, the French authorities having destroyed our papers and done everything possible to protect us." Gertrude and she immediately took the bus back to Bilignin and explained to Madame Peycru in person that their names were never to be used nor their nationality mentioned.

During 1943 the occupying Germans behaved correctly, but as they later lost ground, they grew erratic. Suspecting people of being in the resistance—many were—they shot them indiscriminately—two young boys, a female teacher, an old drunk on the road after curfew. For the first time in her life, Gertrude wore a wristwatch and learned to be inside long before curfew.

During 1944, when a group of Italian soldiers, kindly men who liked to talk to them about the Germans, was billeted with them, the invasion of their lives seemed bearable. The Italian officer unfortunately allowed his men to destroy their papers, although Gertrude warned him that they should keep them; otherwise, they would have no protection. Alice and she later learned that all six hundred of the Italian soldiers leaving Belley were killed by the Germans as they approached the frontier of Italy.

Obsessively hungry and often afraid, Gertrude continued writing *Wars I Have Seen* throughout these literal occupations. Alice never typed any of this manuscript, knowing full well that no enemy would be able to read Gertrude's sprawlingly illegible handwriting (Gertrude was often unable to decipher it herself). As a further precaution, she seldom used either the word *German* or people's surnames. While she depicted emotional states vividly, she never described military movements: one of the book's titles in draft was "An Emotional Autobiography."

There was little news from the outside world. Matisse had moved to Vence, where he was completely isolated. Picasso remained safe in Paris, lionized and courted by the Germans—and denounced by such old friends as Vlaminck, partly because of his luxurious, protected lifestyle and partly because he would not sign Jean Cocteau's letter to German authorities pleading for Max Jacob's release from Drancy. Both men were dear friends of Picasso's. Early in 1944 Jacob had been arrested and taken from his monastery to the detention camp, where he died of pneumonia. Gertrude wrote loving tributes to him for *Confluences* and *Aquédal,* while a collaborationist publication denounced Jacob as "a Jew by birth, Breton by birth, Roman Catholic by religion, sodomist by habit."

In June 1944 the tone of Gertrude's *Wars I Have Seen* changed dramatically. After the long year of danger in Culoz, Gertrude and Alice learned that the Allies had taken Normandy. The success of that immense invasion—thousands of bombers, transport planes, and ships and millions of men—was credited to information given Britain by the French resistance. As Gertrude wrote about June 6, D-Day, "To-day is the landing and we heard Eisenhower tell us he was here they were here and just yesterday a man sold us ten packages of Camel cigarettes, glory be, and we are singing glory hallelujah, and feeling very nicely, and everybody has been telephoning to us congratulatory messages upon my birthday which it isn't but we know what they mean. And I said in return I hoped their hair was curling nicely, and we all hope it is, and to-day is the day." Gertrude and Alice celebrated, once more, in a code that only seemed idiosyncratic and personal. Not the least of their pleasures was the fact that Alice, after years of smoking dried leaves of whatever kind could be found, had real tobacco again.

The End of One War

After D-Day the Allies spent weeks trying to break through to France, which they did at Saint-Lô on July 26. By August 14 Paris had been liberated. During the long, uneasy summer, Gertrude and Alice fended off deserting Germans, hoped theirs would not be one of the French villages burned in the retreat, and tried to "just naturally play possum until the Germans are gone."

The last occupation of Gertrude and Alice's house on Culoz occurred during that summer. When a hundred Germans came to the house, Alice sent Gertrude, the manuscript of *Wars I Have Seen,* and Basket into hiding upstairs in a bedroom, and she and the servants prepared the house for the five officers and seven noncoms who would stay inside. The rest slept on the terraces and in the gardens. It was "hideous confusion" as Alice found mattresses for the men and tried to stay out of their way. The next day the Germans "killed a calf on the terrace nearest the house and cooked it on an improvised spit." Luckily, they then left.

The retreating men could not go far, however. The maquis had destroyed enough bridges and sections of main road that many were trapped, and, as Alice wrote, "the boys of the Résistance came down quietly from their mountain top one morning, drove the seven hundred Germans from Culoz and the neighbourhood into the marshes, surrounded them and wiped them out. It was glorious, classic, almost Biblical. We celebrated by taking one of the liberated taxis to Belley." Gertrude, too, spoke of the "mountain boys," the maquis, killing "fifty Germans right there across the road." In early August the maquis took over Culoz and proclaimed the Fourth Republic.

From then on, it was only a matter of time until the Americans arrived. When they did, Alice and Gertrude burst into action—Alice, baking the long-awaited "liberation" cake with candied fruit she had hoarded throughout the war, killing the fatted chicken that Gertrude had been awaiting, and exploding into culinary delight whenever a GI could be lured to dinner. Gertrude finished *Wars I Have Seen.* In the midst of their almost-daily celebrations, Eric Sevareid and a companion reporter, Frank Gervasi, appeared at their door (Sevareid had interviewed Gertrude in the late 1930s and knew her approximate location, but the move to Culoz had delayed his finding her). He wanted an interview for the CBS station installed at Voiron, forty miles away.

Going to the radio station in two American jeeps and eating with the troops ("ham and eggs, tinned corn, sweet pickles, biscuits and tinned California peaches, coffee with evaporated milk") was more exciting than the broadcast, though Gertrude's exuberance made that a success. She began by saying, "What a day is today, that is, what a day it was day before yesterday," describing her joy at seeing Americans arriving in their Jeeps. When she took some of the men home for lunch—where they could talk together in that "pleasant American way"—the whole village shouted, "The Americans have come! The Americans have come! . . . They are here. God bless them!" The most important part of the broadcast was her tribute to France and to the maquis:

> I can never be thankful enough that I stayed with them [the French] all these dark days, when we had to walk miles to get a little extra butter a little extra flour when everybody somehow managed to feed themselves, when the Maquis under the eyes of the Germans received transported and hid the arms dropped to them by parachutes, we always wanted some of the parachute cloth as a souvenir. . . . I can tell you that liberty is the most important thing in the world more important than food and clothes more important than anything on this mortal earth, I who spent four years with the French under the German yoke tell you so.

The war, of course, continued. There would be no return to Paris, even though it was liberated, until things were safer, but at least communication was possible. Gertrude wrote to all their Parisian and American friends. Alice typed *Wars I Have Seen,* which ended with scenes of their conversations with American GIs in Culoz, and Frank Gervasi carried it to Bennett Cerf in New York. But then Gertrude and Alice grew inordinately homesick. Five years away from Paris seemed like an eternity. They heard that Hemingway was in the city, claiming he had liberated Paris. Sylvia Beach had come out of hiding. Bernard Faÿ, to Gertrude and Alice's sorrow, had been arrested, and many, many other collaborators shot.

In Culoz, in November, Gertrude and Alice read a friend's letter telling them the story of the Gestapo's attempt to take their paintings from the rue Christine apartment. During the last days of the occupation, a group of Germans had entered the flat and, when discovered by a young American neighbor woman who had quickly called the police, were threatening to burn the paintings, which they called "Jewish filth." Turned away by the authorities because they had improper papers, the men removed only some smaller objects, but they had taken Gertrude's photograph with them. Had the Allies not been successful, the Stein-Toklas story might have ended very differently.

Nervous about their possessions and their friends, Gertrude and Alice rented a truck and a car, loaded everything they wanted to take, said goodbye to their friends in Culoz, and braced themselves for the long night's drive to Paris. It was the middle of December. Returning might not have been their most prudent act, but they had not lived through the German occupation by being prudent. Or, as Gertrude had written in *Wars I Have Seen,* she and Alice had seemed to be "rather favored strangers" during the long season of war, never seriously harmed despite the dangers of living in occupied France. Whatever choices they had had to make, they had made them in good conscience: their purpose throughout the war had been to help the French people, and, as Gertrude had written so innocently in 1939, her frustration was only that there seemed to be nothing she could do to help.

The Last Deaths

Gertrude Stein liked to believe in miracles. She had called winning Alice a miracle, and she called her writing "the daily miracle." When American GIs came to talk with her and Alice at the rue Christine (both she and Picasso were inundated with visits once the word got around that they would receive GIs), she said the salvation of their art—and their lives—during the occupation was "a miracle, just like the miracle that prevented Von Choltitz from blowing Paris to bits as Hitler intended." Still another miracle occurred on their night drive from Culoz back to Paris, when their vehicles were stopped by an armed woman and several men. What was Gertrude's identity now, in December 1944—the conservative art patroness protected by collaborator Bernard Faÿ, or the Jewish American who had helped the resistance, or an old Frenchwoman moving back to Paris? Luckily, one of the men leaned against Picasso's portrait of Gertrude, and Alice involuntarily snapped, "Take care, that is a painting by Picasso, don't disturb it." As if she had spoken some kind of password, the resistance members said, "We congratulate you, madame, you may go on."

Gertrude's Postwar Celebrity

Back in Paris, Alice grieved that many of their objets d'art had been stolen, though she was happy that a bundle of smaller paintings, already tied together for carrying, had been left. The next morning Picasso arrived to welcome his friends, and the reunion was ecstatic. Although he had disliked Gertrude's staying away from Paris, and she had doubts about his companionship with the Nazis, their old friendship countered everything. As he gazed at his paintings, he murmured, in what was to become a constant refrain, that their preservation was a miracle.

Paris was nothing like the city they had known. Filled with military forces, debris, and confusing one-way streets, it offered fewer food supplies than had Culoz. Alice was worried: would they be able to survive? But when mail began coming through in early January, people sent food, and the friends who reappeared from hiding also brought supplies. Picabia moved back to Paris. Donald Gallup, who was to be curator of the Stein collection at Yale, made the first of what would be weekly visits; Norman Holmes Pearson came, bringing with him H.D.'s daughter, Perdita (Gertrude and Alice remembered her as a child); William S. Sutton interviewed Gertrude for Robert Haas. Katharine Cornell, in Paris to star in *The Barretts of Wimpole Street* for the USO, arranged for Gertrude and Alice to dress in uniform and attend a performance. Stein and Hemingway crossed paths unexpectedly and cordially, although a friend's recounting of Gertrude's version differs from Hemingway's. Hemingway said they still loved each other; Gertrude remembered that when Hemingway said, "I am old and rich. Let's stop fighting," she had replied, "I am not old. I am not rich. Let's go on fighting."

At the rue Christine the women entertained old friends Sylvia Beach, Donald Sutherland, Harold Acton, and Francis Rose and new friends Henry Rago, George John, Joseph Barry—who became Jo the Loiterer in Stein's next opera—and hundreds of GIs. Gertrude loved the attention—being greeted on the streets, photographed, asked for her autograph, visited. Most of all, she loved being in Paris once more: "Basket and I walk and walk and the house is always full of old friends and new G.I.'s."

Emotionally, however, both women were still traumatized by their war experiences. In Gertrude's case, the residue of the years of fear worked itself out through her writing: *Wars I Have Seen,* with its necessary disguises and childlike expression, was only a start. In the fall of 1944, tired of trying to explain the French to Americans and tired of being maligned herself for her political stance during the early war years, she turned to drama and fiction. At this time, she wrote what was to be her clearest statement of the unreconcilable conflicts of the various French political positions, the two-act play *Yes Is for a Very Young Man.*

A marvel of economical structure, the play opens with the characters' divided opinions about the 1940 armistice. One man is fascist, one is in the resistance, the third is for Pétain so long as his own life is not interrupted. But as this last tells his nagging sister-in-law, "Can't you see, can't you feel, this is no time to talk about anything but what has happened to France." As Gertrude had in *Wars I Have Seen,* here she valorizes French attitudes even as they conflict. Part of the lighter text of the drama consists of narratives that show the Germans (who already occupy the country) being fooled completely by the French and their stories—for example, that the resistance could not exist in the hills because there is no water there; why, there even animals must drink from bottles.

That these narratives are the same ones Alice and Gertrude told about the war in Belley adds a personal authenticity to the drama, but within the play random events are fused into a tight dramatic plot. Gertrude also drew from their Culoz experiences—an old man shot and left dead on the road all night, the woman protagonist passing information at the train station, the fifty Germans shot like rabbits in the marsh after the liberation of Paris.

The most important character in the play, the catalyst who resolves the seemingly disparate French positions, is the young American woman, Constance. Politically astute, philosophically deft, and clearly sexual (Ferdinand is in love with her), Constance fits her name: she endures throughout the five years of the drama (and the occupation), playing the devil's advocate for most of the characters, drawing them out of their provinciality to see the rationale behind dissenting viewpoints. By the play's end, Constance has solved some of the human problems. Denise and Henry stay together, with him loving the child that is probably not his. The young Ferdinand, learning to see beyond sexuality, leaves to support a political position he has chosen. And Constance is free to return to her own life and her own country, understanding that she cannot stay in France. She does not belong: France is for the French.

While *Yes Is for a Very Young Man* is a sympathetic presentation of the French, it is also a self-portrait of Gertrude. Exuding the sensual, Constance owes part of her charm for the young Frenchmen to her femininity. Stein said she had Clare Booth Luce in mind when she created Constance, and she may have—the Luces had spent several days with them in Belignin just before war was declared in 1939—but she was also envisioning her younger self. Like Gertrude, Constance was homesick for the quays of Paris, and a good roast chicken. She carried information, warned the resistance, and devised plans for demolishing wrecked trains. She saw herself as consistently affirmative and claimed the word *yes,* with all its sexual overtones. Constance's compassion for the very young Frenchmen, which the title emphasizes, echoes throughout Gertrude's dealings with both the young men of Belley and the American GIs in Paris.

After the brilliant clarity of this work, Gertrude turned to two other major projects, writing them in sequence. Each grew in its own way from the seminal, and impassioned, *Yes Is for a Very Young Man.* The opera *The Mother of Us All* fuses the characters of Denise and Constance as Gertrude explores the firmly disciplined but complacent Susan B. Anthony. A fiercely independent and female-identified woman, Anthony, in her dialogue scene in prose with her companion, Anne, is bluntly critical of men: "So conservative, so selfish, so boresome . . . so ugly." (She exempts some men—Gallup, Jo the Loiterer, Daniel Webster—from her criticism.) Interchanges about sexual prowess, names, marriage, racial difference, and the vote constitute the ostensible narrative, but the most effective segment of the libretto is Anthony's musing, hesitating soliloquy at the end. Has what she accomplished been worthwhile? There is no way to retrace her steps or to know whether she has gone forward. And her long life, edged with the suggestion of Claribel Cone's "Life is strife" maxim, is not in itself inherently promising. With the weary pace of Anthony's closing, Gertrude conveys the pervasive mood of "mothering." "Where is where. . . . But do I want what we have got, has it not gone, what made it live."

Gertrude wanted to do this libretto because she loved writing for the stage and she loved working with Virgil Thomson, who had returned to Paris to help plan the work. But as he watched the aging Gertrude, now sometimes drawn into herself even in the midst of conversation, Thomson wondered how much time she had left to work.

She was even happier about her other project, the short narrative she called by the unlikely title "Brewsie and Willie," for in it she showcased her keen ear. *Brewsie and Willie* is the voice of one young American GI—in dialogue with several recalcitrant others (chief among them, Willie)—listened to, questioned, prodded to answers, and respectfully loved and enjoyed during that year of Stein's great postwar celebrity, 1945.

On her return to Paris, Gertrude was ready to leave behind all the political controversy over Pétain and Vichy France. She was ready to leave behind the sophistry, the intricate explanations for this stand or that, for betrayal or treason or patriotism—though she never forgot her friends, no matter where they stood politically, and sent a constant barrage of letters about the imprisonment of Bernard Faÿ to American officials. She had ignored Bennett Cerf and Saxe Commins's dismay over her suggestion that Random House publish Pétain's speeches; she simply dropped the project. Cerf, who had been appalled when she sent him the materials, noted on the typescript, "For the records. This disgusting piece was mailed from Belley on Jan. 19, 1942." Time salved his outrage, however, and he understood that *Wars I Have Seen*—and the ill-fated Pétain speech collection—fit into Stein's oeuvre as autobiography, not as political treatise. He was eager to publish the autobiography. Because Kathleen Winsor (the author of *Forever Amber*) had recently appeared on the front cover of *Publishers Weekly,* he arranged for similar treatment of Stein's photo and book, using the caption "Shucks, we've got glamour girls too." Gertrude enjoyed the joke hugely. *The Saturday Review of Literature* also featured her photo on its cover.

Some readers were not impressed with *Wars I Have Seen* when it appeared in early spring, though it sold ten thousand copies within the first few months of publication. Among the offended was Random House editor Saxe Commins, who said later that Gertrude sounded like a collaborationist, that her views were "at best reactionary and at worst reprehensible," and that the book "reveals the essential shallow mindedness of a woman who is indifferent to a world cataclysm while she remains absorbed in her own private word game—a word game that assumes no responsibility." Some readers were put off by her generally pleasant understatement of horrors, failing to see that the speaker's voice might well be ironic. But more reviews—including one by Richard Wright—were positive, and such critics as Ben Ray Redman, Delmore Schwartz, and W. T. Scott said it was Gertrude's best book.

Leo and Nina's Survival

In early September 1944, when the Germans were driven out of northern Italy, Leo and Nina knew they would make it. Leo walked haltingly along the road, content simply to watch the young Americans. He took their chocolate gladly, commenting that his wife would appreciate it, so the soldiers gave the frail old man who spoke English more for himself. They gave him new batteries for his hearing aid so he could hear again. And he wolfed down a meal with them, smiling broadly at their various generosities, and managed to walk into the village for extra ration cards. Now the fact that he was American counted for something: "Nothing like being top dog." By November 11 Nina and he were drinking real coffee with their breakfasts of toast, margarine, and once in a while a little jam.

But in the midst of the defeat of the Germans—although it took the Allies another six months of hard fighting to reach the Po Valley—a discouraging tiredness set in. Leo wanted to begin writing his book, as he wanted to begin painting in earnest, but an intermittent weariness drugged him. Even so, at seventy-two, fatigued from lack of rest, fragile from poor nutrition, he yet pushed on to what was to be the most productive period of his career.

As he prepared the manuscript of the book that would be *Appreciation: Painting, Poetry and Prose* from notes and sections of text written in his voluminous notebooks before and during the war, Leo felt vindicated. His letters to friends show that surviving the war was one of the healthier passages of Leo's life. Though he never called it a miracle, in many respects it was. And Nina basked in his successes, growing stronger herself as their diet improved and the villa was repaired.

Never envious of the comfort Bernard Berenson had enjoyed through the war, Leo was pleased to have him—and his valuable books and paintings—return to I Tatti, which he and Mary had fled shortly after the 1943 armistice. Several of their mutual friends were angry for years about Berenson's lack of concern for Nina and Leo: Maurice Sterne wrote that while the Berensons found refuge with an Italian nobleman, "The Steins were close to starving in Settignano. Nina was helpless in bed with arthritis and Leo burned their furniture to get some warmth in the house. He had to stand in line for hours for whatever bread was available and rationed to them." But Leo seemed to be beyond envy. He never complained to relatives about the war and was simply grateful for the food packages that arrived, finally, during 1944 and 1945. Except for entries in his journals, he seldom wrote about the war at all. It was as if he had realized that what time remained to him should go into his real work.

When Leo wrote Sterne in June 1945, he sounded purposeful and happy; he was writing, he said, and considered himself to be in a "perfect state of grace." Thankful to have survived, he mentioned four friends—including Rudolph Levy—who had been imprisoned, sent north to the murder camps, and never returned. To Fred Stein, he wrote that Nina and he would stay in Settignano for the winter, no longer afraid of freezing. He was writing well, he reported: "My private interior life is one endless round of excitements." By February 1946 he reported to Howard Gans that his finished manuscript was being sent to the States by the USA Information Bureau. In early April Fred Stein had the manuscript but had some trouble marketing it; finally, Hiram Hayden, the editor at Crown, accepted it enthusiastically. Leo was pleased but not surprised. He had at last reached the easy fluency he had worked toward his entire life, and he was writing steadily now on a new manuscript.

The End of the Other War

Much of the world, however, was still at war. On April 12, 1945, Franklin Delano Roosevelt died, leaving many Americans feeling lost. A few weeks later Janet Flanner returned to France and toured Buchenwald and Ravensbruck, the women's concentration camp near Stettin: eyewitness accounts left readers shuddering in disbelief. As the world watched, on April 28 Mussolini and his mistress were executed near Lake Como, Italy, and a few days later Hitler's death was reported. On May 7 the Articles of Surrender were signed, and on May 9, at 12:01 P.M., hostilities in the European theater of war ceased. Gertrude had been speaking to small audiences of the military near Paris and in Nancy, but now in June Alice and she flew by bomber with a group of GIs for a tour of Germany (they were photographed in Salzburg and Frankfurt and on the terrace at Berghof). Gertrude's account of the trip was published in the August issue of *Life.*

That month brought the unspeakable atomic bombing of Hiroshima on August 6 and, three days later, of Nagasaki. Japan accepted the Allied terms of unconditional surrender on August 14, bringing to a close the truly cataclysmic Second World War, with its probable casualty count of forty million people dead. Stunned with this recent series of horrors, Gertrude again found solace in her writing. As she began the book she had promised in the epilogue to *Wars I Have Seen,* something for the GIs who wanted her to write about them, she focused more directly on what the war had meant to the individual. *Brewsie and Willie* represented people the world over, most of them living in shocked disbelief at the carnage of war.

> Brewsie: Well let's think about how everybody perhaps will get killed in the next war.
> Willie: Well they sure will if they fight the war good enough. If you fight a war good enough everybody ought to get killed.
> Brewsie: You mean the other side.
> Willie: No not the other side, that's only when one side fights good enough, but when they both do, and that can happen too, well when they both do, then everybody will be dead, all dead, fine, then nobody's got to worry about jobs.

Reflecting the sad end of human optimism, Willie's laconic bitterness spoke for Gertrude, and for everyone she knew; Brewsie, however, drawing on William James ("I don't know the guy," Willie replied), argued that the will to live was stronger than mere fatalism. Willie admonished him, "Thinking is what you do Brewsie, but living is what we all got to do, now what are we going to do, how we going to live. . . . Somehow everybody just does keep on living, look at everybody over here, by rights they ought all to be all dead, all of them over and over again dead, all of them and they ain't Brewsie, they ain't at all dead, far from it. . . . Everywhere is lousy with them." That segment of the book ended, "Yes, said Donald Paul, that is what William James called the will to live."

Although Gertrude wrote her GI book rapidly, Alice and she looked as if they were simply enjoying Paris and its contingent of young Americans. They traveled around the countryside with Clyde Sweet, a military friend from the California tour, and took him along to a fitting at Balmain's, where Gertrude had his gift of antique Chinese brocade made into a vest. They dined with Harold Acton at an officers' club, taking along the beautifully behaved Basket as they did when Ellen Bloom (Julian Stein's stepdaughter from Baltimore) took them to Red Cross headquarters for Sunday lunch. Gertrude frequently spoke to audiences of American soldiers, both in Paris and in other parts of Europe. Alice and she listened to Janet Flanner's anguish covering the trial of Pétain. And when Gertrude appeared with Basket at an art exhibit to which Caresse Crosby had invited her and stole the show by walking off with the best-looking GI in the gallery, Caresse forgave her. At seventy-one, Gertrude was even more the American character than she had been twenty years earlier.

Invited to Pierre Balmain's first showing as an independent designer, Gertrude and Alice dressed in his clothes—Stein in a tailored suit and Toklas in a garden dress—and, accompanied by Basket and Cecil Beaton, who promised to take photographs, sat in the front row. Unfortunately, Balmain's airedale was being led by the first model, and there was an immediate "furious battle." Balmain, making the best of the situation, pretended he thought it set a tone of informality that may have helped the show. He also was pleased that the two women were circumspect about the fact that he often made their clothes; for that winter, for example, he had made for Gertrude "an imperial evening suit" in brown velvet heavily embroidered in jet, with a matching cap with a long tassel.

But on a trip to Belgium for another talk, Gertrude was prostrate with abdominal pain. The doctor she saw in Brussels alarmed her by telling her to consult a specialist immediately. Gertrude, however, did nothing. She was finally able to deliver her talk, and when she returned to Paris, she sent two-thirds of the *Brewsie and Willie* manuscript to Cerf. She also saw to it that the imprisoned Bernard Faÿ received a package of food and cigarettes, as well as some American vitamin pills she had asked a friend to send over to her. Watching her busy herself with trivia, Alice understood that Stein had already decided how to treat—or refuse to treat—her increasingly painful colitis.

Gertrude's Death

Slowly, the Allies were pulling out of France. Gertrude and Alice said good-bye to more and more friends and acquaintances. Donald Gallup left on December 1, shortly after helping Gertrude celebrate the completion of the first scenes of *The Mother of Us All*; Virgil Thomson, too, returned to the States. Daniel-Henry Kahnweiler's wife languished, and Gertrude and Alice paid a last call, struggling up the four flights of stairs to her bedside. Kahnweiler later said that Gertrude's visit "seemed to represent a great effort for her."

Most people did not notice that Stein was failing. She spent much of the winter sorting through her manuscripts and papers, readying large boxes for Yale. With Janet Flanner, she worried over the outcomes of the Nuremberg trials. Yet as her own writing grew more and more direct—as when she wrote Robert Graves that his relationship with Laura Riding failed because Laura hid her materialism under a feigned intellectualism—she kept up her cordial heartiness with the young. Ellen Bloom wrote thanking them for their hospitality and good humor, saying she was "trying to remember your admonition not to take life too seriously."

And times were xciting. Carl Van Vechten was editing an omnibus collection of Gertrude's work for Random House, and there was much correspondence about the selections and introduction. After the cancellation of one production of *Yes Is for a Very Young Man,* a USO group that had read it in Paris produced it in Pasadena, California. In March Gertrude sent the completed *The Mother of Us All* to Thomson, who was ecstatic about it and wrote that he would return to Paris in May so they could work on final details together. On April 1 she sent the completed manuscript of *Brewsie and Willie* to Van Vechten, with instructions that he forward it to Cerf after he had read it.

But amid the good news about publication and the beautiful Paris spring she and Alice had missed so terribly during their five years away came a growing sense of relinquishment. Perhaps Gertrude had accepted her coming death in Brussels when she decided to disregard the doctor's advice. As she had then written in a loving—and last—letter to the young Wilcox, "Everything is quite alright, and that's the way it is, quite really is, bless you Wendell, lots of love. . . . Gtrde." Now only faintly cognizant of details of her mother's long death in California from a cancer that had been treated . . . and treated . . . and treated, she drew strength to stand the process of dying. As she had described death in *Paris France,* "It is so friendly so simply friendly and though inevitable not a sadness and though occurring not a shock."

She wrote Julian and Rose Ellen, asking again for family news. In March she wrote a long deposition for the court about what she saw as the truly patriotic intent of Bernard Faÿ's activities during the war. In May she met Richard Wright at the train station and helped him meet the American literary crowd in Paris. That same month Natalie Barney returned to Paris, and Gertrude and she resumed their walks, though they were shorter now. Barney recalled one evening on which they had had a disappointing supper out and then gone to Rumpelmayer's for dessert. When a photographer followed Stein to the patisserie, taking her picture through the window as they ate, Gertrude sadly "dropped her head between her hands and shook it from side to side." Later that month, at an amusing dinner at Virgil Thomson's complete with a gangster he thought would interest her, Gertrude was very quiet. When Virgil began teasing her in a familiar and loving way, Alice said quietly to him, "Don't scold her. She may cry."

Ill much of the time with what she called colitis and impatient at the discomfort and her inability to go where she wanted, Gertrude bought a new car. When Picasso criticized her choice (he had advised her to get a used one), Stein said coldly, "It's what I wanted and I've gotten it. So good-bye Pablo." Staying friends with even those she loved took energy she no longer had: she and Picasso never met again. In the new car, Jo Barry drove Alice and Gertrude to Orgeval so they could visit with Noël Murphy. And finally, in late June, Gertrude wrote Kiddy Rogers about what she called a bowel infection. His scolding reply was dated July 1, 1946: "In letter after letter I ask how you are and you never say a single solitary word and all of a sudden it's a bowel infection and it's been going on for nobody knows how long and nobody knows how bad.'"

On July 11 she wrote Donald Gallup that Alice and she had just mailed Yale a large case of manuscripts and letters. Her work was done. Shortly after, again with Jo Barry driving them, they left for a brief vacation in the country, this time to stay at Bernard Faÿ's house in Luceau. On a drive several days after their arrival, Gertrude became too ill to continue. They stopped at an inn in Azay where a doctor was called; he arranged for Gertrude to see a specialist in Paris, and Alice called Allan Stein to meet them at the train. When they arrived, Allan had an ambulance waiting to take his aunt to the American Hospital in Neuilly—and she allowed it only because, in Alice's words, "she was not prepared for this."

Over the next week, Alice's life hung in a torment of almost unbearable worry. Gertrude, though watching observantly, seemed beyond worry. Doctors and friends of Allan and Roubina had consulted and were consulting. They decided that Gertrude was too weak to withstand surgery, and they set about building her up. Instead, her condition worsened. Still the doctors would not operate. She was in greater and greater pain. Finally, one of the younger surgeons said he had told Miss Stein that he would operate and he would.

On July 23 Gertrude drew up her will. Advance copies of *Brewsie and Willie* arrived, as did a cable that *Yes Is for a Very Young Man* was going to be produced on Broadway. On July 26, Allan and Roubina visited her, and when they had gone Gertrude said slyly to Alice, "Now we don't have to see them again." On July 27, with surgery scheduled for the afternoon, Alice sat near Gertrude and held her hand. From her anesthetized reverie, Stein asked comfortingly, "What is the answer?" When Alice was too tearful to answer, she continued, "In that case, what is the question?" Every inch the meditative philosophy student, every minute the inquiring mind, Gertrude Stein was then taken from the room. At 6:30 P.M., she died without recovering consciousness.

Leo's Death

Grieving is a pale, polite term to describe Alice's state of mind for the next few months. The suddenness of Gertrude's death paralyzed her. Though she wired the news to friends, she could not face the burial, and months passed. It was October 22, 1946, before Gertrude was interred at Père Lachaise Cemetery after a "special ceremony" that reflected her Jewish birth was held at the American Cathedral Church of the Holy Trinity. Besides Allan and Roubina, few people knew of the service, and most of the cables and letters Alice received came from the States. The outpouring of sympathy for Toklas repeated the incredulity: no one could believe that Gertrude was dead. As their Boston friend Thomas Whittemore wrote, telling Alice of his feeling of "cosmic loss": "I was as sure that Gertrude would be in Paris as that the Seine would be flowing to the sea. It is true we didn't write to each other but I always felt sailing in her affection. There seemed to be a permanence in Gertrude that belongs to no one else I have ever known."

Leo, living with Nina in their Villina Rosa near Settignano, did not know of Gertrude's death until he read about it in *Newsweek*. In fact, they had celebrated Nina's sixty-fourth birthday on July 27, the day of his sister's death. A month later, in a letter to Fred Stein, Leo mused, "It is strange. I always expected that Mike and Gertrude, both of whom had apparently better constitutions than I, and who took much better care of themselves, would outlive me. I have spent myself recklessly, and after the terrific strain of the neurosis underwent the greater strain of curing it, and now am the only one left." To Howard Gans he was cooler, saying that the news of her death "surprised me, for she seemed of late to be exceedingly alive. I can't say it touches me. I had lost not only all regard, but all respect, for her." Other of Leo's comments, however, do not bear out that tone of dismissal, and in some he discussed her vibrant personality and commanding presence. Just as he had finally admitted that, for all the factual inaccuracy of *The Autobiography of Alice B. Toklas,* the book "maintained very well the tone of sprightly gossip rising at times to a rather nice comedy level," he was finally admitting some of his deep affection for Gertrude. Although Leo said he did not mourn for her, when his second book—*Appreciation: Painting, Poetry and Prose*—was selected by the Book-of-the-Month Club, he realized that he had had nothing to fear from Gertrude.

Even as he pondered his sister's death, Leo wrote Howard Gans that he had anal bleeding, which was "a nuisance." During the fall, he had his first operation for cancer, and while he was hospitalized in Italy, one of his best friends, Gans, died in the States. In January 1947 Leo underwent a second operation—what he termed a "deep cauterization"—behaving like "a model patient" and reconciled to his imminent death. His concern was all for Nina, who was so depressed she could hardly function. In June, apologizing to Fred Stein for his short temper over the publication process of *Appreciation* and other matters, which were largely financial (he needed cash to pay for radium treatments), Leo maintained that he wanted to finish the new book. The radium had stopped the major hemorrhaging, though he was to return to the hospital soon for more internal radium treatment.

But the return to the hospital was for yet another surgery; his colon was completely "rotten," said an Italian specialist, and had to be removed. Alternating between favoring radium and favoring surgery, the consulting doctors finally decided on two operations, one comparatively slight, the other, major. They worried about Leo's age—he was now seventy-five—and about his failing health. But Leo worried only about the reviews of *Appreciation: Painting, Poetry and Prose* and quibbled with Fred over some clippings he had sent. Very well received when it had appeared in June, Leo's book was said to be a hallmark of aesthetic statement, a book that clarified the philosophy of art and literature for the general reader—a book that, in some ways, vindicated the erudition that Gertrude had found tedious.

Again to Fred, Leo commented on his relationship with Gertrude, explaining that so many of the reviews of *Appreciation* brought it up that he wanted to "put this matter straight." He said that they "never quarreled except for a momentary spat. We simply differed and went our own ways," although he admitted, "The differences between Gertrude's character and mine were profound. My interest was a critical interest in science and art. Gertrude had no interest whatever in science or philosophy. . . . Her critical interest was entirely in character, in people's personalities. She was practically inaccessible to ideas and I was accessible to nothing else."

On July 20, 1947, Leo was taken back to the hospital, and on July 29, a year and two days after Gertrude's death, he died of very much the same cause. Had he been conscious enough to hear that his cousin Fred, his publisher, and friends were planning to publish a collection of his unpublished work, he would have been pleased. Like Gertrude, Leo Stein would live in the minds of readers for some time.

Even in death, the symbiosis between brother and sister remained: in almost every review of Leo's book, and in every obituary, Gertrude made her appearance, just as she had forty years earlier in her quiet imposition on his rue de Fleurus studio. As Nina was later to write, "I sometimes feel that Leo's and Gertrude's breaking caused him an immense pain and delusion, perhaps part of his misery! He was so complicated."

And so, naturally and interestingly, was his sister.

Staying on Alone

Of the three widows, Alice B. Toklas may have made the best peace with her circumstances. Luckily, though bereft of Gertrude, she began writing herself, and so the literate world has not only her memoir, *What Is Remembered,* but her informative and autobiographical recipe book, *The Alice B. Toklas Cook Book.* She also published *Staying on Alone,* a collection of her letters, and with Poppy Cannon wrote *Aromas and Flavors,* a second cookbook; she also wrote essays and reviews for the New York media, *The New Republic,* and *Vogue.*

Much of Toklas's writing, unfortunately, was mandated by the circumstances of Gertrude's will. In leaving Alice all the possessions—art collection, furniture, papers—for her lifetime, Gertrude was less specific than she might have been. Some of the possessions she claimed as hers were jointly held and should have belonged outright to Alice; she and Alice together had purchased furniture, for example. Moreover, Alice herself had property: she had bought Italian furniture when she first arrived in France, and she also owned paintings and drawings, even if the art collection was listed as Stein's.

One reason Gertrude's will faltered, leaving Alice with too little income for decent living, was that Toklas lived until 1967, and during those twenty years, the art was appreciating dramatically. Gertrude's nephew Allan, who was to inherit what was left of the estate after Alice had had a good living from it, grew worried about the paintings: when Alice vacationed, he had the paintings removed to a bank vault. The tragedy of this loss for Alice—who had lived nearly fifty years with some of the art—was her feeling both of displacement and of betrayal. Giving her life to caring first for Gertrude and then for the memory and works of Stein as writer, Alice deserved the family's full trust: she had fulfilled her charge well. No survivor could have been more dedicated and more expert in getting what Gertrude wanted accomplished. As it was, Alice was forced to live on contributions from friends, and much of her writing occurred because she needed the money she made from it.

Just as Alice led her life to promote, and maintain, Gertrude Stein's reputation, so she modestly had her own epitaph inscribed on the back of Stein's Père Lachaise rose-colored marker, designed by their friend the artist Francis Rose.

Financial insecurity and loneliness may have driven Nina Auzias Stein to her suicide. The letters that remain between her and Fred Stein inscribe the tragedy of a woman who had no resources to meet bereavement. Completely dependent on Leo, particularly during the difficult war years, Nina could hardly bear to visit him in the hospital during the tests and the surgeries that his cancer required. When Leo died, she was thoroughly disoriented, although her halting English in her letters to Leo's cousin Fred may have disguised the depth of her pain. Staying in the Italian villa also depressed her, but when Fred encouraged her to travel with friends, Nina had no strength for such an endeavor. The shock in Fred's letter to Toklas telling her the news is clear: no one would have anticipated Nina's death, but then none of the American Steins faced the kind of poverty Nina did. Absolutely dependent on the kindness of Leo's cousins, whom she knew only slightly (in forty years Nina had never gone to the States with Leo), and fearing that her depression was going to be costly, as well as permanent, Nina killed herself in the autumn of 1949, two years after Leo's death.

For Sally Stein, "staying on alone" was also a trial. She missed Mike terribly. Gabrielle de Monzie stayed on awhile, but life in the foothills of California was not life in Europe, and she eventually returned to France. Sally was left with a diminished art collection, which she sold piece by piece—and often imprudently—to cover both her living expenses and the debts of her beloved young grandson. Rash sales, furtive deals, and the personal instability that Mike's presence had balanced made Sally's last years less than they might have been. Confused about what people would think about her role in the explosion of Paris art, Sally eventually destroyed her correspondence with Henri Matisse. Enmity between her and Alice Toklas also surfaced, and the latter's acerbity about Sally's Christian Science, fantasy life, and previous cruelty to both Gertrude and Alice was surprising. It became clear that Mike had been the adhesive that held the members of the Stein family together.

After Sally died of natural causes in 1958, the San Francisco Museum tried to collect some of the pieces from Mike and Sally's collection, but more of that art is a part of the Baltimore Museum's Cone Collection. After Etta and Claribel decided to become serious collectors, they had bought extensively from Mike and Sally, Leo, and Gertrude because they trusted the Steins. That the more well-to-do Cone sisters' collection remained whole testifies to the difficulty of being only middle class in the world of collecting. When Gertrude wrote about making her first dollar with the publication of *The Autobiography of Alice B. Toklas,* when she was nearly sixty, she pointed up an important aspect of the Stein family.

It was not, ever, wealthy. It was not, finally, well educated. For its place and time, the Daniel Stein family was a maverick creation, especially after the death of Milly and the disruption of the children's lives. But it somehow had the trait that Gertrude defined as "American": that of knowing what it wanted and of knowing that persistence and directed attention might help in getting what it wanted. During the exciting years of "The Stein Corporation," when Leo and Gertrude and Mike and Sally shocked the art world as they purchased one painting after another by Cézanne, Renoir, Matisse, Picasso, Braque, Gris and then moved on to live from those incredible early purchases, no other collectors took such chances or invested such a high percentage of capital. The Steins spent everything they had on their acquisition of paintings and sculpture. They then husbanded those resources, for the most part, so that they and their families could lead comfortable, quiet lives. They moved quickly from flamboyance to security, each into the kind of life that seemed most productive—Mike monitoring everyone's lives and watching the art markets, Leo questioning what art had to do with larger aesthetic systems and eventually writing about his deliberations, and Gertrude writing and writing, daily, working on the oeuvre that she saw as her contribution to the modernist dream of seeking the new, unhooking language from years of stifling context that misrepresented the times and the period's evolving wisdom.

The Stein family as a unit gave the world a great deal. In their aggressively and humorously idiosyncratic American way, they took from the smorgasbord of the new at its center—in Paris—and made from their takings an American kind of success: financial, aesthetic, and artistic, with all the trappings, during some of the years at least, of "gloire." And Alice Toklas, Nina Auzias, and Sally Samuels, the three women who remained to preserve their memories and their collections, were no small part of the Stein story.

1 Coming to America

1 "Meyer, who had" Sprigge, *GS,* 1; Mellow, *CC,* 20; Stein family genealogy, Jewish Heritage Center, Baltimore; Meyer Stein obituary, YALC.

1 "Although Jews in Germany" Blau and Baron, *JUS,* 803–9.

1 "'the ease with . . . were paid'" Ibid., 809.

1 "from two hundred families" Rosenwaike, *OTE,* 31; Fein, "BJ," 323.

1 "business opportunities for" Rosenwaike, *OTE,* 101; Karp, *JE,* 217–18.

4 "'professing the Jewish religion' . . . office" Karp, *JE,* 217–18.

4 "the state legislature . . . Sloan, *JIA,* 6.

4 "Michael Stein, who" Sprigge, *GS,* 2; Mellow, *CC,* 20.

4 "In 1845 Lloyd" Sloan, *JIA,* 8; Karp, *JE,* 52, 217.

4 "Most early German Jewish" Fein, *MAJC,* 38, 81, 158.

4 "While it was" Rosenwaike, *OTE,* 58.

4 "'almost feudal lives . . . servants [slaves]'" Fein, *MAJC,* 158.

4 "At war's end," Fein, *MAJC,* 99.

4 "U. S. Grant" Sloan, *JIA,* 9.

5 "The Baltimore Steins" Stein family genealogy, Jewish Heritage Center, Baltimore.

5 "on March 23" A. Stein, "Diary," March 23, 1882, records their eighteenth anniversary.

5 "a higher place" Toklas, Duncan interview, 41.

5 "although Moses, a" G. Stein, *EA,* 199.

5 "Both the Stein" Raffel, "TOWAF," 127–38; L. Stein, *JIS,* 187.

5 "Daniel Stein's personal" Most information about the children's early lives is from L. Stein, *A, JIS,* and letters (YALC); A. Stein, "Diary"; G. Stein, *AABT, EA, TMOA, WIHS,* notebooks (YALC), essays, and lectures; see also Raffel, "TOWAF"; and Toklas, Duncan interview.

6 "in dirty, industrial" G. Stein, *EA,* 198.

6 "on Beach Street" L. Stein to Mrs. King, n.d., YALC.

6 "In 1872 the" Meyer Stein obituary, YALC.

6 "'a perfect baby'" G. Stein, *WIHS,* 1.

6 "her unmarried sister" Keyser correspondence, YALC.

7 "'three winters of schooling'" L. Stein, *JIS,* 187.

7 "'going on to the Rhine . . . grape cure'" M. Stein to Moses Keyser, 1875, YALC.

7 "in 1876 that his" M. Stein to Moses Keyser, 1876, YALC.

7 "'where there was . . . must obey'" G. Stein, *TMOA,* 49.

7 "'rather Topsy-like'" L. Stein, *A,* 85.

7   "'"disagreeable" memories of'" L. Stein, *JIS,* 187.
8   "'the struggling, crying . . . brutality'" Ibid., 186.
8   "Children are, of" See A. Miller, *FYOG,* 6–7, for her discussion of the impact of parental desires on infants: "he or she can be molded . . . scolded, and punished—without any repercussions for the person raising the child and without the child taking revenge." Miller warns that if children do not defend themselves by expressing pain and anger, severe psychological damage may result.
8   "'walks all alone . . . imitates everything'" R. Keyser, postscript to M. Stein's 1875 letter, YALC.
8   "'Our little Gertie . . . said or done'" R. Keyser as quoted by L. Stein to G. Stein, Dec. 4, 1914, YALC.
8   "'His whole time . . . with his studies'" R. Keyser, 1876, YALC.
8   "Her short entries" A. Stein, "Diary." Hereafter mentioned in text without citation.
9   "'Whoever teaches his . . . obscenity'" Quoted in Baum, Hyman, and Michel, *JW,* 5. See also Rochlin and Rochlin, *PJ,* 135–36; Glanz, *JOC,* 112; and Levy, *920 O'F,* 129.
9   "German 'salon Jewesses'" Baum, Hyman, and Michel, *JW,* 17–24.
9   "'Woe to the . . . girls'" Quoted in Ibid., 4.
10   "Uncle Meyer Stein, active" Meyer Stein obituary, YALC.
10   "'one little Indian . . . Indian boys'" G. Stein, *WIHS,* 3.
10   "'One is always . . . come from'" Ibid., 11.
10   "moving to California" Glanz, *JOC,* 28; Danziger, "JSF."
10   "'the Paris of the West'" Lewis, *BWB,* 267; Lewis, *TWSF,* 252.
10   "the best-educated" Glanz, *JOC,* 31; Danziger, "JSF," 392.
11   "Public education was" Ferrier, *OAD,* 315, 377; Rochlin and Rochlin, *PJ,* 135–36.
11   "San Francisco's Jewish" Glanz, *JOC,* 38–39, 42.
11   "imaginative business ventures" Danziger, "JSF"; Glanz, *JOC,* 43; Lewis, *TWSF,* 207.
11   "Oakland was proud" Rather, *GSAC,* 14–15; Kahn, *CCD,* 120.
11   "'the most healthful . . . continent'" Rather, *GSAC,* 15–16.
11   "The excited family" Ibid.
11   "Despite his somewhat" M. Stein to Meyer Stein, 1891, YALC; Danziger, "JSF," 395.
11   "'The Old Stratton Place,'" Rather, *GSAC,* 20–25.
12   "'Saint Helena where . . . repeating himself'" G. Stein, *EA,* 255.
12   "'The sun was . . . and running'" G. Stein, *TMOA,* 90.
12   "'a great deal . . . an orgy'" G. Stein, *WIHS,* 17.
12   "Guided by the" Rather, *GSAC,* 19; Rochlin and Rochlin, *PJ,* 107.
12   "'standard of excellence . . . be somebody'" Levy, *920 O'F,* 160–62.
12   "'More and more . . . among them'" G. Stein, *TMOA,* 89.
13   "the Tivoli Opera" Admission included refreshments—beer for men, Queen Charlottes (icy raspberry soda) for ladies and children (Levy, *920 O'F,* 99).
13   "walked up and . . . scheming'" G. Stein, *TMOA,* 132.
13   "Bertha's teeth" G. Stein, *EA,* 115.
13   "'makes everything a pleasure . . . with you'" Ibid., 55.
13   "'California meant knowing . . . surprised'" G. Stein, *WIHS,* 4.
14   "'I was never . . . supplies'" L. Stein, *JIS,* 198.
14   "'You had to . . . little longer'" G. Stein, *EA,* 70.

2   Family Narratives

15   "women's writing often" DuPlessis, *WBTE;* Gilbert and Gubar, *MITA.*
17   "'all of them . . . carry him'" G. Stein, *TMOA,* 135.

17   "'The children would . . . really heard'" Ibid., 51.
18   "'the children would . . . winning'" Ibid., 129.
18   "'My father was . . . the day'" L. Stein, *JIS,* 188.
19   "'all the dried . . . munching'" Ibid., 1.
19   "'radishes pulled with . . . calling'" G. Stein, *TMOA,* 36.
20   "'I wish I . . . dying'" Ibid., 399.
20   "The hormonal changes" Chodorow, *ROM;* Smith-Rosenberg, "PTM," 23–29.
20   "The silences of" Benstock, *PS;* Jelinek, *TWA.*
21   "'women's complaints'" Ehrenreich and English, *FHOG,* 101–40; Baum, Hyman, and Michel, *JW,* 4–8.
21   "'She broke down . . . around them'" G. Stein, *TMOA,* 134.
21   "'his command . . . in general'" Benjamin, *BOL,* 99.
21   "'fathers are depressing . . . as fathers'" G. Stein, *EA,* 112.
21   "'It was when . . . death'" G. Stein, *WIHS,* 8.
21   "'nothing is clear . . . safe'" Ibid., 16.
22   "Mike, graduated from" In a career more diligent than brilliant, Mike had transferred from the University of California (with a recommendation letter that praised his "manly conduct" and "ambition to excel") to Johns Hopkins after his first year. Majoring in chemistry and biology, with minors in French and German, he took a full complement of logic, ethics, political science, drawing, Latin, and Greek classes. In fact, he did a year of graduate work in biology and psychology before returning to the West.
22   "'we went on doing . . . had been'" G. Stein, *EA,* 118.
22   "'You may rest . . . of animals'" D. Stein to S. Stein, June 13, 1890, YALC.
23   "'Her bookish life'" G. Stein, *AABT,* 74.
23   "'not any of . . . important ever'" G. Stein, *TMOA,* 520.
24   "'My brother and . . . been together'" G. Stein, *EA,* 57.
24   "'William Cather, Jr.'" See O'Brien, *WC,* 98–99.
24   "she then read" She may not have known that women could attend the University of California; Harriet Levy had graduated from there in 1886.
24   "'People commonly considered . . . really contented'" L. Stein, *JIS,* 192.
24   "'It was a . . . about hers'" Ibid., 185.
25   "'shuts himself up . . . at a time'" Sprigge, *GS,* 48.
25   "'Disagreeable condition at . . . with me'" G. Stein, Notebooks, 11-14.
25   "'All stopped . . . mother'" Ibid., 11-7.
25   "'to outlive papa . . . lead him'" Ibid., 12-13.
25   "'coming in to . . . him warm'" Ibid., 11-8.
25   "'my experiences . . . Uncle Sol'" Ibid., 2-30.
25   "'scene like . . . with Sol'" Ibid., 2-14.
25   "'like me . . . to do'" Ibid., 9-17.
25   "'Fathers loving . . . to them'" Ibid., 131.
25   "'Mike stands up . . . be eaten'" Ibid., 2-25.
25   "'father angry hit her'" Ibid., MA-23.
25   "'He never knew . . . of pain'" M. Stein to Meyer Stein, Jan. 28, 1891, YALC.
25   "profit and loss," G. Stein, *EA,* 122.
27   "'Then our life . . . pleasant one'" Ibid., 121.

3   Colleges and Marriages

28   "their aunt and uncle's" Pollack, *C,* 13–16; G. Stein, March 21, 1895, (untitled) theme, Radcliffe, English 22, quoted in Miller, *GS,* 139.
29   "David Bachrach, though" Welling, *PIA;* I. Blum, "David Bachrach," in *HOJOB,* 199.
29   "Sociables, as the" Richardson, *DC,* 52–53.
29   "'homely'" G. Stein, Notebooks, 6-7.

29   "Stein's high color," Sprigge, "GSAY," 50; selected friends' memoirs, Radcliffe College Archives.

29   See also Lachman, "GS."

29   "Gertrude's informality caused" Pollack, *C*, 13, 15; Levy, *920 O'F*, 129, 155.

29   "Sharp-tongued Etta" Richardson, *DC*, 53.

30   "in a September" L. Stein to M. Stein, Sept. 12, 1892, YALC.

30   "(yearly fees at" Harvard College catalog, Harvard College Archives.

30   "(the Longfellow house" G. Stein to John C. Minot, undated, YALC.

30   "Meeting other women" Howells, *CC*, 43, 104; Franke, "MT," and Paton, "AM," Radcliffe College Archives; Anniversary Books, Harvard College Archives.

30   "a special, which" See G. Stein records, Radcliffe College Archives. She was exceptional: most Annex students passed comprehensive entrance exams, given in June in New York, Cincinnati, and Cambridge. Passing grades admitted students to all women's colleges—Smith, Bryn Mawr, Vassar, Wellesley, and the Annex. Few Southerners went to the Annex because Harvard was known to accept black students.

31   "She reveled in" Howells, *CC*, 94–99.

31   "She made friends" Class lists and addresses, grade lists, Radcliffe Archives; Drew, "Notes for Talk."

31   "'a terrific talker . . . was saying'" Sprigge, "GSAY," 49.

31   "'rare, warm, human quality'" L. W. S., M. L. E., and L. S. E., "In Memoriam."

31   "'We were all . . . not light'" Sprigge, "GSAY," 49.

31   "Idler Club plays" Some of the Idler Club's readings or plays were given in Fay House's large double parlor, with actors in the back parlor and audience in the front; others were at Agassiz Auditorium. Nearly every Annex student belonged to the Idlers and looked forward to the group's social meetings, after which the women could dance until 5:59 P.M. when campus buildings closed.

31   "'She never wrote . . . to her'" Sprigge, "GSAY," 49.

32   "'knew how to . . . with her'" L. W. S., M. L. E., and L. S. E., "In Memoriam."

32   "'a society of scholars'" Eliot, *HM*, 73.

32   "'sitting monumentally in one corner'" Hopkinson, Letter.

32   "'ideal student,' one" H. Münsterberg to G. Stein, June 10, 1895, in Gallup, *FOF*, 4.

32   "understanding of grammar" Santayana, "Form in Words," in *ELC*, 345.

32   "Saint Teresa's mysticism," Santayana, *PAP*, 102–3.

32   "'a stage in . . . language'" Santayana, "Form in Words," 345.

32   "'"bread" is as . . . psychosis'" Ibid., 345 n. 2.

32   "'contemplation,' what he" Irving Singer, introduction to ibid., 345 n. 2 xxvi.

32   ("'the sense of existence'") Santayana, *ROB*, 47.

33   "'Woman,' an obvious" All quotations from Stein's themes (YALC) are from "The Radcliffe Manuscripts," appendices to Miller, *GS*, 108–55, beginning with "The Red Deeps," Oct. 10, 1894, and continuing through May 22, 1895, "The Temptation."

34   "Her twenty-page" G. Stein, "The Modern Jew Who Has Given Up the Faith of His Fathers Can Reasonably and Consistently Believe in Isolation," handwritten manuscript, YALC.

"attended every meeting" "The Clubs," *The Radcliffe Magazine* (June 1899), 47–48; *The Harvard Graduates' Magazine*, vols. 2–6.

34   "'Consciousness, Knowledge, the . . . Body, etc.'" Catalog description, Harvard Archives.

34   "The engagingly unorthodox" Morison, *TCOH*, 377–78; Myers, *WJ*; Münsterberg, "PJ," 97.

35   "and popular ones" "What Is an Emotion?" was a seminal essay; others were "Are We Automata?" "The Association of Ideas," "The Importance of Individ-

uals," "The Sentiment of Rationality," "The Perception of Time," and "The Hidden Self."

35 "'the important person'" G. Stein, *AABT*, 78–79.

35 "'We were quite . . . was doing'" G. Stein, *EA*, 229–30.

35 "in the paranormal" Myers, *WJ*, 6–11, 369–73; Allen, *WJ*, 281–83, 342–43, 373; Matthiessen, *JF*, 226; Goodwin, *AAW*, 189, Research included work in hypnotism, mescal, faith cures, yoga, telepathy, clairvoyance, nitrous oxide, mediumship, and seances. A founding member of the British Society for Psychical Research in 1882, James founded the American Society in 1884.

35 "'Normal Motor Automatism'" Quotations from G. Stein, with Solomons, "NMA," 492–512.

36 "'automatic writing'" Only in the broadest sense—of writing that draws on the writer's complete resources, as Brewster Ghiselin defines the term ("spontaneous and involuntary production in a state of heightened awareness")—is the term applicable to what was investigated (*CP*, 6–7).

36 . . . xamples of a . . . attention'" G. Stein to R. Church, Dec. 17, 1932, YALC. [Note that *xamples* reflects her usual way of spelling words beginning with *ex-*.]

36 "'I am so . . . philosophy today'" In Allen, *WJ*, 305; G. Stein, *AABT*, 79.

36 "Her senior project" Quotations from "MA," 295–306.

36 "she was secretary" In that role, she invited Santayana, Royce, and James, as well as Stanley Hall of Johns Hopkins, to lecture. The group also discussed James, Balfour, and German idealism, and they went to meetings of the Harvard Club, where they heard Hindu mystic Swami Vivekanada speak on Vedanta philosophy. See, e.g., *The Harvard Graduates' Magazine*, 4 (June 1896), 599.

36 "and campus lectures" *The Harvard Graduates' Magazine*, vols. 2–7. She heard Irving Babbitt, Booker T. Washington, novelist Margaret Deland, poet Harriet Monroe, and lectures on Emily Dickinson, St. Francis of Assisi, *Faust*, the structure of the brain, and modern art.

36 "'small group of . . . people'" Lachman, "GS."

37 "'long walk . . . with Leon'" G. Stein, Notebooks, 6-11.

37 "'Lying out in . . . never his'" Ibid., 11-17.

37 "'semi-flames'" Ibid., 2-24.

37 "'free life in the mountains'" Ibid., 2-23.

37 "'What right . . . to feel'" Ibid., 2-24.

37 "'a triumphant argument'" Ibid., 2-19.

37 "the 'definite mark'" G. Stein, *AABT*, 77.

37 "'widely read, deeply . . . stimulating'" Arthur Lachman, "GS," YALC, 4.

37 "increasing 'ponderosity'" M. Stein to G. Stein, Jan. 2, 1901, YALC. The letter also mentioned Simon's ulcerating veins and trouble with designing women.

37 "Valedictorian at fifteen" Golson, "MS," 38.

37 "a fortune teller" Levy, unpublished memoir, 1.

37 "After their 1893 wedding" All records from this time were destroyed in the 1906 earthquake and fire.

37 "1118 O'Farrell Street in" See Levy, *920 O'F.*

37 "'the Jewish money aristocracy'" S. Stein to G. Stein, undated, probably 1893, YALC.

37 "put up with" S. Stein letters to both G. Stein and L. Stein, 1893–1900, YALC.

38 "'exceedingly put out'" S. Stein to G. Stein, March 9, 1895, YALC.

38 "'probably $240 . . . Market Street'" M. Stein to G. Stein, Sept. 5, 1895, YALC.

38 "troublesome characteristics" Levy, memoir; Jelenko, "Reminiscences."

38 "'much stronger than . . . near heroic'" S. Stein to G. Stein, Oct. 29, 1893, YALC.

38 *The Green Carnation*" Various S. Stein letters to G. Stein, 1893–1896, YALC.

38   "'dear doctor'" S. Stein to G. Stein, 1893, YALC.
39   "'the idea of experiment'" Ehrenreich and English, *FHOG,* 78 ff.
39   "On January 17" *Harvard Graduates' Magazine,* 4, no. 15 (March 1896), 419.
39   "she was 'curetted'" S. Stein to G. Stein, Sept. 18, 1894, YALC.
39   "'diabolical' uterine massage" S. Stein to G. Stein, Oct. 20, 1894, YALC.
39   "'the longest seven months of my life'" S. Stein to G. Stein, Oct. 28, 1895, YALC.
39   "'My head aches . . . my condition'" S. Stein to G. Stein, undated, 1896, and March 27, 1896, YALC.
40   "'wasn't accustomed to . . . outside Baltimore'" Raffel, "TOWAF," 129.
40   "'liable to suspicion'" Baum, Hyman, and Michel, *JW,* 7. Jewish women who remained single were so termed by the *Shulhan Arukh,* the sixteenth-century code of Jewish law.
40   "Uncle Sol invited" L. Stein to G. Stein, Aug. 19, 1895, YALC.
40   "The fascination of" See Parter, *HJ.*
40   "'a different world . . . about you'" L. Stein to G. Stein, July 30, 1895, YALC.
41   "'a 7-room . . . waiting girl'" L. Stein to G. Stein, Dec. 22, 1895, YALC.
41   "'How I hate . . . my return'" L. Stein to G. Stein, March 13, 1896, YALC.
41   "'Weeks ago I . . . without you'" L. Friedman to G. Stein, June 29, 1896, YALC.
41   "'scurrilous scrawl'" L. Stein to G. Stein, May 12, 1896, YALC.
41   "'the love between . . . beautiful'" Sprigge, "GSAY," 49.
41   "'Japs' to Shylock" L. Stein to M. and S. Stein, Dec. 24, 1895, YALC.
41   "Japan seem charming" L. Stein to M. and S. Stein, Feb. 3, 1896, YALC.
41   "white elephant" S. and M. Stein to L. Stein, Nov. 16, 1896, YALC.
42   "'for sending indecent . . . the mails'" S. and M. Stein to L. Stein, May 29, 1896, YALC.
42   "'them Jews—all . . . in business'" L. Stein to M. and S. Stein, Nov. 15, 1895, YALC.
42   "'the first view . . . to Carlsbad'" L. Stein, *A,* 145–46.
42   "'If you came . . . are infinite'" L. Stein to G. Stein, March 13, 1896, YALC.
42   "the banquet years" See Shattuck, *BY.*

4   The Sexual Century

43   "Woods Hole marine" Stein Collection, YALC.
43   "Mike complained about" M. Stein to G. Stein, n.d., YALC.
43   "Lena Lebender, a" L. Lebender to G. Stein, YALC.
43   "'keep house and . . . theories'" quoted in G. Stein to S. Stein, Jan. 20, 1897, YALC.
43   "cousin Helen Keyser" H. K. Bachrach to G. Stein, April 18, 1945, YALC.
43   "graduated magna cum" Drew, Notes.
43   "James had advised" Sprigge, *GS,* 36; Mellow, *CC,* 37; Hobhouse, *E,* 17.
44   "Alfred Dreyfus's conviction" Adler, *AJYB.*
44   "Harvard opened the" Sloan, *JIA,* 13–14.
44   "'ought to be playing'" Quoted in Irwin, *AAA,* 127.
44   "eleven were female" Alan Mason Chesney Medical Archives, Johns Hopkins Medical Institutions.
44   "textbooks and jokes" Mellow, *CC,* 40–41.
44   "'missiles of . . . quids'" Ehrenreich and English, *FHOG,* 65.
44   "'for women and Chinamen'" Quoted in Mellow, *CC,* 40.
44   "'Human beings may . . . physicians'" Quoted in Irwin, *AAA,* 146.
44   "the first American" Ehrenreich and English, *FHOG,* 79.
44   "By 1890 there" Pollock, *C,* 21; Richardson, *DC,* 50.
44   "The American Medical Association" Ehrenreich and English, *FHOG,* 66.

44   "Part of the professional" Ibid., 66, 79, 122.
44   "'senseless injections' of" Wood, "FD," 30.
45   "The 1897 publication" P. Robinson, *MOS,* 3–11.
45   *"The Ballad of"* Sprigge, *GS,* 28–29.
45   "Studying at Johns Hopkins" Class lists, Johns Hopkins University Archives.
45   "Claribel Cone among" Richardson, *DC,* 53.
45   "'A "career" is . . . ideals'" Margaret Snyder to G. Stein, April 29, 1896, YALC; reprinted in Gallup, *FOF,* 8.
46   "'Therefore my dear . . . like babies'" S. Stein to G. Stein, June 12, 1897, YALC.
46   "Claribel asked Gertrude" G. Stein "OTV"; all references are to this manuscript.
47   "Leo received 1s" Student records, Johns Hopkins University Archives.
47   "Leo entered an" Leo Stein file, Johns Hopkins University Archives.
47   "Leo disliked laboratory" L. Stein, *JIS,* 194; Mellow, *CC,* 41.
48   "a Harvard acquaintance" Lachman, "GS."
48   "'Almost every week'" Quoted in Sprigge, "GSAY," 50.
48   "Emma Lootz, from" Class lists, Johns Hopkins University Archives.
48   "In her second-year" G. Stein grade lists, Johns Hopkins University Archives.
48   "Her ungraded short" Confidential file, Johns Hopkins Medical School Archives.
48   "'anecdotal midwifery'" Quoted in Bensley, "GS," 36–37.
48   "Osler's sexism was" Ehrenreich and English, *FHOG,* 91–93.
49   "'If a poor . . . done more'" W. Osler, *A,* 286.
49   "'where to be . . . on earth'" G. Stein, forensics essay, Radcliffe, YALC.
49   "'an aristocrat and a snob'" Quoted in Mellow, *CC,* 45.
49   "'She talked to . . . their race'" Hapgood, *VMW,* 533–34.
49   "'untimely and never . . . death'" W. James to G. Stein, Oct. 17, 1900, in Gallup, *FOF,* 19–20. To Hugo Münsterberg, however, James wrote that while Solomons was "the keenest intellect we ever had . . . there was always a mysterious side to me about his mind; he appeared so critical and destructive. . . . He was the only student I have ever had of whose criticisms I felt afraid" (quoted in Allen, *WJ,* 413).
50   "'They would ask . . . not forget'" G. Stein, *AABT,* 82.
50   "'It would be . . . back on it'" L. Stein to G. Stein, Feb. 3, 1901, in Gallup, *FOF,* 22.
50   "On June 5, 1901" Minutes, Alan Mason Chesney Medical Archives, Johns Hopkins Medical Institutions.
50   "'I have so . . . bores me'" G. Stein, *AABT,* 82–83.
51   "'Of course she . . . roses on it'" Quoted in Sprigge, *GS,* 41.
51   "three references to" Barker, *NS,* 721, 725, 875.
51   "On January 30, 1902" L. Barker to G. Stein in Gallup, *FOF,* 24.
51   "Knower rejected the" H. M. Knower to L. Barker, April 7, 1902, Alan Mason Chesney Medical Archives, Johns Hopkins Medical Institutions.
51   "'I am convinced . . . to them'" L. Barker to H. M. Knower, April 9, 1902, loc. cit.
52   "'The embryological series . . . hopeless mess'" G. Stein to L. Barker, undated, loc. cit.
52   "Knower apologized to" H. M. Knower to L. Barker, April 15, 1902, loc. cit.
52   "'ought to be . . . *Anatomy*'" L. Barker to Franklin Mall, October 23, 1903, loc. cit.
52   "May (Mary Abletta)" Bryn Mawr College Archives.
53   "Her notebooks record" G. Stein, Notebooks, 1-17.
53   "through the 'smashings'" Sahli, "S," 17–27.
53   "'raw virginity'" Katz, introduction, xii.
53   "Gertrude's attraction" Wise, "COSP"; Ellis, "SIIW," 16; Krafft-Ebing, *PS.* See

also Rosenberg and Smith-Rosenberg, "FA," 332–46; Showalter, *SA;* and Gilbert and Gubar, *NML.*

53   "letters were destroyed" Years later, at the angry insistence of Alice Toklas.

53   "her homoerotic years" Despite a tolerance of male homosexuality in some educated circles, lesbianism was still covert. Victorian belief in "separate spheres" mandated that women be asexual: that a sexually passive woman would initiate a lesbian relationship was unbelievable. This restrictive definition of women's sexual behavior led to society's masculinizing one of the female couple. See Chauncey, "FITH," 114–46; and Newton, "MML," 557–75.

54   "'passion in its many disguised forms'" Katz, introduction, xiii.

54   "May admitted that" Recorded in Mellow, *CC,* 127.

54   "'Adele [Gertrude] was . . . the words'" G. Stein, *Q.E.D.,* 91.

54   "described from within Adele's consciousness" Ibid., 102.

55   When friends insisted" G. Stein, *AABT,* 82.

55   "(A later notebook" G. Stein, Notebooks, MA-17.

55   "'monomania,' second only" James, *POP,* 2:543.

55   "he had studied" Information about Leo's courses and grades is from the Harvard Archives. As a special student, he sometimes missed exams, in one case, still receiving an A in Professor Taussig's economic theory class but failing a course in government. His grades in philosophy and English courses (Shakespeare from Francis James Child and Barrett Wendell's English 12) were Bs; his other grades either As or high Bs.

55   "'discovered pragmatism'" L. Stein, *A,* 147.

56   "'filled with beautiful . . . and hangings'" L. Stein to G. Stein, Oct. 9, 1900, in L. Stein, *JIS,* 3.

56   "'that tremendous excess of the I'" L. Stein to G. Stein, Oct. 11, 1900, *JIS,* 4.

56   "'I have numerous . . . convictions'" L. Stein to G. Stein, Dec. 20, 1900, in L. Stein, *JIS,* 5.

56   "'strange atmosphere of . . . its surroundings'" Rewald, *CAA,* 134.

56   "inventing the umbrella" See Mellow, *CC,* 44.

56   "invested the family" M. Stein to G. Stein, Dec. 22, 1900, YALC.

57   "During the season" Mellow, *CC,* 47–48.

57   "Her visits to" Raffel, "TOWAF", 131.

57   "'cram herself . . . window'" King, "GSAFP," 2.

5   The Steins in Paris

61   "'I've got my . . . the summer'" L. Stein to M. Weeks, April 1903, YALC.

61   "'growing into an artist'" L. Stein, *A,* 151.

61   "'To have bought . . . for the rich'" Ibid., 150.

61   "'I didn't have . . . contemporary art'" L. Stein, *JIS,* 203–4.

62   "conversion to Francophilia" Quoted in Prokosch, *V,* 20.

62   "'Jewish parents do . . . their keeping'" G. Stein, Notebooks, 33 f.

62   "Alfred Stieglitz said" Young, "LWG," 92.

63   "'The stomach . . . more helpless'" G. Stein, Notebooks, 111, ch. 5.

63   "'sexual base'" Ibid., C-31.

63   "Haynes as 'masculine'" Ibid., C-30.

63   "'pure servant . . . to dominate'" Ibid., C-31.

63   "'a naughty little girl'" D. Guggenheimer to G. Stein, Feb. 6, 1901, YALC. References are to Dolene's letters on this date and on Feb. 26, 1901, as well as to other undated correspondence.

63   "Brenda Richardson makes" See Richardson, *DC,* 63 ff.

64   "it all 'interesting'" One of Gertrude's coded words, present in much of her

later writing and often intentionally overused—a passive, academic term that ironically belies the excitement she often used it to describe.

64   "emphasis on 'construction'" L. Stein, *A*, 153.
64   "'the nastiest smear . . . waiting for '" Ibid., 158.
64   "'adventure' in the" Ibid., 154.
64   "'really intelligent. He . . . with painters'" Ibid., 159.
64   "'We is doin . . . the Cézanne'" G. Stein to Mabel Weeks, undated, YALC.
64   "'like an Egyptian . . . my desires'" Quoted in L. Stein, *JIS*, 25; also available in Nina Auzias Stein papers, YALC.
65   "early in 1904" Mellow, *CC*, 62–63.
65   "Photographs of the atelier" See pp. 88–89 ff. in Golson, "MS."
65   "by Alexander Schilling" G. Stein, *LIA*, 69. She spells his name "Shilling." See also Gallup, *FOF*, 27 n.
65   "Mike found" Saarinen, *PP*, 183.
66   "In December 1903" Jelenko, "R" (1967), 1–2.
66   "'meagerly.' On outings" Ibid., 5.
66   "'a delicious hot . . . chocolate'" Rosenshine, "LNAP," 98.
66   "Therese recalled" Jelenko, "Reminiscences," 2.
66   "the Haig diet" M. Stein to G. Stein, Jan. 2, 1901, YALC.
67   "not new habits" The Steins' move from San Francisco to Paris was less radical than it might appear. No longer a pioneer town, San Francisco was a center for music, theater, and art. The San Fransisco Art Association held exhibits in the Mark Hopkins Nob Hill mansion; during the 1880s the University of California began collecting American paintings and old masters, though most were copies. Starting in 1895, exhibits in the Memorial Museum in Golden Gate Park were opened to the public. That Mrs. Phoebe Asperson Hearst, the William Crockers, Leland Stanford, and Collis P. Huntington collected art increased its currency as an intellectual pursuit. See Golson, "MS," 36–37.
67   "Pablo Casals recalled" Casals, *JAS*, 106 ff.
67   "When relatives and" Correspondence with M. Stein, YALC.
67   "'were properly respectful . . . to see'" Rewald, *CAA*, 60; Levy, *920 O'F*, 13.
67   "'I still can . . . himself away'" Jelenko, "Reminiscences," 5.
67   "Memoirs written by" G. Stein, *AABT*, 41–42; L. Stein, *A*, 158–59; S. Stein to Jeffery Smith, 1948, quoted in Barr, *M*, 58.
67   "Vauxcelles named Matisse" Golson, "MS," 42. These painters were also called the "Incoherents" and the "Invertebrates."
67   "Alfred Barr, the foremost biographer" Barr, *M*, 57.
68   "He later recalled" Quoted in Barr, *M*, 58, from Matisse's statement in the *transition* supplement entitled "Testimony against Gertrude Stein."
68   "a surprise breakfast" Levy, unpublished memoir, 13.
68   "'bundles of pictures . . . argue about it'" Jelenko, "Reminiscences," 2.
68   "'remarkable'" L. Simonson to L. Stein, undated, YALC.
69   "'He was almost . . . with him.'" Hapgood, *VMW*, 119.
69   "'The Stein Corporation'" Sterne, *SAL*, 52.
69   "Leo and Gertrude bought" Rewald, *CAA*, 61.
69   "Saturday salons" Saarinen, *PP*, 187.
69   "'almost dawn'" Pollock, *C*, 76.
69   "seldom spending more" Golson, "MS," 40.
69   "Leo told the" L. Stein, *A*, 150.
69   "Mike took Allan" Rosenshine, "LNAP," 97; Rewald, *CAA*, 60.
69   "Isabella Stewart Gardner" Frackman, "SF," 41–43.
70   "'As to the Steins . . . buy Manets'" M. Cassatt to A. Borie, July 27, 1910, quoted in Rewald, *CAA*, 73.

70   "'wonderful how the . . . but new men'" Quoted in Reid, *MFNY*, 105.
70   "Ambroise Vollard, recalling" A. Vollard, *ROPD*, 136.
70   "'was virtually open . . . Morosov'" Rewald, *CAA*, 61.
70   "'people who came . . . man's house'" Vollard, *R*, 137.
70   "'When Matisse comes . . . virility'" Quoted in Toklas, "SM," 2.
70   "'always standing up . . . on his face'" Luhan, *EE*, 321.
70   "'expounding with Socratic . . . the moment'" Simonson, *POL*, 14–15. American painter Andrew Dasburg echoed the point that Leo spoke less about ideas than "about the pictures he had" (quoted in Rewald, *CAA*, 84 n. 35).
70   "'Leo's brilliant conversation . . . collection'" Meyer, *OOTR*, 81.
71   "'like a Cambodian . . . else did'" Davidson, *BS*, 174.
71   "'laughed out loud . . . admired inside'" Quoted in L. Stein, *JIS*, 24.
71   "Harriet Levy recalled" Levy, unpublished memoir, 10.
71   "In 1906" G. Of letter to L. Stein, Nov. 25, 1906, YALC.
71   "'with whom I . . . background'" M. Cody with H. Ford, *WOM*, 79–80.
71   "Picasso saw Leo" Katz and Burns, "TW," 110, repeating Stein's statement in Burns, *GSOP*, 13; Brinnin, *TR*, 70; Mellow, *CC*, 90; Olivier, *PHF*, quoted in Simon, *GS*, 20.
71   "Another version" Crespelle, *PHW*, 105. Varying among all the versions of this narrative is the order in which the two Picasso paintings were purchased. Commentary under the reproduction of *The Acrobat's Family* in Burns says the Steins bought that painting second (*GSOP*, 125). Another version of the story also moves Picasso's invitation to pose well before the Autumn Salon because Etta Cone recorded spending 120 francs at Picasso's, when Gertrude took her along to a sitting (Richardson, *DC*, 90).
72   "paintings worth 800" Frackman, "SF," 42.
72   "Later, at table, Gertrude" G. Stein, *AABT*, 46.
72   "Sometimes she walked" Pollock, *C*, 74.
72   "without either electricity" Gosling, *P*, 70.
72   "'a good-looking bootblack'" G. Stein, *AABT*, 46.
72   "'Fat, short, massive . . . entire bearing'" Oliver, *PHF*, quoted in Crespelle, *PHW*, 105.
72   "John Richardson claimed" Richardson, "PGS."
73   "Ingres, Cézanne, and" P. Daix, "PT," speaks of the influence of Ingres's exotic female nudes. Richardson says the portrait face resembles that of "an old Pyrenean smuggler" whom Picasso painted often that summer, a process that may have given him the key to Stein's features ("PGS," 36).
73   "As she said," G. Stein, *GSOP*, 8.
73   "'random bit of . . . Montmartre'" Simonson, *PL*, 16.
73   "Years later, Gertrude" G. Stein, *AABT*, 6.
74   "his 'Rabelaisian' personality" Mackworth, *GA*, 76.
74   "'surprise' he urged" Shattuck, *BY*, 262; Apollinaire also used the word *abruptness* (*SW*, 237).
74   "weekly poetry gatherings" Shattuck, *BY*, 201–2.
74   "at the Closerie" Mackworth, *GA*, 96.
74   "'frequently drunk, shouting and declaiming'" Quoted in Gosling, *P*, 72.
75   "'The clowns had . . . his friends'" G. Stein, *AABT*, 51.
75   "and strap sandals" Apollinaire, calling the Steins "unexpected" patrons, described their being refused service at café because of their sandals and wrote the couplet "Their bare feet shod in sandals Delphic, / They raise toward heaven their brows scientific" (*AOA*, 29).
75   "motivated as they" Gosling, *P*, 80.
75   "Matisse asked, when" G. Stein, *AABT*, 65.

75 "'Nobody but Guillaume . . . greater effort'" Ibid., 99.
75 "'is so suave . . . is doing'" G. Stein to M. Dodge, YALC; reprinted in Luhan, *MAS*, 29–30.
75 "'a compulsive punster'" Moishe Black, introduction to Jacob, *HF*, xiii–xvi.
75 "'The Plain and . . . Virtue's Reward'" Bernier, *MPM*, 109.
75 "mysterious 'fourth dimension.'" Mackworth, *GA*, 86.
75 "from early in" Published in *Alcools* (1914) and in *Calligrammes* (1918).
76 "'Lady of my . . . Orient rival'" Apollinaire, *Alcools*, 41. The sensual text occurs in "Annie," also from *Alcools*: "On the shores of Texas / Between Mobile and Galveston there is / A great garden filled with roses / There is also a villa / Which is one huge rose. . . . / As she is a Mennonite / Her rose trees and her garments have no buttons . . ." (49). Here, multiple associations for rose both confuse and enlarge the ostensible meaning of the work; Stein was to play with multiple meanings for rose and for buttons in the same way. Bates, appendix B, *GA*, 172–74, includes a dictionary of the poet's sexually coded language.
76 "'We were settled . . . was writing'" G. Stein, *EA*, 58.
76 "'working tremendously'" Quoted in Brinnin, *TR*, 75.
76 "Matisse, she noted" G. Stein, *AABT*, 39.
76 "(As Henri Peyre" Peyre, "TLM."
76 "'middle class'" G. Stein, "TMOA," in *FQOEW*, 145.
77 "'interesting quartet' of" G. Stein, *F*, 43.
77 "'eager, anxious and moral'" Ibid., 39.
77 "'It is the . . . importance'" Ibid., 38.
77 "'discreet homosexuality was . . . both sexes'" Gosling, 36.
77 "Critics have cited" Brinnin, *TR*, 56–64; Mellow, *CC*, 71–77; Hobhouse, *E*, 70–73.
77 "About this time" E. L. Erving to G. Stein, 1906, YALC.
78 "'arduous and troubled life'" G. Stein, "The Good Anna," in *TL*, 11.
78 "'strong, strained, worn-out body'" Ibid., 82.
78 "'only romance'" Ibid., 52.
78 "'wandering'" G. Stein, "Melanctha," in *TL*, 97.
78 "'always loved too . . . too often'" Ibid., 89.
78 "watched blacks in" Church, "RIR," 7.
78 "'It was not . . . her wisdom'" G. Stein, "Melanctha," 104.
78 "'long hours . . . room'" Ibid., 105.
79 "Although the dialogue" M. Weeks to G. Stein, 1908, quoted in Mellow, *CC*, 127.
80 "'dirty'" G. Stein, Notebooks, D13-47.
80 "'mysticism and . . . the intellect'" Ibid., 41.
80 "'the simple . . . black people'" G. Stein "Melanctha," 60.
80 "Gertrude then sent" G. Stein, *AABT*, 51–52.
80 "'superficially irritating and difficult'" H. Hapgood to G. Stein, April 22, 1906, YALC; reprinted in Gallup, *FOF*, 31–32.

6   Tremors of Change

81 "Mike and Sally" M. Stein and S. Stein to G. Stein, May 10, 1906, YALC; reprinted in Gallup, *FOF*, 32–33.
81 "'a sensation'" S. Stein to G. Stein, Oct. 8, 1906, YALC; reprinted in Gallup, *FOF*, 37.
81 "grandfather's household" Levy, *920 O'F*, 24. See also Toklas, *WIR*, 3–12.
82 "'each one opposite . . . more bread'" G. Stein, *AABT*, 15.
82 "'deep and understanding interest in art'" Aldrich, "CB," M-114.
82 "with Etta Cone" The Cone brothers had expanded from their father's whole-

sale grocery business into textiles, and much of their fortune now came from North Carolina mills. It was at brother Caesar's Greensboro home that Gertrude, visiting with Claribel, stretched out on her back in the sun and frightened the servant, who ran to the house crying that there was a dead body on the lawn (Saarinen, *PP,* 187–91; Richardson, *DC,* 66–93; Pollock, *C,* 52–53).

82 "being drunk together" Burke, "GS," 548.
82 "'lack of . . . and richness'" G. Stein, Notebooks, DB-50.
82 "'I sincerely trust . . . both ways)'" Quoted in Pollock, *C,* 62.
82 "Etta, too, began" Richardson, *DC,* 90.
82 "'The Steins introduced . . . new and old'" Pollock, *C,* 64.
83 "'in a crouching . . . pants down'" Sterne, *SAL,* 51.
83 "'shocking . . . unnecessary and harsh'" Howard Gans to L. Stein, Dec. 3, 1906, YALC.
83 "she left Paris" G. Stein to H. Hapgood, Feb. 25, 1906, YALC.
83 "May Bookstaver had" E. L. Erving to G. Stein, YALC. The Newport wedding took place on August 16.
83 "in Baltimore Dolene" Julie Guggenheimer to G. Stein, n.d., YALC.
83 "'Sometimes it is . . . are puzzling'" G. Stein, *TMOA,* 607.
83 "When Sally, Mike" S. Stein to G. Stein, Oct. 8, 1906, YALC.
84 "Annette remembered her" Padgette, "SBHL."
84 "'a striking contrast'" G. Stein, Notebooks, DB-50.
84 "that 'sex was'" Rosenshine, "LNAP," 76.
84 "'in most cases . . . temperament'" G. Stein, Notebooks, NB, 56, 4.
85 "Annette confessed that" Rosenshine, "LNAP," 76.
85 "George Of had" Barr, *M,* 83.
85 "Paul Signac, vice" Ibid., 82.
85 "'*representing* the model . . . copying it'" Henri Matisse, "Matisse Speaks to his Students, 1908, (Notes by Sarah Stein)," appendix A in Barr, *M,* 552.
85 "'(Both Félix Fenelon" Rubin, *PAB,* 346.
85 "'The Philosophic Brothel,'" Mackworth, *GA,* 81–82.
86 "'analytic tendency which . . . of geometry'" Roger Shattuck, introduction to Apollinaire, *SWGA,* 16.
86 "'Don't hesitate and . . . no use to'" Quoted in Pollack, *C,* 85.
86 "Etta was pleased" Ibid., 89.
86 "'Gertrude, about money did not joke'" Thomson, *VT,* 247.
86 "'surplice' in his" S. Stein to M. Stein, Dec. 3, 1909, YALC.
87 "After rejections from" Gallup, *FOF,* 42–43; correspondence to G. Stein, YALC.
87 "but Etta declined" E. Cone to G. Stein, June 23, 1909, in Gallup, *FOF,* 45.
87 "'I am not . . . they or you'" Recounted in Toklas, *WIR,* 44.
87 "Ralph Church recalled" Church, "AR," 7.
87 "'I hate labels . . . long ago'" Quoted in Sterne, *SAL,* 49.
87 "'Pablo and Matisse . . . *aussi* perhaps'" G. Stein, Notebooks, quoted in *GSOP,* 97.
87 "Gertrude usually placed" Stein, Notebooks, 43, 1.
87 "'indolent'" Ibid., DB-52.
87 "'Maddalena'" Ibid., DB-47.
87 "'Mr. Stein's phrase 'cocktail'" Carl Van Vechten, "How to Read Gertrude Stein," in Simon, *GS,* 53.
87 "'utter abomination . . . only stupid'" L. Stein to M. Weeks, Feb. 4, 1913, YALC.
88 "'When my interest . . . to withdraw'" L. Stein, *A,* 201.
88 "the painters of" Van Vechten, "How to Read Gertrude Stein," in Simon, *GS,* 52.
88 "'fur-lined steamer coat'" Levy, *920 O'F,* 271.

88   "the femme fatale" Toklas, *RSAT*, 46.

88   "Harriet had lent" Levy, unpublished memoir, 2.

88   "'a golden brown presence'" Toklas, *WIR*, 23–24.

88   "'only three times . . . Whitehead'" G. Stein, *AABT*, 5. In unpublished manuscript notes, Toklas placed her first meeting with Gertrude at the rue de Fleurus, with Stein "sitting very calmly in strange contrast" to the bright paintings: "When she finally spoke it came from under the very dark coral brooch. . . . Her voice had that color and quality. Her laugh was deep full and hard." In this version of Alice's lateness, she wrote that Gertrude was "angry as I had never seen anyone before. She paced around . . . her ineffably beautiful voice booming, 'no one has ever treated me so inconsiderately—so lightly and I am not accepting it'—the . . . violence of the attack frightened me. I was weak. Tears came to my eyes. I could not speak." In another version of their meeting, she described Stein's physical beauty, her "wonderful eyes," and the sense of the "enormous life that she'd led. . . . She had so much sense of life" (Toklas, unpublished manuscript, 1, Lake Collection; and Duncan interview, 15).

88   "'new full life'" Toklas, unpublished manuscript, 1, Lake Collection.

89   "first dinner at" Levy, unpublished memoir, 5–6.

89   "Alice remembered vividly" Toklas, *WIR*, 26–30.

89   "and others constituted" Barr, *M*, 116–19. Jean Biette (Matisse's friend), Karl Palme, and several others, perhaps including a "Miss von Knierien."

89   "'the father of us all'" Quoted in Ibid., 118.

89   "'During those . . . than words'" Quoted in Rewald, *CAA*, 82.

90   "remained so vehement" Levy, unpublished memoir.

90   "'scandalise the [Steins] American puritanism'" Mackworth, *GA*, 110.

90   "him 'the miraculous'" Apollinaire, 1914 column reprinted in Apollinaire, *AOA*, 339.

90   "The evening started" Maurice Raynal's version, quoted in Mackworth, *GA*, 110–12; originally from Apollinaire's *Les Soirées de Paris* (1914).

90   "Alice remembered" Toklas, *WIR*, 55–57; see also G. Stein, *AABT*, 103–7.

90   "Fernande Olivier's account" Olivier, *PAHF*, 68–71. In Harriet Levy's unpublished memoir, Alice's hat is described as a turban from which the rose had been eaten, and Gertrude's hat was a yellow and brown felt sailor. Salmon later claimed that he and a friend staged attacks of delirium tremens, chewing soap to make their mouths foam, in order to bait the stuffy Americans in their formal dress (Shattuck, *BY*, 67; see Salmon, *SF*, 48–65).

90   "'Sometimes people who . . . were free'" L. Stein, *A*, 196.

91   "'looked at the . . . any other?'" Sprigge, "GSAY," 49.

91   "'made with wide . . . one's eyes'" Berenson, *MB*, 130.

91   "Picasso's squeezing Alice's" Levy, unpublished memoir.

91   "considered a siren" Toklas, *RSAT*, 46.

91   "'an awful Jewess . . . her eyebrows'" Quoted in Samuels, *BB*, 106. See Souhami, *GAA*, for people's comments about the two.

91   "'somehow mixed up . . . and Sally'" G. Stein, Notebooks, NB, 56-1.

91   "'crooked, a liar'" Ibid., DB 59-2.

91   "'whore clothes'" Ibid., DB 63.

92   "'tasting'" Ibid., 56-4.

92   "'She listens . . . superior'" Ibid., 46-2.

92   "'have to do . . . success'" Ibid., C-4.

92   "'elderly spinster mermaid'" Toklas, *WIR*, 44.

92   "In 'Americans,' a text" G. Stein, "Americans," in *GAP*, 39, 43, 41, and 45.

92   "had been engaged" Rose, "GS," 135.

93   "anti-female Weininger" Katz, "W." See also Robinson, *MOS*, and Wickham, *I*.

93   "'outcome of her . . . development'" Weininger, *SAC*, 66.
93   "copies to American" She took Weininger seriously, unlike Marion Walker
Williams, who wrote in 1909 that she had finally read *Sex and Character* and
wanted to correct Stein's thinking: the fact was that Weininger did not go in-
sane after he wrote the book but before (M. W. Williams to G. Stein, June 11,
1909, YALC; reprinted in Gallup, *FOF*, 45).
94   "'Alice wept and . . . a day'" Levy, unpublished memoir, 46.
94   "Alice's friend and" Toklas, *WIR*, 54.

7   Portraits

95   "practice that worried" Toklas, *WIR*, 55.
95   "'kinds in men and women'" G. Stein, *TMOA*, 672.
95   "Alice prepared American" Toklas, *ABTCB*, 29.
95   "Trembling was all . . . be living'" G. Stein, "Ada," in *GAP*, 16. No one is sure
when the portrait was written. Leon Katz's dissertation dates it December
1910, ("FM," 144); Janet Flanner assigns it to the winter of 1908–09 (introduction to G. Stein, *Two*, x); the Yale catalog places it midway between 1908
and 1912. See also G. Stein, *AABT*, 139; and R. Bridgman, *GSIP*, 93, 210–11.
Bridgman notes that much of the draft is written in Alice's hand and may be an
early joint effort. The Yale collection of Stein's many manuscripts for the next
years is dated 1908–1912, indicating that Gertrude did not date this work
specifically; Bridgman attempted to do so in "Key to the Yale Catalogue," in
GSIP, 365–85.
96   "'Are these drawings . . . person represented'" Henri Matisse, "Exactitude Is
not Truth," appendix H in Barr, *M*, 561.
96   "I had to . . . was inside'" G. Stein, *LIA*, 183.
96   "'furious saying, He . . . doing now?'" Toklas, *WIR*, 64.
97   "'Why did he . . . said everything.'" G. Stein, *Two*, 76, 83, 6, 88.
97   "'He said everything'" Ibid., 83.
97   "'he was different from her'" Ibid., 6.
97   "'She works'" Ibid., 88.
97   "'unflattering' lecture about" Mary Berenson, quoted in Samuels, *BB*, 50.
97   "'clad in nothing but her Fat'" Berenson, *MB*, 146.
97   "'so horribly inapropos that one shivered'" Mary Berenson, quoted in
Samuels, *BB*, 61.
97   "Gertrude's borrowing valuable" Sprigge, *GS*, 143 n.
97   "'tribe of queer . . . in the library'" B. Berenson to I. S. Gardner, Aug. 27, 1909,
in Berenson, *LBB*, 454.
97   "'an extraordinary book'" *Boston Morning Herald*, Jan. 8, 1913, in Stein's
clipping notebook, YALC.
97   "H. G. Wells" G. Stein, typed manuscript of reviews, 1–2, 6, Harry Ransom
Humanities Research Center.
97   "'You know it yourself'" Auzias, unpublished manuscript, reprinted in L. Stein,
JIS, 27.
98   "'little airtight room . . . rue Dulin'" Auzias, unpublished manuscript.
98   "like a modern Scheherazade'" Auzias in L. Stein, *JIS*, 28.
98   "'There are three . . . romance'" L. Stein to M. Weeks, Feb. 15, 1910, in L.
Stein, *JIS*, 22–23.
98   "described him, at" Sterne, *SAL*, 48.
98   "prostitutes because of" L. Stein, *JIS*, 198.
98   "'a perfect devil . . . admission'" L. Stein to G. Stein, Oct. 25, 1901, in L. Stein,
JIS, 9.

98   "'intellectuals with fine . . . experience'" Sterne, *SAL*, 47–48.
98   "Leo tested Nina" Once, after he told her he loved her, he withdrew the pledge, and she wrote to him, "Steiney, How stupid I was to believe that your 'I love you' was anything but a test. I was so happy about it and so proud all day yesterday . . . that my vanity will not be able to get over it. . . . Don't be angry, Steiney dear. As for me, I shall always love you, and I long to be quite cured of my grief to see you again in a happier frame of mind" (N. Auzias to L. Stein, undated, reprinted in L. Stein, *JIS*, 23–24; last sentence from the YALC translation).
99   "He also wrote Gertrude" See series of L. Stein letters to G. Stein beginning July 10, 1910, YALC.
99   "'This one was . . . some women'" G. Stein, *Two*, 316–18.
99   "'that she took . . . studio'" S. Stein to G. Stein, undated, 1909, 5, YALC. She also mentions having read a letter from May Bookstaver that Mabel Weeks had brought to Paris; that letter has disappeared.
99   "'delightful' month of" M. Stein to G. Stein, June 14, 1909, YALC.
99   "The four women" Toklas, *WIR*, 59–61.
99   "Marie Laurencin and" The Steins accepted Marie once Apollinaire began seeing her, but visiting her home was unusual (see Mackworth, *GA*, 103).
100   "'beautiful ideas which . . . of women'" Gosling, *P*, 161 ff. For the political implications of this aesthetic, see Gilbert and Gubar, *NML*, 1: 22.
100   "'There has never . . . artistic systems'" Apollinaire, *AOA*, 74.
100   "his huge paintings" Barr, *M*, 104.
100   "'I came around . . . to you all'" S. Stein to M. Stein, Dec. 3, 1909, YALC.
100   "when Gertrude was" G. Stein, *EA*, 115.
100   "'Son you are . . . not do it'" G. Stein, *TMOA*, 489–90.
101   "'a son irritates . . . irritated'" Quoted in G. Stein, *EA*, 118–19.
101   "'kind of nasty . . . can be'" G. Stein, Notebooks, 11-8.
101   "role of 'beloved'" H. Hapgood, *VMW*, 247. Virgil Thomson later made the same point; see discussion in C. Stimpson, "GA," 127.
101   "(he and Mike" Rewald, *CAA*, 129.
101   "he criticized the" L. Stein to G. Stein, Aug. 1910, YALC.
101   "'splendid isolation'" L. Stein to G. Stein, n.d., YALC.
101   "lunch be served" L. Stein to G. Stein, n.d., YALC.
101   "Alice had not yet" Albert S. Bennett, forward to Salinger, *JVPG*, xiii. According to Bennett, Harriet's nephew, Alice never repaid the money.
101   "Mike wrote that" M. Stein to G. Stein, Nov. 30, 1910, YALC. See also letters from July 7, July 9, and Oct. 29, 1910. Showing typical concern for his family, Mike's July 9 letter noted where he had hidden Gertrude and Alice's jewelry and umbrellas and that he had left them a thousand francs in the secret drawer "where your wills are."
102   "'Leo's new room'" M. Stein to G. Stein, Jan. 10, 1911, YALC.
102   "'Leo lives alone . . . very beautiful'" Salinger, *JVPG*, 1.
102   "'a false alarm'" Toklas, *WIR*, 63.
102   "'All my fellow-feeling . . . modesty'" Kahnweiler, introduction to *PL*, x.
102   "one of Sally" S. Stein to G. Stein, Aug. 17, 1910, YALC.
102   "'the hazardous Fridays'" Quoted in Wickes, *AOL*, 240.
103   "Miriam Sutro Price" Referring to Gertrude's criticism that Miriam (or Marion) had not gotten past the "gullible 90s," Price replied that judging a person "by one test" seemed unfair (M. S. Price to G. Stein, April 17, n.d., YALC).
103   "'feels the neglect so keenly'" R. Keyser to G. Stein, May 3, 1911.
103   "'Lots and lots . . . in Paris'" P. Jacobs to "Dear Girls," Dec. 18, 1910, YALC (series of letters, 1910–1913).

103   "'the conversation was . . . limited'" P. Jacobs to A. Toklas and G. Stein, March 2, 1911, 5, YALC.
103   "'all-absorbing'" P. Jacobs to A. Toklas and G. Stein, Oct. 8, 1911, 2, YALC.
103   "'every Jew these . . . summer home'" P. Jacobs to A. Toklas and G. Stein, June 12, 1913, 6, YALC.
103   "in Marin county" M. Stein to G. Stein, March 18, 1911, YALC.
103   "'Sarah is so wonderful . . . homelike'" Salinger, *JVPG,* 10.
104   "'Construction is a . . . genuinely creative'" G. Stein to H. P. Roché, June 12, 1912, Harry Ransom Humanities Research Center.
104   "as Sonia and Robert" Gosling, *P,* 210.
104   "This last recalled" Ludington, *MH,* 79, 81, 98–99.
105   "'There is a . . . it here'" M. Stein to G. Stein, 1912, YALC.
105   "'as there might . . . newspaper line'" M. Stein to G. Stein, n.d., YALC.
105   "'The academicians must . . . their boots'" M. Stein to G. Stein, n.d., YALC.
105   "'reasonably poor'" Quoted in Rogers in *WTYS,* 27. Letters in YALC show Mike paying at least one set of taxes for Gertrude each year.
105   "'small' income suggest" Toklas, Duncan interview, 9.
105   "Leo satirized her" See his parody of Gertrude's "Mabel Dodge" in *JIS,* 50.
105   "he wrote with genuine" See L. Stein, *JIS,* 32–57; and YALC correspondence.
105   "'sufficiently happy'" W. James to G. Stein, May 25, 1910, in Gallup, *FOF,* 51–52. He apologized for not finishing *Three Lives,* which he called "a fine new kind of realism."
106   "'intellectual silvery giggle'" A. Rönnebeck, "GWAG," 4.
106   "'that quiet yet . . . place'" Harley also described the salon as having "a kind of William James intimacy" in its bringing "the universe of ideas to your door in terms of your own sensations" (*AIA,* 194–95).
106   "nursing one modest glass" Rönnebeck, "GWAG," 4.
106   "that he danced" L. Stein, *JIS,* 164, 120.
106   "that 'any manifestation'" Carl Van Vechten, notebook, Carl Van Vechten Collection, Manuscripts Division, New York Public Library.
106   "'It is almost . . . this way'" M. Dodge to G. Stein, April? 1911, in Gallup, *FOF,* 52. See Rudnick, *MDL,* for the most informative account of the Steins' friendships with Mabel.
106   "'gloried in her . . . laugh at me'" Luhan, *EE,* 327.
106   "'all in a . . . to steam'" Quoted in Hahn, *M,* 48.
106   "'a really gay evening'" Luhan, *EE,* 389.
106   "Florence Blood's tearing" Samuels, *BB,* 56.
107   "'more thrilling than . . . ballet'" Toklas, *WIR,* 70; see also 67–74.
107   "'Susie Asado,' was" Thomson, "VDA," 3.
107   "'a delightful companion . . . the ludicrous'" Quoted in Luhan, *EE,* 397.
107   "Constance Fletcher, the" Toklas, *WIR,* 75–76.
107   "'football player of 22'" M. Dodge to G. Stein, June 24, 1912, in Gallup, *FOF,* 60.
107   "a 'strong' look" Hahn, *M,* 49.
108   "Gertrude—if you . . . Dam everything'" M. Dodge to G. Stein, n.d., YALC.
108   "'The days are . . . pleasant'" G. Stein, "Portrait of Mabel Dodge," in *SW,* 527.
108   "joined Arthur Davies" Brown, *SAS,* 49–53.
108   "When Mike and" Rubin, *PAB,* 413.
108   "'as proud as punch'" G. Stein to M. Dodge, n.d., in Luhan, *MAS,* 35.
108   "for 'inherent quality'" Dodge, "Speculations," reprinted in Luhan, *MAS,* 28.
109   "Duchamp's *Nude*" Brown, *SAS,* 110.
109   "'I called the . . . Gertrude Stein'" Ibid., 111.
109   "'a portfolio bursting with manuscripts'" Stieglitz, "IM," 192–95. See A. Stieglitz to G. Stein, Feb. 26, 1912, in Gallup, *FOF,* 57.

109   *"struggling, certain,* and *clearly expressing"* G. Stein, "Matisse," in *SW,* 330.
109   "'One whom some . . . charming'" Ibid., 333–34.
110   "John Galsworthy asked" Abrahams, *LL,* 160. There was also a controversy between Walter Weyl and Morton Schamberg over Stein's portraits.
110   "'I was doing . . . one thing'" G. Stein, *LIA,* 177. Always conscious of the effect of her writing, she reminded Stieglitz that punctuation must remain as she had written it, none added or deleted.
110   "'Don't be surprised . . . let me know'" G. Stein to M. Dodge, n.d., in Luhan, *MAS,* 29.
110   "Encouraged by a California" Toklas, *WIR,* 79–81.
110   "The Drapers invited" G. Stein to M. Dodge, n.d., in Luhan, *MAS,* 34.
110   "'she would talk . . . dialectic'" Draper, *MAM,* 152.
110   "Logan Pearsall Smith" L. P. Smith to G. Stein, Feb. 26, 1913, in Gallup, *FOF,* 75. See also *FOF,* 82 (A. L. Coburn to G. Stein, Aug. 23, 1913). She received sharp rejections from several people (Austin Harrison at *The English Review* returned what he called her "curious Studies" [A. Harrison to G. Stein, Jan. 29, 1913, in Gallup, *FOF,* 73]).
110   "Oliver St. John" O. St. J. Gogarty to G. Stein, Jan. 24, 1914, in Gallup, *FOF,* 92.
110   "Mitchell Kennerley" Besides publishing Ibsen and Strindberg, Kennerley was editor of *The Forum,* a magazine of new writing.
111   "in the fall of 1913" Samuels, *BB,* 160, 154–55.
111   "'Certainly he was . . . out of him'" G. Stein, *Two,* 6.
111   "'Gertrude's tempo was . . . and active'" Sterne, *SAL,* 49.
111   "'mentor, dictionary, and . . . she required'" Rosenshine, "LNAP," 86.
111   "'charming'" G. Stein, *Two,* 7.
110   "'terrifying'" Ibid., 8.
111   "'then I was not . . . interested'" G. Stein, *EA,* 60.
111   "'was cheerful as . . . chief speaker'" Pollack, *C,* 49.
111   "'He would linger . . . answered him'" Luhan, *EE,* 326.
112   "'sheer nonsense'" Cody, *WOM,* 79–80.
112   "'Jews mostly . . . great minds'" G. Stein, Notebooks, A-3.
112   "'resolution and . . . purpose'" Ibid., C-20.
112   "his own paintings" See the Leo Stein collection of 71 oils, 379 sketches, and other artwork in YALC. Several oils are at the Univ. of Texas, Austin.
112   "Gertrude also had" See exhibition catalog, Moore, *PFP.* See G. Stein, *AABT,* 62, for her comments on Vallotton's painting her.
112   "'the miserable time'" Toklas, *SOA,* 195.
112   "'was offended by . . . on his part'" Pollack, *C,* 105. See Rosenshine, "LNAP," 87.
112   "accepted Florence Blood's" Toklas, *WIR,* 67. Hutch Hapgood warned that both Leo and Gertrude were "capable of absolute esthetic and moral condemnation" (*VMW,* 219); one remembers Gertrude's break with Harvard friend Francis Pollak because he married a woman she did not like.
112   "'Leo did not . . . an also-ran'" Cody, *WOM,* 82.
112   "Alice later said" See Toklas, Duncan interview, 114.
112   "'a couple of new Picassos'" G. Stein to M. Dodge, n.d., in Luhan, *MAS,* 29. One was *The Architect's Table,* which included Gertrude's calling card and the print *Ma Jolie* (Rubin, *PAB,* 388).
112   "*The Man in Black*" H. Kahnweiler to G. Stein, Oct. 17, 1913, in Gallup, *FOF,* 86–87. Kahnweiler appraised *Boy Leading a Horse* at twelve thousand francs and *Portrait of Gertrude Stein* at only six thousand francs (Rubin, *PAB,* 418).
113   "Kahnweiler paid Gertrude" Kahnweiler, introduction to *PL,* x.
113   "Sally Stein found" Cannell, "SAGS."
113   "'(with other pictures) . . . to the Cones'" Toklas, *SOA,* 315–16.

113   "'the Picasso oeuvre . . . the Renoir'" L. Stein to G. Stein, n.d., in L. Stein, *JIS*, 56–57.
113   "Leo kept it" Rewald, *CAA*, 66–67.
113   "'I will paint . . . apples,'" Quoted in "Catalog," n.p., in G. Stein, *GSOP.*
113   "'and wait for . . . survive them'" L. Stein to L. Simonson, Oct. 11, 1913, YALC.
113   "'The presence of Alice . . . our work'" L. Stein to M. Weeks, Feb. 7, 1913, in L. Stein, *JIS*, 52.
113   "'tell Pablo that . . . Espana!'" L. Stein to G. Stein, n.d., YALC, in L. Stein, *JIS*, 51.

8 Wars

115   "'grand mutter . . . real core'" G. Stein, "In the Grass," in *GP*, 80. The phrase occurs in the midst of segments about brothers and sons ("A son is not a sister diamond") and references to "whispers" and "whiskers," suggesting Leo's beard. Language becomes "a wet syllable is we are (81)," merging the sexual with the voiced.
115   "'how women are . . . Olga'" G. Stein, manuscripts, *Many Many Women*, YALC.
115   "early short plays" Influenced by the Spanish love of drama, attending theater as part of daily life, Gertrude began writing plays after she and Alice returned from Spain; she also followed French traditions.
115   "'Ladies' voices give pleasure'" G. Stein, *Ladies' Voices*, in *GAP*, 203.
115   "'Thank you, I'll be there'" Pankhurst quoted in Thomson, notes to G. Stein, *BTV*, 43.
115   "'Compose compose beds'" G. Stein, "Sacred Emily," in *GAP*, 178.
115   "'tenderness'" Ibid., 179.
115   "'Apples went'" Ibid., 185.
115   "'extra stress'" Ibid., 184.
115   "'able able able'" Ibid., 185.
115   "'Rose is . . . ice-cream'" Ibid., 187. So important did Gertrude and Alice consider the rose motif that they designed stationery headed by the line in a decorative circle. Toklas's letter to R. Haas, July 14, 1947, YALC, dates the stationery as "1912–1914."
115   "'Cow come out . . . a little'" Ibid., 181.
115   "suggestive of orgasm" Apollinaire had earlier used the metaphor of button for clitoris; see appendix B, Bates, *GA*, 172–74. Virgil Thomson noted that Stein relied on translation in her puns—"Tender Buttons" in French is amusing ("VDA," 3).
116   "'I am often . . . to be right'" G. Stein, manuscript, "He Didn't Light the Light," YALC.
116   "'Spoken. . . . pressed figs'" G. Stein, manuscript, "He Said It," YALC.
116   "'So to measure . . . line together'" G. Stein, manuscript, "Publishers," YALC.
116   "'Laugh, to laugh . . . any yesterday'" G. Stein, "France," in *GAP*, 30.
116   "New York edition" Toklas, *SOA*, 86.
116   "Eva Groul" Also known as Marcelle Humbert. K. Cannell recounts Picasso's fascination with comic strips ("SAGS").
117   "Dodge, who had warned" M. Dodge to G. Stein, March 29, 1914, in Gallup, *FOF*, 96–97.
117   "my dear Miss Claire'" G. Stein to "Miss Claire," n.d., YALC.
117   "'To be a . . . is pus'" G. Stein, "Shoes," *TB*, in *SWGS*, 474.
117   "specialized in psychology . . . take degree'" Enclosed with G. Stein to "Miss Claire," n.d., YALC.

117   "'Build is all right'" G. Stein, "Oranges," *TB*, in *SWGS*, 496.
118   "'Climb up in . . . hanging'" G. Stein, "Milk," *TB*, in *SWGS*, 487.
118   "'No song is . . . certainly is'" G. Stein, "Rooms," *TB*, in *SWGS*, 500–1.
118   "'The sister was . . . It was'" Ibid., 499.
118   "'Replacing a casual . . . a son'" Ibid., 500.
118   "'Why is there . . . is there'" Ibid., 508.
118   "'Almost very . . . seduction'" Ibid., 503.
118   "'Press juice from . . . ice cream'" G. Stein, manuscript, "Americans," YALC.
118   "'What is a bud . . . ancient'" G. Stein, "A Long Gay Book," in *G.M.P.*, 114.
118   "'a good deal . . . and fun'" Anderson, "The Work of Gertrude Stein," introduction to G. Stein, *GAP*, 5. Readers were impressed with Stein's sexual text. Van Vechten wrote to his second wife, the actress Fania Marinoff, about the work, calling it "extraordinary": "The last part refers, I am sure, to things you and I do very well indeed" (June 5, 1914; *LCVV*, 11).
118   "'an everyday event'" Apollinaire, "New Spirit and the Poets," in *SWGA*, 234. Her language experiments reflected what Apollinaire called "the synthetic tendency which stressed creation, surprise, and spontaneity" (Roger Shattuck, introduction to Apollinaire, *SWGA*, 16).
119   "'pure interior sound'" A. Rönnebeck to G. Stein, April 1, 1913, in Gallup, *FOF*, 77. See *Klänge* in Kandinsky, *CWOA*.
119   *"Playboy of the"* Leo wrote her on June 14, 1912, that Florence Bradley had sent them a copy of the play (YALC).
119   "Through Henry McBride" H. McBride to G. Stein, Aug. 28, 1913, in Gallup, *FOF*, 82–83.
119   "Marsden Hartley later" M. Hartley to G. Stein, Oct. 1913, in Gallup, *FOF*, 85–86. See T. Ludington, *MH*, 104.
119   "'drama consists here . . . spectator'" Kandinsky, "On Stage Composition," in *CWOA*, 264.
120   "Simon—who was" See M. Stein to G. Stein, Aug. 26, 1913, YALC.
120   "'very nervous like Simon'" G. Stein, Notebooks, G-6, 2-11.
120   "(full meals and" See Salinger, *JVPG*, 103–8.
120   "'The bathing is . . . superb'" M. Stein to G. Stein, June 14, 1909, YALC.
120   "instead loaning nineteen" Barr, *M*, 177–78, 540–41.
121   "Sally's obsession with" Toklas, *SOA*, 140. Alice said that a conversation with Sally meant a lecture on Christian Science. Sylvia Salinger recalled that Sally wrote to her family about her "splendid physical healing" after studying Christian Science; Sylvia's migraines were gone, Sally said, because she had learned to "rejoice" (Salinger, *JVPG*, 39–40).
121   "David Edstrom recalled" Edstrom, *TOC*, 245.
121   "isolated life in" L. Stein to G. Stein, April 7, 1914, 3, YALC.
121   "'favorite authors were . . . judge what'" L. Stein to G. Stein, Sept. 23, 1913, YALC.
121   "Mary Berenson disliked" In *MB*, 187, she wrote that she saw "red" when she thought of the Steins, "such a weight on me for *years* . . . so persistent, so insoluable, so—well, dirty, so horrible in their ideas—(as for instance that the disgustingly silly book by Weininger on 'Sex and Character' was 'the greatest and most important book that had been written for 50 years') that I cannot endure the thought of them—*pas meme* [sic] *l'odeur—surtout pas l'odeur!*"
121   "'You are for me . . . human value'" L. Stein to N. Auzias, April 3, 1914; reprinted in L. Stein, *JIS*, 58.
121   "of 'fatherliness' toward" L. Stein to N. Auzias, undated, YALC.
121   "'absolute confidence, perfect . . . goodwill'" L. Stein to M. Weeks, Feb. 7, 1913, YALC; reprinted in L. Stein, *JIS*, 55.

122   "'I cherish you enormously . . . complicated'" L. Stein to N. Auzias, undated, YALC; reprinted in L. Stein, *JIS*, 83.

122   "'how anyone of . . . breeding'" Sterne, *SAL*, 50–51.

122   "to call 'co-feeling'" Quoted in Benjamin, *BOL*, 48.

122   "'ability to share . . . control'" Benjamin, *BOL*, 48.

123   "'perfect peace' of" Aldrich, *HOM*, 5.

123   "'Since the 4th . . . determined eyes'" Ibid., 60.

123   "'happy in Paris'" E. Groul to G. Stein, quoted in Rubin, *PAB*, 432.

123   "long queues to" Tylee, *GWAWC*, 23.

124   "her knees were" Simon, *BABT*, 97.

124   "'long lines of grain-sacks'" Quoted and discussed in ibid.

124   "'go to a . . . an hour'" Toklas, "SM," 16.

125   "'We invented that'" Quoted in Penrose, *P*, 199.

125   "offered to send him" Cooper, "GSAJG."

125   "Leo's letters in" L. Stein to G. Stein, Aug. 16, 1914, YALC.

125   "he wrote that" L. Stein to G. Stein, Dec. 4, 1914, YALC.

125   "a joint letter" Quoted in L. Stein to N. Auzias, April 21, 1915, in L. Stein, *JIS*, 61–62.

126   "then wrote Nina" L. Stein to N. Auzias, April 21 and April 26, 1915, YALC.

126   "'go to America . . . isolation'" L. Stein to N. Auzias, Feb. 6, 1914, YALC.

126   "'My dear Nina . . . together'" L. Stein to N. Auzias, Sept. 5, 1915, YALC; reprinted in L. Stein, *JIS*, 63.

126   "'I love you . . . something real'" L. Stein to N. Auzias, Sept. 19, 1915, YALC; reprinted in L. Stein, *JIS*, 65.

126   "'If you'd like . . . down here'" L. Stein to G. Stein, Jan. 11, 1915, YALC.

126   "'the traveling to . . . of better'" M. Stein to G. Stein, March 23, 1915, YALC.

126   "'thoroughly agreeable'" L. Stein to G. Stein, Feb. 15, 1916, YALC.

126   "Bertha Raffel's daughter, Gertrude" Gertrude Stein Raffel, in Haas, "BOE," 131.

127   "Katherine Dreier and" McCarthy, *WC*, 183. In 1920, Dreier, with Man Ray and Duchamp, founded the Société Anomyme of the Museum of Modern Art, which exhibited Paul Klee, Kandinsky, Léger, Miró, and others (190). It may be that personal rivalry between Dreier and Gertrude led to the latter's leaving her portrait by Picasso to the Metropolitan Museum rather than to the Museum of Modern Art.

127   "'Leo meant a . . . for thinking'" Luhan, *MAS*, 406.

127   "her 'cooperative commonwealth'" Rudnick, *MDL*, 125.

127   "'talking cure' she" Luhan, *MAS*, 439–57, 505–12. The best coverage of Brill's philosophy at the time Leo worked with him is found in his *Fundamental Conceptions of Psychoanalysis* (1921), complete with discussions of symptoms, dreams, forgetting, wit, and insanity.

128   "'Everybody is occupied . . . exciting things'" L. Stein to G. Stein, Feb. 15, 1916, YALC, reprinted in L. Stein, *JIS*, 71.

128   "'three major complexes . . . pariah complex'" Quoted in Saarinen, *PP*, 194.

128   "In the next issue" L. Stein, "IT."

128   "Barnes wrote that" Barnes, "WCAF." See L. Stein, "SHP"; and Barnes, "TPA."

128   "'old fashioned . . . quarrel'" M. Stein to G. Stein, June 3, 1916, YALC.

128   "fresh from Pennsylvania" G. Stein to M. Dodge, n.d., in Luhan, *MAS*, 29.

129   "finally told him" Schack, *AAA*, 93.

129   "In December 1915 Leo" L. Stein to N. Auzias, Dec. 28, 1915, YALC; reprinted in L. Stein, *JIS*, 68.

129   "'I have just . . . not understand'" L. Stein to N. Auzias, undated, YALC; reprinted in L. Stein, *JIS*, 69.

129 "'I have just . . . Get Papers'" L. Stein to N. Auzias, undated (second), YALC; reprinted in L. Stein, *JIS,* 69.

129 "'I am astonished . . . France'" L. Stein to N. Auzias, Jan. 22, 1916, YALC; reprinted in L. Stein, *JIS,* 70.

129 "'Everything I do . . . success'" L. Stein to N. Auzias, 1916, YALC.

130 "'a kind of . . . the theatre'" L. Stein to N. Auzias, May 5, 1916, YALC.

130 "'a conspicuous hearing aid . . . and can't'" Davidson, *BS,* 175.

130 "operations for 'fistula'" M. Stein to G. Stein, June 3, 1916, YALC.

130 "Battle Creek, Michigan" L. Stein correspondence, letters from sanitoria, YALC. See L. Stein to N. Auzias, Sept. 17, 1916.

130 "Dr. Jelliffe pioneered" Luhan, *MAS,* 440–41.

130 "'Art, and about . . . in Paris'" Ibid., 406.

130 "'those amazing dunes . . . one's eyes'" Hartley, "SAP," 272.

131 "'Money is worth . . . my income'" L. Stein to N. Auzias, Aug. 28, 1916, YALC; reprinted in L. Stein, *JIS,* 72–73.

131 "'about 1,000 francs . . . month [$171]'" L. Stein to N. Auzias, n.d., YALC; reprinted in L. Stein, *JIS,* 73.

131 "'Most of the time . . . to fight'" Ibid.; reprinted in L. Stein, *JIS,* 74.

131 "'not nationally . . . patriotic'" L. Stein to M. D. Luhan, quoted in Luhan, *MAS,* 425.

131 "'split personality: cold . . . my analysis'" Sterne, *SAL,* 49–50.

131 "'I continue my . . . my being'" L. Stein to N. Auzias, April 21, 1916, YALC.

131 "'If I cannot . . . on the way'" L. Stein, *ABC,* 35.

9 World War I and the Steins

132 "'sardines as big as cartwheels'" Toklas, *SOA,* 214. From a letter to Claude Fredericks, Nov. 19, 1950.

132 "'screaming and gesticulating'" Toklas, *ABTCB,* 42.

132 "'quite a number of funny things'" G. Stein to C. Van Vechten, April 10, 1916, in G. Stein, *Letters,* 52.

133 "Gertrude's independence" Luhan, *EE,* 327.

133 "a vine's strangling" Ibid.

133 "'The war will not be over'" G. Stein, "All Sunday," in *PL,* 104. Other titles as in Gertrude's manuscript notebooks (YALC) rather than according to published versions.

133 "being displeased with Mike" Ibid., 101.

133 "German word *Fatherland*" Ibid., 104.

133 "'My brother went to America'" Ibid., 105.

133 "that remained unpublished" Ms. of "Lifting Belly," YALC. See Bridgman, *GSIP,* 148–50.

133 "'Alas about every . . . Alas'" G. Stein to C. Van Vechten, April 18, 1916, in G. Stein, *Letters,* 53.

134 "'a friend like you'" P. Picasso to G. Stein, Jan. 8, 1916, quoted in Penrose, *P,* 202.

134 "From Agay, Mike" M. Stein to G. Stein, Dec. 23, 1914; Feb. 12, March 8, and March 23, 1915, YALC.

134 "Inez Haynes Irwin" Irwin, war diary, 18, 22, 16, 44, 47, 39, 9.

134 "Gertrude asked a" G. Stein, *AABT,* 171–72.

135 "princesse de Polignac" Virginia Woolf wrote to Dorothy Strachey Bussy about "Winnie Singer" who "ravished half the virgins in Paris" during these years (Jan. 1, 1937, in *LVW,* 100).

135 "Erik Satie, who" Hobhouse, *E,* 106.

135   "admirers of Philippe Pétain" Flanner, *P,* 1–26; G. Stein, *WIHS,* 86–87.
135   "Alice learned of the" Toklas, *WIR,* 93–94.
135   "'delegates' so long" Simon, *BABT,* 102.
135   "Bird's husband, Howard" H. Gans to G. Stein, Sept. 14, 1916, in Gallup, *FOF,* 113–14.
135   "never in retreat" Toklas, *ABTCB,* 61.
135   "as a 'chuffer'" M. Stein to G. Stein, Aug. 6 and 12, 1916, YALC.
136   "'who always behaved . . . flattered'" G. Stein, *AABT,* 172.
136   "the truck stalled on" Ibid., 172–74.
136   "'Oh that I . . . to do it'" Toklas, *ABTCB,* 62.
136   "Auntie needed both" Mellow, *CC,* 228.
136   "'engaged in good . . . am working'" G. Stein to C. Van Vechten, Feb. 23, 1917, in G. Stein, *Letters,* 57.
136   "a Saint-Cloud" Toklas, *WIR,* 94.
136   "Yvonne Davidson, wife" Mellow, *CC,* 228.
137   "'Well I am . . . could not do'" M. Aldrich to G. Stein and A. Toklas, April? 1917, YALC.
137   "Because Gertrude hated" Simon, *BABT,* 103.
137   "building steps out" Toklas, *WIR,* 95.
137   "theme of sexual" Several dozen pieces from the 1916–1918 period might be discussed here, among them, "Marry Nettie," "Why We Are Pleased," and "A Very Good House."
137   "'There is no . . . your wife'" G. Stein, "Marry Nettie," *Painted Lace,* 43.
138   "comfort bag, complete" Toklas, untitled article, July 4, 1918.
138   "'the next day . . . it take?'" Toklas, "NWAN."
138   "Committed to aiding" Simon, *BABT,* 103.
138   "'It is the limit'" L. Stein to A. Toklas, May 17, 1917, Lake Collection, Harry Ransom Humanities Research Center, Univ. of Texas; L. Stein to G. Stein undated, YALC.
138   "Allan, graduated from" M. Stein to G. Stein, May 8, June 4, June 23, Oct. 2, and Nov. 8, 1917; Jan. 2, Nov. 12, and Dec. 8, 1918, YALC. In this last, Mike includes Virginia Moffat's Dec. 4, 1917, letter (YALC), in which she spoke of visiting Simon's grave and recalled his happiness when she fried chicken for him, his laughing hard at stories about the past, and his appreciation of some mementos that Bertha had sent him from Baltimore.
139   "'I enjoyed the . . . so smoothly'" M. Stein to G. Stein, 1919. These stories seem to have disappeared.
139   "'hundreds and hundreds . . . handkerchiefs'" Toklas, "NWAN."
139   "'The wounded have . . . and staffs'" Toklas, untitled article, Nov. 8, 1918.
139   "'so brave in his suffering'" Toklas, "FOOOD," 2. See Toklas, *SOA,* 226; and idem, *ABTCB,* 69.
139   "'frightfully wounded,' Alice" Skinner, "AAGMP," 39.
139   "Dr. Irving Waldberg" I. Waldberg to G. Stein, Oct. 31 and Nov. 13, 1917, YALC. In her "Poem about Waldberg" (*GAP,* 166), she stated, "I don't care for him."
140   "'godsons'; they exchanged" Simon, *BABT,* 104.
140   "'the solid museum . . . battlefields'" Rogers, *WTYS,* 90.
140   "'She never suggested . . . hard floor'" Ibid., 102–3.
140   "'heavy-duty corduroy . . . pockets'" Ibid., 101.
140   "Samuel L. M. Barlow, Jr." Barlow, "AD," 2, 5, 11, 13, and 20.
141   "'Gertrude Stein has . . . conflict than she'" *Vanity Fair* 10 (June 1918), 31.
141   "Mike had the water" M. Stein to G. Stein, Jan. 28, 1918, YALC. See also M. Stein to G. Stein, Jan. 2, March 13 and 20, April 8 and 12, June 8, 19, and 26, and July 23, 1918, YALC.

142   "Late in 1918" M. Stein to G. Stein, Nov. 16, Nov. 27, and Dec. 18, 1918, YALC.
142   "Mike grieved over" Barr, *M*, 178.
142   "Though he claimed" L. Stein, *JIS*, 192.
142   "'tremendous number of . . . raining women'" L. Stein to N. Auzias, Dec. 1917, YALC; reprinted in L. Stein, *JIS*, 75–76.
142   "'the mystery' of psychoanalysis" L. Stein to M. Dodge, Sept. 22, 1915, in L. Stein, *JIS*, 65.
142   "haphazard adobe buildings" Luhan, *TAIA*, 16.
143   "'the only landscape . . . great painters'" Quoted in Luhan, *TAIA*, 21.
143   "'negotiating for an . . . $200'" M. Stein to G. Stein, Aug. 1918?, YALC.
143   "Indian dances, which" Harley, *SAP*, 273.
143   "Leo suggested that" L. Stein to N. Auzias, Aug. 11, 1918, YALC.
143   "'the strange and wonderful world'" L. Stein to M. Weeks, Feb. 7, 1913, in L. Stein, *JIS*, 55.
143   "'Leo preferred the . . . mother's womb'" Sterne, *SAL*, 156.
143   "Howard Gans, too" H. Gans to G. Stein, March 23, 1918, 4, YALC. Gans also said that Leo seemed to have "found peace" and was in "a fairly cheerful frame of mind." It is also clear that Howard's secretary did Leo's typing.
143   "'I shall be . . . so many years'" L. Stein to N Auzias, Sept. 24, 1919, YALC; reprinted in L. Stein, *JIS*, 77.
143   "'Compose yourself. You . . . be killed'" Toklas, *WIR*, 101.
144   "rushed back to" Toklas, *ABTCB*, 71.
144   "'a mix-up'" Toklas, *WIR*, 102. See also idem, *ABTCB*, 72.
144   "some link sausage" Mellow, *CC*, 236.
144   "'great elegance and luxury'" Toklas, *ABTCB*, 74.

10   The Twenties Begin

147   "Overflowing now with" See Flanner, interview, 7–8, 10; and Huddleston, *BTM*, 130–31, 151, 238, 259.
147   "two 'sourly' sipping" Biddle, *AAS*, 209.
148   "'gossiping in four . . . civilized universe'" Ibid., 208.
148   "'Paris was filled . . . and restaurants'" Toklas, *ABTCB*, 78.
149   "They saw him only" Toklas, "SM," 15.
149   "'I can still . . . had happened'" Kahnweiler, introduction, xi.
149   "I found in . . . interior logic'" Ibid., xii.
150   "'second class hearse'" Toklas, *WIR*, 105.
150   "'her 'stern expression'" Imbs, *C*, 125.
150   "a fussy grandmother" Ibid., 166.
150   "'cut off coal scuttles'" Beach, *SAC*. Comments from various sources detail the fact that Gertrude had discovered that men's boxer shorts made the best undergarment for summer, and both she and Alice wore long johns in winter.
151   "Hans Purrmann's negotiations" Barr, *M*, 178, 199.
151   "While Leo was in" L. Stein to N. Auzias, undated and December 21, 1916, YALC. There is extensive correspondence between them, much of it undated, most in French, also in YALC. See, e.g., L. Stein, *JIS*, 73–74.
152   "'Apart from a . . . shrinks recently'" L. Stein to A. Barnes, Dec. 29, 1920, YALC; reprinted in L. Stein, *JIS*, 84.
152   "Sally bought *Tea*" Barr, *M*, 206.
152   "'do about them . . . than in mine'" L. Stein to A. Barnes, March 8, 1921, YALC; reprinted in *JIS*, 86.
153   "'a steal, that . . . a break'" Schack, *AAA*, 114. Leo's silence need not be read as agreement. During the later 1920s, as he watched prices in the art world

skyrocket, he realized that selling when he did, and for what he did, had been foolish.

153   "(*Still Life with*" Rewald, *CAA*, 256.
153   "their 'Family Romance'" L. Stein to G. Stein, Dec. 14, 1919, YALC; reprinted in L. Stein, *JIS*, 78.
153   "his next letter" L. Stein to G. Stein, undated, YALC.
153   "She poured at" Imbs, *C*, 176.
153   "heaped with homemade . . . paper lanterns'" Rose, "GS," 89.
154   "'writing was a contagious craft'" Toklas, "TWCTP," 1.
154   "'Our Lady,' 'The Presence,' 'Le Stein'" Stearns, *CHM*, 151; Cody, *WOM*, 77.
154   "What are you . . . homework for her'" Quoted in Putnam, *PWOM*, 136.
154   "his sister did" Carpenter, *GT*, 25.
154   "'I suppose some . . . modern movement'" G. Stein to H. P. Gibb, Dec 23, 1921, YALC.
155   "'an ethical Jewess . . . rather a rare type'" Bryher, *HTA*, 210.
155   "'Gertrude led everything'" J. Flanner quoted in Wineapple, *G*, 77.
155   "'found to his . . . deal to her'" Kreymborg, *T*, 292.
155   "'throw the rest into the fire'" Williams, *AWCW*, 254.
156   "'content to be . . . they would take'" Steffens, *ALS*, 834.
156   "'as unmistakably American . . . McKinley era'" J. P. Bishop, quoted in Cowley, *AGT*, 193.
156   "Van Wyck Brooks" Brooks, *OOA*, 240.
156   "'like a banner'" Prokosch, *V*, 16, 19.
156   "'Gertrude's style was . . . into her rhythms" Ibid., 94.
156   "'She created an . . . instant visions'" Ibid., 95.
156   "'with unerring accuracy . . . and pure'" Imbs, *C*, 120.
157   "'meant discipline and . . . loyalties'" Ibid., 122.
157   "'If you have . . . in writing'" Ibid., 121.
157   "Stein was trying" Bryher, *HTA*, 210.
157   "'In my own . . . to writing'" Imbs, *C*, 121.
157   "Wambley Bald asked" Putnam, *PWOM*, 137.
157   "'toward abstractionism . . . without mysticism'" Ibid., 139.
158   "'Her lips moved . . . all believed'" Cody, *WOM*, 74–76.
158   "'the easiest, most . . . with sunlight'" Imbs, *C*, 118.
158   "'She spun webs . . . to death'" Young, "LWG," 92.
158   "'from Catullus to . . . aggressive'" Tytell, *EP, SV*, 186.
159   "The later story" See Mellow, *CC*, 252.
159   "'not entirely on unfriendly terms'" Biddle, *AAS*, 210–11.
159   "'made the tactical . . . but her own'" Porter, "Gertrude Stein: Three Views," in *DB*, 45–46.
159   "'a lively cross-examination'" Loeb, *WIW*, 62.
160   "'there was no . . . unconscious mind'" K. Buss, quoted in Sorrell, *TW*, 103.
160   "'thought she had . . . her writing'" Flanner, foreword to G. Stein, *Two*, xvii ff.
160   "'Great Jehoshaphat,' she" Ibid., xvi.
160   "'Annie from Chicago'" Putnam, *PWOM*, 134–35.
161   "Loy linked her" Loy, *LLB*, 289–99.
161   "'the fractional tones . . . sculpture'" Ibid., 289.
161   "'power of evocation . . . *Book of Job*'" Ibid., 294.
161   "Shakespeare and Company" See Fitch, *SB*; and Beach, *SAC*.
161   "Andre Gide, Jules" Toklas, "SAHF," 24.
162   "'Not a country . . . remember'" G. Stein, "Rich and Poor in English, Sylvia Beach," 95.

162 "'Sorry I said . . . do not know'" Stein, *PF*, 10–11.
163 "'a winning brusquerie . . . irresistible'" Toklas, "TWCTP," 1.
163 "'sweet and healthy' bread" Anderson, "FAI," 171.
163 "'The woman is . . . the telling'" Quoted in White, *SA/GS*, 9.
163 "'large liquid eyes . . . facial planes'" Bibesco, "LWGS," 11.
163 "Gertrude's breasts must" Sokoloff, *H*, 50.
163 "'a far more . . . marvelous laugh'" Wescott, foreword, xvii.
163 "'alarming' sexual attraction" Sutherland, "AAG," 297.
163 "Alice insisted regularly" Daniel, "SLWG," 17.
164 "(like Edith Wharton)" See Benstock, *NGFC*, 161–63 and 201 for her description of Wharton's reenactment of Sand in her life (naming her motor "George," for instance).
164 "'As you like . . . the story'" Sand, preface to *B*.
164 "Proud of being" Ardagh, *WF*, 69, 12.
164 "Flaubert called her" Moers, introduction, xiv–xviii, xx–xxi. See also Barry, preface to *IW*.
164 "I have spent . . . beatitude'" Quoted in Barry, *IW*, 328.
165 "persona 'Jane Sands'" G. Stein, *G.M.P.*, 30.
165 "'two little leaves . . . and Chopin'" G. Stein to H. P. Gibb, July 1913, YALC.

11   Legends of Hemingway and Others

166 "Alice's carried the" Mellow, *CC*, 247.
166 "practical Alice was" See Toklas's "FY," 55–57, and Stein's "Flirting at the Bon Marché" and "Bon Marché Weather," descriptions of sorties there with Etta Cone.
166 "'were all in perfect . . . and ospreys'" Rose, "GS," 89.
166 "'frail Chinese terra-cotta pottery'" Ibid. See also ibid., 133.
167 "group of Spanish" Flanner, forword to G. Stein, *Two*, xiii.
167 "part of the dialogue" Beach, *SAC*, 27.
167 "Her doctor told . . . have it out'" Thomson, "RG," 3. According to Bravig Imbs (*C*, 180), Gertrude used to joke that Alice had lost her taste for highly seasoned food as a result of cooking and eating Stein's diet.
167 "The surgery she did" Sprigge, *GS*, 128; and Steward, *DS*, 74.
167 "'Miss Ellen Sedgwick'" See the Sedgwick-Stein correspondence, YALC.
167 "with Edmund Brown" See the Brown-Stein correspondence, late 1921 (early letters undated) through May 29, 1925, Univ. of Virginia Libraries.
167 "'I have a large selling public'" G. Stein to E. Brown, undated, Univ. of Virginia Libraries.
167 "Man Ray photos" For a full account of this skirmish, which is suggestive of Gertrude's stubbornness when roused, see Baldwin, *MR*, 103 and 162.
168 "'She Bowed to Her Brother'" Toklas, *WIR*, 105–6.
168 "Sherwood had told" Hemingway to G. Stein, n.d., Hemingway Collection, Kennedy Library.
168 "'In a couple . . . of ships'" Hemingway to S. and T. Anderson, Dec. 23, 1921, in Baker, *EH*, 59.
168 "Blaise Cendrars, the" Cendrars, interview, 51.
168 "'became an unofficial . . . of her thumb'" Imbs, *C*, as quoted in Simon, *BABT*, 167.
168 "'Gertrude Stein and . . . lot of her'" E. Hemingway to S. Anderson, March 9, 1922, in Baker, *EH*, 62.
168 "'extraordinarily good looking'" G. Stein, *AABT*, 212.

169   "his 'direct' poems" Ibid., 213.
169   "writing 'inaccrochable' fiction" Hemingway, *MF,* 15.
169   "'I've been working . . . better'" E. Hemingway to G. Stein, Feb. 18, 1923, in Baker, *EH,* 79. Hemingway's references to Gertrude's advice become clearer in the context of her many statements about the way the best artists work.
169   "'The trouble with . . . America?'" As quoted in Daniel, "TSL," 18.
169   "'between Avignon and . . . the sea'" Toklas, *ABTCB,* 94.
170   "Gertrude later said" G. Stein, *AABT,* 209–10.
170   "'I'm so sick . . . salaries'" E. Hemingway to H. Hemingway, Nov. 28, 1922, in Baker, *EH,* 73. For his use of *kike,* see note below on "they both liked 'niggers.'"
170   "'a belly full . . . Vendee [*sic*]'" E. Hemingway to C. E. Hemingway, March 26, 1923, in Baker, *EH,* 81.
170   "'Miss Stien and Miss Toclaz'" H. Hemingway to G. Stein and A. Toklas, Nov. 25, 1922, Hemingway Collection, Kennedy Library.
170   "Mike and Sally were" Richardson, *DC,* 173–83; M. Stein letters to G. Stein, June 6 and Friday, otherwise undated, YALC.
170   "Picasso's mother, Señora" G. Stein, *AABT,* 221.
170   "'were phenomenal together . . . witnessing it'" Tomkins, *LWIBR,* 39.
170   "'the run of the studio'" E. Hemingway to D. Gallup, Sept. 22, 1952, in Baker, *EH,* 781.
170   "'more about them . . . as painters'" Hemingway, *MF,* 17.
171   "'Stein made me . . . of hearing'" Church, "ARI," 24–25.
171   "she thought was 'hilarious'" Sokoloff, *H,* 61.
171   "'lived in a . . . toreros'" E. Hemingway to W. Horne, July 17–18, 1923, in Baker, *EH,* 87–88.
171   "'I've been trying . . . to him'" Daniel, "SL," 17.
172   "'Deeply interested in . . . redemption'" Church, "ARI," 29.
172   "'healthy and happy . . . handsome'" H. Hemingway to G. Stein, Nov. 28, 1923, Hemingway Collection, Kennedy Library.
172   "'try not to be turgid'" E. Hemingway to "Dear Friends," Nov. 9, 1923, in Baker, *EH,* 102.
172   "'They [readers in . . . papers etc.'" Ibid., 101.
172   "praise from Edith" See Sitwell, "MSS," 492; Hecht, review, 2; Van Vechten, "MFMS," 20; Burke, "EWW," 408–12; and Wilson, "GTGS," 60, 80.
172   "'a young Chicago . . . abroad'" *Poetry,* 21 (Jan. 1923), 193.
173   "would use excerpts" E. Hemingway to G. Stein, Feb. 17, 1924, in Baker, *EH,* 111.
173   "'bouncing into the . . . bit tired'" Anderson and Kelly, *ME,* 169.
173   "Bumby's six-month" Diliberto, *H,* 173.
173   "been 'very hectic'" G. Stein to H. P. Gibb, Aug. 18, 1924, YALC.
174   "the 'enchanted' valley" Toklas, *ABTCB,* 100.
174   "'I'm trying to . . . job though?'" E. Hemingway to G. Stein, Aug. 15, 1924, in Baker, *EH,* 122.
174   "one of the stockholders" That fall Ford wrote Gertrude asking if he might hold a meeting of those shareholders—Natalie Barney, Nancy Cunard, Bill Bird, the duchesse de Clermont-Tonnerre, Romaine Brooks, Ezra Pound, others—at her flat (F. M. Ford to G. Stein, quoted in Poli, *FMF,* 125).
174   "'That little check . . . in handy'" G. Stein to E. Hemingway, n.d., Hemingway Collection, Kennedy Library.
174   "'drop in after dinner'" Bowen, *DFL,* 171.
174   "'It seems that . . . foolish'" G. Stein to E. Cone, June 22, 1924, YALC.
175   "she claimed heavy" Quoted in Pollack, *C,* 160.
175   "Alice was busily" Toklas, *WIR,* 114–15.

175   "sales were small" See McAlmon, *BGT,* 206–7 and 91; G. Stein, *AABT,* 223–25; and Gallup, "MOTMOA," 63–73.

176   "'It's hard to . . . royalties'" A. Toklas to D. Gallup, April 29, 1951, in Toklas, *SOA, 229.*

176   "critic Edmund Wilson" Wilson, "MHDP," 340–41.

176   "relationships with protégés" Interview with Virgil Thomson, in Lowe, *GW,* 170. Thomson said Stein was so effective in this role because, though she had the authority of a father figure, her appeal was feminine, so the young were not blocked from her as they were from their own fathers. Her advice was always general and easier to accept.

176   "Pavlik Tchelitchew, whose" See Lowe, *GW,* 157–65, for a good account of Stein's friendship with "the New Romantics," many of whom were also surrealists.

176   "Although Gertrude was" See Josephson, *LAS,* for descriptions of their beliefs and their "happenings" from 1920 on.

176   "the only woman" Benstock, *WLB,* 380–81.

177   "they both liked 'niggers'" Duberman, *PR,* 92–93. Unlike Hemingway's pervasive use of *kike* and *nigger,* Stein's use of *nigger* to Van Vechten, who sponsored a great many black artists, seems to have carried no censure. At the height of Josephine Baker's rage in Paris (Stein wrote a portrait of Baker) and the popularity of all-black casts in such productions as Cendrars's 1923 ballet *La Création du monde* and the Revue nègre, the tone of the word was probably understood; Van Vechten's new novel was *Nigger Heaven.* See also G. Stein to C. Van Vechten, Nov. 9, 1925, in G. Stein, *Letters,* 123; also in Gallup, *FOF,* 197; and G. Stein to C. Van Vechten, Aug. 11, 1927, in G. Stein, *Letters,* 152–53.

177   "'The door opened . . . prove it'" Daniel, "SL," 17.

177   "her 'weakness' for" G. Stein, *AABT,* 220.

177   "they discussed the" Ibid., 219.

177   "ninety percent Rotarian," Ibid., 220.

177   "'Neither reading . . . for him'" Ibid., 216.

178   "'Neither reading nor'" Toklas, "TWCTP," 25.

178   "'terrible things' Toklas" E. Hemingway to D. Gallup, Sept. 22, 1952, in Baker, *EH, 781;* also in Diliberto, *H, 191.*

178   "Mike and Sally's" M. Stein to G. Stein, Aug. 10, 1924, YALC.

178   "a cement house" Pach, *QT, 143.*

178   "The William Cooks" Curtis, *LC, 75.*

178   "to Yvonne Daunt" Cannell, "SAGS," 15.

178   "substantial work" Richardson, *DC,* said that "Michael became almost an official representative of the Cones in Paris," acting as "administrator and provocateur" throughout the 1920s. In 1922, for example, Mike shipped seven crates with fifty-seven works of art back to the States for them (107).

178   "giving her the" M. Stein to G. Stein, undated [1922], YALC.

178   "'the Ruth Elkins . . . Jewish girl'" M. Stein to G. Stein, Oct. 28, 1923, YALC.

178   "'Michael's hair would . . . he knew'" L. Stein to N. Stein, undated [probably 1925], YALC.

178   "'the cult of the machine'" Curtis, *LC, 50.*

178   "cousin, Pierre Jeanneret" Ibid., 71.

178   "'une maison un palais'" Ibid., 79.

178   "'an asymmetrical . . . open-air rooms'" Ibid., 81.

178   "By early 1927" Ibid., 80–82.

178   "Mike visited the" M. Stein to G. Stein, undated, YALC.

178   "'machines for sitting in'" Curtis, *LC,* 84. Despite the fame—and the cost—of their home, Mike and Sally were still modest Americans who entertained

droves of visitors curious to see both their art and its setting by serving home-made ice cream and listening to Mike's player piano. In 1928, Etta brought Mike all the new songs on piano rolls. (Rogers, *LB*, 93.)

178   "willing to comment" Loeb, *WIW*, 79.
180   "'Despite my disapproval . . . yet acquired'" Ibid., 165–66.
180   "'tall, thin, slow-moving . . . in black'" Glassco, *MOM*, 15.
180   "'his sensibility and his creative strain'" McAlmon, *BGT*, 135.
180   "'Leo Stein, Gertrude . . . Paris modernists'" Flanner, *PWY*, 9.
180   "as Hapgood analyzed" Hapgood, *VMW*, 533.
180   "As his borrowing" L. Stein, borrowing lists from Shakespeare and Company, 1923–1932, Sylvia Beach Archive, Princeton University.
181   "Leo's correspondence also" L. Stein, correspondence, YALC. See also L. Stein, *JIS*, 88–94, 99–107 ff.
181   "reviews were positive" See M. J. Adler, *New York Evening Post*, Oct. 15, 1927, 15; D. Phillips, *Yale Review*, Sept. 28, 1927, 192; W. Frank, *The New Republic*, Nov. 2, 1927, 292; H. M. Kallen, *Dial*, Feb. 1928, 146.
181   "Alfred Stieglitz, who" A. Stieglitz to L. Stein, Feb. 2, 1928, YALC.
181   "Correspondence between the" L. Stein to N. Stein, correspondence, YALC.
181   "'they were furious . . . forgave her'" Toklas, Duncan interview, 44.
182   "'when she is sad'" L. Stein to N. Stein, undated, YALC.
182   "'I have heard . . . look at you'" M. Hartley to G. Stein, in Gallup, "WOAP," 259.

12   "The Most Famous Jew in the World"

183   "like a monk" G. Stein, *AABT*, 247.
183   "'was not at all . . . and jolly'" Grosser, "VGAA," 36.
183   "'the Young Men's . . . of course'" Sitwell, *TCO*, 81.
184   "Osbert recalled that" Sitwell, *LNR*, 245. See Baker, "SPDH," 24, 30–31.
184   "'It has gone off very well'" G. Stein to Julian and Rose Ellen Stein, 1926, YALC.
184   "'Jews swarmed. It . . . exacerbating affair'" V. Woolf, letter 1644, to V. Bell, June 2, 1926, in Woolf, *LVW*, 3: 269–70.
184   "the Woolfs' Hogarth" L. Woolf to G. Stein, June 11, 1926, in Gallup, *FOF*, 193.
184   "'May June and Jew lie'" G. Stein, "A Lyrical Opera Made by Two," *OAP*, 53.
184   "'my little jew'" G. Stein, "A Sonatina," *BTV*, 31.
184   "the adjective *Jewish*" Katz, "FM," 207.
184   "Pound's blatant criticism" Cunard, *TWTH*, 129. Benstock notes that Pound conveniently broke with all the women editors in Paris—many of whom were Jewish—after he became established and that in 1928, writing to Louis Zukof-sky about forming a New York poetry group, Pound warned "NOT too many women" (*WLB*, 333, 363).
185   "'the Jews have . . . and myself'" Mellow, *CC*, 290.
185   "been a disguised anti-Semitism" Secor, "GS," 34.
185   "'kowtowing to a Jewess'" Quoted in Imbs, *C*, 123.
185   "'Sitting Bull' and" Cooper, *SP*, 201.
185   "'The Jewish women . . . not marry them'" Tchelitchew to G. Stein (trans.), March 18, 1926, in Gallup, *FOF*, 187.
185   "'Gertrude is the . . . Jewish traits'" Quoted in Imbs, *C*, 123.
185   "'No Jew ever . . . last cent'" Quoted in Jackson, "WGS," 245.
185   "'A Jew is . . . new Christians'" Quoted in Grosser, "VGAA," 37.
185   "for the *New*" S. Wallach to G. Stein, Nov. 12, 1928, YALC.
185   "'the most famous Jew in the world'" Quoted by Rose Raffel (Arthur's widow), in conversation with the author, Nov. 10, 1991.

185 "Dayang Muda of" Boyle and McAlmon, *BGT*, 261. Most versions of the story emphasize Stein's rapport with Raymond Duncan, whose later entrance saved the party, but her affability can surely be seen as a means of saving face and charming the royal visitor with tales of "wild" American behavior.

186 "'a Jewish strain'" Carl Van Vechten notes, quoted in Kellner, "BWII," 9.

186 "separatist attitudes—which" Sachs noted that, while in New York "Catholics never associate with Protestants, and the Israelites form a society apart," Paris was thought to pay little attention to such labels (*DOI*, 12).

186 "'I should like . . . student life'" M. W. Williams to G. Stein, June 28, 1928, in Gallup, *FOF*, 223.

186 "'being able to . . . poisoned'" Toklas, "TA," 94.

186 "'the Indecision Board'" Toklas, Duncan interview, 42.

186 "the Baroness Else" Toklas, "TA," 95.

186 "'setting people at sixes and sevens'" Imbs, *C*, 162–63.

186 "'One must always yield to temptation'" G. Stein, *PAP*, 48.

186 "'Le Grand Gertrude Stein'" Mellow, *H*, 316. See Wagner-Martin, "RASC."

187 "editor Harold Loeb" Harold Loeb in his essay "Hemingway's Bitterness" said that the novel "hit like an upper-cut" and he was amazed at the unflattering portrait of himself as Cohn (in Sarason, *HATSS*, 126).

187 "'If that nice . . . like a shot'" Daniel, "SL," 17.

187 "piece about his break" Hemingway, "MOL," 23–24. See items 423a and 593a, Hemingway Collection, Kennedy Library.

187 "beautiful Laura Riding" See correspondence among G. Stein, Robert Graves, and L. Riding, YALC, and Riding's story about Stein's confiding in her: "What she told had for me the quality of a natural womanly feeling towards a man. . . . She said to me 'Picasso knows and I know that he is the only man for me and I the only woman for him'" (Jackson, "WGS," 256).

187 "Georges Hugnet, who" Lowe, *GW*, 191–95.

187 "Eugene Berman, whose" Grosser, "VGAA," 36–37.

187 "Both Kay Boyle and Bryher" Boyle, *BGT*, 333; Bryher, *HTA*, 211.

187 "she got 'low in her mind'" Imbs, *C*, 229.

187 "food was 'pernicious'" Daniel, "SL," 17.

187 "'That Pound. Neither . . . amuse me'" Ibid., 18.

187 "'Ford and his women! . . . gets 'em'" Ibid., 17.

187 "'What is the use . . . to be a man?'" G. Stein, *GHOA*, 25.

187 "When Sherwood Anderson" Anderson and Kelly, *ME*, 163.

189 "Natalie Barney's salon" Rogers, *LB*, 56; Josephson, *LAS*, 324.

189 "by buying his" Cooper, "GSAJG," 28–35.

189 "arguments with Picasso" During those years, Gertrude sold the Cone sisters works from her collection—sculptures by Picasso, Laurencin's *Group of Artists*, the Vallotton portrait of her, and Cézanne's *Bathers*. (Richardson, *DC*, 175–76).

189 "'a very great . . . is dying'" G. Stein to C. Van Vechten, May 5, 1927, in G. Stein, *Letters*, 146.

189 "'The Life and Death of Juan Gris'" G. Stein, *PAP*, 48–50.

189 "'Go away, Pablo. Not today'" Toklas, *RSOAT*, 43.

189 "'You have no right . . . he replied'" G. Stein, *AABT*, 212.

190 "Besides friendship with" Toklas, *WIR*, 122–23.

190 "became Gertrude's dream" Toklas, *ABTCB*, 102; idem, *WIR*, 123.

190 "Gertrude wrote Baltimore" G. Stein to Julian and Rose Ellen Stein, July 23, 1928, YALC.

190 "she saw weeds" Simon, *BABT*, 141.

191 "'meditating or writing . . . or talking'" Laughlin, "AGS" 528.

191   "'The first gathering . . . has grown'" Toklas, *ABTCB,* 283.
191   "'one of those . . . you on'"'" Barney, foreword, ix–x.
191   "to Orgeval to see" Wineapple, *G,* 121. (Toklas spells the name *Orgival.*)
191   "Mildred Aldrich died" Toklas, *WIR,* 112–13.
192   "'made a very . . . Always, Gertrude'" Quoted in Pollack, *C,* 197.
192   "As Hemingway said" Church, "ARI," 26.
192   "That she consulted" G. Stein to J. and R. E. Stein, July 23, 1928, YALC. The
       Yale papers include several handwritten astrological charts, undated, saying
       much the same thing.
192   "'Alice is managing . . . purchasers'" G. Stein to C. Van Vechten, Jan. 17, 1931,
       in G. Stein, *Letters,* 233.
193   "called the Plain Edition(s)" G. Stein, *AABT,* 242–45; Toklas, *WIR,* 136–37;
       Ford, *PIP,* 236–46. The stationery for the company used the plural; most crit-
       ics have used the singular form.
193   *"Woman with Bangs"* Richardson, *DC,* 183, 186. The fourteen Picasso draw-
       ings sold for fifty thousand francs. Many critics identify the sold painting as Pi-
       casso's *Woman with a Fan,* suggesting that the venture took the proceeds from
       more than one sale (see Mellow, *CC,* 348). Ford says that two Picasso paintings
       were sold but describes "girl sitting on horse," sold through Van Vechten's New
       York dealer, as one of them (*PIP,* 236).
193   "the Library of Congress" To Plain Edition from Library of Congress, March
       25, 1931, YALC.
193   "'Out of her early . . . modern writing'" Toklas, statement on *Geography and
       Plays,* Stein Collection, Univ. of Virginia Libraries.
193   "'Copies of HOW . . . settled quarterly'" Toklas, promotion letter, YALC;
       reprinted in Rogers, *WMFH,* 133.
193   "'a colossal impertinence'" Imbs, *C,* 296–97.
194   "'Alice was furious. Doors slammed'" Ibid., 299.
194   "'Miss Gertrude Stein . . . Virgil Thomson'" Grosser, "VGAA," 38. See B. Imbs,
       C, 300.

13   Alice's Book and "La Gloire"

195   "poem 'Patriarchal Poetry'" G. Stein, *BTV,* 265, 268–69.
195   *"A Bouquet. Their"* G. Stein, *OAP,* 204, 210. The best account of this period of
       Stein's writing is Dydo's "LING."
196   "'You poor Kid'" M. Stein to G. Stein, undated, YALC.
196   "'Gertrude and I . . . the street'" L. Stein to Annette Rosenshine, Feb. 12,
       1947, Bancroft Library, Univ. of California, Berkeley.
196   "'would finish opera . . . old painting'" Quoted in C. Van Vechten to G. Stein,
       Feb. 18?, 1929, in Gallup, *FOF,* 228.
196   "Aaron Copland arranged" A. Copland to G. Stein, Nov. 10, 1931, in Gallup,
       FOF, 253.
197   "'giant sort of feasts'" M. Gellhorn, letter to author, July 28, 1991.
197   "In 1931 Alice" Fitch, *SB,* 311.
197   "'squatted in a . . . chair'" Ibid., 296.
197   "Finally, at the" Ibid., 311.
197   "'lots of pleasant xcitement'" G. Stein to C. Van Vechten, Nov. 29, 1930, in
       G. Stein, *Letters,* 231. Later that winter she wrote, "Paris is rather wonderful"
       (Jan. 29, 1931, in ibid., 235).
198   "as she said later" A. Toklas to L. Katz, quoted in Dydo, *"SIM,"* 119.
198   "regardless of meaning" Another odd word exchange during this period is the
       use of *smile* for *write.* In "The Story of a Book," for instance, Stein wrote, "I
       did not smile to anybody about the autobiography" (MS of title, 3, YALC).

198   "'I myself have . . . for violence'" Discussion about the cahiers as well in "The Story of a Book" MS, 123.
198   "'Who is winning . . . she is'" "The Story of a Book" MS, 116.
198   "'Where they are . . . forget it'" *Stanzas* MS, vol. 10, YALC.
198   "about possible 'arrangements'" Ibid., vol. 9.
199   "six weeks Gertrude" G. Stein, "The Story of a Book," 1933 MS, YALC.
199   "'We were a . . . they were'" G. Stein to L. Hubbell, Sept. 22, 1933, YALC.
199   "Gertrude 'as a joke'" Ford, *PIP,* 246.
199   "'This is not . . . hard to say'" *AABT* MS, YALC.
200   "(Pages in Alice's" See MS, Lake Collection, Harry Ransom Humanities Research Center.
200   "'feeling himself to be the coming man'" Ibid., 72.
200   "'nothing but a fat head'" Ibid., 206.
200   "'30 Years with Gertrude Stein'" *AABT* MS, YALC. For a sampling of the extensive discussion about who wrote the *Autobiography,* see Bridgman, *GSIP;* Mellow, *CC;* and Thomson, *VT.*
200   "The Autobiography of Alice . . . Stein'" Frontispiece of Notebooks, vol. 4.
200   "'How the Saturday . . . Roger Fry'" *AABT* MS, YALC.
200   "his being 'yellow'" G. Stein, *AABT,* 216 18. After reading the *Atlantic,* Sherwood Anderson wrote Stein that he was "a bit sorry and sad" that she "took such big patches of skin off Hemmy with your delicately held knife" (in White, *SA/GS,* 76).
201   "'The Autobiography of Alice B. Hemingway'" Hemingway, unpublished text, Hemingway Collection, Kennedy Library. Besides much sexual innuendo, the piece also slams Louis Bromfield and Bernard Faÿ for being sycophants and says of Alice, "She runs the show you know. She's a very severe disiplinarian [*sic*]. . . . She's very charming." The last comment echoes Hemingway's refrain all through the parody, that he "likes" Gertrude Stein.
201   "'Testimony Against Gertrude Stein'" Published in February 1935 as a pamphlet by Servire Press, The Hague.
201   "'Matisse was very . . . horse beautiful'" Toklas, "SM," 5.
201   "'made up word . . . conversation'" Grosser, "VGAA," 36. See Adato, transcript of interview; see also Thomson's autobiography, *VT,* 176–77.
201   "more than a hundred" See White, *GSAABT,* 35–52.
202   "'gently bred . . . and kind'" G. Stein, *AABT,* 3.
202   "casual comparison" Ibid., 237.
202   "'I am adoring . . . adoring it'" G. Stein to L. Hubbell, June 1933, YALC.
202   "extravaganzas in the" Sachs, *DOI,* 20.
203   "Stravinsky's *Oedipus Rex*" Flanner, *PWY,* 24.
203   "dada performances of" See Josephson, *LAS,* 127.
203   "'the most important . . . season'" Young, *IS,* 150.
204   "a bubble-shaped Dymaxion" Mellow, *CC,* 368.
204   "'anyone who counted . . . on the train'" Bryher, *HTA,* 271–72.
204   "Beatrice Robinson-Wayne" John Houseman explained that Thomson found the "plain middle-aged lady" in a church in Brooklyn or Queens; "she had all the things Virgil was looking for—the clear speech and the rapt, simple, dedicated quality of a Saint" (*R-T,* 107).
204   "'To know to . . . love her so'" G. Stein, *Four Saints in Three Acts,* 15.
204   "'What happened today . . . country'" Ibid., 15–16.
204   "'a masterpiece'" Ibid., 39.
204   "'Saint Sarah' and" Stein had also used Mike and Sally, as well as Gabrielle and grandnephew Danny, in *Louis XI and Madame Giraud,* a 1930 play that describes visitors admiring "Mike and the house" (*OAP,* 345–46).
204   "'Rejoice saints . . . reinvite'" G. Stein, *Four Saints in Three Acts,* 20.

204 "'The working artist's working life'" Thomson, *VT*, 91.

204 "'Alice is of the St. Theresa type'" G. Stein, Notebooks, D-3.

204 "'Saint Therese something . . . out of doors'" G. Stein, *Four Saints in Three Acts*, 20.

205 "'would and would and would'" Ibid., 20.

205 "'Any one to . . . seriously'" Ibid., 21.

205 "'One at a . . . time'" Ibid., 55.

205 "Grosser's careful scenario" See Grosser, "VGAA," 37–38.

205 "'a knockout and a wow'" C. Van Vechten to G. Stein, Feb. 8, 1934, in G. Stein, *Letters*, 295.

205 "'a *wonderful* night . . . can imagine'" C. Van Vechten to G. Stein, Feb. 21, 1934, in G. Stein, *Letters*, 300.

205 "fifteen 'enchanted weeks'" Houseman, *R-T*, 126.

205 "Alfred Harcourt described" Mellow, *CC*, 369.

205 "'meant nothing, means'" Canby, "DFA," 572.

205 "Gilbert Seldes commented" Seldes, "DIT," 138–41.

205 "Gertrude's holding Thomson" Thomson, *VT*, 228–35.

205 "'pigeons on the grass'" Thomson ("VDA," 5) explained that Stein told him that the passage is meant to describe a true vision—but of doves, not pigeons, in the sky, not on the grass. The magpies hanging in the sky are visionary and create the sense of Spanish landscape, and "Let Lucy Lily" represents the "heavenly lingo" of the angel choir.

206 "Gertrude to pretend she" Imbs, *C*, 159. Criticism of Stein's work, especially in German, has often claimed that she created musical structures (see Helmut Heissenbuttel's discussion of "As a Wife Has a Cow" in "RS").

206 "'The important thing . . . good luck'" G. Stein to V. Thomson, June 11, 1933, quoted in *VT*, 233.

206 "Mike and Sally" G. Stein to Julian and Rose Ellen Stein, winter 1933/34, YALC.

14   Lions in America

208 "'to tell very . . . literature is'" "Gertrude Stein, Home, Upholds Her Simplicity," *New York Herald-Tribune*, Oct. 25, 1934, sec. 1, p. 3. See also "Gertrude Stein Arrives and Baffles Reporters by Making Herself Clear," *New York Times*, Oct. 25, 1934, 25.

208 "Gertrude saw her" Cerf described her as "the publicity hound of the world—simply great; she could have been a tremendous hit in show business. They wrote funny stories about her, but they were mixed with love and admiration, because she was a great woman—a woman of authority. When she talked, she talked as plain as a banker. She knew what she was talking about, too, and all the incomprehensible mishmash appeared only in her writing. The press met a very direct, brilliant woman" (*AR*, 102).

209 "'Gertrude Stein was . . . do likewise'" Rogers, *WTYS*, 151.

209 "'Gertrude Stein has . . . New York'" Toklas, *WIR*, 144.

209 "'All these people . . . careful of me'" Quoted in Barney's foreward, ix.

210 "'highly-amused'" Quoted in Cerf, *AR*, 103.

210 "'My dear, you . . . understand'" Commins, *WIE*, 28.

210 "'stopped him cold . . . am talking'" Cerf, *AR*, 103.

210 "of 'mutual rejection'" Tyler, *FS*, 147.

210 "Thanksgiving with the Harcourts" Toklas, *ABTCB*, 132.

210 "'The elder Bromfield . . . he asked'" Harriman, *VC*, 149–50.

211 "'the people on . . . happy in it'" G. Stein to W. Lundell, Nov. 12, 1934, typescript, YALC.

211 "Gabrielle liked to" Saarinen, *PP*, 201.

211 "Frances Steloff at" Steloff, "MOAAV" 9, 11–12.
211 "she had refused" A. Barr to G. Stein, June 29, 1934, YALC (reply written on back).
212 "more than five hundred" Most such lectures would have drawn fewer people than this; Rogers suggests the figure was named tongue in cheek (*WTYS,* 152).
212 "'The first glimpse . . . once-over'" Matthews, "GSCH," 100.
212 "Ross lost his" Stein had been suspicious of Ross from the beginning, calling him "the kind of angel lamb who is red riding hood's grandmother after she changed" (G. Stein to C. Van Vechten, July 13, 1934, in G. Stein, *Letters,* 321). She broke with Bradley, her agent, during that same summer because he was too "commercial . . . there are some things that a girl can't do" (G. Stein to C. Van Vechten, July 21, 1934, in G. Stein, *Letters,* 323).
213 "'perfect *cuisine,*' beginning" Toklas, *ABTCB,* 134.
213 "'showed dark spots . . . father's had'" Thomson, *VT,* 246.
213 "'It is wonderful . . . to me'" G. Stein to J. and R. E. Stein, 1934, YALC.
213 "'I want to stay . . . forever'" G. Stein to W. Rogers, Nov. 7, 1934, YALC.
213 "'I will yet . . . lovely opera'" G. Stein to L. Hubbell, Nov. 27, 1934, YALC.
213 "'I was always . . . country town'" G. Stein, *EA,* 161.
214 "'We had a . . . odd students'" G. Stein to B. Goodspeed, Dec. 17, 1934, Harry Ransom Humanities Research Center.
214 "'For years they . . . will change'" G. Stein, quoted in *Olivet College Echo,* Dec. 19, 1934, 1.
214 "'Don't worry, we'll . . . on time'" G. Stein, quoted in typescript of remarks by Glenn Gosling, Dave Baker, Joseph Brewer, and Mildred Lignin, Olivet Archives, 5–6.
214 "Gertrude also disliked" Toklas, *ABTCB,* 135.
214 "'just like Switzerland . . . inadequate food'" G. Stein to B. Goodspeed, Jan. 12 and 25, 1935, Harry Ransom Humanities Research Center.
214 "lavish dinner party" Toklas, *ABTCB,* 139; C. Van Vechten, "Fragments from an unwritten autobiography," 1, YALC.
214 "University of North Carolina" Cornelia Love describes the Department of English's reluctance to cosponsor Stein: "conservatives of the deepest dye," some of the members "got upset about it," although they finally agreed (Feb. 9, 1935, Southern Historical Collection, Univ. of North Carolina).
214 "Sherwood Anderson, who" Toklas, *WIR,* 151.
214 "'on the road'" G. Stein to B. Goodspeed, Feb. 17, 1935, Harry Ransom Humanities Center.
214 "she found the trip tiring" Toklas wrote later to Norman Holmes Pearson that Gertrude knew it was just a Yale key but she carried it in her coin purse for its sentiment (Nov. 1, 1952, YALC).
215 "Random House sold" Mellow, *CC,* 410.
215 "(Laughlin's task—aside" See Laughlin, *RE,* 139–68.
215 "'About your income . . . you owned'" M. Stein to G. Stein, Feb. 8, 1935, YALC.
215 "'But, Miss Stein . . . of ideas'" Quoted in Goldstone, *TW,* 104–5.
215 "'Not at all . . . more interesting'" G. Stein, *EA,* 177–78.
216 "the police were" Toklas, *WIR,* 148–49.
216 "'always talk. They like to talk'" Quoted in ibid., 148. See also G. Stein, *EA,* 183–84.
216 "'Everyone had some . . . listened to'" Quoted in Sorrell, *TW,* 121–22.
216 "'Being a really . . . very interesting'" G. Stein to C. Van Vechten, March 7, 1935, in G. Stein, *Letters,* 406–7.
217 "a Drive-Yourself" Rogers, *WTYS,* 98.
217 "'warm friendship. Endless . . . city streets'" Toklas, "TWCTP," 25.
217 "'not much,' she . . . could use'" Steffens, *ALS,* 834.

217 "'It was frightening . . . driving there'" Skinner, "AAGMP," 20.

217 "'indulged in gastronomic . . . ate them'" Toklas, *ABTCB*, 143.

218 "'It is very . . . school with'" G. Stein to B. Goodspeed, April 12, 1935, Harry Ransom Humanities Center. See G. Stein, "ICAHIA" 167.

218 "'calm, commanding presence . . . flow of ideas'" Haas, "BOE," 15.

218 "'She really cares . . . Fine!'" H. Levy, quoted in ibid., 16.

218 "'an enfant terrible'" Toklas, *WIR*, 152.

218 "'won his heart'" Rather, *GSAC*, 72.

218 "'did invent all . . . invent women'" G. Stein, *EA*, xxiii.

219 "'wanted the sentiment . . . by himself'" Ibid., 246.

219 "'a sentence for . . . metronome'" G. Stein, *AABT* MS, 200, Harrison Collection, UCLA.

219 "Opening the Christmas" In G. Stein to Steins, Dec. 1935, YALC, she reminisced about the 1934 holiday: "Alice still unearths weird treasures and I say where did you get that and she says out of my Xmas stocking, she mends things and cures things and all out of the Christmas stocking."

219 "Gertrude refused her" Pollack, *C*, 231.

219 "Scott's somewhat embarrassing" Mellow, *CC*, 394. As Stein was leaving, Fitzgerald "blurted out, 'Thank you. Having you come to the house was like—it was as if Jesus Christ had stopped in!'"

219 "'not a bit . . . almost weird'" G. Stein to B. Goodspeed, Dec. 31, 1934, and Jan. 4 and 9, 1935, Harry Ransom Humanities Research Center.

219 "'the disaster of the U.S.'" G. Stein to Steins, July 23, 1934, YALC.

220 "Leo Stein's *New*" Montale's item, "Poet's Brother," appeared in the March 23, 1935, *New Yorker*, and Leo's response, dated April 23, 1935, appeared in the May 18, 1935, issue, under the heading "We Stand Corrected." Stein's letter comments that Montale's statement is "monstrously false" and "falsely and foully poisons the atmosphere" (72).

220 "'told me how much . . . we would do'" Cerf, *AR*, 105.

220 "'Just like that'" Quoted in Ford, *PIP*, 252.

220 "'I don't know . . . to Texas'" "Gertrude Stein Adores U.S. but Not California," *New York Herald-Tribune*, April 30, 1935, 15.

220 "'an experience and . . . ever equal'" Toklas, *ABTCB*, 143.

220 "'I am already . . . so beautiful'" G. Stein, *New York Herald-Tribune*, May 13, 1935.

15 The Second Autobiography

223 "'to be fairly luxurious'" G. Stein to J. and R. E. Stein, 1930, YALC.

223 "practice bombing alerts" Porter, *DB*, 48.

224 "'The french army . . . machine guns'" G. Stein to B. Goodspeed, May 21, 1935, Harry Ransom Humanities Research Center.

224 "'For the first . . . Any truth'" G. Stein, *WIHS*, 114.

224 "'I suppose there . . . on being'" Ibid., 120.

224 "'the terrifying SS'" Wineapple, *G*, 145.

224 "German Jewish refugees" Flanner, *PWY*, 93–94.

224 "'pro-Fuehrer' by" Wineapple, *G*, 146.

224 "'so political'" Quoted in ibid.

224 "'It's funny that . . . on your mind'" Quoted in ibid., 147.

225 "'Hush, young man . . . talking about'" Toklas, *WIR*, 139. Laughlin, in turn, deciding that Stein was nutty for even listening to such profascist talk, saw the d'Aiguys' position as a class marker (*RE*, 147; and letter to author, June 11, 1992).

225 "'How can a nation . . . do to them'" G. Stein, *WIHS*, 120.

225 "the Führer's qualities" Laughlin remarked on the strangeness of their approval, since Gertrude was Jewish and Faÿ "had nearly gotten himself killed fighting the Boches" (*RE*, 147).

225 "by suppressing" Warren, "GSVL," 9. Stein's irony here echoed Max Jacob's when he wrote in chalk on the walls of the Butte in Montmartre, "Matisse drives mad!" "Matisse is worse than war!" Everyone but Matisse understood that this mix of "morbidity and love of fun" was praise (Mackworth, *GA*, 80).

226 "although Van Vechten" C. Van Vechten to G. Stein, Aug. 19, 1935, in G. Stein, *Letters*, 441.

226 "six hundred of those" G. Stein to C. Van Vechten, Aug. 29, 1935, in G. Stein, *Letters*, 442.

226 "Ivan Kahn was" I. Kahn to G. Stein, Aug. 28, 1935 (about placement at MGM or Paramount) and Nov. 21, 1936 (about *AABT* instead of "Lena"), YALC.

226 "'all writing is a Leap'" Wilder, *JTW*, 45.

226 "Gertrude's 'meditation'" Stein wrote in "Meditations on Being About to Visit My Native Land" that she was so busy that "I have not been meditating not meditating very much" (*PL*, 254).

226 "Wilder's 'reflection,' and" Wilder, *JTW*, xix.

226 "'The difficult thing . . . at one time'" Quoted in ibid., 185.

226 "'In Bilignin she . . . previous day'" Wilder, introduction, to G. Stein, *FIA*, ix.

227 "'What we know . . . daily life'" G. Stein in conversation, quoted in ibid., xi. And see Thomson, "VDA," 3.

227 "'I am not I when I see'" G. Stein, quoted in Wilder, introduction to G. Stein, *GHOA*, xiii, balances this sentence with "I am I because my little dog knows me" (ibid., 108).

227 "'a series of spiritual exercises'" Wilder, introduction, to G. Stein, *FIA*, xiii.

227 "'Everybody's life is . . . their stories'" G. Stein, quoted in ibid., x.

227 *"The Geographical History"* Largely because of Wilder's enthusiasm for this difficult work, as well as his opinion of *Four in America*, Stein asked him to write introductions for both works; that he called them studies in "metaphysics" endeared him further to her (see Wilder, introduction to G. Stein, *GHOA*, 8–9).

227 "'human nature' and" G. Stein, *GHOA*, 80. She further said, privileging "human mind," that "human nature is not interesting not at all interesting" (112). In a 1934 letter to Gilbert Harrison, she had said, "I am finding out a lot about the human mind and about America, not so much about human nature but human nature is really very much less interesting" (Harrison Collection, 2108, box 1, UCLA).

228 "'nice and quiet . . . and unworried'" G. Stein to C. Van Vechten, Dec. 18, 1935, in G. Stein, *Letters*, 466.

228 "France might have" G. Stein to C. Van Vechten, Nov. 21, 1935, in G. Stein, *Letters*, 456; G. Stein to L. Lewis, n.d., Harrison Collection, UCLA.

228 "being 'too forethoughtful'" Quoted in Mellow, *CC*, 426.

228 "later admitted to" G. Stein to C. Van Vechten, March 25, 1936, in G. Stein, *Letters*, 491. See G. Stein to C. Van Vechten, Feb. 8, and later letters for comments about the ten-day visit (in G. Stein, *Letters*, 477–94).

228 "'talked about the . . . and stirring'" Chase, "FLP," 513–14.

229 "'Each country if . . . go on living'" G. Stein to J. and R. E. Stein, May 30, 1936, YALC.

229 "'Creative people have . . . true enough'" G. Stein to H. McBride, n.d., YALC. See also G. Stein to C. Van Vechten, Feb. 8, 1936, in G. Stein, *Letters*, 477.

229 "'England and France . . . they wished '" Quoted in Wineapple, *G*, 147–48.

229 "risked their lives" As recounted by J. Laughlin, Paul Bowles, and others, lighting the gas burner for the *chauffe-bains à gaz* could singe a hand or a face (Laughlin, *RE*, 142). Stein's overseeing her guests' cleanliness was the comic

dimension; Bowles described her "standing outside my bedroom door in the morning, calling out in a low melodious voice, 'Freddy. Are you taking your bath? . . . I don't hear anything'" (WS, 120, 123).

229 "her 'obsessive energy'" Laughlin, RE, 142.

229 "Max Jacob, who" Thomson, VT, 285.

229 "witnessing a meeting" G. Stein to W. Wilcox, Oct. 10, 1936, in Galanes, "GS," 366.

229 "'And then gradually . . . all over'" G. Stein, EA, 277.

229 "'have no capital to fall back on'" G. Stein to F. Rose, June 28, 1938, YALC.

229 "'as if there were a time limit'" Steward, DS, 13.

229 "'cut off dreadfully . . . past 70'" Ibid., 63.

229 "by saying 'What'" Ibid., 7.

229 "Like a bragging" Ibid., 47.

229 "'No one expected . . . I pleased'" Ibid., 9.

231 "'Now take Hart . . . false sense '" Ibid., 17.

231 "'like a road'" Quoted in Rogers, WTYS, 189. See G. Stein to C. Van Vechten, in G. Stein, Letters, 563–64.

231 "the suicide of" Simon, BABT, 173.

231 "'You don't understand . . . I must'" G. Stein, EA, 5.

231 "Reassured that Mike" Family correspondence, YALC.

231 "States only once" See Adele Wolman to N. Stein, June 30, 1948 (reminiscing about Leo's visit), YALC.

231 "(According to rumor" Sterne, SAL, 183.

231 "In 1932 Leo's" H. Gans to L. Stein, July 13, 1932, YALC.

231 "his cash account" H. Gans to L. Stein, June 4, 1932, YALC.

232 "'clear the entire matter up'" E. Bruce to L. Stein, June 8, 1932, YALC.

232 "In July Gans" H. Gans to L. Stein, July 13, 1932, YALC.

232 "but six months" H. Gans to L. Stein, Jan. 31, 1933, YALC.

232 "'a very important person'" Sterne, SAL, 233.

232 "'never to speak . . . disagreeable'" Hartley, "SP," 290.

232 "Hartley visited the Berensons" Ibid., 297.

233 "Howard replied that" H. Gans to L. Stein, Jan. 9, 1939, YALC.

233 "In a later note" H. Gans to L. Stein, Jan. 13, 1939, YALC.

233 "Luckily, they found" G. Stein to C. Van Vechten, Nov. 25, 1937, in G. Stein, Letters, 578.

233 "'remarkable seventeenth century . . . reading cabinet'" Flanner, PWY, 187.

233 "called it 'magical'" Thomson (VT, 286) described it as "propitious to sorcery, curses, and Black Masses . . . the neighborhood of alchemy."

233 "'blue pigeon in . . . wall paper'" G. Stein to C. Van Vechten, Jan. 20, 1938, in G. Stein, Letters, 587.

233 "however, was 'frightful'" G. Stein to W. Wilcox, Jan. 11, 1938, in Galanes, "GS," 369.

233 "'pretty dead'" G. Stein to C. Van Vechten, Feb. 21, 1938, in G. Stein, Letters, 591.

233 "'not in . . . yet but xhausted'" G. Stein to C. Van Vechten, Jan. 20, 1938, in G. Stein, Letters, 587.

233 "'gave me a . . . which I did'" Flanner, PWY, 187–88.

233 "new home 'immensely'" G. Stein to J. and R. E. Stein, January 1938, YALC.

233 "'in our quiet . . . side streets'" Barney, foreword to G. Stein, AFAM, viii.

234 "'the most affirmative person I ever met'" Ibid., vii.

234 "'She never appeared . . . hit the mark'" Ibid., viii.

234 "'I have just . . . English language'" G. Stein to W. Sears, Jr., Dec. 10, 1937, YALC.

234   "terms, his 'splendor'" G. Stein, *GSOP*, 50.
234   "'very polite and and respectful'" M. Gellhorn to author, July 28, 1991.
234   "'essays in tactlessness . . . lapse in tact'" Quoted in Prokosch, *V*, 281.
234   "'a woman who . . . of that time'" Hemingway, *"The Farm."*
234   "'a new and very simple drama'" G. Stein to William Sears, Jr., Oct. 18, 1938, YALC.
234   "'that madman in Germany'" Quoted in Steward, *DS*, 37.
234   "'Aryan' or 'non-Aryan'" Quoted in Wineapple, *G*, 153.
234   "In April Mike" M. Stein to G. Stein, April 14, 1938, YALC.
234   "Allan wrote that" A. Stein to "Aunty Gertrude," July 10, 1938, YALC.
234   "she assured Gertrude" S. Stein to G. Stein, Oct. 13, 1938, YALC.
234   "'stay fearfully on'" G. Stein to B. Goodspeed, Jan. 13, 1941, Harry Ransom Humanities Research Center.
234   "the hundreds of" Flanner, *PWY*, 157.
236   "All foreigners in" Ibid., 197.
236   "Belley instituted a" G. Stein to J. and R. E. Stein, Aug. 1939, YALC.

16   World War II (1939–1942)

237   "'I was scared . . . come here'" G. Stein, "A Picture of Occupied France," in *SW*, 623.
237   "'one foot on . . . the picture'" Kahnweiler, introduction to G. Stein, *PL*, xvii.
237   "(unable to locate" Toklas, *WIR*, 162.
238   "'We have no . . . America on it'" G. Stein to C. Van Vechten, Sept. 17, 1939, in G. Stein, *Letters*, 651.
238   "'there is nothing . . . do to help'" G. Stein to C. Van Vechten, Oct. 1, 1939, in G. Stein, *Letters*, 651.
238   "Gans replied that" H. Gans to L. Stein, Sept. 17, 1940, YALC.
238   "By October 23" From this time on, according to Edward Burns, editor of the Stein–Van Vechten correspondence, all letters were censored, marked with the phrase *Ouvert 6B93 Par L'Autorité Militaire Contrôle Postal Militaire* (G. Stein, *Letters*, 654).
238   "Natalie Barney wrote" N. Barney to G. Stein, Dec. 3, 1930, in Gallup, *FOF*, 347.
238   "'it takes an . . . not too cold'" G. Stein to C. Van Vechten, Sept. 9, 1941, in G. Stein, *Letters*, 736.
238   "Van Vechten warned" C. Van Vechten to G. Stein, Nov. 7, 1939, in G. Stein, *Letters*, 657.
238   "the American consul" Toklas, *WIR*, 162.
238   "'We love France . . . wonderful'" G. Stein to C. Van Vechten, Sept. 17, 1939, in G. Stein, *Letters*, 651.
238   "evening gatherings lasting" G. Stein to C. Van Vechten, Jan. 10, 1940, in G. Stein, *Letters*, 663. Stein based the ending section of *Paris France* on this interaction.
238   "'Hubert de R.,' a" Toklas, *ABTCB*, 219.
239   "'usual twelve kilometers'" G. Stein, *WIHS*, 124.
239   "'Everything is dangerous . . . is everybody'" Ibid., 121.
239   "a 'phony war'" Man Ray wrote that he could detect "no sign that France was at war" (quoted in Baldwin, *MR*, 22).
239   "'Paris does not . . . at home'" D. H. Kahnweiler to G. Stein, May 2, 1940, YALC.
239   "Virgil Thomson said" Thomson, *VT*, 297.
239   "as Gertrude wrote" Her phrasing was "none of us talked about the war because there was nothing to say" ("The Winner Loses," in *SW*, 618, 622).

239 "bombings and parachutists" Ibid., 620–22.
239 "Remembering the chances" Each recorded several occasions; see G. Stein, "The Winner Loses," in *SW*, 623–25, and Toklas, *WIR*, 162, 164.
240 "They regretted not" Bulletin from W. C. Bullitt, Paris, May 14, 1940, YALC.
240 "'Paris was empty . . . few, foreigners'" Thomson, *VT*, 299.
240 "'Laws and dicta . . . were published'" Baldwin, *MR*, 227.
240 "the 'Liste Otto'" Lottman, *LB*, 154. On the list were the books of Malraux, Benda and Léon Blum, Freud, Thomas Mann, Arthur Koestler, Louis Aragon, Paul Nizan, Remarque, Vicki Baum, Stefan Zweig, and Heinrich Heine. By 1942 all books by Jews, except scientific works, and all biographies of Jews were included on the list.
240 "'Jewish writers have . . . second rank'" de Man, "The Jews and Contemporary Literature," *Le Soir*, 1940-4-42.
241 "'(miles and miles . . . went away'" G. Stein, *SW*, 633.
241 "'Pétain was right . . . understood it'" G. Stein, *WIHS*, 87.
241 "'So everybody is very . . . to everything'" G. Stein, *SW*, 637.
241 "When Bernard Faÿ" B. Faÿ to G. Stein, July 18, 1940, in Gallup, *FOF*, 351.
241 "Gertrude's voice was" Toklas, *WIR*, 162–63.
241 "'My God, the woman's Jewish!'" Quoted in Bowles, *WS*, 108.
241 "Gertrude wrote Julian" G. Stein to J. and R. E. Stein, Sept. 6, 1940, YALC.
241 "She wrote Marshall" G. Stein to M. M. Vance, Sept. 20, 1940, YALC. Vance's reply was that a copy of her request had been forwarded to Bern to inform the "appropriate Swiss authorities."
241 "'Come back to us soon'" G. Stein to J. Flanner, June 1940, quoted in Wineapple, *G*, 164.
242 "'interminable winter' of" Toklas, *ABTCB*, 219.
242 "people used skis" G. Stein to J. and R. E. Stein, Jan. 16, 1941, YALC.
242 "'We didn't feel . . . been enforced'" Toklas, *ABTCB*, 215.
242 "'Suddenly we realized . . . not mentioned'" Ibid., 218.
242 "'Life is interesting . . . of complications'" G. Stein to B. Goodspeed, Jan. 31, 1941, Harry Ransom Humanities Research Center.
242 "'Wars change the . . . hungry too long'" Toklas, *ABTCB*, 4.
242 "'in practice it . . . German coercion'" Huddleston, *P*, 17. This comfortable view was opposed by the journal *Combat* and its proponents (Kedward, *RVF*, 145–46).
242 "as when Gertrude talked" G. Stein, *WIHS*, 132, 197.
243 "like them, Gertrude" Toklas, *SOA*, 314.
243 "'we are all . . . occupying'" G. Stein to C. Van Vechten, June 22, 1941, in G. Stein, *Letters*, 728.
243 "sentences about other things" G. Stein to C. Van Vechten, September 1941, in G. Stein, *Letters*, 735–39.
243 "clearly shows her" Besides Stein's own late writing, see Hubly, "GS," 65–74.
243 "'The Germans say . . . an armistice'" G. Stein, *WIHS*, 12.
243 "'Now in 1943 . . . and burning'" Ibid., 22.
243 "'this meaningless war'" Ibid., 12.
243 "she should have" G. Stein to C. Van Vechten, Sept. 9, 1941, in G. Stein, *Letters*, 736.
243 "'Victor, he is . . . I am afraid'" G. Stein, *WIHS*, 24.
244 "he wrote Hutch" L. Stein to H. Hapgood, Feb. 18, 1941, in L. Stein, *JIS*, 207–10.
245 "'Failure in the . . . of invasion'" L. Stein, journal entry, Jan. 14, 1942, in *JIS*, 230.
245 "he wrote about" L. Stein to H. Gans, March 22, 1941, and L. Stein, journal entries, Oct. 16, 17, 18, in *JIS*, 213, 224–25.

245   "Rudolph Levy, a" L. Stein, journal entries, Oct. 5, 9, 10, 12, in *JIS*, 221–24.
245   "'clothes, linen, bedding'" Ibid., Jan. 8, 1942, in *JIS*, 228.
246   "Bernard Faÿ wrote" B. Faÿ to G. Stein, Sept. 13, 1941, in Gallup, *FOF*, 356. Fay's letters are usually in thanks for a book Gertrude has sent him, suggesting that she initiated the interchange.
246   "which included overseeing" Kedward, *RVF*, 163–64.
246   "historian Herbert Lottman" Lottman, *LB*, xii.
246   "'Nothing counts any more'" Quoted in Toklas, *WIR*, 162.
246   "'a little thing . . . Marshal Pétain'" G. Stein to C. Van Vechten, May 31, 1941, in G. Stein, *Letters*, 725.
247   "Gertrude's main point" G. Stein, manuscript of introduction, Butler Library, Rare Book and Manuscript Collection, Columbia Univ.
247   "'Pétain dictated a . . . special mission'" Simon, *BABT*, 182.
247   "Goebbels's journal shows" Huddleston, *P*, 14.
247   "'inevitable moment' when" Ibid., 210.
247   "Pétain still insisted" Griffiths, *BOMPP*, 321. See also Flanner, *P*; and Kedward, *RVF*, 165–75.
247   "new little magazines" See Lottman, *LB*, 162, 208–10; and Kedward, *RVF*, 192–96.
247   "'The literary magazines . . . of *Confluences*'" Quoted in Lottman, *LB*, 209.
248   "René Tavernier, was" See R. Tavernier to G. Stein, June 23, 1943, in Gallup, *FOF*, 362–63. In this letter he thanked Stein for "your welcome, your advice, and your collaboration."
248   "'everybody collaborated';" Lottman, *LB*, 162.
248   "as Simone de Beauvoir," Ibid., 168, 174.
248   "Official French resistance" Huddleston, *P*, 199; Kedward, *RVF*, 80–81.

17   World War II (1942–1945)

249   "'Jews were barred . . . and libraries'" Lottman, *LB*, 154.
249   "cooperated in rounding up" Wyman, *AJ*, 31.
249   "in United States papers" Ibid., 29.
249   "fifty thousand Jews were" Ibid., 31.
249   "'Final Solution' plan" Ibid., 40.
249   "What was believed" Ibid., 19, 40, 335.
250   "her letters spoke" G. Stein to J. and R. E. Stein, March 27 and 29, 1942, YALC; to C. Van Vechten, March 23, 1942, in G. Stein, *Letters*, 748–49; and to Wendell Wilcox, March 27, 1942, in Galanes, "GS," 377. To the last she admitted having had "a very long and very dreary winter."
250   "Saint Odile, an" G. Stein to C. Van Vechten, March 23, 1942, in G. Stein, *Letters*, 749.
250   "'a possible danger . . . to face'" Toklas, *ABTCB*, 227.
250   "'In my home . . . their safety'" G. Stein to M. M. Vance, Sept. 20, 1942, YALC.
250   "Sometime during this" G. Stein, *WIHS*, 112.
251   "'We were broken-hearted . . . Bilignin'" Toklas, *ABTCB*, 223.
251   "'by fraud'" G. Stein, *WIHS*, 50.
251   "'Tell those ladies . . . concentration camp'" G. Stein, *WIHS*, 50.
251   "'by collecting and . . . to them'" The words of Professor Trenard, Univ. of Lilles, quoted in Hubly, "GS," 71. See also DeKoven, *RAS*, 200.
251   "'at the close of . . . appreciation'" Grahn, *RRGS*, 141.
252   "she had found two" Toklas, *ABTCB*, 224.
252   "eating the Cézanne" Balmain, *MYAS*, 76.
252   "'bright spots' of" G. Stein, manuscript of "From Dark to Day," 1, Harry Ransom Humanities Research Center.

252   "'All in the . . . naturally'" Toklas, *ABTCB,* 226. See Gallup, FOF, 362.
252   "'Play Hemingway! Be fierce!'" Rogers, *WTYS,* 109.
252   "Leo steadily wrote" See his extensive journals, 1940–45 and undated, YALC.
253   "through intolerable times" Zuccotti, *IAH,* 140ff. See also Fargion, "JDGO," 109–138.
253   "'Batteries have been . . . and wounded'" in *JIS,* 233.
253   "'a number of . . . the street'" L. Stein, journal entry, Aug. 3, 1944, ibid., 232.
253   "'I have not . . . of waiting'" L. Stein, journal entry, Aug. 3, 1944, ibid.
253   "'I have noted . . . thrill of fear'" Ibid.
254   "'I'm beginning to . . . noisome'" L. Stein, journal entry, Aug. 12, 1944, in *JIS,* 241.
254   "'They were always . . . locksmith again'" Quoted in Sevareid, *NSW,* 458.
254   "mayor, had stopped" Ibid., 459.
254   "'Every neighbour is . . . for theft'" G. Stein, *WIHS,* 37.
254   "'a little wooden . . . front door'" Ibid., 42.
254   "'The Two American Ladies in Culoz'" Toklas, *ABTCB,* 226.
254   "they grew erratic" G. Stein, *WIHS,* 91ff.
255   "wore a wristwatch" Rogers, *WTYS,* 209.
250   "The Italian officer" Toklas, *ABTCB,* 231.
255   "Alice never typed" G. Stein, *WIHS,* 229.
255   "denounced by such" Lottman, *LB,* 201.
255   "'a Jew by . . . by habit'" Quoted in Lottman, *LB,* 163.
255   "'To-day is the landing . . . is the day'" G. Stein, *WIHS,* 194.
256   "'just naturally play . . . are gone'" Ibid., 200.
256   "'hideous confusion' as" Toklas, *ABTCB,* 231.
256   "'the boys of . . . to Belley'" Ibid., 232.
256   "'fifty Germans right . . . the road'" G. Stein, Sept. 4, 1944, transcript of CBS radio broadcast, Butler Library, Rare Book and Manuscript Collection, Columbia Univ.
256   "'ham and eggs . . . evaporated milk'" Toklas, *ABTCB,* 235.
256   "'What a day . . . yesterday'" G. Stein, transcript of CBS broadcast.
257   "'I can never . . tell you so'" Quoted in Sevareid, *NSW,* 462.
257   "many other collaborators" Lottman, *LB,* 209.
257   "the Gestapo's attempt" Hobhouse, *E,* 226.
257   "'rather favored strangers'" G. Stein, *WIHS,* 114.
257   "nothing she could do" G. Stein to C. Van Vechten, Oct. 1, 1939, in G. Stein, *Letters,* 651.

18   The Last Deaths

258   "'the daily miracle'" G. Stein, *PF,* 3.
258   "'a miracle, just . . . Hitler intended'" Quoted in Shaw, "EWGS," 22–23.
258   "'Take care, that . . . disturb it'" Toklas, *WIR,* 167.
259   "'I am old . . . fighting'" Quoted in Sutherland, "TPOGS," 28.
259   "'Basket and I . . . new G.I.'s'" G. Stein to C. Van Vechten, Feb. 7, 1945, in G. Stein, *Letters,* 766–67.
259   "'Can't you see . . . to France'" G. Stein, *Yes Is for a Very Young Man,* in *LO,* 4.
259   "for example, that the resistance" G. Stein, *WIHS,* 34.
260   "'So conservative, so . . . so ugly'" G. Stein, *The Mother of Us All,* in *LO,* 60.
261   "'Where is where . . . made it live'" Ibid., 87.
261   "'For the records . . . Jan. 19, 1942'" B. Cerf, notation on typescript of Stein introduction to Pétain, *Paroles aux Français,* Butler Library, Rare Book and Manuscript Collection, Columbia Univ.
261   "Kathleen Winsor (the author" Cerf, *AR,* 107.

261   "'at best reactionary . . . reprehensible'" Quoted in Commins, *WIAE?* 32.
261   "one by Richard" Wright, "GSS."
262   "'Nothing like being top dog'" L. Stein, journal entry, Sept. 4, 1944, in *JIS*, 244.
262   "'The Steins were . . . rationed to them'" Sterne, *SAL*, 199–200.
262   "'perfect state of grace'" L. Stein to M. Sterne, June 29, 1945, in L. Stein, *JIS*, 251.
263   "'My private interior . . . excitements'" L. Stein to F. Stein, Sept. 16, 1945, in L. Stein, *JIS*, 255.
263   "Hiran Hayden, the editor" The Hayden-Stein correspondence also concerns an essay he had taken to use in *American Scholar;* see L. Stein to H. Hayden, Aug. 7, 1946, and Jan. 15, Feb. 4, April 3, May 5 and 27, and July 3 and 17, 1947, YALC.
263   "Janet Flanner returned" Flanner, *D*, 50–72.
263   "'Brewsie: Well let's . . . about jobs'" G. Stein, *BAW*, 12.
264   "'Thinking is what . . . lousy with them'" Ibid., 85–87.
264   "stole the show" Crosby, *PY*, 225.
264   "Gertrude and Alice dressed" Balmain, *MYAS*, 95.
265   "'seemed to represent . . . for her'" Kahnweiler, introduction to G. Stein, *PL*, xviii.
265   "she wrote Robert" G. Stein to R. Graves, Feb. 4, 1946, YALC.
265   "'trying to remember . . . too seriously'" E. Bloom to G. Stein and A. Toklas, Dec. 3, 1945, YALC.
265   "'Everything is quite . . . Gtrde'" G. Stein to W. Wilcox, Nov. 14, 1945, in Galanes, "GS," 378.
265   "'It is so . . . not a shock'" G. Stein, *PF*, 13.
266   "'dropped her head . . . to side'" Barney, foreword to G. Stein, *AFAM*, ix.
266   "'Don't scold her. She may cry'" Thomson, *VT*, 373.
266   "'It's what I . . . Pablo'" Quoted in Toklas, *WIR*, 172.
266   "'In letter after . . . how bad'" W. G. Rogers to G. Stein, July 1, 1946, quoted in Simon, *BABT*, 188.
266   "'she was not prepared for this'" Toklas, *WIR*, 172.
266   "one of the younger surgeons" Ibid., 173.
266   "'Now we don't . . . them again'" Quoted in Thomson, *VT*, 377.
267   "'What is the answer?'" Toklas, *WIR*, 173.
267   "after a 'special ceremony'" Mellow, *CC*, 471.
267   "'I was as . . . ever known'" T. Whittemore to A. Toklas, Aug. 12, 1946, YALC.
267   "it in *Newsweek*" L. Stein to Fred Stein, Aug. 1946, in L. Stein, *JIS*, 275.
267   "'It is strange . . . one left'" Ibid.
267   "'surprised me, for . . . for her'" L. Stein to H. Gans, Aug. 1946, in L. Stein, *JIS*, 276.
267   "'maintained very well . . . comedy level'" L. Stein to M. Weeks, Dec. 28, 1933, in L. Stein, *JIS*, 134.
267   "was 'a nuisance,'" L. Stein to H. Gans, Aug. 24, 1946, in L. Stein, *JIS*, 278.
268   "a 'deep cauterization'" L. Stein to O. Coubine, Jan. 28, 1947, in L. Stein, *JIS*, 284.
268   "In June, apologizing" L. Stein to F. Stein, June 5, 1947, in L. Stein, *JIS*, 286.
268   "completely 'rotten'" L. Stein to F. Stein, June 22, 1947, in L. Stein, *JIS*, 289.
268   "'put this matter straight'" L. Stein to F. Stein, July 17, 1947, in L. Stein, *JIS*, 298.
268   "'I sometimes feel . . . complicated'" N. Stein to H. Hayden, undated (summer 1948), 3, YALC.

Primary Sources

Both Leo and Gertrude have extensive collections of manuscripts, papers, and letters in the American Literature Collection of the Beinecke Library at Yale University (YALC). Other large holdings are at the Baltimore Museum of Art; the Bancroft Library, University of California, Berkeley; and the Harry Ransom Humanities Research Center, University of Texas, Austin. Libraries and centers at the following locations have also been helpful in providing correspondence and manuscripts for this study: American Jewish Archives, Cincinnati, Ohio; Barnard College Library; Mugar Memorial Library, Boston University; American Jewish Archive, University Library at Brandeis University; Bryn Mawr College Archives; Special Collections, the libraries of the University of California at Los Angeles; the Ella Strong Denison Library, the Claremont Colleges; Butler Library, Rare Book and Manuscript Collection, Columbia University; Cornell University Library; the University Library, University of Delaware; Theatre Collection of the Pusey Library, the Houghton Library, and Harvard College Archive, Harvard University; Hebrew Union College Library, Cincinnati, Ohio; the University of Illinois Library and Special Collections; the Hemingway Collection at the John F. Kennedy Library; the Lilly Library, Indiana University; Jewish Heritage Center, Baltimore; the Alan Mason Chesney Medical Archives and Johns Hopkins Medical School Archives, the Johns Hopkins Medical Institutions, and the Johns Hopkins University Archives, Baltimore; Maryland Historical Society, Baltimore; Special Collections, Michigan State University Library; New England Memorial Hospital; the Berg Collection and the Carl Van Vechten Collection, Manuscripts Division, New York Public Library; the Poetry/Rare Books Collection, State University of New York at Buffalo; Special Collections at the Newberry Library; Special Collections, University of North Carolina, Chapel Hill; Oakland, California, Public Library; Olivet College Library and Archives, Olivet, Michigan; Sylvia Beach Archive, Princeton University; the Radcliffe College Archives and Schlesinger Library, Radcliffe; the Rosenbach Collection, Philadelphia; Southern Illinois University at Carbondale Library; University of Virginia Libraries; Z. Smith Reynolds Library at Wake Forest University; and the Fromkin Memorial Collection, University of Wisconsin–Milwaukee.

Works by Gertrude Stein

Alphabets and Birthdays. Introduction by Donald Gallup. New Haven: Yale UP, 1957.
As Fine as Melanctha, 1914–1930. Foreword by Natalie Clifford Barney. New Haven: Yale UP, 1954.

The Autobiography of Alice B. Toklas. New York: Random House, 1933.
Manuscript of *The Autobiography of Alice B. Toklas,* Harrison Collection, Univ. of California at Los Angeles.
Bee Time Vine and Other Pieces, 1913–1927. Preface and notes by Virgil Thomson. New Haven: Yale UP, 1953.
Before the Flowers of Friendship Faded Friendship Faded. Paris: Plain, 1931.
Brewsie and Willie. New York: Random House, 1946.
Composition as Explanation. London: Hogarth, 1926.
"Cultivated Motor Automatism: A Study of Character in Its Relation to Attention." *Harvard Psychological Review,* May 1898, 295–306.
Everybody's Autobiography. New York: Random House, 1937.
Fernhurst, Q.E.D., and Other Early Writings. Edited by Leon Katz. New York: Liveright, 1971.
Four in America, Introduction by Thornton Wilder. New Haven: Yale UP, 1947.
Four Saints in Three Acts. New York: Random House, 1934.
G.M.P. or Matisse Picasso and Gertrude Stein with Two Shorter Stories. 1933. Reprint, New York: Something Else, 1972.
The Geographical History of America; or, The Relation of Human Nature to the Human Mind. Introduction by Thornton Wilder. New York: Random House, 1936.
Geography and Plays. Foreword by Sherwood Anderson. New York: 1922. Reprint, Something Else, 1968.
Gertrude Stein on Picasso, ed. Edward Burns. New York: Liveright, 1970.
How To Write. Paris: Plain, 1931.
"I Came and Here I Am." *Cosmopolitan,* Feb. 1935, 18–19, 167–68.
Ida. New York: Random House, 1941.
Last Operas and Plays. Introduction by Carl Van Vechten. New York: Rinehart, 1949.
Lectures in America. New York: Random House, 1935.
The Letters of Gertrude Stein and Carl Van Vechten, 1913–1946. Edited by Edward Burns. 2 vols. New York: Columbia UP, 1986.
Lucy Church Amiably. Paris: Plain, 1930.
The Making of Americans. 1925. Reprint, New York: Something Else, 1966.
"The Modern Jew Who Has Given Up the Faith of His Fathers Can Reasonably and Consistently Believe in Isolation," Radcliffe forensics essay (unpublished). Yale American Literature Collection.
Mrs. Reynolds and Five Earlier Novelettes, 1931–1942. Foreword by Lloyd Frankenberg. New Haven: Yale UP, 1952.
Narration: Four Lectures by Gertrude Stein. Introduction by Thornton Wilder. Chicago: U of Chicago Press, 1935.
Notebooks for *The Making of Americans* and other work, annotated by Leon Katz. Yale American Literature Collection.
A Novel of Thank You. Introduction by Carl Van Vechten. New Haven: Yale UP, 1958.
"On the Value of a College Education for Women." Unpublished essay. Baltimore Museum of Art.
Operas and Plays. Paris: Plain, 1932.
Painted Lace and Other Pieces, 1914–1937. Introduction by Daniel-Henry Kahnweiler. New Haven: Yale UP, 1955.
Paris France. London: Batsford, 1940.
Portraits and Prayers. New York: Random House, 1934.
Reflection on the Atomic Bomb. Vol. 1 of *The Previously Uncollected Writings of Gertrude Stein,* ed. Robert Bartlett Haas. Los Angeles: Black Sparrow, 1973.

Selected Writings of Gertrude Stein, ed. Carl Van Vechten. New York: Random House, 1946.
Stanzas in Meditation and Other Poems, 1929–1933. Preface by Donald Sutherland. New Haven: Yale UP, 1956.
A Stein Reader, Gertrude Stein, ed. Ulla F. Dydo. Evanston, Ill.: Northwestern UP, 1993.
Tender Buttons. New York: Claire Marie, 1914.
Three Lives. New York: Grafton, 1909.
Two: Gertrude Stein and Her Brother and Other Early Portraits, 1908–1912. Foreword by Janet Flanner. New Haven: Yale UP, 1951.
Useful Knowledge. New York: Payson and Clarke, 1928.
Wars I Have Seen. New York: Random House, 1945.
What Are Masterpieces and Why Are There So Few of Them. Foreword by Robert Bartlett Haas. Los Angeles: Conference, 1940.
With Leon Solomons. "Normal Motor Automatism," *Harvard Psychological Review*, September 1896, 495–512.

Works by Leo Stein

The ABC of Aesthetics. New York: Boni and Liveright, 1927.
"Aesthetic Fundamentals," *New Republic*, 18 (March 1, 1919), 138–50.
"Albert Ryder," *New Republic* 14 (April 27, 1918), 385–86.
"American Optimism," *Seven Arts*, May 1917, 72–92.
Appreciation: Painting, Poetry and Prose. New York: Crown, 1947.
"Arch in New York City," *New Republic*, 17 (Jan. 11, 1919), 303–5.
"Art and Common Sense," *New Republic*, 11 (May 1917), 13–15.
"Art and the Frame," *New Republic*, 46 (March 24, 1926), 143–44.
"Art and Society," *New Republic*, 46 (April 14, 1926), 224–25.
"Art versus Its Estimation," *New Republic*, 18 (Feb. 1, 1919), 18–20.
"Cézanne," *New Republic*, 5 (Jan. 22, 1916), 297–98.
"Defeat of John Ruskin," *New Republic*, 18 (Feb. 8, 1919), 51–53.
"Degas and Draughtsmanship," *New Republic*, 13 (Nov. 3, 1917), 13–14.
"Distortion," *Dial*, 83 (July 1927), 28–32.
"If Rubens Were Born Again," *New Republic*, 15 (June 1, 1918), 153–54.
"An Inadaquate [*sic*] Theory," *New Republic*, 5 (Jan. 29, 1916), 339–40.
"Integrity and Integration," *New Republic*, 46 (April 7, 1926), 196–97.
"Introductory to the Independent Show," *New Republic*, 10 (April 7, 1917), 288–90.
Journey into the Self: Being the Letters, Papers and Journals of Leo Stein, ed. Edmund Fuller. New York: Crown, 1950.
"Knowing and Feeling," *New Republic*, 46 (March 17, 1926), 102–3.
"Meanings," *Seven Arts*, Feb. 1917, 402–5.
"New Return to Nature," *New Republic*, 6 (March 18, 1916), 179–81.
"New Salon in Paris," *New Republic*, 39 (July 30, 1924), 271–73.
"On Teaching Art and Letters," *New Republic*, 46 (March 3, 1926), 47–48.
"Pablo Picasso," *New Republic*, 37 (April 23, 1924), 229–30.
"Painting of Arthur B. Davies," *New Republic*, 13 (Jan. 19, 1918), 338.
"Personality and Identification," *New Republic*, 46 (March 31, 1926), 172–73.
"Reality," *Dial*, 83 (Sept. 1927), 201–7.
"Rembrandt's Etchings in the Public Library," *New Republic*, 14 (March 2, 1918), 137–38.
"Renoir and the Impressionists," *New Republic*, 14 (March 30, 1918), 259–60.
"Ritual and Reality," *The American Scholar*, 16 (Spring 1947), 140–47.

"Supports His Psychology," *New Republic*, 6 (Feb. 26, 1916), 105.
"Tradition and Art," *The Arts*, 7 (May 1925), 265–69.
"William James," *American Mercury*, 9 (Sept. 1926), 68–70.
"William M. Chase," *New Republic*, 10 (March 3, 1917), 133–34.
"Zuloaga," *New Republic*, 9 (Dec. 23, 1916), 210–12.

Secondary Sources

Abrahams, Edward. *The Lyrical Left*. Charlottesville: UP of Virginia, 1986.

Acton, Harold. *More Memoirs of an Aesthete*. London: Methuen, 1970.

Adato, Perry Miller. Transcript of interview with Virgil Thomson, Janet Flanner, and Maurice Grosser for NET Gertrude Stein Special, Bilignin, France, May 30, 1970, YALC.

Adler, Cyrus, ed. *The American Jewish Year Book 5660, Sept. 5, 1899 to Sept. 23, 1900*. Philadelphia: Jewish Publication Society of America, 1899.

Aldrich, Mildred. "Confessions of a Breadwinner" (unpublished autobiography, 1926). Microfilm. Schlesinger Library Archive, Radcliffe College.

———. *A Hilltop on the Marne*. Boston: Houghton Mifflin, 1915.

———. *The Peak of the Load*. Boston: Small, Maynard, 1918.

Allen, Gay Wilson. *William James, A Biography*. New York: Viking, 1978.

Anderson, Elizabeth, and Gerald R. Kelly. *Miss Elizabeth, A Memoir*. Boston: Little, Brown, 1969.

Anderson, Margaret. *The Fiery Fountains*. New York: Hermitage House, 1951.

Anderson, Sherwood. "Four American Impressions: Gertrude Stein." *New Republic*, 32 (Oct. 11, 1922), 171.

Apollinaire, Guillaume. *Alcools*, trans. Anne Hyde Greet. Berkeley: U of California P, 1965.

———. *Apollinaire on Art: Essays and Reviews, 1902–1918*, trans. Susan Suleiman, ed. Leroy C. Breunig. New York: Viking, 1960.

———. *Selected Writings of Guillaume Apollinaire*, trans. Roger Shattuck. New York: New Directions, 1971.

Ardagh, John. *Writers' France*. London: Hamish Hamilton, 1989.

Auzias, Nina. Unpublished manuscripts and letters. YALC.

Baker, Carlos, ed. *Ernest Hemingway, Selected Letters, 1917–1961*. New York: Scribner's, 1981.

Baker, William. "Stein Put Down Hecklers After University Lecture," *Lost Generation Journal*, winter 1976, 24, 30–31.

Baldwin, Neil. *Man Ray, American Artist*. New York: Clarkson N. Potter, 1988.

Balmain, Pierre. *My Years and Seasons*, trans. Edward Lanchbery, with Gordon Young. London: Cassell, 1964.

Barker, Lewellys F. *The Nervous System and Its Constituent Neurones*. New York, 1899.

Barlow, Samuel L. M., Jr. "Ave Dione, A Tribute." Lake Collection, Harry Ransom Humanities Research Center, U of Texas, Austin.

Barnes, Albert C. "That Psychology Again" (letter). *New Republic*, 6 (March 18, 1916), 188.

———. "What Causes Aesthetic Feeling" (letter). *New Republic*, 6 (Feb. 19, 1916), 75.

Barney, Natalie Clifford. *Adventures of the Mind*, trans. John Spalding Gatton. New York: New York UP, 1992.

———. Foreword to G. Stein, *As Fine as Melanctha, 1914–1930*. New Haven: Yale UP, 1954, vii–xix.

Barr, Alfred, Jr. *Matisse: His Art and His Public*. New York: Museum of Modern Art, 1951.

Barry, Joseph. *Infamous Woman, The Life of George Sand.* Garden City, N.Y.: Doubleday, 1977.

Barry, Naomi. "Paris à Table: A Memory of Alice B. Toklas," *Gourmet,* Aug. 1967, 13, 28–30.

Bates, Scott. *Guillaume Apollinaire.* Boston: Twayne, 1967.

Baum, Charlotte, Paula Hyman, and Sonya Michel. *The Jewish Woman in America.* New York: Dial, 1976.

Beach, Sylvia. *Shakespeare and Company.* New York: Harcourt, Brace and World, 1959.

Beaton, Cecil. *Self Portrait with Friends, the Selected Diaries of Cecil Beaton, 1926–1974,* ed. Richard Buckle. New York: Quadrangle, 1979.

Benjamin, Jessica. *The Bonds of Love: Psychoanalysis, Feminism, and the Problem of Domination.* New York: Pantheon, 1988.

Bensley, Edward H. "Gertrude Stein as a Medical Student," *The Pharos,* 47 (spring 1984), 36–37.

Benstock, Shari. *No Gifts from Chance, A Biography of Edith Wharton.* New York: Scribner's, 1994.

———. *Women of the Left Bank: Paris, 1900–1940.* Austin: U of Texas P, 1986.

———, ed. *The Private Self.* Chapel Hill: U of North Carolina P, 1988.

Berenson, Bernard. *A Matter of Passion,* ed. Dario Biocca. Berkeley: U of California P, 1989.

———. *The Letters of Bernard Berenson and Isabella Stewart Gardner, 1887–1924,* ed. Rollin Van N. Hadley. Boston: Northeastern UP, 1987.

Berenson, Mary. *Mary Berenson, A Self-Portrait from Her Letters and Diaries,* ed. Barbara Strachey and Jayne Samuels. London: Victor Gollancz, 1983.

Bernier, Rosamond. *Matisse, Picasso, Miró As I Knew Them.* New York: Knopf, 1991.

Bibesco, Count. "Lunch with Gertrude Stein." *New Boston Review,* 5 (Nov.–Dec. 1980), 11–13.

Biddle, George. *An American Artist's Story.* Boston: Little, Brown, 1939.

Blau, Joseph L., and Salo W. Baron, eds. *The Jews of the United States, 1790–1804, A Documentary History,* vol. 3. New York: Columbia UP, 1963.

Bloom, Ellen F. "Three Steins, A Very Personal Recital." *Texas Quarterly,* 13 (summer 1970), 15–22.

Blum, Isidor. *The History of the Jews of Baltimore.* N.p., 1910.

Bowen, Stella. *Drawn from Life.* 1941. Reprint, London: Virago, 1984.

Bowles, Paul. *Without Stopping, An Autobiography.* New York: Putnam's, 1972.

Boyle, Kay, and Robert McAlmon. *Being Geniuses Together, 1920–1930.* 1968. Reprint, San Francisco: North Point, 1984.

Bridgman, Richard. *Gertrude Stein in Pieces.* New York: Oxford UP, 1970.

Brinnin, John Malcolm. *The Third Rose: Gertrude Stein and Her World.* Boston: Little, Brown, 1959.

———. "Mushroom Pie in the Rue Christine." In *Sextet.* New York: Delacorte/Seymour Lawrence, 1981, 233–48.

Brooks, Van Wyck. *Opinions of Oliver Allston.* New York: Dutton, 1941.

Brown, Milton W. *The Story of the Armory Show.* New York: H. Wolff, Joseph H. Hirshhorn Foundation, 1963.

Bryher. *The Heart to Artemis.* New York: Harcourt, Brace, Jovanovich, 1961.

Burgess, Gelett. "The Wild Men of Paris." *The Architectural Record,* 27 (May 1910), 400–14.

Burke, Carolyn. "Gertrude Stein, the Cone Sisters, and the Puzzle of Female Friendship." *Critical Inquiry,* 8 (spring 1982), 543–64.

Burke, Kenneth. "Engineering with Words." *Dial,* 74 (April 1923), 408–12.

Camfield, William A. *Francis Picabia, His Art, Life and Times.* Princeton, N.J.: Princeton UP, 1979.

Canby, Henry Seidel, "Dressmakers for Art." *Saturday Review of Literature,* 10 (March 24, 1934), 572.

Cannell, Kathleen. "Gertrude Stein—'The Rhythm Is the Person.'" *Christian Science Monitor,* March 5, 1970, 15.

———. "Nightingales of Perpignan." *Christian Science Monitor,* May 4, 1963, 14.

———. "Saturdays at Gertrude Stein's," *Christian Science Monitor,* March 4, 1970, 15.

Carpenter, Humphrey. *Geniuses Together, American Writers in Paris in the 1920s.* Boston: Houghton Mifflin, 1988.

Casals, Pablo. *Joys and Sorrows, Reflections by Pablo Casals.* New York: Simon and Schuster, 1970.

Cendrars, Blaise. Interview. *Paris Review,* 10 (spring 1966), 105–32.

Cerf, Bennett. *At Random, the Reminiscences of Bennett Cerf.* New York: Random House, 1977.

Chase, Mary Ellen. "Five Literary Portraits." *Massachusetts Review,* spring 1962, 511–16.

Chauncey, George, Jr. "From Sexual Inversion to Homosexuality: Medicine and the Changing Conceptualization of Female Deviance," *Salmagundi,* 58–59 (fall 1982–winter 1983), 14–46.

Chodorow, Nancy. *The Reproduction of Mothering: Psychoanalysis and the Sociology of Gender.* Berkeley: U of California P, 1978.

Church, Ralph. "A Rose is a Rose is a Rose" (memoir). Bancroft Library, U of California, Berkeley.

Cody, Morrill, with Hugh Ford. *The Women of Montparnasse, The Americans in Paris.* Cranbury, N.J.: Cornwall, 1984.

Coffelt, Beth. "The Incredible Stein Influence." Part 1. *California Living Magazine,* Aug. 29, 1971, 14–15, 17–22.

Commins, Dorothy. *What Is an Editor? Saxe Commins at Work.* Chicago: U of Chicago P, 1978.

Cone, Edward T. "The Miss Etta Cones, The Steins, and M'sier Matisse: A Memoir." *American Scholar,* 42 (summer 1973), 441–60.

Cooper, Douglas. "Gertrude Stein and Juan Gris." *Apollo,* n.s., 93 (January 1971), 28–35.

Cooper, Emmanuel. *The Sexual Perspective: Homosexuality and Art in the Last 100 Years in the West.* London: Routledge and Kegan Paul, 1986.

Cowley, Malcolm, ed., *After the Genteel Tradition: American Writers, 1910–1930.* Carbondale: Southern Illinois UP, 1964.

Crespelle, Jean-Paul. *Picasso and His Women,* trans. Robert Baldick. New York: Coward-McCann, 1969.

Crosby, Caresse. *The Passionate Years.* New York: Dial, 1953.

Cunard, Nancy. *These Were the Hours, Memories of My Hours Press, Reanville and Paris, 1928–1931,* ed. Hugh Ford. Edwardsville: Southern Illinois UP, 1969.

Curtis, William J. R. *Le Corbusier: Ideas and Forms.* New York: Rizzoli, 1986.

Daix, Pierre. "Picasso's Time of Decisive Encounters." *Art News,* 86 (April 1987), 136–41.

Daniel, Alix Du Poy. "The Stimulating Life with Gertrude & Co." *Lost Generation Journal,* 6 (summer 1979), 16–18.

Danziger, Gustav Adolf. "The Jew in San Francisco, The Last Half Century." *Overland,* 25 (April 1895), 382–410.

Davidson, Jo. *Between Sittings.* New York: Dial, 1951.

Dearborn, Mary V. *Pocahontas's Daughters, Gender and Ethnicity in American Culture.* New York: Oxford UP, 1986.

DeKoven, Marianne. *Rich and Strange: Gender, History, Modernism.* Princeton, N.J.: Princeton UP, 1991.

de Morinni, Clara More. "Miss Stein and the Ladies." *New Republic,* 157 (Nov. 11, 1967), 17–19.

Diedrich, Maria. "'A Book in Translation About Eggs and Butter': Gertrude Stein's World War II." In *Women and War: The Changing Status of American Women from the 1930s to the 1950s,* ed. Maria Diedrich and Dorothea Fischer-Hornung. New York: Berg, 1990.

Diliberto, Gioia. *Hadley.* New York: Ticknor and Fields, 1992.

Draper, Muriel. *Music at Midnight.* New York: Harper and Bros., 1929.

Drew, Bertha Vincent. Notes for a Talk, 1948, Radcliffe Archives.

Duberman, Martin B. *Paul Robeson.* New York: Knopf, 1988.

Duchamp, Marcel. "Matisse and the Physics of Painting." *Homage to Matisse, Yale Literary Magazine,* 123 (fall 1955), 14.

DuPlessis, Rachel Blau. *Writing Beyond the Ending.* Bloomington: Indiana UP, 1985.

Dydo, Ulla. "Landscape Is Not Grammar: Gertrude Stein in 1928." *Raritan,* 7 (summer 1987), 97–113.

———. "*Stanzas in Meditation*: The Other Autobiography." In *Gertrude Stein Advanced, An Anthology of Criticism,* ed. Richard Kostelanetz. Jefferson, N.C.: McFarland, 1990, 112–27.

Edstrom, David. *The Testament of Caliban.* New York: Funk and Wagnalls, 1937.

———, "Why Gertrude Stein Is What." *Los Angeles Times Sunday Magazine,* April 14, 1935, 3.

Ehrenreich, Barbara, and Deirdre English. *For Her Own Good, 150 Years of the Experts' Advice to Women.* Garden City, N.Y.: Doubleday, 1979.

Eliot, Charles W. *Harvard Memories.* Cambridge: Harvard UP, 1923.

Ellis, Havelock. "Sexual Inversion in Women." *Alienist and Neurologist,* 16 (1895).

Fargion, Liliana Picciotto. "The Jews During the German Occupation and the Italian Social Republic." In *The Italian Refuge,* ed. Ivo Herzer. Washington, D.C.: Catholic Press, 1989, 109–38.

Faÿ, Bernard. *Les Précieux.* Paris: Librairie Académique Perrin, 1966.

Fein, Isaac M. "Baltimore Jews During the Civil War." In *The Jewish Experience in America,* vol. 3. New York: KTAV, 1969, 323–52.

———. *The Making of an American Jewish Community, The History of Baltimore Jewry from 1773 to 1920.* Philadelphia: Jewish Publication Society of America, 1971.

Ferrier, William W. *Origin and Development of the University of California.* Berkeley, Calif.: Sather Gate Book Shop, 1930.

Fitch, Noel Riley. *Sylvia Beach and the Lost Generation.* New York: Norton, 1983.

Flanner, Janet. *Darlinghissima, Letters to a Friend,* ed. Natalia Danesi Murray. New York: Random House, 1985.

———. Interview with Tom Wood, 1964. *Lost Generation Journal,* 10 (1990), 2–10.

———. *Janet Flanner's World, Uncollected Writings, 1932–1975.* New York: Harcourt, Brace, Jovanovich, 1979.

———. *Paris Was Yesterday, 1925–1939.* New York: Viking, 1972.

———. *Pétain, The Old Man of France.* New York: Simon and Schuster, 1944.

Ford, Hugh. *Published in Paris, American and British Writers, Printers, and Publishers in Paris, 1920–1939.* New York: Macmillan, 1975.

Foucault, Michel. *The History of Sexuality,* vol. 1, trans. Robert Hurley. New York: Random House, 1978.

Frackman, Noel. "The Stein Family and the Era of Avant-Garde Collecting." *Arts Magazine,* 45 (Feb. 1971), 41–43.

Franke, Katharine Gilbert. "My Time at the Harvard Annex." Radcliffe Archive.

Galanes, Philip, ed. "Gertrude Stein: Letters to a Friend." *Paris Review,* 28 (summer/fall 1986), 359–74.

Gallup, Donald. "Always Gtde Stein." *Southwest Review,* 34 (summer 1949), 54–58.

————. "Du Côté de Chez Stein." *Book Collector,* 19 (summer 1970), 169–92.

————. "Gertrude Stein and the *Atlantic.*" *Yale University Library Gazette,* 28 (January 1954), 109–12.

————. "The Making of *The Making of Americans,*" *New Colophon,* 3 (1950), 54–74.

————. "The Weaving of a Pattern: Marsden Hartley and Gertrude Stein." *Magazine of Art,* 41 (Nov. 1948), 256–61.

————, ed. *The Flowers of Friendship, Letters Written to Gertrude Stein.* New York: Knopf, 1953.

"Gertrude Stein Comes Home." *New Republic,* 81 (Dec. 5, 1934), 100.

Gertrude Stein. Conference proceedings (in French), Le Clos Poncet, Culoz, 1987.

Gervasi, Frank. "The Liberation of Gertrude Stein." *Saturday Review,* 54 (Aug. 21, 1971), 13–14, 57.

Ghiselin, Brewster, ed. *The Creative Process: A Symposium.* Berkeley: U of California P, 1952.

Gilbert, Sandra M., and Susan Gubar. *The Madwoman in the Attic: The Woman Writer and the Nineteenth-Century Literary Imagination.* New Haven: Yale UP, 1979.

————. *No Man's Land: The Place of the Woman Writer in the Twentieth Century,* Vols. 1 and 2. New Haven: Yale UP, 1988, 1989.

Glanz, Rudolf. *The Jews of California, From the Discovery of Gold until 1880.* New York: Waldon, 1960.

Glassco, John. *Memoirs of Montparnasse.* New York: Oxford UP, 1970.

Goldstone, Richard H. *Thornton Wilder, An Intimate Portrait.* New York: Dutton, 1975.

Golson, Lucile M. "The Michael Steins of San Francisco: Art Patrons and Collectors." In *Four Americans in Paris.* New York: Museum of Modern Art, 1970.

Goodwin, Donald W. *Alcohol and the Writer.* New York: Penguin, 1988.

Gordon, Irene. "Leo Stein." In *Four Americans in Paris.* New York: Museum of Modern Art, 1970.

Gosling, Nigel. *Paris 1900–1914, The Miraculous Years.* London: Weidenfeld and Nicolson, 1978.

Grahn, Judy. *Really Reading Gertrude Stein, A Selected Anthology with Essays.* Freedom, Calif.: Crossing Press, 1989.

Griffiths, Richard. *A Biography of Marshal Philippe Pétain of Vichy.* Garden City, N.Y.: Doubleday, 1972.

Grosser, Maurice. "Visiting Gertrude and Alice." *New York Review of Books,* 33 (Nov. 6, 1986), 36–38.

Haas, Robert Bartlett. "A Bolt of Energy, or Why I Still Read Gertrude Stein." *The Widening Circle,* 1 (fall 1973), 14–17.

Hahn, Emily. *Mabel, A Biography of Mabel Dodge Luhan.* Boston: Houghton Mifflin, 1977.

Hapgood, Hutchins. *A Victorian in the Modern World.* New York: Harcourt, Brace, 1939.

Hapgood, Hutchins, and Neith Boyce. *Intimate Warriors,* ed. Ellen Kay Trimberger. New York: Feminist Press, 1991.

Harriman, Margaret Case. *The Vicious Circle* (Algonquin). New York: Rinehart, 1951.

Harrison, Gilbert A. *The Enthusiast, A Life of Thornton Wilder.* New York: Ticknor and Fields, 1983.

Hartley, Marsden. *On Art,* ed. Gail R. Scott. New York: Horizon, 1982.

————. "Somehow a Past" (unpublished manuscript). YALC.

Hecht, Ben. *Review of G. Stein, Geography and Plays. Chicago Literary Times,* 1 (July 1, 1923), 2.

Hecht, Lucille. "Gertrude Stein's Conquest of the Midwest." *Real America*, 6 (Feb. 1936), 40–42.

Heissenbuttel, Helmut. "Reduzierte Sprache. Ueber ein Stuck von Gertrude Stein." *Augenblick*, 1 (1955), 1–16.

Hemingway, Ernest. "The Farm." *Cahiers d'Art*, 9 (1934).

———. *A Moveable Feast.* New York: Scribner's, 1964.

———. "My Own Life." *New Yorker*, February 12, 1927, 23–24.

Hirshler, Eric E., ed. *Jews from Germany in the United States.* New York: Farrar, Straus and Cudahy, 1955.

Hobhouse, Janet. *Everybody Who Was Anybody.* New York: Putnam's, 1975.

Hopkinson, Leslie W. Letter. *Undergraduate Times.* Radcliffe Archives.

Houseman, John. *Run-Through.* New York: Simon and Schuster, 1972.

Howells, Dorothy Elia. *A Century to Celebrate, Radcliffe College, 1879–1979.* Cambridge, Mass.: Radcliffe College, 1978.

Hubly, Erlene. "Gertrude Stein." *North American Review*, 271 (Sept. 1986), 65–74.

Huddleston, Sisley. *Back to Montparnasse.* London: Harrap, 1931.

———. *Paris Salons, Cafés, Studios.* Philadelphia: Lippincott, 1928.

———. *Pétain, Patriot or Traitor?* London: Andrew Dakers, 1951.

Imbs, Bravig. *Confessions of Another Young Man.* New York: Henkle-Yewdale, 1936.

Irwin, Inez Haynes. *Angels and Amazons, A Hundred Years of American Women.* Garden City, N.Y.: Doubleday, Doran, 1934.

———. Unpublished materials, diary from 1904 to 1927, including March 27–May 3, 1908, and the war dairy, Feb. 19–Oct. 26, 1916. Schlesinger Library, Radcliffe College.

Jackson, Laura Riding. "The Word-Play of Gertrude Stein." *Critical Essays on Gertrude Stein*, ed. Michael J. Hoffman. Boston: G. K. Hall, 1986, 240–60.

Jacob, Max. *Hesitant Fire, Selected Prose of Max Jacob*, trans. and ed. Moishe Black and Maria Green. Lincoln: U of Nebraska P, 1991.

James, William. *The Principles of Psychology.* 2 vols. New York: Henry Holt, 1890.

Jelenko, Therese. "Reminiscences." Bancroft Library, U of California, Berkeley.

Jelinek, Estelle C. *The Tradition of Women's Autobiography: From Antiquity to the Present.* Boston: Twayne, 1986.

Josephson, Matthew. *Life Among the Surrealists.* New York: Holt, Rinehart and Winston, 1962.

Kahn, Edgar M. *Cable Car Days in San Francisco.* Stanford, Calif.: Stanford UP, 1940.

Kahnweiler, Daniel-Henry. Introduction to Gertrude Stein, *Painted Lace and Other Pieces, 1914–1937.* New Haven: Yale UP, 1955.

Kandinsky, Wassily. *Complete Writings on Art.* Vol. 1 *(1901–1921)*, ed. Kenneth C. Lindsay and Peter Vergo. Boston: G. K. Hall, 1982.

Karp, Abraham J. *The Jewish Experience in America.* Vol. 3, *The Emerging Community.* New York: KTAV, 1969.

Katz, Jonathan. *Gay American History: Lesbians and Gay Men in the U.S.A.* New York: Crowell, 1976.

Katz, Leon. "The First Making of *The Making of Americans:* A Study Based on Gertrude Stein's Notebooks and Early Versions of Her Novel (1902–8)." Ph.D. dissertation, Columbia University, 1963.

———. Introduction to Gertrude Stein, *Fernhurst, Q.E.D., and Other Early Writings.* New York: Liveright, 1971, xi–xxii.

———. "Weininger and *The Making of Americans*," *Twentieth Century Literature*, 24 (spring 1978), 8–26.

Katz, Leon, and Edward Burns. "'They Walk in the Light,' Gertrude Stein and Pablo

Picasso." Afterword to Gertrude Stein, *Gertrude Stein on Picasso,* ed. Edward Burns. New York: Liveright, 1970.

Kedward, H. R. *Resistance in Vichy France.* New York: Oxford UP, 1978.

Kellner, Bruce. "Baby Woojums in Iowa." *Books at Iowa,* 26 (April 1977), 3–18.

———, ed. *A Gertrude Stein Companion: Content with the Example.* New York: Greenwood, 1988.

King, Georgiana Goddard. "Gertrude Stein and French Painting." *Bryn Mawr Alumnae Bulletin,* May 1934.

Kouidis, Virginia M. *Mina Loy, American Modernist Poet.* Baton Rouge: Louisiana State UP, 1980.

Krafft-Ebing, Richard von. *Psychopathia Sexualis,* trans. F. J. Rebman. 1886. Reprint, Brooklyn, New York: Physicians and Surgeons Book Co., 1908.

Kreymborg, Alfred. *Troubadour.* New York: Sagamore, 1957.

Lachman, Arthur. "Gertrude Stein as I Knew Her." YALC.

Laughlin, James. "About Gertrude Stein." *Yale Review,* 77 (Oct. 1988), 528–36.

———. *Random Essays, Recollections of a Publisher.* Mount Kisco, N.Y.: Moyer Bell, 1989.

Leider, Emily Wortis. *California's Daughter, Gertrude Atherton and Her Times.* Stanford, Calif.: Stanford UP, 1991.

Levy, Harriet. *920 O'Farrell Street.* 1947. Reprint, New York: Arno, 1975.

———. Unpublished memoir. Bancroft Library, U of California, Berkeley.

Lewis, Oscar. *Bay Window Bohemia.* New York: Doubleday, 1956.

———, ed. *This Was San Francisco.* New York: David McKay, 1962.

Loeb, Harold. *The Way It Was.* New York: Criterion, 1959.

London, Blanche. "The Career of a Modernist." *New York Jewish Tribune,* March 6, 1931, 2, 6.

———. "Gertrude Stein." *New Palestine,* 16 (April 5, 1929), 298–300.

Longstreet, Stephen. *We All Went to Paris, Americans in the City of Light, 1776–1971.* New York: Macmillan, 1972.

Loos, Anita. *A Girl Like I.* New York: Viking, 1966.

Lord, James. *Six Exceptional Women.* New York: Farrar, Straus and Giroux, 1994.

Lottman, Herbert R. *The Left Bank, Writers, Artists, and Politics from the Popular Front to the Cold War.* Boston: Houghton Mifflin, 1982.

Lowe, Frederick W., Jr. "Gertrude's Web, A Study of Gertude Stein's Literary Relationships." Ph.D. dissertation, Columbia University, 1956.

Loy, Mina. *The Last Lunar Baedeker,* ed. Roger L. Conover. Highlands, N.C.: Jargon Society, 1982.

Ludington, Townsend. *Marsden Hartley, The Biography of an American Artist.* Boston: Little, Brown, 1992.

Luhan, Mabel Dodge. *Edge of Taos Desert,* Vol. 4 of *Intimate Memories.* 1937. Reprint, Albuquerque: U of New Mexico P, 1987.

———. *European Experiences,* Vol. 2. New York: Harcourt, Brace, 1935.

———. *Movers and Shakers,* Vol. 3. 1936. Reprint, Albuquerque: U of New Mexico P, 1985.

———. *Taos and Its Artists.* New York: Duell, Sloan and Pearce, 1947.

McAlmon, Robert. *Being Geniuses Together, 1920–1930,* ed. Kay Boyle. Garden City, N.Y.: Doubleday, 1968.

McCarthy, Kathleen D. *Women's Culture, American Philanthropy and Art, 1830–1930.* Chicago: U of Chicago P, 1991.

MacDonald, Edgar. "Hunter Stagg: 'Over There in Paris with Gertrude Stein,'" *Ellen Glasgow Newsletter,* 15 (Oct. 1981), 2–17.

Mackworth, Cecily. *Guillaume Apollinaire and the Cubist Life.* London: John Murray, 1961.

Mariano, Nicky. *Forty Years with Berenson.* New York: Knopf, 1967.

Matthews, T. S. "Gertrude Stein Comes Home." *New Republic,* 81 (Dec. 5, 1934), 100–1.

Matthiessen, F. O. *The James Family, A Group Biography.* New York: Knopf, 1961.

Mellow, James R. *Charmed Circle, Gertude Stein and Company.* New York: Praeger, 1974.

———. *Hemingway, A Life Without Consequences.* Boston: Houghton Mifflin, 1992.

———. *Invented Lives, F. Scott and Zelda Fitzgerald.* Boston: Houghton Mifflin, 1984.

Meyer, Agnes E. *Out of These Roots, The Autobiography of an American Woman.* Boston: Little, Brown, 1953.

Miller, Alice. *The Drama of the Gifted Child (Prisoners of Childhood),* trans. Ruth Ward. New York: Basic, 1981.

———. *For Your Own Good, Hidden Cruelty in Child-Rearing and the Roots of Violence,* trans. Hildegarde and Hunter Hannum. Toronto: Collins, 1984.

Miller, Rosalind. *Gertrude Stein: Form and Intelligibility.* New York: Exposition, 1949.

Moers, Ellen. Introduction to George Sand, *George Sand, In Her Own Words,* ed. Joseph Barry. Garden City, N.Y.: Doubleday, 1979.

Moore, Lamont, ed. *Pictures for a Picture of Gertrude Stein as a Collector and Writer on Art and Artists.* New Haven: Yale UP, 1951.

Morison, Samuel Eliot. *Three Centuries of Harvard, 1636–1936.* Cambridge: Harvard UP, 1936.

Münsterberg, Hugo. "Professor James as a Psychologist." *Harvard Illustrated Magazine,* 8 (Feb. 1907).

Myers, Gerald E. *William James, His Life and Thought.* New Haven: Yale UP, 1986.

Nesfield, K. M. "From a Gentile Standpoint." *Overland,* 225 (April 1895), 410–20.

Neuman, Shirley, and Ira B. Nadel, eds. *Gertrude Stein and the Making of Literature.* Boston: Northeastern UP, 1988.

Neville, Amelia Ransome. *The Fantastic City.* 1932. Reprint, New York: Arno, 1975.

Newton, Esther. "The Mythic Mannish Lesbian: Radclyffe Hall and the New Woman." *Signs: Journal of Women in Culture and Society,* 9, no. 4 (1984), 557–75.

O'Brien, Sharon. *Willa Cather: The Emerging Voice.* New York: Oxford UP, 1987.

Olivier, Fernande. *Picasso and His Friends,* trans. Jane Miller. Reprint, New York: Appleton Century, 1965.

Orenstein, Gloria Feman. "The Salon of Natalie Clifford Barney: An Interview with Bertha Cleyrerque." *Signs: Journal of Women in Culture and Society,* 4, no. 3 (1979), 484–96.

Osler, William. *Aequanimitas: With Other Addresses to Medical Students, Nurses and Practitioners of Medicine.* Philadelphia: P. Blakiston's Sons, 1932.

Pach, Walter. *Queer Thing, Painting, 40 Years in the World of Art.* Freeport, N.Y.: Books for Libraries Press, 1938.

Padgette, Paul. "Sculpture Became Her Language." *Lost Generation Journal,* 3 (fall 1975), 20–21.

Parter, Dennis. *Haunted Journeys, Desire and Transgression in European Travel Writing.* Princeton, N.J.: Princeton UP, 1991.

Paton, Lucy Allen. "Annex Memories." Radcliffe Archives.

Penrose, Roland. *Picasso, His Life and Work.* 3rd ed. Berkeley: U of California P, 1981.

Peyre, Henri. "The Lesson of Matisse." *Homage to Matisse, The Yale Literary Magazine,* 123 (fall 1955), 7–10.

Poli, Bernard J. *Ford Madox Ford and the Transatlantic Review.* Syracuse, N.Y.: Syracuse UP, 1967.

Pollack, Barbara. *The Collectors: Dr. Claribel and Miss Etta Cone.* Indianapolis: Bobbs-Merrill, 1962.

Porter, Katherine Anne. *The Days Before.* New York: Harcourt, Brace, 1952.

Preston, John Hyde. "A Conversation with Gertrude Stein." *Atlantic,* 156 (Aug. 1935), 187–94.

Prokosch, Frederic. *Voices, A Memoir.* New York: Farrar, Straus, and Giroux, 1983.

Putnam, Samuel. *Paris Was Our Mistress, Memoirs of a Lost and Found Generation.* New York: Viking, 1947.

Raffel, Gertrude Stein. "There Once Was a Family Called Stein." In *A Primer for the Gradual Understanding of Gertrude Stein,* ed. Robert Bartlett Haas. Los Angeles: Black Sparrow, 1971, 127–38.

Rather, Lois. *Gertrude Stein and California.* Oakland, Calif.: Rather, 1974.

Redman, Ben Ray. "The Importance of Being Ernest." *Saturday Review of Literature,* 28 (March 10, 1945), 8, 30.

Reid, B. L. *The Man from New York: John Quinn and His Friends.* New York: Oxford UP, 1968.

Rewald, John. *Cézanne and America, Dealers, Collaborators, Collectors, Artists and Critics 1891–1921.* Princeton, N.J.: Princeton UP, 1989.

Reynolds, Michael. *Hemingway: The Paris Years.* London: Basil Blackwell, 1989.

Richardson, Brenda. *Dr. Claribel and Miss Etta.* Baltimore: Baltimore Museum of Art, n.d.

Richardson, John. "Picasso and Gertrude Stein: Mano a Mano, Tête-à-Tête." In *A Life of Picasso,* vol. 1. New York: Random House, 1991.

Richey, Elinor. *Eminent Women of the West.* Berkeley, Calif.: Howell-North, 1975.

Robinson, Paul. *The Modernization of Sex.* New York: Harper and Row, 1976.

Rochlin, Harriet, and Fred Rochlin. *Pioneer Jews, A New Life in the Far West.* Boston: Houghton Mifflin, 1984.

Rogers, Mary Wilkins. "The Story of a Mid-Victorian." Radcliffe Archives.

Rogers, W. G. *Gertrude Stein Is Gertrude Stein Is Gertrude Stein. Her Life and Work.* New York: Crowell, 1973.

———. *Ladies Bountiful.* New York: Harcourt, Brace, and World, 1968.

———. *When This You See Remember Me: Gertrude Stein in Person.* New York: Holt, Rinehart, 1948.

———. *Wise Men Fish Here, The Story of Frances Steloff and the Gotham Book Mart.* New York: Harcourt, Brace and World, 1965.

Rönnebeck, Arnold. "Gertrude Was Always Giggling." *Books Abroad,* 18 (October 1944), 3–7.

Rose, Sir Francis. "Gertrude Stein." *Vogue,* Jan. 1, 1971, 89, 133.

———. *Gertrude Stein and Painting.* London: Book Collecting and Library Monthly, 1968.

Rosenberg, Charles, and Carroll Smith-Rosenberg. "The Female Animal: Medical and Biological Views of Women." *Journal of American History,* 60 (1973), 332–56.

Rosenshine, Annette. "Life's Not a Paragraph" (memoir). Bancroft Library, U of California, Berkeley.

Rosenwaike, Ira. *On the Edge of Greatness: A Portrait of American Jewry in the Early National Period.* N.p.: American Jewish Archives, KTAV, 1985.

Rubin, William. *Picasso and Braque, Pioneering Cubism.* New York: Museum of Modern Art, 1989.

Rudnick, Lois Palken. *Mabel Dodge Luhan, New Woman, New Worlds.* Albuquerque: U of New Mexico P, 1984.

S., L. W., M. L. E. and L. S. E, "In Memoriam." *The Radcliffe Quarterly,* 30 (Aug. 1947).

Saarinen, Aline B. *The Proud Possessors, The Lives, Times and Tastes of Some Adventurous American Art Collectors.* New York: Random House, 1958.

Sachs, Maurice. *The Decade of Illusion, Paris 1918–1928.* New York: Knopf, 1933.

Sahli, Nancy. "Smashing: Women's Relationships Before the Fall." *Chrysalis,* 8 (1979), 17–27.

Salinger, Sylvia. *Just a Very Pretty Girl from the Country, Sylvia Salinger's Letters from France, 1912–1913,* ed. Albert S. Bennett. Carbondale: Southern Illinois UP, 1987.

Salmon, André. *Souvenirs sans fin,* Vol. 2. Paris: Gallimard, 1956.

Samuels, Ernest. *Bernard Berenson, The Making of a Legend.* Cambridge: Harvard UP, 1987.

Sand, George. *The Bagpipers.* Chicago: Cassandra, 1977.

———. *George Sand, In Her Own Words,* ed. Joseph Barry. Garden City, N.Y.: Doubleday, 1979.

Santayana, George. *Essays in Literary Criticism of George Santayana,* ed. Irving Singer. New York: Scribner's, 1956.

———. *Persons and Places.* New York: Scribner's, 1963.

———. *Realms of Being.* New York: Scribner's, 1937.

Sarason, Bertram D. *Hemingway and the Sun Set.* Washington, D.C.: Microoard Editions, 1972.

Schack, William. *Art and Argyrol, the Life and Career of Dr. Albert C. Barnes.* New York: Thomas Yoseloff, 1960.

Schwartz, Delmore. "Gertrude Stein's Wars." *Nation,* 160 (March 24, 1945), 339–40.

Scott, W. T. "Gertrude Stein's Particular Warfare." *Providence Sunday Journal,* March 11, 1945, sec. 6, p. 6.

Secor, Cynthia. "Gertrude Stein: The Complex Force of Her Femininity." In *Women, the Arts, and the 1920s in Paris and New York,* ed. Kenneth W. Wheeler and Virginia Lee Lussier. New Brunswick, N.J.: Transaction, 1982, 27–35.

Seldes, Gilbert. "Delight in the Theatre." *Modern Music,* 11 (March–April 1934), 138–41.

Sevareid, Eric. *Not So Wild a Dream.* New York: Knopf, 1947.

Shattuck, Roger. *The Banquet Years, The Arts in France, 1885–1918.* New York: Harcourt, Brace, 1958.

Shaw, B. "Encounter with Gertrude Stein, Paris, 1944." *Texas Quarterly,* 9 (autumn 1966), 22–23.

Showalter, Elaine. *Sexual Anarchy.* New York: Penguin, 1990.

Simon, Linda. *The Biography of Alice B. Toklas.* Garden City, N.Y.: Doubleday, 1977.

———, ed. *Gertrude Stein, A Composite Portrait.* New York: Avon, 1974.

Simonson, Lee. *Part of the Lifetime, Drawings and Designs 1919–1940.* New York: Duell, Sloan and Pearce, 1943.

Sitwell, Edith. "Miss Stein's Stories." *Nation and Atheneum,* 33 (July 14, 1923), 492.

———. *Taken Care Of, An Autobiography.* London: Hutchinson, 1966.

Sitwell, Osbert. *Laughter in the Next Room.* Vol. 4 of *Left Hand, Right Hand!* London: Macmillan, 1949.

Skinner, Lloyd. "Alice and Gertrude Meet the Press." *San Francisco Magazine,* July 1970, 20–22, 39–40.

Sloan, Irving J., ed. *The Jews in America, 1621–1970.* Ethnic Chronology Series No. 33. Dobbs Ferry, N.Y.: Oceana, 1971.

Smith-Rosenberg, Carroll. "Puberty to Menopause: The Cycle of Femininity in Nineteenth-Century America." In *Clio's Consciousness Raised,* ed. Mary Hartman and Lois Banner. New York: Harper, Torchbooks, 1974, 23–29.

Sokoloff, Alice Hunt. *Hadley, The First Mrs. Hemingway.* New York: Dodd, Mead, 1973.

Sorrell, Walter. *Three Women, Lives of Sex and Genius,* Indianapolis: Bobbs-Merrill, 1975.

Souhami, Diana. *Gertrude and Alice.* San Francisco: HarperCollins, 1992.

Sprigge, Elizabeth. *Gertude Stein: Her Life and Work.* New York: Harper and Bros., 1957.

———. "Gertude Stein's American Years." *Reporter,* 13 (Aug. 11, 1955), 46–52.

Stearns, Harold E. *The Street I Know.* Rev. ed. of *Confessions of a Harvard Man.* New York: Lee Furman, 1935. Santa Barbara, Calif.: Paget, 1984.

Steffens, Lincoln. *The Autobiography of Lincoln Steffens.* New York: Harcourt Brace, 1931.

Stein, Amelia (née Keyser). Diary, from Jan. 1878 through March 1886, with interruptions. Bancroft Library, U of California, Berkeley.

Steloff, Frances. "The Making of an American Visit: Gertrude Stein." *Confrontation,* 8 (spring 1974), 9–19.

Stendhal, Renate, ed. *Gertrude Stein in Words and Pictures: A Photobiography.* Chapel Hill, N.C.: Algonquin, 1994.

Sterne, Maurice. *Shadow and Light, The Life, Freinds, and Opinions of Maurice Sterne,* ed. Charlotte Leon Mayerson. New York: Harcourt, Brace, and World, 1952.

Steward, Samuel M., ed. *Dear Sammy, Letters from Gertrude Stein and Alice B. Toklas.* Boston: Houghton Mifflin, 1977.

Stieglitz, Alfred. "In Memoriam. Alfred Stieglitz: Six Happenings, III, Camera Work Introduces Gertrude Stein to America." *Twice-a-Year,* nos. 14–15 (fall–winter 1947), 192–95.

Stimpson, Catharine R. "Gertrice/Altrude, Stein, Toklas and the Paradox of the Happy Marriage." In *Mothering the Mind, Twelve Studies of Writers and Their Silent Partners,* ed. Ruth Perry and Martine Watson Brownley. New York: Holmes and Meier, 1984, 122–39.

Sulzberger, Cyrus L. *A Long Row of Candles, Memoirs and Diaries, 1934–1954.* New York: Macmillan, 1969.

Sutherland, Donald. "Alice and Gertrude and Others." *Prairie Schooner,* 45 (winter 1971–72), 284–99.

———. "The Pleasures of Gertrude Stein." *New York Review of Books,* 21 (May 30, 1974), 28–29.

Thomson, Virgil. "Remembering Gertude," *Columbia Library Columns,* 31 (Feb. 1982), 3–16.

———. "A Very Difficult Author." *New York Review of Books,* 16 (April 8, 1971), 3–8.

———. *Virgil Thomson.* New York: Knopf, 1966.

Toklas, Alice B. *The Alice B. Toklas Cook Book.* Garden City, N.Y.: Doubleday, 1954.

———. "Between Classics." Review of *The Short Stories of F. Scott Fitzgerald, New York Times Book Review,* March 4, 1951, 4.

———, trans. *The Blue Dog and Other Fables for the French,* by Anne Bodart. Boston: Houghton Mifflin, 1956.

———. Duncan interview. Bancroft Library, Univ. of California, Berkeley.

———. "Fifty Years of French Fashions." *Atlantic,* 201 (June 1958), 55–57.

———. "Food, Artists and the Baroness." *Vogue* (March 1, 1950), 165, 189–91.

———. "From One of Our Depots." *American Friends of French Wounded Weekly Bulletin,* Nov. 28, 1917.

———. "The Nice Wounded at Nîmes." *American Fund for French Wounded Weekly Bulletin,* Dec. 29, 1917.

———. *The Roman Spring of Alice Toklas, 44 Letters by Alice Toklas in a Reminiscence by Donald Windham.* Verona, Italy, 1987.

————. "The Rue Dauphine Refuses the Revolution." *The New Republic*, 139 (Aug. 18, 1958), 8.

————. "Some Memories," *Homage to Matisse, The Yale Literary Magazine*, 123 (fall 1955), 15–16. (MS, U of Virginia Libraries.)

————. *Staying On Alone, Letters of Alice B. Toklas*, ed. Edward Burns. New York: Liveright, 1973.

————. "Sylvia and Her Friends." *The New Republic*, 141 (Oct. 19, 1959), 24.

————. "They Who Came to Paris to Write." *New York Times Book Review*, Aug. 6, 1950, 1, 25.

————. "Two Acorns, One Oak." *New Yorker*, Jan. 23, 1954, 92–98.

————. Untited article. *American Fund for French Wounded Weekly Bulletin*, July 4, 1918.

————. Untitled article. *American Fund for French Wounded Weekly Bulletin*, Nov. 8, 1918.

————. *What Is Remembered.* New York: Holt, Rinehart and Winston, 1963.

————. Unpublished manuscript. Lake Collection, Harry Ransom Humanities Research Center, U of Texas, Austin.

————. Unpublished manuscript. YALC.

Toklas, Alice B., with Poppy Cannon. *Aromas and Flavors of Past and Present.* New York: Harper and Brothers, 1958.

Tomkins, Calvin. *Living Well Is the Best Revenge.* New York: Viking, 1962.

Tylee, Claire M. *The Great War and Women's Consciousness.* London: Macmillan, 1990.

Tyler, Parker. *The Divine Comedy of Pavel Tchelitchew, A Biography.* New York: Fleet, 1967.

————. *Florine Stettheimer, A Life in Art.* New York: Farrar, Straus, and Giroux, 1963.

Tytell, John. *Ezra Pound: The Solitary Volcano.* New York: Anchor, 1987.

Van Vechten, Carl. *Letters of Carl Van Vechten*, ed. Bruce Kellner. New Haven: Yale UP, 1987.

————. "Medals for Miss Stein." *New York Tribune*, May 13, 1923, sec. 9, p. 20.

Vaughan, M. I. "Annex and Harvard." AWWA papers, Radcliffe Archives.

Vollard, Ambroise. *Recollections of a Picture Dealer.* Boston: Little, Brown, 1936.

Wagner-Martin, Linda. "Racial and Sexual Coding in Hemingway's *The Sun Also Rises.*" *Hemingway Review*, 10 (spring 1991), 39–41.

Warren, Lansing. "Gertrude Stein Views Life and Politics." *New York Times Magazine*, May 6, 1934, 9, 23.

Weininger, Otto. *Sex and Character.* London: Heinemann, 1906.

Welling, William. *Photography in America: The Formative Years, 1939–1900.* New York: Crowell, 1978.

Wendell, Barrett. "English at Harvard." *Dial*, 16 (March 1, 1894).

Wescott, Glenway. Foreword to Hugh Ford, *Four Lives in Paris.* San Francisco: North Point, 1987.

White, Mary Hawthorne. "Reminiscences of 1894." Radcliffe Archives.

White, Ray Lewis. *Gertrude Stein and Alice B. Toklas, A Reference Guide.* Boston: G. K. Hall, 1984.

————, ed. *Sherwood Anderson/Gertrude Stein, Correspondence and Personal Essays.* Chapel Hill: U of North Carolina P, 1972.

Wickes, George. *The Amazon of Letters, The Life and Loves of Natalie Barney.* New York: Putnam, 1976.

Wickham, Harvey. *The Impuritans.* New York: Dial, L. Mac Veagh, 1929.

Wilder, Thornton. *The Journals of Thornton Wilder, 1939–1961*, ed. Donald Gallup. New Haven: Yale UP, 1985.

Williams, William Carlos. *The Autobiography of William Carlos Williams.* New York: Random House, 1951.

Wilson, Edmund. "A Guide to Gertrude Stein." *Vanity Fair,* 21 (Sept. 1923), 60, 80.

————. "Mr. Hemingway's Dry Points." *Dial,* 77 (Oct. 1924), 340–41.

Wineapple, Brenda. *Genet, A Biography of Janet Flanner.* New York: Ticknor and Fields, 1989.

Wise, P. M. "Case of Sexual Perversion." *Alienist and Neurologist,* 4 (1883).

Wood, Ann Douglas. "The 'Fashionable Diseases': Women's Complaints and Their Treatment in Nineteenth Century America." *Journal of Interdisciplinary History,* 4 (summer 1973), 25–52.

Woolf, Virginia. *The Letters of Virginia Woolf,* ed. Nigel Nicolson and Joanne Trautman. Vol. 3. New York: Harcourt, Brace, Jovanovich, 1978.

Wright, Richard. "Gertrude Stein's Story Is Drenched in Hitler's Horrors." *PM,* March 11, 1945.

Wyman, David S. *The Abandonment of the Jews, America and the Holocaust, 1941–1945.* New York: Pantheon, 1984.

Young, Mahonri Sharp. "Life with Gertrude." *Art News,* 72 (April 1974), 92.

Young, Stark. *Immortal Shadows.* New York: Scribner's, 1948.

Zuccotti, Susan. *The Italians and the Holocaust: Persecution, Rescue, and Survival.* New York: Basic, 1987.

Index

ABOUT THE AUTHOR

Linda Wagner-Martin (formerly Wagner) is Hanes Professor of English and Comparative Literature at the University of North Carolina, Chapel Hill. The author or editor of many books in modern American literature, she has been a president of the Society for the Study of Narrative Technique and currently serves as president of the Ernest Hemingway Foundation. She has been a Bunting Institute fellow, a Guggenheim fellow, and the recipient of grants from the National Endowment for the Humanities, the Rockefeller Foundation, the American Philosophical Society, and ACLS, as well as institutional and state awards for teaching and leadership. A former editor of *The Centennial Review,* Wagner-Martin serves on the editorial boards of *Studies in American Fiction, American Poetry, Modern Fiction Studies, Narrative, Resources for American Literary Study, Papers in Language and Literature, The Hemingway Review,* and other journals. A member of the *D. C. Heath American Literature Anthology* team, she is coeditor of *The Oxford Companion to Women's Writing in the United States* (1995) and its accompanying anthology of women's writing. Her biographies include books on Ellen Glasgow and Sylvia Plath. Her most recent book is *Telling Women's Lives: The New Biography.*